The Group of Seven

We are now in the era of the G8, although the G7 still exists as a grouping for finance ministers and central bank governors. Why do G7 finance ministries and central banks co-operate? What are the implications of this for the power of the United States and the abilities of the other six states to exercise leadership? What influence do the G7 have on global financial governance? How much authority do they possess and how is that authority exercised?

This is the first major work to address these fundamental questions. It argues that to understand the G7's contribution to global financial governance it is necessary to locate the group's activities in a context of 'decentralized globalization'. It also provides original case study material on the G7's contribution to macro-economic governance and to debates on the global financial architecture over the last decade. The book assesses the G7's role in producing a system of global financial governance based on market supremacy and technocratic trans-governmental consensus and articulates normative criticisms of the G7's exclusivity.

For researchers in the fields of IR/IPE, postgraduate students in the field of international organization and global governance, policy-makers and financial journalists, this is the most comprehensive analysis of the G7 and financial governance to date.

Andrew Baker is Lecturer at the School of Politics and International Studies at the Queen's University of Belfast. He is the co-editor of *Governing Financial Globalisation* (Routledge, 2005) and has published in journals such as *Review of International Political Economy* and *Global Governance.*

Routledge/Warwick Studies in Globalisation

Edited by Richard Higgott and published in association with the Centre for the Study of Globalisation and Regionalisation, University of Warwick.

What is globalisation and does it matter? How can we measure it? What are its policy implications? The Centre for the Study of Globalisation and Regionalisation at the University of Warwick is an international site for the study of key questions such as these in the theory and practice of globalisation and regionalisation. Its agenda is avowedly interdisciplinary. The work of the Centre will be showcased in this new series.

This series comprises two strands:

Warwick Studies in Globalisation addresses the needs of students and teachers, and the titles will be published in hardback and paperback. Titles include:

Globalisation and the Asia-Pacific
Contested territories
Edited by Kris Olds, Peter Dicken, Philip F. Kelly, Lily Kong and Henry Wai-chung Yeung

Regulating the Global Information Society
Edited by Christopher Marsden

Banking on Knowledge
The genesis of the global development network
Edited by Diane Stone

Historical Materialism and Globalisation
Edited by Hazel Smith and Mark Rupert

Civil Society and Global Finance
Edited by Jan Aart Scholte with Albrecht Schnabel

Towards a Global Polity
Edited by Morten Ougaard and Richard Higgott

New Regionalisms in the Global Political Economy
Theories and cases
Edited by Shaun Breslin, Christopher W. Hughes, Nicola Phillips and Ben Rosamond

Routledge/Warwick Studies in Globalisation is a forum for innovative new research intended for a high-level specialist readership, and the titles will be available in hardback only. Titles include:

1 **Non-State Actors and Authority in the Global System**
Edited by Richard Higgott, Geoffrey Underhill and Andreas Bieler

2 **Globalisation and Enlargement of the European Union**
Austrian and Swedish social forces in the struggle over membership
Andreas Bieler

3 **Rethinking Empowerment**
Gender and development in a global/local world
Edited by Jane L. Parpart, Shirin M. Rai and Kathleen Staudt

4 **Globalising Intellectual Property Rights**
The TRIPS agreement
Duncan Matthews

5 **Globalisation, Domestic Politics and Regionalism**
The ASEAN Free Trade Area
Helen E. S. Nesadurai

6 **Microregionalism and Governance in East Asia**
Katsuhiro Sasuga

7 **Global Knowledge Networks and International Development**
Edited by Diane Stone and Simon Maxwell

8 **Globalisation and Economic Security in East Asia**
Governance and institutions
Edited by Helen E. S. Nesadurai

9 **Regional Integration in East Asia and Europe**
Convergence or divergence?
Edited by Bertrand Fort and Douglas Webber

10 **The Group of Seven**
Finance ministries, central banks and global financial governance
Andrew Baker

11 **Globalisation and Poverty**
Channels and policy responses
Edited by Maurizio Bussolo and Jeffery I. Round

12 **Democratisation, Governance and Regionalism in East and Southeast Asia**
A comparative study
Edited by Ian Marsh

13 **Assessment and Measurement of Regional Integration**
Edited by Philippe De Lombaerde

The Group of Seven

Finance ministries, central banks and global financial governance

Andrew Baker

E·S·R·C
ECONOMIC & SOCIAL RESEARCH COUNCIL

Centre for the Study of Globalisation and Regionalisation

Routledge
Taylor & Francis Group
LONDON AND NEW YORK

First published 2006
by Routledge
2 Park Square, Milton Park, Abingdon, Oxon OX14 4RN

Simultaneously published in the USA and Canada
by Routledge
270 Madison Avenue, New York, NY 10016

Routledge is an imprint of the Taylor & Francis Group

Typeset in Baskerville by
HWA Text and Data Management, Tunbridge Wells
Printed and bound in Great Britain by
Antony Rowe Ltd, Chippenham, Wiltshire

British Library Cataloguing in Publication Data
A catalogue record for this book is available from the British Library

Library of Congress Cataloging in Publication Data
Baker, Andrew, 1972–
The Group of Seven: finance ministries, central banks and global financial governance / Andrew Baker.
p. cm. — (Routledge/Warwick studies in globalisation)
Includes bibliographical references and index.
1. Group of Seven (Organisation) 2. International finance. 3. Monetary policy—Group of Seven countries—International cooperation. 4. Banks and banking, Central—Group of Seven countries. I. Title. II. Series.
HG3881.B252 2005
332'.042—dc22 2005008334

ISBN10: 0–415–35492–7

ISBN13: 9–78–0–415–35492–9

For Maeve

Contents

List of illustrations x
Foreword xi
Acknowledgements xiv

1 Introduction: the Group of Seven and global financial governance 1

2 The evolution of the Group of Seven and the re-emergence of global finance: the historical context 18

3 Situating the Group of Seven in a context of decentralized financial globalization: a four-dimensional framework 38

4 The Group of Seven and the politics of financial ideas: the durability of the economic consensus of the 1990s 66

5 The Group of Seven as a multi-spatial transgovernmental actor in world politics: four-dimensional diplomacy in practice 100

6 The Group of Seven and macroeconomic governance: discourse, declaratory policy and market supremacy 143

7 The Group of Seven and the global financial architecture: the institutional and ideational foundations of market supremacy 183

8 Conclusions: global financial governance and the Group of Seven as a senior transgovernmental coalition 228

Notes 247
Bibliography 273
Index 290

Illustrations

Figure

5.1 Linkages between the actors in the G7 Finance Minister's and Central Bank Governor's process and the Annual Summits 112

Tables

5.1 Career details of Finance Ministry and Central Bank deputies in 1996 113
5.2 Fiscal frameworks in G7 countries 119
5.3 Procedures for foreign exchange interventions in G7 countries 123
5.4 G7 countries percentage share of IMF votes 137
6.1 G7 declaratory policy in the 1990s 171

Foreword

If money makes the world go round, and foolish would be the scholar who argues that money has little to do with earthly or other rotations in this era of global market integration, then an increasingly coherent club of the most powerful finance ministers and central bank governors in the world, representing the dollar, the euro, and the other serious 'hard' currencies of the global economy, must be an important focus of scholarly enquiry. This book is surely about one of the most important issues of the day. How is it that there is so little serious scholarship from the political economy corner on this pressing issue?

Of course there is scholarship on the G7 as an institution, and this Baker easily acknowledges. Scholarship on G7 summitry, where agreement is less easily reached and the clash of inter-state conflicts of interest often appears prevalent, however, misses the importance of the more subtle forums which meet in the shadows, but arrive at more consensual and thus more consequential decisions. This forum actually does something, and as such Baker has spotted something which many scholars have missed.

A specific focus on the interactions among finance ministries, central banks, and financial market constituencies is therefore rarely seen. Equipped with a strong awareness of methodological proprieties, Andrew Baker is filling in an important gap in our empirical understanding of the world of globalization, and he does so in an original and theoretically innovative way. He has put his finger on probably the most important 'transgovernmental coalition' of our day, a crucial underpinning and promoter of global integration and market-oriented economic policy-making. Furthermore, he explores the intimate interrelationships between this transgovernmental club, its constituent agencies, and the market constituencies which it ostensibly governs. His analysis clearly reveals how this club of technocratic expertise and guardian of financial orthodoxy has developed the normative and ideational supports, not to mention the policy decisions, which underpin the contemporary global financial architecture from which these states and their most powerful firms largely benefit.

Baker's account is also a sound empirical and theoretical case against theoretical parsimony and in favour of multivariate analysis, which for all its cumbersome attributes has the distinct advantage of fitting reality testing rather better than the alternative. Parsimonious accounts might reveal some of the central questions we need to ask and help orient us in terms of coming to terms with phenomena, but as an explanation of complex processes they usually fall rather short. Most analysis of the G7 has tended towards the state-centric in theoretical terms, especially given that most of this analysis has focused on the summits themselves, and to a much more limited degree on the rest of what is known as the G7 'process'. We instinctively think that the G7 is about states, which of course in part it is. Yet this view is unfortunate, and this unfortunate situation is laid bare in this account of finance ministries and central bankers in global financial governance. State-centric accounts of summitry forget to ask what states are and what lies behind them. Baker finds, based on comprehensive empirical research, that a clear coalition of financial market interests in close relation with central bank and finance ministry officials has given the G7 finance and central bank governors, as a transgovernmental coalition, a set of interests and ideas around macroeconomic prudence, sound money, and integrated capital markets which are largely shared with the very industry which this club ostensibly supervises and governs. Public and private financial interests do not collide as in the traditional state or market-centric literature; far from it, they increasingly *coincide*. Furthermore, Baker succinctly dispenses with the US hegemony issue so crucial to most state-centric analyses of global governance and international relations. Endless attention to US power tells us little about what it might deliver in terms of policy. In an interactive situation of relationships among state agencies, increasingly independent central banks, and private institutions, where the personnel overlap and is involved in revolving-door rotation between the worlds of public and private institutions, 'hegemony' as a concept often explains even less. Even if first among equals, wielding important veto power, simplistic ideas of the US as a hegemon are hardly appropriate as a concept in multivariate analysis. The US finds itself constrained by market forces, the dynamics of decentralizing globalization, emerging multilateral norms, and the cross-cutting forums in which it must operate if its preferences are ever to be translated into policy at the multilateral level.

Baker labels as 'four-dimensional diplomacy' the complex and multivariate relationships of central banks and finance ministries with each other in the G7 process, with their own (steadily transnationalizing) domestic constituencies, with other (e.g. G20) agencies outside the process, and with global financial markets themselves. The concept gives a flavour of the complexity he clarifies and explains in this work. In such a complex and globalizing setting, G7 consensus is regarded as central and has been achieved with difficulty over time, but has proved durable indeed. This consensus has lent continuity to the process, and one might remark a certain inertia and resistance to ideas which lie outside the consensus but which might explain contemporary policy problems somewhat better. This consensus also preserves a range of political and financial gains for finance ministries and central banks relative to other agencies of government in inter-bureaucratic competition, as well as the gains which the consensus represents for global financial market players. Unsurprisingly, material interests are never far from sight in the political economy of financial governance, despite the veneer of technocratic, apolitical ideas through which the consensus is expressed.

Finally, Baker contributes to the crucial debate on the legitimacy of current patterns of global governance, dominated in finance by the G7 central bank and finance ministerial forum. There is little empirical doubt about the importance of the forum for global financial governance – current institutions and policies are directly traceable to G7 preferences and debates. It is also clear that the forum is less than inclusive – finance ministries and central banks, and their corresponding private sector interlocutors, are not the only parties affected by financial governance arrangements. Yet here lies the crux of the matter. G7 central bank and finance ministries are capable of generating effective consensus, and this very effectiveness is related to the exclusionary nature of this transgovernmental coalition and the limited range of private sector interests with which they regularly and systematically interact. It follows that the very effectiveness of the G7 finance ministry/central bank condominium is precisely what contributes to its broader lack of legitimacy. The interests of G7 ministries and central banks are hardly directly commensurate with those of developing countries or those in transition economies. Furthermore, finance ministries and central banks represent a particularly narrow version of government interests and often clash with other branches of government. Adding a G20 central bank and finance ministry forum, composed of like-minded and similarly trained officials from developing countries, is thus far from being a complete answer to the problem. Furthermore, the G7 reliance on market-friendly declaratory policy has put markets firmly in charge, whether they need be or not, and whether this is ultimately good for governance (and for whom?) or not. This tidy consensus ensures that a lot of important questions are not asked. Those who innocently assume that public policy necessarily serves the interests of 'the public' should think again.

So far, this relative lack of legitimacy embodied in the G7 central bank and finance ministry consensus has not led to failure, though financial crises have sorely tried the process in this respect. Apolitical approaches to inherently political issues, however, cannot forever prevail. The last time such approaches failed was in the Great Depression. Exclusion of a broad range of voices also militates against basic democratic principles at either the global or the domestic level. Let us hope that Baker's work encourages sufficient self- and scholarly examination of what is quietly going on around us to broaden the agenda and raise the questions which, so far, are seldom asked in official circles.

Geoffrey R.D. Underhill
Chair of International Governance
University of Amsterdam
June 2005

Acknowledgements

The process of researching and writing this book began nearly ten years ago here in Belfast. At the time, the thought that it would lead to a full length book manuscript on what appeared an impenetrable, opaque, mysterious and secretive process seemed fanciful. The book grew out of a comparative project on the budgetary processes of G7 countries being conducted at the University of Ulster by Professor Colin Thain, funded by Leverhulme Trust Research Grant F144U and on which I was research assistant between 1995 and 1998. Quite simply without Colin's encouragement and enthusiasm the work for this book would never have got off the ground, but by generously allowing access to his research grant I was able to visit some of the world's great cities and to meet an incredible breadth of interesting people. The research for this book took me to London, Washington DC, Paris, Basle, Bern, Baltimore, Rome, New York, Boston, Cambridge MA, Toronto, Brussels and the Hague, where I conducted interviews and discussed and presented my ideas at various academic conferences. Unfortunately, for logistical and financial reasons it was not possible to visit Tokyo, but hopefully this does not distract too greatly from the end product. I'm particularly grateful to Colin Thain for opening the door to HM Treasury, and facilitating access for a vital first round of interviews. The then director of the International Finance Directorate, Sir Nigel Wicks, generously allowed me close to unrestricted access to his officials. It is not possible to thank individuals by name, but a special mention should go to Patsy Izzard, a secretary at HM Treasury, for setting up a number of meetings.

Many others have helped along the way. Angus Wright, Daniel Lowes and Philip Poole allowed me to stay in their apartments, at different times during trips to London, as did Nico Van Dyck during a trip to Brussels. The numerous officials from HM Treasury, the Bank of England, the US Treasury Department, the Federal Reserve System, the Foreign and Commonwealth Office, the State Department and the International Monetary Fund, the Canadian Department of Finance, the German Federal Ministry of Finance, the European Commission and the Bank of International Settlements that I have either spoken or communicated with at various times, on the whole, gave generously and willingly of their time, despite enormously heavy workloads.

Intellectually, I have benefited from discussions and correspondence with a number of individuals who have enhanced my understanding of some of the core theoretical and empirical issues in the study of International Political Economy. Special mentions should go to Geoffrey Underhill (University of Amsterdam, formerly University of Warwick), Robert Putnam (Harvard University), Sir Nicholas Bayne (LSE), Philip Cerny (Rutgers University) and Randall Germain (Carleton University). The Faculty of Business and Management, University of Ulster provided me with office space, computing facilities and a salary for three years and I was eventually able to submit a doctoral thesis based on some of the research for this book, which was shortlisted for the BISA thesis prize in 2000 and was externally examined by Professor Richard Higgott, the editor of this series. Dr David Kitchen in the University's international office helped in arranging some of the details for my Washington trip, while the inter-library loan staff at the Jordanstown campus and at the Queen's University of Belfast library were unfailingly helpful, efficient and cheerful in dealing with my numerous requests.

Later, Professor Mike Smith, the former Director of the Institute for European Studies, Queen's University of Belfast, now Pro-Vice Chancellor of Glasgow Caledonia University, appointed me to the position of research fellow and later lecturer in political economy, allowing me to continue writing and researching. The Institute was my home for nearly five years and I am thankful to Mike for creating a relaxed, collegiate and sometimes stimulating environment in which to work. Despite having little familiarity with the subject area, and only a passing acquaintance with the inter-discipline of IPE, Andrew Evans read numerous draft chapters of the earlier thesis. He was always a polite, but also quite scathing and valued critic. During this time I benefited enormously from discussions in the Queen's Europeanisation seminar series and some of the excellent speakers we invited over including Kenneth Dyson, Claudio Radaelli, Kevin Featherstone, Colin Hay, Andreas Bieler, Alec Stone-Sweet and Ben Rosamond, all of whom contributed to a lively and engaging academic environment. Some of the arguments in this book are derived from and are developments of earlier pieces published in *Review of International Political Economy* and *Global Governance* and I am grateful to the reviewers of these journals for their thoughtful commentary. Two anonymous referees provided insightful, penetrating and sometimes complementary comments on an earlier version of this manuscript submitted to Cambridge University Press and two reviewers of the proposal submitted to Routledge provided interesting thoughts. Later I gave papers based on some of the work for this book at seminars at the Universities of Sheffield, Nottingham and Warwick and benefited from discussions with participants at these sessions, particularly Richard Woodward, David Hudson, Ben Thirkell-White, Andreas Bieler, Xiaoke Zhang and Shaun Breslin. I should also acknowledge the excellent website compiled by the G8 Research Centre at the University of Toronto, by Peter Hanjal and John Kirton. Without their foresight and diligence in constructing one of the world's most valuable sources on international affairs the research for this book would have been much more difficult.

More recently, I've been grateful for the encouragement and support of new colleagues in the School of Politics and International Studies as the manuscript neared completion, particularly Ralph Dietl and Stefan Andreasson. Richard Higgott as the editor of the Warwick Studies in Globalisation series has been supportive throughout, and Heidi Bagtazo, Grace McInnes and Harriet Brinton of Routledge have been unfailingly helpful, co-operative and patient as I missed various deadlines. Paul Stewart and John Mackin have done their best to distract me with offers of the good things in life – fine wine and Liverpool FC. Finally, this book wouldn't have been possible without the puzzled encouragement and support of my parents Alan and Jacqui, or without the reassurance, understanding and supreme patience of the most special person in my life, Maeve Halton.

Andrew Baker
School of Politics and International Studies
Queen's University of Belfast
January 2005

1 Introduction

The Group of Seven and global financial governance

Since the 1980s the international monetary and financial landscape has been dramatically transformed. Foreign exchange and derivatives trading has risen exponentially. By 2001 daily turnover in these markets stood at $1,210 billion, dwarfing trade in goods and services.[1] Many financial markets now operate 24 hours a day, with world financial cities linked by extensive computer networks reducing the immediate importance of time and location.[2] However, in this brave new interconnected financial world, volatility, instability and disturbance have been constant threats. One of the City of London's most venerable institutions, and a seemingly solvent financial concern – Baring's – collapsed almost overnight in 1995. Repeated contagious financial and exchange rate crises, mainly originating in emerging markets from Asia to Latin America, rocked the global financial system, and deprived citizens in these countries of incomes and savings following rapid and hasty capital account liberalization. The European monetary system was also blighted by turbulence in 1992 as central banks experienced severe losses at the hands of speculators, while North America did not escape unaffected by events in emerging market in 1997–8. More recently, the United States has been blighted by corporate financial scandals, most notably Enron. And against this turbulent backdrop European states created a new single currency in an unprecedented act of monetary union amongst sovereign nation states.

In this context, questions of global financial and monetary governance have become ever more prominent. Yet despite a decade of turbulence and change, the meetings of finance ministries and central banks from the world's leading industrialized nations, the Group of Seven (G7 – Canada, France, Germany, Italy, Japan, UK, US), have retained a prominent, if ambiguous and not easily definable role in directing and steering governance and development trajectories in an increasingly diffused, but interconnected global financial system. Since the 1960s, finance ministries and central banks from the wealthiest nations have met several times a year to consult with one another and exchange views on international economic conditions (first as the G10, later as the G5, then as the G7, see Chapter 2).[3] Over time, it is the G7 finance ministers and central bankers round of meetings, or the G7 process, that has become the pre-eminent forum for the formulation of international monetary policy and has been regarded as the most important locus of authority in global financial governance.[4] The meetings of the Group of Seven finance ministries and central banks have been used to discuss national macroeconomic and exchange rate policies, to develop shared policies in relation to the international financial institutions, and to reach agreement on the general design of the global financial system. In other words, the collective choices, policies and decisions of G7 finance ministries and central banks, or indeed the lack of them, are central to global financial governance – the decisions and decision-making processes that determine how the international monetary and financial system is organized, the array of mechanisms for preventing and responding to international financial disturbance and the procedures and norms that set the parameters for and inform transnational market operations.

However, for most of the last decade, save for one short policy-orientated study, academics, particularly political scientists, paid little attention to the interactions of the G7 finance ministries and central banks as an ongoing regularised multilateral process.[5] This changed with the publication of a series of volumes by the Canadian-based G8 Research Centre at the University of Toronto. However, much of the Toronto group's work is informed by a liberal institutionalist assumption that international co-operation is a positive public international good, regardless of its social purpose or content. In my view this has resulted in an insufficiently critical approach to G7 co-operation, which neglects many of the G7's deficiencies, including its unrepresentative exclusive membership and the resulting narrow technocratic approach to global financial governance that leaves many countries and political constituencies feeling excluded. Furthermore, despite a comprehensive commentary on the G7's response to the Asian financial crisis and several volumes on the issue of the global financial architecture,[6] we are yet to see a theoretically grounded and carefully researched up-to-date monograph about the G7 finance ministries and central banks' regular meetings that discusses the dynamics of these institutions' interactions and diplomacy, examines what drives their co-operation, and assesses their wider collective authority and influence including their general contribution to global financial governance.[7] It is this gap that this book intends to fill.

This book sets out to make four broad contributions to the existing literature. First, it seeks to provide the most theoretically informed and critical examination of co-operation between G7 finance ministries and central banks on macroeconomic and financial matters, as well as the most detailed treatment of the dynamics of the politics and the norms of that co-operation. Second, it aims to shed light on debates concerning the extent of US power in global financial governance as evident in the activities of the Group of Seven. Third, it explores the authority of the G7 and its contribution to global financial governance in the context of the emergence of a complex, interconnected, transborder financial system and the governance challenges this poses.[8] Fourth, this book articulates normative criticisms of the G7 process based on its exclusive, unrepresentative membership, its general lack of inclusion, or dialogue with wider societal actors and the very narrow technocratic, and essentially neo-liberal view of global financial governance, that the finance ministries and central banks have promoted and protected. Such an approach has paid insufficient attention to the political and social consequences of liberalized finance, privileging established financial interests in the leading financial centres of developed countries, contributing to a legitimacy crisis and a democratic deficit in global financial governance.[9]

Section 1 of this introduction introduces the G7 process. Section 2 covers the various research agendas to be pursued. Section 3 outlines and justifies the scope of the study. Section 4 sets out the chapter structure of the book. The final section provides a brief note on the methodology used in the research for the book.

Introducing the G7 process

The G7 finance ministers and central bankers' process consists of an annual cycle of three or four meetings at ministerial level, six to ten meetings between senior officials (the deputies) and a number of more informal communications via email and telephone conference calls. The process has no official legal status, no permanent home base and no secretariat. The initial rationale for these meetings was the need to manage a condition of economic interdependence, first recognized in academic writings in the late 1960s.[10] As product and capital markets became increasingly intertwined, so developments in one national economy had a bigger impact on the performance of other economies. State agencies with responsibility for national economic performance therefore had an obvious self-interest in exchanging information on the future intentions and projections of their national counterparts so as to increase the pool of information on which to base their own national policy decisions.[11] Furthermore, due to their responsibilities in relation to national currencies and national financial sectors, finance ministries and central banks have always been concerned with systemic issues relating to financial stability. The G7 process has come to act as a forum for the discussion and formulation of joint positions on many issues relating to the design of the international financial system.

In 1973, finance ministers met as a G4 in the library of the White House to discuss the repercussions of the decision to take the dollar off the gold standard and the collapse of the Bretton Woods exchange rate system. They later met as a G5 and were joined by the central banks governors, subsequently drafting an agreement in 1975 on the legal foundations for the new international monetary system.[12] From 1986 onwards the finance ministries and central banks met as a Group of Seven and intensified their multilateral surveillance activities.

Traditionally, the G7 process has been associated with economic policy co-ordination, or exchange rate management because of episodes like the Bonn locomotive strategy of 1978, or the Plaza and Louvre agreements of the 1980s.[13] The Bonn locomotive strategy consisted of a package deal agreed between the G7 countries in an effort to generate global growth, while the Plaza and Louvre agreements included adjustments to domestic policies and exchange market interventions to stabilize exchange rates between the major currencies. Over the last decade however, there has been an absence of these sorts of grand macroeconomic and exchange rate bargains. Instead recent G7 activities have revolved around managing financial crises, instigating long-term responses to those crises and outlining, protecting and promoting core principles for macroeconomic policy and global financial governance.

Some of the economics literature has attempted to draw a distinction between co-operation and policy co-ordination, which is useful for the purposes of this study.[14] Co-ordination is best viewed as international agreements that include precise pre-negotiated adjustments to domestic policies, or what Putnam and Henning have called reciprocal 'package deals' involving mutual commitments.[15] Such co-ordination can take the form of co-ordinated macroeconomic expansions, or 'international Keynesianism' – so as to generate economic growth, exchange rate agreements and mutually agreed monetary policy adjustments to produce exchange rate stability and ease balance of payments discrepancies, or the collective re-establishment of capital controls to prevent destabilizing foreign exchange speculation.[16] Co-operation on the other hand is best seen as a looser process. Here, it is taken to mean the sharing of information, experiences and opinion, or a combination of 'consultation' and 'enlightenment/learning', as well as the identification of common interests, objectives and causal beliefs by a group of actors who then seek to collectively promote those interests, objectives and beliefs, domestically and elsewhere.[17]

Research agendas

This book has three principal empirical research objectives: 1) to establish the form and determinants of interaction and co-operation between G7 finance ministries and central banks at their regular meetings; 2) to examine and establish the patterns of power and authority evident at G7 meetings, examine how these patterns influence G7 outcomes and the implications of this for the exercise of power and authority in global financial governance more generally and most especially for US power; 3) to assess the wider contribution of the G7 to global financial governance and their collective authority in an era of 'decentralized globalization'.

The form and determinants of interaction and co-operation between G7 finance ministries and central banks

The first empirical research agenda in this book involves the identification and explanation of the type/s of co-operation that characterize the G7 process and asks what factors have most influence in shaping and determining the form of G7 interaction and co-operation. Various factors come into play when considering G7 interactions, including the social practices, routines and conventions of finance ministry and central bank elites; the technical economic beliefs and ideas that these elites hold; perceptions of national interest; the relationship the finance ministries and central banks have with different domestic constituencies and the extent to which they operate on behalf of these constituencies; the degree of domestic institutional autonomy the finance ministries and central banks enjoy, including formal and informal relationships with other state agencies; and the impact of the rise of international capital mobility and the continuous transnational market scrutiny of a range of national policies that has accompanied this.

An obvious research question to explore is why the kind of policy co-ordination referred to in the previous section has been replaced by a looser but more far-reaching form of co-operation and which factors account for the apparent demise in formal bargaining and co-ordinated policy agreements. Existing literature on G7 co-operation and/or co-ordination provides some guidance here. Michael Webb argued that policy co-ordination in the 1980s, and to a lesser extent the late 1970s, involved adjustments to domestic monetary and fiscal policies, rather than symptom-management policies such as exchange market interventions, because domestic action was required to address the larger payments and currency imbalances generated by rising international capital mobility. Webb's argument was that international capital mobility was a structural feature of the international system and was the most important factor explaining instances of G7 policy co-ordination.[18] However, further intensification in the speed and volume of international capital flows has seen a demise in the kinds of policy co-ordination that characterized the 1980s (see Chapter 2 for more of a discussion). Fred Bergsten and Randall Henning of the Institute of International Economics have pointed to a number of inter-related factors that have caused this, such as policy-makers' perceptions of limited macroeconomic effectiveness (other than to deliver a stable low inflationary environment) in the face of financial globalization, domestic institutional changes such as the rise of independent central banks and fiscal rules that make national macroeconomic policy less discretionary and finally what they call a consensus, or non-aggression pact, where states refuse to be too critical of one another's policies.[19]

A further interpretation of international financial relations is provided by Randall Henning in his compelling study of exchange rate diplomacy between the major powers in the 1970s and 1980s. Henning argued that the domestic political economies of the leading states and patterns of domestic interest politics, evident in the relationship between national financial and industrial sectors primarily determined the major states' exchange rate policies.[20] This is particularly important given the perceived division between and different needs of Anglo-American financial sectors with arm's length relations with industry and the less market-oriented and more socially embedded financial sectors of Japan and continental Europe.[21] How much influence do these differences in the political economies of the G7 countries have on G7 diplomacy and financial relations and how much purchase do domestic political economy explanations of international financial relations have? It is also notable that the most authoritative account of the Plaza Agreement of 1985 demonstrated that US domestic interest-based politics was the principal driving force behind that episode of exchange rate co-operation.[22] How certain domestic interests and positions are promoted during the course of G7 deliberations and how certain interests are represented in the institutional arrangements of G7 finance ministries and central banks cannot therefore be ignored in explanations of contemporary G7 co-operation.

What is required is a way of examining the inter-relationship and interactions between elite causal and normative beliefs, shared elite social practices, behavioural routines, procedures and understandings, domestic interests and institutional politics, and the challenges and pressures that a more geographically interconnected but diffused financial system places on policy-makers. The approach adopted here maintains that it is not sufficient to consider solely how elites behave at G7 meetings, or how they interact with one another, rather we need to acknowledge that they are responding to pressures from several discrete but overlapping spatial dimensions simultaneously. Multilateralism, in other words, needs to be placed in a wider spatial social, political and material or structural context.[23] The basic premise of the approach adopted here is that explaining the behaviour and strategies of states in the global political economy requires an effort to examine the relations and multiple linkages between national, international and global realms and between state and non-state actors.

A framework of multi-dimensional diplomacy is adopted throughout this book. It is an attempt to identify several spatial domains, or dimensions, and examine how they interact in the context of the collective efforts of the G7 finance ministries and central banks to maintain and manage the global financial system. The various spatial dimensions identified in this framework (see Chapter 3) include: the meetings of G7 finance ministries and central banks, which is a particular form of social interaction in its own right; domestic political forces and institutional arrangements in the various G7 states; financial markets as transworld or transborder spaces and the processes of signalling to and communicating with these markets; and the broader range of institutions and state agencies that contribute to global financial governance but are not present at G7 meetings – what has recently been termed the wider global financial architecture. This multi-dimensional approach serves two principal purposes. Firstly, it enables us to look at how a range of variables and factors interact across a range of spatial dimensions to influence the form, purpose and content of G7 interaction and co-operation, while avoiding reductionism, or one-way determinism. Secondly, it enables us to consider the contribution of the G7 process to a diffuse process of global financial governance, while sensitizing us to the broader social and political implications of collective G7 activities.

Authority and power relations within the Group of Seven: is the G7 a US-dominated coalition or a modern concert of leading powers?

The next research agenda refers to relations among the G7 finance ministries and central banks and the ability of each to get what they want in relation to G7 outcomes. Obviously this take us into the traditional domain of international relations – intergovernmental bargaining. However, we need to be aware from the outset that interactions between the G7 finance ministries and central banks involve more than just traditional inter-state bargaining.[24] Rather there is an attempt to deliberate and express opinions in an effort to arrive at a consensus, but these debates take place in a wider context of the patterns of structural power that characterize the international financial system. Many scholars of international monetary and financial relations have identified US dominance, exceptionalism and even hegemony in international monetary and financial affairs, although definitions of the latter term vary and remain contested.[25] More recently, authors who previously acknowledged US hegemony in financial governance have begun to question its continued existence, because US capital markets, despite their undoubted importance, no longer determine the trajectory of the entire system. A situation of 'decentralized globalization' has emerged in which large liquid credit markets exist in Europe, Asia and Latin America as well as North America, and no single financial centre provides guidance and direction to the entire global financial system.[26] For example, financial crises in emerging markets have recently had the potential to develop into systemic crisis, demonstrating that the United States has a new sensitivity and vulnerability to developments elsewhere. Moreover, the recent decline of the dollar may be suggestive of significant erosion in US monetary exceptionalism. However, very few have taken this view of diminishing US financial power as far as John Kirton, who has long argued that the G7 represents a modern concert of international powers characterized by an equality of capability among its respective constituent members.[27] Either way, any examination of G7 financial diplomacy and co-operation inevitably has to consider the issue of how much power the US has relative to other G7 states and its capacity to dominate G7 meetings and dictate G7 outcomes.

Two broad views have emerged in scholarship on G7 diplomacy on the subject of US power. The first is that the G7 is a coalition in which the US is the principal power. G7 co-operation has principally been generated by the US, with the US having the ability to get its way, providing it has the support of one or two other major powers.[28] The second view is Kirton's modern concert of international powers thesis that makes claims for equality amongst the G7 and that any G7 power is capable of displaying critical leadership at any given time.[29] Both perspectives have elements of truth about them, but neither are strictly accurate representations of the dynamics of G7 power relations. For example, it is certainly true that lesser G7 powers such as Canada and the UK have the capacity to critically influence G7 debates and push them in a certain direction, but this is quite a different thing from saying that the G7 represents a modern international concert of powers with each member enjoying an effective equality of capability.[30] We have to search for the reason the UK and Canada are able to critically influence G7 debates and I argue in what follows that it has precious little to do with the comparability of their power or capability to that of the United States, because ultimately the United States continues to enjoy privileges in global financial governance stemming from the international use of the dollar, the presence of the world's most important and liquid capital markets, the largest shareholding in the IMF and its position as the world's leading trainer of professional economists.[31]

Particular elite social practices, together with the vulnerability that comes from what Germain calls 'decentralized globalization', means that the United States is finding it increasingly difficult to act alone in international financial affairs. The

United States has to listen to other G7 states, does listen to other states and this in turn provides opportunities for other G7 states to critically influence debates on financial and monetary governance through their finance ministries and central banks. Therefore, while the United States enjoys privileges in the monetary and financial sphere and is very definitely an exceptional power, evident in its continued capacity to run record trade and budget deficits, we must also be careful not to overstate US power. The United States cannot simply act as it pleases but is subject to constraints that need to be identified and understood just as much as US power resources need to be understood and appreciated.

The discussion of US power in global financial governance in this book seeks to bring the debate up to date, and highlight some of the constraints that have restricted even the US in G7 discussions over the last decade or so. In this regard, while the US retains its pre-eminent position in the G7 and in some respects has even enhanced its capability to achieve its objectives,[32] in other respects it has found itself constrained by growing market authority and shared multilateral norms, including the preference for governance by multilateral consensus in the field of money and finance. Studying the exercise of power and authority in global financial governance requires a sensitivity to the particular multilateral setting under consideration and the norms and social practices of the elites that operate in these settings, a sensitivity which until now has been largely absent from existing accounts. This book seeks to demonstrate how looking at the G7 can provide the basis for a more sophisticated and qualified understanding of US power and the exercise of authority in international monetary relations in a globalized era, as well as how we need to be cautious when making grand pronouncements on either the decline or growth in US hegemony.

How important is the G7 process? Its wider role and authority in an era of globalization

If the first two research questions focused on what influenced and determined the nature of the interactions between finance ministries and central banks and the implications of the outcomes of these interactions for patterns of power and authority among the G7 finance ministries and central banks themselves, the third principal research question pursued in this book asks what purpose these interactions serve and what contribution they make to global financial governance. This is clearly related to the previous questions and can be broken down into three further questions. First, what function/s has the G7 process served in relation to governance of the wider global financial system? Second, how do the G7 perform these functions and what kind of relationships and interactions do the G7 have with wider institutions, non-G7 states and market actors? Third, what methods do the G7 employ in their attempts to get these actors to behave in certain ways, how successful are they and how much authority do they subsequently enjoy? These questions are all of critical importance in comprehending the changing nature of state authority and collective multilateral action and its contribution to governance in a globalized era.

Immediately we are faced with a paradox when considering the governance contribution and the authority of the Group of Seven. The Group of Seven are an exclusive inner caucus group of selected state agencies – finance ministries and central banks – possessing critical expertise in monetary and financial governance. They attempt to define priorities, challenges and key principles in global financial governance by constructing an initial consensus amongst themselves as the basis for a more far-reaching consensus encompassing a broad range of multilateral institutions, specialist regulatory bodies, state and market actors. The exclusivity of the Group of Seven is in many respects its defining feature and characteristic. The group operates as a small club-like group of officials that have enjoyed some success in arriving at a consensus on a number of issues. At the same time, however, it is precisely this exclusivity that restricts the effectiveness of the Group of Seven, undermining their legitimacy and ultimately their authority.

The principal problem with the G7 as a governance mechanism therefore, is precisely who is excluded from its meetings. Consensus relies upon argumentation for its creation and some degree of legitimacy for its implementation. In the process of formulating and disseminating consensus, actors have to be persuaded to accept the arguments of others and decide to act in accordance with those arguments on the grounds of their moral or technical authority. Restricted participation in the G7 makes the attainment of consensus within the group easier, but it also makes it more difficult for the group to promote that consensus and have it accepted elsewhere. In this respect, issues of inclusion, legitimacy and implementation of ideas and proposals were repeated challenges for the G7 during the 1990s, mainly due to the continued exclusion of emerging markets and developing countries from deliberations and discussions, which created a situation where the G7 authored approaches to financial governance and then expected emerging markets to implement them, despite the fact that they often had little or no opportunity to contribute to the nature or content of the governance solutions being proposed.

Failure to have ideas accepted and implemented elsewhere has undermined the authority of the G7 and it is no surprise that we have seen an increase in outreach activities, culminating in the establishment of the G20. In part, this new forum was an attempt to address the inclusion problem as means of improving the implementation record of G7-inspired initiatives. On the one hand, the creation of the G20 could constitute an important step forward in giving emerging markets an institutional position in the governance of global finance and offer new opportunities for emerging markets to challenge G7 dominance of global financial governance by creating new alliances which could split the G7 and isolate the key Anglo-American coalition.[33] On the other hand increased consultation with a carefully selected restricted group of finance ministries and central banks from emerging markets, which is what the fairly modest creation of the G20 essentially amounts to, could actually enhance G7 authority and secure improved implementation of G7-generated ideas and initiatives. A more detailed examination of the relationships between the two groups is therefore essential if we are to obtain a better understanding of the impact of the G20 on patterns of inclusion and authority in global financial governance and determine which of the above scenarios is closer to reality.

The focus on the interaction between ideas and norms, domestic institutions and interests, and relations with markets, as well as wider multilateral bodies, referred to earlier draws attention to the constraints the Group of Seven experience as well as their capacity to initiate policy proposals. One interpretation of the G7 has maintained that the wider G7 system, with the annual leaders' summit at its apex, is emerging as an effective centre of global governance, because it has developed follow-up procedures consisting of a thriving system of working groups and various ministerial fora, making the G7 more reliable as an ongoing system of governance with an annual rhythm where commitments are less likely to be forgotten due to a centrally co-ordinated institutional machinery.[34] The problem with this interpretation is that it takes an insufficiently disaggregated view of this so-called G7 institutional machinery. The leaders at the summit do not control the activities of the finance ministries and central banks. On the contrary they have developed a reliance on their technical expertise to develop proposals, agendas and principles to inform financial governance. Given the rise of central bank independence and fiscal austerity, the finance ministries and central banks have enjoyed a surprising amount of autonomy in relation to their chief executives over the last decade. Indeed, the Group of Seven finance ministries and central banks are closer to what Keohane and Nye famously described as a transgovernmental coalition, or network in which sub-units of governments act relatively autonomously from higher authority in international politics, albeit not independently, and even act to build coalitions with like-minded agencies from other governments to reinforce their own institutional position or a shared policy perspective, which might meet with domestic opposition.[35] Crucially of course, the G7 finance ministries and central banks also seek to promote shared views in their dealings with wider international institutions, other states and financial markets.

In this respect, this book challenges the notion that the G7 process has the capacity to act as a centre of global governance, not least because such a notion rests on a flawed state-centric conception of world order, which pays insufficient attention to the diffused nature of power, authority and capability in the realm of global finance and which also fails to adequately disaggregate the state. Multiple, overlapping and interlocking authorities clutter the field of financial governance as multilayered networks of influence, interests and decision-making enmeshed in complex and hybrid webs of governance cut across the state.[36] The G7 is just one element in these complex webs of governance and the meetings of finance ministries and central banks deserve special consideration, precisely because they frequently take the lead on international financial governance initiatives, independent of chief executives and other state agencies.[37] The G7 finance ministries and central banks cannot impose their will on other bodies and authorities. There is no legal basis through which they can ensure other actors comply with their wishes. Through continuous networking, persuasion and deliberations they attempt to set agendas in global financial governance and define the parameters for financial and monetary policy-making more broadly. They do not govern in their own right as such, because global financial governance is a diffuse disaggregated process that is the sum of myriad control mechanisms in which it is difficult to discern any single hierarchical structure.[38] Therefore, one of the central arguments of this book is that the contribution of the G7 process (the finance ministry–central bank cycle of meetings) to global financial governance is more modest than 'the centre of global governance' interpretation, with its legalistic implications relating to the notion of compliance, suggests.[39] The G7 process does perform a hugely significant role in global financial governance based on activities such as discourse construction, the promotion of shared causal and normative beliefs, mutual endorsement, suasion and ultimately attempts to legitimate existing arrangements, because the G7 is an inherently conservative, system-reinforcing process.[40] In other words, G7 activities remain central to the exercise of power and authority in the global political economy, because the views the finance ministries share, refine and promote in the course of their deliberations and statements are so central to the design of the international monetary and financial system.

The scope of this book

Coverage

Macroeconomic policy and the design of the wider international monetary and financial system – the global financial architecture – are focused on throughout the book as the principal substantive areas the finance ministries and central banks have been concerned with. Developing country debt issues are also discussed by the finance ministries and central banks, but the acrimonious nature of these discussions and the absence of consensus for most of the last decade has meant that these issues have tended to be sidelined. Consequently, they are not discussed in any great detail here, although they are briefly touched upon in Chapter 7.[41]

Both macroeconomic policy and the design of the international monetary and financial systems are intrinsically intertwined. The linkages between macroeconomic policy, exchange rate regimes and international capital mobility are well established. They have long been acknowledged by economists in the form of the Mundell–Flemming dilemma, or unholy trinity, which holds that it is not possible to simultaneously have an independent national monetary policy and a fixed exchange rate under conditions of international capital mobility except on an episodic basis.[42] In this respect, exchange rate valuations are one of the principal transmission mechanisms in the international economy and they simultaneously influence, and are influenced by, national monetary policy and interest rate decisions, and by fiscal policy, or the size of state borrowings. Ultimately, under conditions of international capital mobility, policy-makers face a choice between directing policy towards national targets and objectives, or adopting an exchange rate policy.

More recently, those working in the field of IPE have been quick to identify how marketization and de-regulation in the financial services sector have effectively erased the distinction between financial markets on the one hand and the international monetary and exchange rate regime on the other.[43] At one time, the two were distinct, with the latter considered the preserve of governments and the former segmented by national economic space, sector and self-regulating cartels. As market de-regulation and liberalization have eroded distinctions between sectors and attacked the notion of national space, so too macroeconomic management problems and exchange rate issues have become bound up with financial markets.[44] Regulation and supervision of financial sectors affects the ways and rate at which capital can be moved across and within both borders and financial institutions, thereby influencing exchange rates, the financing options for governments and the general stability of the financial sector. Changes in financial regulatory and supervisory arrangements have done much to allow financial institutions to instantaneously move vast amounts of speculative investment capital across political jurisdictions and across market segments, often within a single company structure.[45] Simultaneously, this has caused instances of exchange rate instability and circumscribed the macroeconomic policy options of states. In an era of such capital mobility, there is a strong sense amongst policy-makers that governments face the threat of capital flight if they fail to deliver a hospitable climate for international investors through price stability and low fiscal deficits. Consequently, financial orthodoxy based on macroeconomic austerity has become widespread.[46]

The linkages between the policy area of financial regulation and supervision, macroeconomic policy and the occurrence of financial crises are at last increasingly being recognized by policy-makers, albeit belatedly, as the issue of financial sector governance begins to feature more prominently on the G7 agenda and is consciously being linked to macroeconomic and exchange rate governance under the broad, but grandiose title – the global financial architecture – or the collection of institutions, principles, standards and guidelines that oversee but also give shape to the international financial system. Both macroeconomic policy and the global financial architecture are therefore concentrated on throughout this book as two issues central to global financial governance.

Time frame

In terms of time frame the study focuses on the 1990s up to the present day, but particularly the period after 1992. The 1990s were particularly significant because they were characterized by efforts to respond and react to challenges arising from the reforms of financial liberalization and de-regulation implemented throughout the advanced capitalist world in the 1980s, and the sometimes hasty movement towards capital account liberalization in emerging markets in the 1990s. Technological advancement and innovation further accentuated the impact of these reforms. Significantly, foreign exchange and derivatives trading for example increased exponentially during the first half of the 1990s, and by 1996 the volume of daily trades had risen by 32 times from the comparable figure for 1989.[47] Moreover, it was after 1992 that the nature and extent of the challenges posed by financial liberalization became particularly apparent when a series of exchange rate crises rocked the European Monetary System. Subsequently, financial and exchange rate crises were a repeated feature of the 1990s and this study traces the finance ministries and central banks' collective lesson-drawing endeavours in the aftermath of each crisis.

The year 1992 is also a significant date in that it marked a watershed in patterns of fiscal data in G7 countries. From 1983 to 1992 fiscal deficits rose in all G7 countries from an average of 2.9 per cent of GDP to an average of 3.4 per cent of GDP. After 1992 this trend reversed as the average fiscal deficit in G7 countries fell to 1.9 per cent of GDP in 1997. This was indicative of a genuine fiscal tightening across the G7 in the face of lingering recession and high unemployment in most G7 countries throughout the 1990s. In other words, in the 1990s, the rhetoric of fiscal consolidation took on a more tangible element than had been evident in the 1980s, but more recently there have been signs that the consensus of the 1990s is under strain where budget deficit reduction is concerned. However, it may be premature to say that this has been abandoned altogether. Finance ministries and central banks continue to view fiscal consolidation and reductions in public expenditure as laudable and defensible economic governance principles, even if they have been prepared to adopt a more pragmatic stance, which allows a role for macroeconomic expansion, in the context of the recent slow-down in world economic activity, and in the case of the United States the security challenges identified in the aftermath of 9/11.

The 1990s also witnessed the removal of one of the most notable asymmetries in the international economy. The Clinton administration turned the US from the world's largest sovereign debtor, to a country with a fiscal surplus. This was the first time the United States had delivered a balanced budget since the 1960s. Moreover, it had the effect of bringing down US interest rates and therefore bringing down interest rates throughout the world. More importantly for the purposes of this study, it affected the patterns of power politics, and to some degree the intellectual premises surrounding exchange rate and macroeconomic diplomacy, as did the creation of a single currency in Europe. The impact of these developments on G7 relations are deserving of more consideration.

Structure and argument of the book

The rest of this book is divided into six further chapters and a conclusion. The next chapter looks at the historical context in which the G7 began to meet, how the process began to evolve and how the current G7 membership was arrived at. All of this is located in the context of the re-emergence of global finance, the breakdown of the fixed exchange rate system and the challenges arising from these developments. The G7 policy record is discussed and a rise–fall–rise–fall again cycle of policy co-ordination is identified. This discussion is used to additionally justify the research agenda set out above. In Chapter 3 a framework of multi-dimensional diplomacy, or more precisely four-dimensional diplomacy, is constructed. The framework of four-dimensional diplomacy is subsequently applied throughout the rest of the study so as to structure the analysis developed in later chapters. The linkages and interactions between the respective dimensions are discussed in Chapter 3, as a series of relevant variables are identified.

Chapter 4 examines the extent to which the G7 have developed a consensus relating to monetary and financial governance and considers the politics of financial ideas more generally. The challenges to and limitations of this consensus are also considered, as well as the national tensions that co-exist within this consensus. Despite differences and challenges it is argued that a broad, sound money, open markets consensus continues to inform the interactions and deliberations of G7 finance ministries and central banks. Chapter 5 actually applies the framework of four-dimensional diplomacy developed in Chapter 3. It examines the interactions between G7 finance ministries and central banks and the distinct set of social practices and procedures that characterize these interactions. The rest of the chapter assesses the inter-relationships between these interactions and domestic markets, developments in global financial markets, wider multilateral institutions, bodies and states outside of the G7. The aim of this analysis is to situate the G7 as a transgovernmental coalition of state agencies in a wider political and structural context, referred to throughout this book as decentralized globalization. Chapter 6 examines the discussion of macroeconomic and exchange rate issues at G7 meetings from 1990 through to 2004. It considers the influence that the US Treasury have had on G7 outcomes, relative to other G7 members, how the collegiate nature of the G7 process and the shared social practices of the finance ministries and central banks inform their interactions. The influence the G7 are able to exert over exchange rates and domestic macroeconomic decision-making are evaluated and the overall contribution of G7 meetings to macroeconomic governance is assessed. Generally, it is argued that market pressures determine macroeconomic and exchange rate priorities, but the G7 have actively encouraged and facilitated this state of affairs. In Chapter 7, the G7's relations with wider multilateral institutions, transnational policy communities and authorities in emerging markets in the context of the recent review of the global financial architecture are examined. This chapter argues that the G7 finance ministries and central banks have acted collectively to promote, deepen and extend shared norms, code, standards and practices, producing a form of governance based on peer and market scrutiny of national policies. The recent global financial architecture exercise has created institutional and ideational foundations for a form of market supremacy derived from the implementation of a neo-classical vision of financial markets and related concepts such as transparency. A complex stratified transgovernmental system of global financial governance has resulted in which technocrats dominate a conservative and incremental process. The conclusion ties the arguments together, discussing some of the linkages between shared ideas, G7 norms, domestic institutions and interests, and market structures. It is argued that the United States remains the dominant power within the G7, but that market forces are eroding even its exceptionalness, as the US is subject to an increasing number of constraints. At the same time, the G7 finance ministries and central banks' collective activities have been most concerned with maintaining, reinforcing, promoting and extending their consensual views in a form of multi-dimensional transgovernmentalism. In this respect the G7 involves a series of agencies within democratically elected governments coming together to provide a crucial source of moral, intellectual and normative support for an increasingly global financial system that rests upon liberalized international capital markets, floating exchange rates, macroeconomic discipline and core, prudential, largely market-determined regulatory standards and from which the G7 states and their financial sector are the principal beneficiaries.

A brief methodological note

Finally, two fundamental methodological problems confront us when conducting empirical research into the G7 process. The first of these is establishing what takes place at G7 meetings, what is discussed and what is agreed, given the secrecy that surrounds the G7 process and the absence of formally recorded minutes. The second problem is assessment of the actual impact of G7 meetings. This second problem relates to the issue of counterfactuals. In particular, assessing the impact of a G7 meeting is complicated by the difficulty in assessing what outcomes would have resulted in the absence of the G7 process, whether those outcomes be exchange rate valuations, domestic policy change, market perceptions, or the stance of a multilateral institution.

Without insider status (actually being present at G7 meetings) there are limits to which the first problem can be successfully negotiated. However, the problem can be minimized. In this regard four sources were used and cross-referenced throughout the research for this book. First, G7 communiqués and statements have been used as a primary source that provides some indication of what takes place at G7 meetings. Second, this is supplemented by press coverage of G7 meetings. Third, a series of interviews with officials involved in G7 preparations in the US and UK were conducted, and correspondence has since taken place with Canadian and German officials. Fourth, a series of articles by senior officials, the 'G7 deputies', have been tracked and examined. Cross-referencing these sources makes it possible to build up a reasonable picture of what takes place at G7 meetings.

Communiqués are released at G7 meetings, but they are usually written in a coded language that is difficult to decipher. Moreover, while they provide a loose guide, they are not necessarily an accurate reflection of what has been discussed.[48] They are however often directed at actors in other settings in an effort to influence their activities. Therefore, communiqués remain a useful guide to what the G7 are attempting to accomplish. Furthermore, communiqués can be considered alongside press reports of G7 meetings as an additional source of information. Once again press reports only provide limited insights into the substance of G7 discussions. These two sources are triangulated against a third source of confidential elite interviews. In this way discrepancies in press reports can be identified.[49] A further source for verifying press reports and official G7 statements are the articles and speeches of practitioners. These are particularly important because they provide further insights into the thinking of officials and what is referred to here as the shared G7 'belief system'. This is especially important where officials attempt to explain their thinking and the constraints under which they operate to a wider audience, not least because it gives a sense of officials' perceptions.

Of course, elite interviews raise a number of issues. For example, in the course of the interviews for this study it was necessary to protect the confidentiality of officials in accordance with Chatham House rules. During the interviews it was possible to ask questions relating to the course of events at specific meetings. Information provided was corroborated with information obtained from earlier interviews. After a certain number of interviews there was a degree of repetition in the interview material. On the whole officials were willing to speak candidly off the record and even pointed out where their interpretation of events differed from those of press reports.

The most problematic issue raised by elite interviewing is that of reliability:

> Collecting reliable data through interviews is admittedly a tricky art based on an uncertain process of triangulation guided by inference. Personal rivalries and reputations, political convenience, psychological vested interests, memory lapses, and discretion combine to color what one can learn from talking to those who help shape policy, and there are always those with whom it is not possible to speak at all.[50]

Elite interviews clearly have shortcomings. Therefore, where there is an uncertainty about a source, an assertion is prefaced by terms such as allegedly or reportedly. However, on the whole, different independent sources have led the researcher in broadly the same direction, suggesting that there is reliability to the conclusions presented in the study.

Finally, it was necessary mainly for financial and logistical reasons to initially limit interviews solely to UK and US officials. Since then however it has been possible to communicate with a Canadian and a German official, as well as accessing interview transcripts with senior Canadian figures from the University of Toronto's website and a number of key papers and speeches prepared by Japanese officials. This does make the evidence presented in the course of this book susceptible to the criticism that it reflects an Anglo-Saxon bias. However, interviews with and articles by French and German policy-makers reveal a compatibility with the views expressed by British and American officials, particularly with regard to the broad analytical premises that inform approaches to macroeconomic policy, exchange rates and capital mobility. A similar if less pronounced pattern was evident in the public speeches and papers of senior Japanese officials. It is on this basis that assertions relating to a broad G7 consensus on macroeconomic, exchange rate and financial matters are made.

The second methodological problem, of assessing the impact of G7 meetings, is again one that can only be minimized, particularly in an increasingly interdependent world consisting of multiple and overlapping authorities and structures. In this context, most empirical studies that enquire into the function, role and influence of particular multilateral processes are vulnerable to the criticism that many outcomes would have been arrived at even in the absence of that particular multilateral process. However, by considering developments in three other dimensions or spatial settings and linking these to the outcomes of G7 meetings, through the application of a multi-dimensional approach, it is at least possible to develop a sense of the impact particular meetings have and the constraints under which multilateralism operates.

2 The evolution of the Group of Seven and the re-emergence of global finance

The historical context

The G7 countries have been meeting together as a Group of Seven for thirty years. During that time, the structure of the international financial system and prevailing economic ideas have undergone a transformation. This chapter locates the establishment and historical evolution of the G7 process, as a series of regularised interactions between finance ministries and central banks, in the context of the re-emergence of wide-scale international capital mobility and global financial activities, as well as an ideational shift away from Keynesian economic thought. The chapter also facilitates comparisons between earlier and more recent patterns of G7 co-operation by looking at notable instances of G7 policy co-ordination from the 1970s and 1980s. Significantly, the United States drove many of these instances of policy co-ordination[1] and generally attempted to use the G7 to promote and endorse its own vision of the international financial system.

The chapter begins by looking at how dramatic changes in the international monetary and financial system, which heralded the re-emergence of a liberal financial order, provided the context for the inception of the G5/G7 process. The second section discusses how the G7 process evolved in an institutional sense and how G7 membership was arrived at. Finally, in the third section of the chapter the G7 policy record is discussed and a rise–fall–rise–fall again cycle of policy co-ordination is identified. This section demonstrates that US producer and exporter interests drove G7 co-operation at key times in the 1970s and 1980s. In this respect, the US's ability to use the G7 process to achieve desired policy outcomes was a recurring theme of the first two decades of G7 activity. The concluding discussion additionally justifies the research agendas set out in the introduction. It also raises the possibility that US interests have changed since the 1980s and that it has also become more difficult for the US to realize policy objectives through the G7 process, because of structural and ideational constraints linked to the re-emergence of global finance.

The historical context of international monetary co-operation

International monetary co-operation and the restrictive post-war financial system

Following the economic turmoil and disruption that resulted from efforts to restore the liberal financial order and the gold standard along pre-1914 lines in the 1920s and 1930s, a more restrictive financial order was viewed as a necessity for post-World War II reconstruction efforts.[2] In contrast to the 1920s and in accordance with the writings of John Maynard Keynes, the overriding norm in the post-war international financial system after 1945 was the control of capital movements.[3] States were given the explicit right to control all capital movements. Moreover, capital controls were encouraged by the mandate of the new International Monetary Fund. The IMF was set up with American money following the Bretton Woods conference in 1944 to provide a source of foreign exchange for governments to finance payments imbalances. However the Fund would not finance 'a large and sustained outflow of capital'. This put pressure on governments to try and administer effective capital controls. The IMF was also empowered to 'request' a member to implement controls to prevent the use of Fund resources.

The other major feature of the post-war international monetary system was a fixed exchange rate system in which the US dollar acted as an anchor currency. The dollar was fixed in terms of the price of gold at $35 per ounce. By 1958 European economies were sufficiently recovered to allow free convertibility of their national currencies with the dollar. A 'key currency system' or a 'dollar standard' emerged.[4] The dollar acted as the principal lubricant of international commerce. The international monetary system therefore hinged on confidence in the US dollar, while economic growth and international trade depended on an ample supply of dollars. At the same time however, the more dollars there were in circulation, the more difficult it became for the US to honour its pledge to convert unlimited amounts of dollars into gold on demand at the fixed price of $35 per ounce. Eventually, this dilemma would lead to instability and the collapse of the system.[5] The payments system and the exchange rate mechanism were therefore at the mercy of the US's capacity and willingness to restrain the outflow of dollars, in keeping with the needs of a stable international system. This required the US to run an economic policy aimed at maintaining the international trade competitiveness of American industry, while controlling capital outflows linked to private overseas investment and government expenditure. US authorities had to exercise their responsibilities with caution. In effect, the US Treasury and the Federal Reserve, rather than the Bretton Woods institutions, were the dominant authorities in the post-war international monetary and payments system, and acted as the world's banker.[6]

During the post-war period international monetary co-operation revolved around balance of payments financing and exchange rate co-ordination.[7] Co-ordinated exchange market interventions were the principal policy instrument used by authorities in episodes of international monetary co-operation, in a form of symptom management.[8] Until the late 1960s the small level of international capital movements restricted the size of exchange rate and payment imbalances that could emerge. This made both exchange market interventions and payments financing relatively effective policy instruments for tackling such imbalances.[9] As a consequence, national macroeconomic policies could be made independently and were able to focus on national objectives of economic growth and low unemployment in accordance with Keynesian prescriptions, rather than being used to correct international imbalances.[10] Moreover, the relative insulation of national economies from international effects minimized incentives for co-ordination of national policies. Consequently, it was rare for governments to adjust fiscal or monetary policy in accordance with balance of payments data.[11]

The collapse of the adjustable fixed/pegged rate system

The emergence of the Eurodollar markets in the City of London in the 1960s as an offshore centre in which dollars could be traded in a regulation free environment, served to create a glut of dollars in the system, further undermining the ability of US authorities to guarantee the value of their currency.[12] The eventual breakdown of the fixed exchange rate regime was caused by a combination of growing payment imbalances among the major OECD countries and a widespread feeling among market operators that the central banks were defending unsustainable exchange rates.[13] Confidence in the dollar plummeted and speculative flows including hedging, swaps and futures to offset currency risk proliferated. The problem of currency instability was compounded when the Eurodollar markets were flooded with petrodollars following the oil price rise of 1971. The US devalued the dollar first in 1971 and again in 1973 in an effort to export its way out of difficulty, before taking the dollar off gold altogether and advocating a floating exchange rate regime.

The Mundell–Flemming hypothesis holds that it is not possible to have both a fixed exchange rate and national monetary policy autonomy under conditions of international capital mobility except on an episodic basis.[14] This economic hypothesis effectively asserts that under conditions of international capital mobility, governments face a choice between an exchange rate policy, or an independent national monetary policy. In this respect, US authorities were able to justify and rationalize the move to floating rates in terms of economic theory.[15] In particular, they were able to point to the growing tension between international capital mobility and the fixed exchange rate regime, as well as the detrimental impact this was having on US policy autonomy and economic performance. A floating rate regime on the other hand would allow the US to base monetary policy decisions on national considerations rather than international obligations.

By the 1970s, two of the most pressing problems facing the US were growing trade and budget deficits. The combination of a floating exchange rate regime and increasing international capital mobility would afford US authorities the opportunity of using macroeconomic policy as a means of attracting foreign capital, thus financing their twin deficits, but only if they were freed of their obligation to guarantee the value of the dollar in terms of the price of gold. In this regard, these twin deficits and the United States' need to finance them, has shaped international monetary diplomacy since the end of the 1960s. Significantly, the eventual abandonment of the fixed exchange rate regime was therefore very much a unilateral US decision, motivated by the US's changing position in the international financial system, as the United States moved from a position as a creditor country to a position as a debtor country, consuming more than it produced. In other words, the restrictive post-war financial system and fixed exchange rate regime only existed for as long as US interests and the US payments position permitted.

Global finance, floating exchange rates and international monetary co-operation

In accordance with the need to attract foreign capital to fund balance of payments and fiscal deficits, processes of financial liberalization and de-regulation were also initiated and promoted by the US government in the late 1960s and 1970s. US policy-makers calculated that if given the freedom to choose, international investors would decide to hold dollars and invest in the US, because of the reserve role of the dollar and the depth of US capital markets.[16] This combined with pressure from the US financial sector, to push the US towards the abolition of capital controls and some de-regulation of capital markets. Furthermore, an ideational shift away from Keynesian economic thought towards the position advocated by economic liberals such as Friedman and Hayek was gathering momentum.[17] This position essentially advocated a liberal financial order on the grounds that it would promote a more efficient global allocation of capital, while state powers to implement controls were seen as an infringement of individual liberties.[18] Concerns that speculative financial flows would disrupt a stable exchange rate regime were rejected, as the Keynesian premises that had informed the Bretton Woods system began to be challenged. As a consequence of this combination of pressures, the US eventually abolished its capital controls in 1974 and de-regulated financial markets in New York in 1975.

Following the abandonment of fixed exchange rates and the US decision to abolish capital controls, speculative financial movements increased. Both the British Labour government in 1976 and the French socialists in 1983 found that national Keynesian strategies were thwarted. Both governments were forced to accept the disciplines of the market and adopt monetary and fiscal rectitude after experiencing capital flight and exchange rate crises. A growing disillusionment with the impracticality of Keynesian reflationary macroeconomic prescriptions in a context of increasing international capital mobility became prevalent across the G7 countries and a convergence on the priority of sound money in macroeconomic policy followed.[19]

The combination of increasing international capital mobility and the new floating exchange rate regime also combined to increase the US's capacity to unilaterally disrupt the international monetary system. This disruptive capacity became evident in the form of a 'catastrophic liquidation' in the international value of the dollar, prompting European countries to establish the managed floating rate system of the European Monetary System in 1978–9, in an effort to insulate themselves from the repercussions of US monetary policy.[20] In connection with this, US interest rate policy was one of the reasons for the difficulties the French experienced with the Franc in 1983, as investors attracted by high interest rates, moved capital out of France and into the US.[21] In other words, growing international capital mobility accentuated the significance of the performance of the largest economy, the United States, and the decisions of its policy-makers, for other countries. Rising international capital mobility also meant the effectiveness of symptom management policies, such as exchange market interventions and payments financing, declined as exchange rate and payments imbalance grew in size. States were consequently propelled towards adjustments to domestic policies and exchange rate management schemes such as the EMS (European Monetary System), or a combination of both, in an effort to address growing international imbalances. In other words, international capital mobility increased the extent to which national macroeconomic (monetary and fiscal) policies were co-ordinated in the 1980s.[22]

The momentum of the move towards financial liberalization, initiated by the United States, was further consolidated by the election of the monetarist-leaning Thatcher government in Britain. Foreign exchange controls in the UK were abolished within a year of the Conservative Party's election victory, in a bid to increase the attractiveness and competitive position of the City of London, and because such a move was ideologically attractive. The removal of limits on bank lending and a series of financial de-regulatory measures in the City of London in 1986 abolished many of the restrictive practices that had held the Bretton Woods financial order together. A remarkable trend of financial liberalization across the industrialized world followed. By 1988, all European Community countries had committed themselves to complete abolition of capital controls in the context of efforts to construct a European single market, so as to improve the competitive position of Europe in world terms.[23] Japan too gradually dismantled its controls throughout the 1980s. In effect, policy-makers in Europe and Japan dismantled post-war financial controls and regulations to avoid losing business and capital to the liberalized financial centres of London and New York.[24]

Possibly the most notable effect of this wave of financial liberalization has been the apparent financial pressures this has placed on national welfare states. They have had to attempt to make economic activities within the national territory more competitive in international or transnational terms, or risk losing mobile finance capital to rival states.[25] Governments have to pursue the goals of low inflation and price stability, rather than economic growth and full employment, if 'credibility' with global investors is to be retained. Consequently, public ownership and welfare spending have come under increasing pressure,[26] although there is an element of self-fulfilling prophecy about this.

By the mid-1990s transactions in foreign exchange markets had reached $1.3 trillion a day, far exceeding the amount traded in goods and services, and representing an exponential average yearly increase of 23 times per annum since 1989.[27] In this context of expanding financial transactions, financial instability and crises have been repeated features of the past decade. Exchange rate turmoil affected the European Monetary System in 1992. There were currency and liquidity crises in Mexico in 1994/5, again in East Asia, Russia and Latin America in 1997/8 and most recently in Turkey and Argentina. Reductions in direct controls and taxation on financial transactions, the elimination of long-standing regulatory restrictions on financial intermediaries, the expansion of lightly regulated offshore financial centres, and the introduction of new technologies have all sped the movement of capital across borders. The re-emergence of global finance has brought with it increased systemic risk and it is the dangers of this systemic risk and how to respond to it that have increasingly framed G7 discussions over the last decade or so.

The institutional evolution of the G7 process

From the G10 to the Library Group and the G5

Understanding how the exchanges of the Group of Seven finance ministries and central banks evolved and emerged as the pre-eminent forum for the discussion of international monetary and financial affairs, what officials continue to refer to as 'first among equals',[28] requires an appreciation of how informal but institutionalized exchanges between finance ministries and central banks from the leading industrialized countries, emerged in the context of the G10 and the WP-3, in the 1960s. Eleven major industrialized countries assumed primary responsibility for the international monetary system with the formation of the Group of Ten in 1961. Formal institutions and international organizations (IMF, OECD, BIS) provided supporting services for the meetings of central bank and finance ministry representatives, but the key officials – the G10 deputies, who met most often and prepared for ministerial meetings, remained centrally placed in national bureaucracies.[29] The G10 finance ministries and central banks met throughout the 1960s in order to administer a collective pool of capital designed to finance payments imbalances and to provide a source of liquidity in emergency situations.[30] Both the General Agreement to Borrow (GAB) and Special Drawing Rights (SDR) were created for these purposes. The WP-3 had a country membership nearly identical to the G10 and was instituted in 1961 for the purpose of the promotion of better international payments equilibrium.[31] The basic proposition behind these regular consultations was that national balance of payments policies and positions could prove to be conflictual and could lead to worse outcomes for all concerned if left unresolved. Intergovernmental discussions were consequently designed to induce greater compatibility of national policy targets.[32] As Russell has noted, the regular consultations amongst the finance ministry and central bank deputies produced enduring friendships and discussions increased mutual understandings of balance of payments questions and national problems and issues, but on the whole governments used these meetings to obtain information on other authorities' future policy intentions and to intellectually rationalize policies they were already intent on pursuing. There was little evidence to suggest that these discussions had a decisive impact on national policies, although they did improve understanding of technical balance of payments questions.[33] This is a picture that fits with the thesis later developed by Webb, that in the 1960s, international monetary co-operation focused on symptom management policies – exchange market interventions and payment financing, rather than adjustments to domestic policies, because of the relatively small size of payments imbalances generated in a restrictive international monetary order.

However, with the breakdown of the fixed exchange rate system international payments questions became increasingly politicized. It was during the critical juncture following the dollar's suspension from gold that the finance ministers from what eventually became the G7 first began meeting. Initially finance ministers met as a Group of Four, before becoming a Group of Five. Both were the forerunners of the G7. Significantly, the heavy European representation in the G10 (eight out of the eleven members), made the US reluctant to transact much business at G10 meetings. In particular, the Americans prevented the G10 from conducting any surveillance of its members' policies and crucially discussion of the dollar was also kept off the agenda. This apparent US aversion to the G10 led to the Americans exploring possible alternative groupings in which to conduct discussions concerning the future of the international monetary system.[34]

In the spring of 1973, US Treasury Secretary George Schultz invited his counterparts from France, Germany and the UK to meet with him in the Library of the White House to discuss the turmoil resulting from the collapse of the fixed exchange rate system. The decision to call such a meeting was of symbolic significance. Although initially a one-off, it signified the US's desire to transact business on systemic financial issues in a more exclusive and informal setting than the G10. George Schultz (US), Valéry Giscard d'Estaing (France), Helmut Schmidt (Germany), and Anthony Barber (UK), all finance ministers, were accompanied by senior officials or deputies, Paul Volcker (US), Claude Pierre Brossolette (France), Karl Otto Pohl (Germany) and Derek Mitchell (UK).[35] The meeting did not arrive at any conclusions of substance, but participants valued the informal, frank and candid exchange of information and opinion and reached a common understanding that there would be merit in further meetings.

At the annual meeting of the IMF in Kenya the following September, Japanese finance minister Kiichi Aichi invited the four library group ministers to the Japanese ambassador's residence in Nairobi and managed to get agreement from his counterparts that the five finance ministers would continue to meet. In the process, the so-called 'Library Group' not only went from four to five, but also became a regular fixture. Chairman of the Federal Reserve, Arthur Burns, was present at the next Library Group meeting, on his own insistence, and this set a precedent for central bank governors to accompany their finance ministry colleagues. Thus, the G5 framework of finance ministers and central bank governors' consultations was born.[36] Clearly the beginnings of the G5 (later to become the G7) process were heavily informal, somewhat ad hoc and had an incremental and evolutionary dynamic. From the outset the process was heavily dependent upon the personalities involved and to some extent it has retained these qualities of personalism and informality. Such qualities have meant that it has revolved around personal networks and shared understandings, although like all multilateral forums, the G7 process has undergone a degree of institutionalization over time.

The G7/G8 summits

Today, there are two principal separate but related branches of the G7 process. Perhaps best known are the annual summits attended by heads of state and government (now G8). Helmut Schmidt of Germany and Valéry Giscard d'Estaing of France subsequently went from being finance ministers, who attended initial Library Group meetings, to becoming leaders of their countries. Both were keen to recreate the 'Library Group' meetings at head of state/government level. They decided to hold a summit meeting in Rambouillet, France in 1975, to which the heads of the existing G5 were invited, along with the Italian leader. The following year the US hosted a similar summit meeting in Puerto Rico and invited the Canadians so as to further offset perceived Eurocentrism. Thus the G7 summits were born (now G8). Now only four out of the seven members of the new G7 were European. From the perspective of US policy-makers this was a much more favourable ratio than the eight out of eleven that persisted in the G10, while the smaller numbers made the G7 more manageable. The leaders of G7 countries have continued to meet on an annual basis since 1975. The finance ministers and central bank governors also continued with their own G5 meetings. On the surface therefore, G7 membership would appear to be something of a historical accident, but this belies the reality of common ties that have bound the group together and facilitated their operation as a coalition.

From G5 to G7: the ascendancy of the finance ministers' process

From the mid-1980s onwards, the leaders increasingly abdicated from discussing financial and monetary issues at their annual summits and allowed the finance ministers and central bank governors to take a more active role. At the Versailles summit in 1982 the leaders decided that the G5 finance ministers and central bank governors should meet periodically in the presence of the managing director of the IMF.[37] From 1982, G5 finance ministers and central bank governors were also instructed by the leaders to develop a more comprehensive multilateral surveillance exercise.[38] This was to become more systematic and with the aid of the Managing Director of the IMF was to promote policy convergence and exchange rate stability. Despite having undergone a marginal degree of formalization, the G5 meetings continued to involve a mere sixteen individuals (excluding translators): the five finance ministers, central bank governors and finance ministry deputies, and the Managing Director of the IMF. Initially, these meetings took place in secret without the press scrutiny that surrounded the summits.

The privacy of G5 meetings ended with a formal announcement at a meeting at the Plaza Hotel in Manhattan in September 1985.[39] The finance ministries and central banks announced that national monetary authorities would engage in exchange market interventions to encourage the orderly depreciation of the dollar. This resulted in intensified pressures from the Italians and the Canadians to extend the G5 forum and bring it into line with the seven power summits. Unilaterally, Ronald Reagan agreed to invite the Italians after threats were made to close US military bases in Italy. US Treasury Secretary James Baker was embarrassed by the intervention of the US president and later apologized to disappointed G5 colleagues.[40] Subsequently, the extension of membership was announced at the Tokyo summit of 1986 and an invitation was also extended to the Canadians. There was now a finance ministers and central bank governors' Group of Seven to go with the leaders' Group of Seven. A further intensification and formalization of the multilateral surveillance process involving a series of seven economic indicators were also announced at Tokyo. This was another US initiative and it reflected James Baker's desire to deliver a more competitive dollar by encouraging both Japan and Germany to follow more expansionary macroeconomic policies.

Initially, the G5 finance ministers continued to meet ahead of G7 meetings, but by 1989 G7 finance ministers' meetings had almost entirely replaced G5 meetings. At the same time, the surveillance exercise enabled the finance ministers and central bank governors to build up their own momentum and to play an increasingly prominent role in the conduct of international monetary policy. Moreover, the independence of several of the national central banks made it very difficult for the annual summits to issue instructions to the G5/G7 process concerning exchange rate policy. Consequently, the G7 finance ministers and central bank governors' process has become the pre-eminent forum for the formulation of international monetary and exchange rate policy and related financial questions. Today, it is accepted that the finance ministries and central banks take the lead on international financial questions and the leaders look to the expertise of their finance ministries and central banks to formulate proposals and set agendas in the field of global financial governance. The more detailed reports of the finance ministries and central banks tend to feed into the documentation released at the summits. Finance ministry and central bank officials take their own series of interactions and communications far more seriously than the summits.[41] It is also interesting to note that in career terms the finance ministry deputies are almost always more senior officials than their summit counterparts – the sherpas, also indicating that national bureaucracies tend to take the finance ministry and central bank process rather more seriously than summitry.

The rationale for G7 meetings

In terms of explanations for the establishment of the G7, the definitive account of G7 summitry identifies increasing economic interdependence, and the need for collective management of this condition, as one of the principal factors behind the initiation of a new group of countries to reach decisions on key international issues.[42] Interdependence is a condition whereby policies pursued in one country affect economic conditions in other countries. Certainly, there were obvious advantages to be gained from holding joint meetings at which policy-makers explained their problems, listened to others and discerned the future policy intentions of their overseas counterparts. An awareness of international effects, causes and values, the cultivation of shared world-views, the development of common historical lessons and more informed national policies, were all potential benefits to be derived from such meetings. However, there were other settings such as the G10 that could be used for purposes of discussion and information sharing. Interdependence alone cannot explain why the G5/G7 was created. In this respect, the timing of the emergence of the Library Group and the G7 are crucial in explanations of the rationale behind the process. The collapse of the fixed exchange rate system gave consensus formation a particular sense of urgency, as the future design of the international monetary system became a principal concern for policy-makers. The United States saw the creation of a smaller less Eurocentric group of countries than the G10 as the quickest and easiest route to such a consensus.

A new notion of trilateralism, involving a trilateral approach to the international economy, based upon co-operation, and even co-ordination, between Europe, North America and Japan to replace US hegemony, has also been advanced as an explanation of the creation of the G7. However, as the rest of this chapter demonstrates, during the first two decades of its existence, the G7 primarily operated as a vehicle for providing support and endorsement for US-generated initiatives and ideas.[43]

One other factor was significant in the establishment of the G7. Both the Library Group and the summits were intended to give finance ministers and leaders the opportunity to meet alone without an excessive bureaucratic presence. Participants valued the informal familiarity and the personal relations they were able to build up through their interactions.[44] G7 meetings allowed frank and unfettered face-to-face discussions of policies and problems. Certainly finance ministers valued the sense of common purpose and solidarity regular meetings provided them with, reflecting the fact that they often had more common ground and shared understandings than with colleagues at home.[45]

G7 policy phases

Establishing principles for the governance of the international monetary system

Following the collapse of the dollar exchange rate system in the early 1970s, the first challenge facing G5/G7 countries was to establish some broad consensual principles to inform the future international monetary system. During 1973–4 a dispute between France and the USA on the most appropriate international exchange rate regime acted as an obstacle to the formation of such a consensus. The French wanted to return to some version of a fixed exchange rate regime and were inclined to support capital controls. The Americans insisted on retaining their ability to let the dollar float and vociferously opposed capital controls. Restoration of the legality of the international monetary system therefore floundered on the basis of doctrinal differences between the US and France.[46]

Library Group meetings and the emerging G5 process acted as an important source of exchanges between finance ministry officials. They lubricated French–American monetary negotiations in 1973–5. In the autumn of 1975, a series of secret meetings were held between Edwin Yeo and Jacques de Larosiere, the US and French finance ministry (G5) deputies. The French maintained that the US enjoyed an 'exorbitant privilege' because the dollar's reserve status enabled them to finance internal and external deficits with their own currency. Such a privilege, the French argued, had been abused as evidenced by widening external and internal deficits and rising inflation. The principal US negotiator, Edwin Yeo, a banker by profession, had some sympathy with this view. However, Yeo held that countries with persistent surpluses such as Germany and Japan should also bear some of the costs of international adjustment efforts. At the same time, the US Congress expressed concern that countries might seek to gain a competitive advantage through currency devaluations under a free-floating regime.[47]

Yeo advocated not fixed exchange rates but a 'stable' system of exchange rates. This would be maintained by individual countries' efforts to deliver domestic price stability. At the same time, the mandate of the IMF would be expanded and renewed so that the institution would exercise 'surveillance' over the international adjustment process. The rationale behind this was that international market forces supplemented by peer pressure, exercised through the Fund, would discipline countries and foster domestic conditions conducive to international stability.[48] France was prepared to accept this thinking, possibly over-estimating the potential impact of such discipline on the US. The term 'surveillance' was chosen, primarily because it had the right connotation for the US congress.[49] It implied some sort of international oversight without deference to a higher international authority.[50]

Eventually the text of the French–American agreement was released in 1975 at the first Rambouillet summit, after it had been endorsed by leaders from the G5 and Italy, and after senior IMF staff had been consulted. The text contained an acknowledgement that monetary authorities could occasionally usefully intervene in the markets to counter disorderly conditions, however this was to be the exception rather than the rule.[51] The first principle of the new international monetary system was clear. The market rather than states would assume primacy in determining exchange rates. When governments' perceived that the market failed to reflect underlying economic realities, they could intervene to correct imbalances. This was essentially a US concession to appease French distrust of markets. Any decision to return to a system of fixed exchange rates would require an 85 per cent majority within the IMF. This gave the US a comfortable veto on the matter.

The text of the agreement also covered changes to the IMF's articles of agreement concerning exchange rate arrangements. The new article IV stated that IMF members had an obligation to pursue economic policies conducive to monetary stability as a means of producing exchange rate stability.[52] This was the second major principle for the governance of the international monetary system.

Governments had a duty towards monetary stability in the formulation of their domestic macroeconomic policies. The full implications of this obligation on governments have only emerged over time as the process of capital liberalization has proceeded. The Rambouillet agreement also established that the IMF was to exercise oversight over the international monetary system by exercising firm surveillance over the exchange rate policies of members. Members were to provide the Fund with the information necessary for such surveillance and to consult with it on exchange rate policies.[53]

Almost from its very inception therefore, the post-1970 liberal international financial order has had a legal and institutional foundation that has reflected US preferences. Moreover the G7/G5 process was used to endorse this. The new G5/G7 process began life with a series of protracted negotiations among officials over a two-year period, which eventually led to the endorsement of a new, albeit minimal, legal framework for the international monetary system. The US Treasury used the G7 process to ensure that this initial legal and institutional framework placed an onus on domestic price stability and sound money well before Keynesian approaches to macroeconomic policy-making had been abandoned across the G7, while continuing to pursue growth-orientated macroeconomic policies itself. However, the consent of European finance ministries via the G7 process implies that this was part of a concerted effort to create a supportive international context for 'sound money' policies. It had long been the responsibility of officials from finance ministries and central banks involved in international monetary affairs to promote monetary discipline in the domestic setting.[54] This new international agreement increased their strategic capacity to ensure that national policies concerned themselves with price stability. In this respect, the agreement announced at Rambouillet constituted a crucial strategic turning-point in the battle to establish the supremacy of finance ministries and central banks and of financial and monetary criteria over socially orientated ones in national policy processes.

The subsequent operations of the G7 process, including the summits, can be divided into four broad phases that have characterized international financial diplomacy since the 1970s. This involves a rise–fall–rise and fall again cycle of policy co-ordination. US interests have been to the fore, but these appear to have been progressively constrained by market, intellectual and institutional developments.

Phase I 1975–8: rise of policy co-ordination

The first four annual G7 summits followed an increasingly ambitious path of international policy co-ordination to promote economic recovery and international growth. The culmination of this was 'a paradigmatic case of policy co-ordination'[55] involving a cross-issue package deal brokered at the Bonn summit of 1978. This agreement was known as the 'locomotive strategy' and was based on a series of reciprocal concessions among participant governments in key sectors of the economy. Because it brought leaders together, the summit was able to bring in other areas such as trade and energy, making reciprocal concessions possible and thus increasing the potential for genuine policy co-ordination.[56] This kind of cross-issue international Keynesian fine tuning was possible because of the presence of a range of voices from national bureaucracies and the fact that political commitment from leaders enabled them to co-ordinate the various bureaucracies. As finance ministries and central banks have gradually monopolized international monetary and financial policy and have increasingly portrayed it as a highly specialist technical task due to rising international capital mobility and the growing complexity and sophistication of financial markets, the potential for the negotiation of such package deals has receded in inverse proportion to the growing autonomy of the finance ministries and central banks, who in turn increasingly operate in a sectoral fashion and are largely unresponsive to the concerns and demands of other bureaucracies. The increasing fragmentation of international politics into a series of specialist transgovernmental networks also acts to restrict the range of joint outcomes that are open to governments.[57]

At Bonn, the German government pledged to submit expansionist measures equivalent to 1 per cent of GDP to the Bundestag. Japan agreed to increase its real growth by 1.5 per cent, whilst holding exports at 1977 levels. In return, the US introduced some anti-inflationary measures and offered to remove controls on domestic oil prices. It was hoped that this strategy would address the stagnation in world growth caused by the existence of a large US current account deficit, a low dollar and rising inflation, as well as a stagnation in production and current account surpluses in Japan and Germany. The locomotive approach launched at Bonn was essentially a form of international Keynesianism involving efforts to administer a co-ordinated international demand stimulus. On the whole however, the agreement addressed immediate US concerns rather more directly than Japanese and German ones. The agreement attempted to create the conditions for an export-driven recovery in the US, thereby stemming the fall of the dollar. Significantly, the agreement was secured because internationalist forces within each government were able to exploit divisions within more domestically orientated coalitions and reinforce arguments for the domestic courses of action that they favoured.[58]

In Germany, high inflation and budget deficits followed, although the second oil shock of 1979 and the Iranian revolution undoubtedly contributed to this. Unfortunately, the association with the Bonn agreement did much to discredit the idea of internationally co-ordinated growth strategies in German academic and policy-making circles thereafter.[59] The memory of Bonn has created an in-built resistance from German policy-makers and public to subsequent attempts by the US to get Germany to share in international adjustment efforts, particularly when this has involved addressing external surpluses through macroeconomic expansion.

Phase II 1979–84: the fall of policy co-ordination

The next sequence of summits in 1979–84 had to handle the recession provoked by the second oil crisis and reacted against the complexity of the cross-issue package launched at Bonn. The election of Thatcher, Reagan, Kohl and Nakasone shifted the political balance in the G7 countries to the right. Every summit declaration in 1979–82 advocated prudent monetary and fiscal policy. The recommendation throughout the period was that governments and central banks should give priority to checking inflation through strict monetary control and by cutting back on public spending. In other words, policy co-ordination was rejected and it was emphasized that governments had to first 'put their own houses in order'. G7 statements repeatedly claimed that government's role was to create the conditions for the private sector to become the engine of growth, rather than attempting to stimulate the economy through macroeconomic policy. This contrasted starkly with the Keynesian orientation of the Bonn summit communiqué and its references to 'stated growth targets'.[60] Such a change in sentiment was indicative of the gradual rejection of Keynesian economic thought throughout the industrialized world.[61]

The first half of the 1980s was also a period in which US Treasury Secretary Don Regan and deputy Beryl Sprinkel denied that the dollar exchange rate had any significant implications for the US economy, arguing that 90 per cent of the US economy was domestic.[62] The dollar was allowed to rise to unprecedented levels. This was the result of an unfortunate conjuncture of domestic policies. US tax cuts and spiralling military expenditures created a large US budget deficit. At the same time, the tax cuts fuelled a consumer boom, which not only increased the US trade deficit, but also created inflationary pressures. In the face of widening trade and budget deficits, Paul Volcker, Chairman of the Federal Reserve, presided over short-term interest rate rises. This sucked capital into the US from all over the world, leading to a rapid appreciation in the dollar. The rising dollar exacerbated the US trade deficit and created problems for a weak French franc and for developing countries' debt repayments, as interest rates around the world were forced up by the Fed's policies.

The period has subsequently been referred to as a phase of 'benign neglect' of the dollar. Influenced by the Jurgensen Report, published by a Working Group on Exchange Market Intervention in 1983, the G7 rarely engaged in exchange market interventions during this period. The working group had reached the conclusion that sterilized intervention[63] had a much smaller impact than unsterilized intervention[64] and could have a short-term effect on exchange rates but would not have a long-term impact unless it was accompanied by supportive domestic policy action. The onus for delivering financial stability was therefore placed firmly on national policies.

Unfortunately, the process of multilateral surveillance established at Rambouillet did not have the desired disciplinary affects on US policies. As an exceptional country the US was able to use the dollar's reserve status and its highly developed financial markets to finance its twin deficits with foreign, predominantly Japanese, capital. Consequently, the dollar became overvalued and together with high short-term US interest rates this had disruptive effects on the international monetary system as a whole. Moreover, US-based manufacturers began to suffer. Exports fell because of the high value of the dollar and intense competition in domestic markets, which was due to an influx of cheap foreign imports to meet the bloated domestic consumer demand resulting from the Reagan tax cuts. Unsurprisingly, powerful protectionist pressures emerged in the US Congress, as manufacturing lobbies signalled their frustration at the 'benign neglect' of the dollar.

Phase III 1984–9: the re-emergence of policy co-ordination

The next phase in international monetary co-ordination was the result of a change of personnel in the Reagan administration,[65] illustrating the significance of US preferences for patterns of G7 co-operation. In 1985, James Baker and Richard Darman replaced Treasury secretary Donald Regan and deputy Beryl Sprinkel. Baker was interested in using surveillance to counteract the emerging protectionist pressures in Congress and to correct external and fiscal imbalances. He wanted surveillance to promote increased consumer demand abroad in the hope it would help correct the US trade deficit and avert the emerging recession. Unlike Don Regan, Baker also acknowledged the dollar's valuation as a problem, primarily because of his close connections to manufacturing and his avowed opposition to protectionism.[66] To the relief of G7 colleagues, Baker was quick to spot the potential for some form of exchange rate co-operation and the domestic political capital he could accumulate in his effort to counter protectionist pressures.[67]

By 1985–6, the US was in a similar position to that of 1978. A massive external deficit had been accumulated, whilst Germany and Japan had large external surpluses and low inflation. In September 1985, the G5 went public with the announcement of the Plaza agreement. In an effort to counter the effects of a soaring and an overvalued dollar, concerted exchange market interventions were agreed upon in the hope that this would correct what officials viewed as a clear misalignment. By December, the dollar had lost 16 per cent against the yen and 12 per cent against the deutschmark.[68] Subsequently, there has been some debate on whether the dollar would have depreciated without the G5 initiative.[69] The dollar's rise was undoubtedly excessive and a market-initiated correction may have taken place anyway.[70] However, after a brief interlude the rise of the dollar continued right up to the time of the Plaza interventions and showed no signs of relenting.[71]

The Plaza agreement was successful in accomplishing its objectives of minimizing the dollar volatility caused by the US's twin deficits and combating the protectionist pressures emerging in Congress.[72] This gave the G5/G7 process a role as a sort of part-time international financial council. In the retrospective words of one participant, 'the G7 used to perform a kind of loose management function. Markets gave the G7 some credit for its efforts and in times of stress looked to it for co-ordinated action'.[73] However, most notable was the fact that Plaza happened only because US authorities wanted it to. For some time prior to Plaza other G7 governments had been expressing their disquiet at the overvaluation of the dollar. However, collective action only came about when US authorities came to recognize the domestic value of that collective action. Moreover, Plaza was an example of collective international adjustment because of US authorities' failure to manage the dollar through domestic policies, which were also disrupting the international monetary system in the form of higher world interest rates. Rather than adjusting domestic policies (in particular addressing the fiscal deficit) and putting their own house in order, US policy-makers were able to use the G5 process to initiate a managed depreciation of the dollar. In other words, the US was able to use exchange rate agreements in the 1980s to ensure that it retained the sort of autonomy in fiscal policy that was being denied to other G7 countries.

The main motivation behind the US Treasury's initiation of the Plaza agreement was the desire to quell protectionist pressures in Congress. In this respect, multilateral co-operation on exchange rates was seen by the US Treasury as a way of convincing Congress that foreign governments were willing to make a contribution to solving US trade problems, thus offsetting the widespread view on Capitol Hill that other governments' trade and exchange rate policies were unfair. US domestic interests and preferences were in fact the biggest influence on the Plaza agreement of 1985, because economic ideas appear to explain relatively little where Plaza is concerned. As Destler and Henning have noted:

> if anything the fraternity of professional economists and government practitioners was marginally more skeptical in 1985 of the efficacy of intervention and declaratory policy than it had been in 1981. On the other hand, political pressures and wider societal preferences in the US were such that an administration with philosophical preference for free markets, was willing to adopt a more active exchange rate stance.[74]

The second half of the 1980s produced speculation that G5/G7 co-operative efforts might evolve into a new system for the management of the international monetary system consisting of moveable and flexible reference ranges.[75] The Louvre accord, announced by the G7 in February 1987, adopted a system of currency reference ranges to stabilize the yen–dollar–deutschmark relationship at unpublished central rates for the dollar of 1.825DM and 153.5Y.[76] The motivation behind this was a strong US desire to stabilize the fall of the dollar initiated at Plaza, combined with German and Japanese concern over export competitiveness. In this respect, inflation had become a pressing concern for the Reagan administration and a dollar stabilization would assist in efforts to tackle inflation. Once more, US domestic priorities drove the G7 agenda. The post-Louvre statement indicated that ministers would co-operate to 'foster stability of exchange rates around current levels'.[77] Like Plaza, the Louvre accord was relatively successful in achieving exchange rate stability. Despite this, policy-makers remained sceptical that an optimum exchange rate equilibrium existed. A reactive method was used to identify appropriate levels to be maintained by future policy action, namely the level the markets closed at the previous day.[78] Throughout this period the G7 continued to intermittently manage international currency relationships as a substitute for a formal rule-binding regime. It was an ad hoc process of adjustment based upon continuous consultation. A meeting standard, as opposed to a formal regime, maintained the momentum of co-operation.[79] The process differed from the EMS because exchange rates were expressed in nominal bilateral terms, while ranges remained confidential.[80]

The G7 process was also used to manage the stock market crash of 1987. Central banks appeared to co-ordinate interest rate reductions in an attempt to restore confidence. Finance ministry officials remained in contact throughout the adjustment process. These extensive communications proceeded smoothly and were aided by the familiarity and solid relationships built up through regular G7 meetings.[81]

On 23 December 1987, a G7 communiqué was released which contained policy commitments and renewed agreements on exchange rates. The markets tested the authorities' commitments to reference ranges. Central banks mobilized in a concerted fashion. After reaching a low in mid-January, heavy intervention supported the dollar throughout January. By February 1988, there was evidence of the desired adjustment in the US trade balance. Unfortunately, interest rate cuts in Japan later resulted in asset inflation in stock and property markets, and the so-called 'bubble economy'. At the same time, despite pressure from G7 partners and supportive rhetoric from Treasury officials, the US took no serious steps to cut its budget deficit.

Ultimately, the key point about the second half of the 1980s is that the G7 showed a willingness to negotiate quite specific exchange rate agreements that required joint exchange market interventions and sometimes adjustments to domestic monetary policies. In other words, the G7 regularly co-ordinated their policies throughout the period, while the broad thrust of their activities was to advocate financial liberalization and macroeconomic discipline, even if the former appeared contrary to the objective of exchange rate stabilization, and the US only partially adhered to the latter. Subsequently, exchange rate co-operation of the sort witnessed in the second half of the 1980s declined, as the perverse national policy mixes often implied by exchange rate targeting became progressively more evident.

Phase IV since 1991: the fall of co-ordination

Most commentators have agreed that the record of the G7 in the 1990s did not match earlier periods of activity.[82] In this respect, we can refer to a rise, fall, rise and fall again cycle of economic policy co-ordination. There were some instances of loose co-operation in the 1990s. For example, the G7 responded to the collapse of communism with an aid package designed to encourage market reforms in the Eastern Bloc, but the sums of money involved were meagre compared with the amount of US aid that was provided to Europe after WWII. In 1991, Japanese and German membership of the G7 enabled it to be used as the forum for working out financing arrangements for the Gulf War.[83] The Brady plan unveiled a system of debt relief in 1989. This was updated and reinforced through the initiation of Naples terms of debt in 1994, but further progress has been impeded by a disagreement between the US and Germany.[84] On the question of modernizing international financial institutions the G7 has acted as the catalyst for some reforms of the IMF and World Bank (see Chapter 7). However, the ambitious policy co-ordination of the 1980s has largely been abandoned. In other words, the evidence would suggest that, while as Webb has argued, international capital mobility increases the need for domestic macroeconomic adjustment if attempts at policy co-ordination are to be successful, it is an insufficient condition for co-ordinated domestic policy adjustments to take place.[85] Rather as international capital mobility proceeds it can actually make policy co-ordination less likely, restricting governments' ability to deliver collective international public goods.[86] As the introduction to this book explained, for such a hypothesis to be verified, it is necessary to link international capital mobility to changing institutional and ideational contexts. The framework of four-dimensional diplomacy outlined in the next chapter takes steps in this direction.

In the 1990s the G7 was the subject of fierce criticism.[87] The early 1990s saw severe recession linked to debt deflation throughout most of the G7. Financial liberalization and de-regulation also led to speculative excesses. Indebtedness in the USA and UK grew at all levels, while Japanese monetary authorities sought to dampen asset inflation. The allegation was that the G7 experienced a series of missed opportunities and outright failures by not co-ordinating policies as in the 1970s and 1980s. Bergsten and Henning have referred to a non-aggression pact that emerged in the place of active policy co-ordination, where countries refused to be openly critical of one another's policies.[88] A number of possible explanations for this absence of policy co-ordination present themselves for consideration. First, intellectually, international Keynesianism of the sort evident in the Bonn locomotive strategy of 1978 had become unfashionable, largely because of a concern that such co-ordinated macroeconomic expansions were inflationary. Second, domestic institutional changes in G7 countries and a convergence towards independent central banks and rules for the conduct of fiscal policy made national policy-making less discretionary and therefore less conducive to international co-ordination. Connected to this, societal interests favouring competitively valued exchange rates have found it increasingly difficult to influence exchange rate policies throughout the G7 countries. Third, expansion in the volume and scope of international capital flows has led to the widespread perception that government-executed foreign exchange market interventions are of limited utility. The evidence for this view however, is the subject of some debate, suggesting that such a view may be primarily socially constructed.[89] These possible explanations are explored in more detail throughout the rest of this book.

Conclusions

The G7 process came into existence in the context of the breakdown of the fixed exchange rate system and the emergence of an increasingly liberal and open international financial order. It has evolved in an incremental and ad hoc fashion and has had a somewhat haphazard and accidental development. The G7 process has also been characterized by informality, personalism and a highly discretionary form of co-operation. Finance ministries and central banks have used the G7 process to develop shared understandings and maximize their influence by promoting shared objectives, notably macroeconomic austerity and financial liberalization. The G7 have also collaborated to minimize exchange rate disruptions caused by the shift from a fixed rate system in an era of capital controls to a floating rate system in an era of liberalized capital. In effect, the timing of the emergence of the G7 has meant that the process has presided over the emergence of a more liberalized international financial order and a more disciplined set of macroeconomic policies that have prioritized price stability.[90]

Initially, discussions at G7 meetings were dominated by the breakdown of the post-war international monetary system. The US decision to consult with other leading powers more actively can be interpreted as an implicit acknowledgement that it was no longer able or willing to act as guarantor for the system. In reality, the US continued to enjoy exorbitant monetary privileges and remained easily the most influential power within the G5/G7, but was less willing to accept the responsibilities this entailed. The eventual design of the new international monetary system and the new articles of agreement of the IMF bore the imprint of US preferences. Multilateral surveillance of national policies was at the heart of the new system and became a crucial component of the G7 process.

Instances of policy co-ordination have been sporadic and have taken the form of a rise–fall–rise and fall again cycle. Significantly, co-ordination has taken place when the US has wanted it to and when societal interests in the US have created political pressures for some form of multilateral exchange rate management, or economic policy co-ordination. Practically all notable instances have been driven by and have reflected US interests. During the course of the 1980s, the US argued for market-determined outcomes when the dollar was strong, and 'policy co-ordination' through the G7 process when the domestic results of market-determined outcomes became a liability.[91] The G5/G7 process has effectively been used by the US as a means of trying to pass some of the burden of management of the international financial system on to other governments. The clearest endorsements of policy co-ordination came at the end of the Carter administration and after 1985, through the Plaza and Louvre agreements. Political pressures from domestic constituents in the US drove both of these episodes.

Co-ordinated adjustment among the leading industrialized states remains one of the few ways of stabilizing the world economy. The G7 has been the principal forum for such efforts, but its record has at best been sporadic and based on a highly discretionary form of negotiation. From a historical perspective, research into the G7 process should seek to explain why policy-makers have adopted a much less ambitious approach to policy co-ordination over the last decade. Payments imbalances between the leading industrialized countries have continued to increase and exchange rate volatility has shown no signs of abating.[92] If anything therefore, the incentives for policy co-ordination have actually increased.[93] A number of possible contributory factors present themselves for further consideration where the seeming demise of policy co-ordination is concerned. Given that in the 1970s and 1980s co-ordination was predominantly driven by and reflected US preferences, the diminishing influence or the changing interests of the US could both be feasible explanations. Other explanations include a changing intellectual consensus, domestic institutional constraints and the expansion in the scope, volume and intensity of international capital flows. Finally, in the 1960s the finance ministries and central banks largely concerned themselves with technical balance of payments fine tuning. By the late 1970s and 1980s they were using the G7 process to initiate sporadic ad hoc adjustments to domestic macroeconomic policies and to establish a legal basis and governance mechanisms for the new post-Bretton Woods international monetary system. In the 1990s however, with the demise of economic policy co-ordination and the expanding role of various multilateral institutions, it became less clear what role the G7 process performed. Despite this the finance ministries and central banks continued to meet regularly and valued their consultations and deliberations. So how then should we characterize the governance role of the G7 in an era of financial globalization in which some assumed states to be retreating in the face of expanding market authority?[94] Subsequent chapters will explore these issues and questions in more detail, not least in the context of a process of 'financialization', the growing importance of equities markets for US economic performance and wealth and the emergence of a new share owning constituency in the United States.

3 Situating the Group of Seven in a context of decentralized financial globalization

A four-dimensional framework

Assessing the contribution of the G7 process to global financial governance requires that the process be located in a wider context. If we are to obtain an understanding of the role, function and purpose of the meetings of G7 finance ministries and central banks, looking solely at what takes place between national representatives at G7 meetings is insufficient. As Robert Cox has argued, 'multilateralism can only be understood in the context in which it exists and that context is the historical structure of world order'.[1] The relationships the G7 process has with domestic settings, market forms, and the range of bodies and organizations that clutter the domain of financial governance, should be essential components of any attempt to decipher the purpose and authority of the G7 process. Crucially however, while acknowledging that interactions between states will be affected by the wider context in which they take place, it would be mistaken to assume that inter-state relations and interactions are entirely shaped by exogenous global structures.[2] Inter-state diplomacy and its outcomes can be an active force shaping world order. Multilateral processes will be constrained by and have to respond to structural factors, such as the way in which the international monetary and financial system is organized, yet multilateralism also retains the capacity to shape and influence such structures.[3] In other words, analyses of the interactions between the G7 finance ministries and central banks inevitably have to wrestle with the structure–agency dilemma that has long preoccupied international relations scholars.[4] Mindful of the structure–agency problem, this chapter develops an analytical framework which examines structure–agency interactions and rests on the belief that the primacy of neither structure nor agency can simply be assumed. It devises a framework for locating the G7 in a wider world context and for organizing analysis of some of the inter-relationships that have an effect on the functioning of the G7 process.

In the first section there is a discussion of how the contemporary financial order is characterized by what Randall Germain calls 'decentralized globalization'. I argue that this context creates multiple incentives for the finance ministries and central banks to construct a transgovernmental coalition. Keohane and Nye's original formulation of transgovernmentalism is revisited and revised and I suggest that a revised version of transgovernmentalism, in which excessively state-centric assumptions are relaxed, can have a useful application in an extended study of G7 finance ministry–central bank collaboration. In the second section, the concepts of power and authority in global financial governance are discussed. In particular, the concepts of structural power and technical authority are distinguished from one another. In the third section, the structure–agency dilemma is wrestled with and I advocate a stucturation, or neo-integrationist perspective based on theoretical complexity, rather than parsimony. There is also an extended discussion of the shortcomings of two-level games, as an approach that was developed on the basis of a case study of G7 co-operation and which is often used as a metaphor for G7 co-operation. In this section I make the case for an approach I call multi-dimensional diplomacy. In the fourth section I identify four spatial dimensions that need to be considered when evaluating the role of the G7 and their contribution to global financial governance. A range of literatures and analytical tools which can be usefully employed in a study of the Group of Seven are also identified.

States, transgovernmentalism and global financial governance in an era of decentralized financial globalization

The G7 process is essentially a form of multilateralism consisting of relations among three or more states based on certain shared principles.[5] On the one hand then, the G7 process can be viewed as little more than a series of state–state interactions. On the other hand, this acknowledgement needs to be accompanied by an awareness that G7 interactions do not take place on a blank canvas but are shaped by previous instances of interaction and the inherited legacies of knowledge, beliefs and social practices that have accumulated as a consequence of the history of that interaction. Nor do interactions between the G7 finance ministries and central banks take place in a societal vacuum, but in a wider context comprising the complexities of domestic politics, the evolution of an emerging complex global financial system and a diffused and highly differentiated inter-state and inter-agency system of decision making which is supposed to govern the global financial system. Any attempt to examine the role and politics of the Group of Seven has to be sensitive to this wider context.

Global financial governance in a context of decentralized financial globalization

Global financial governance is an ambiguous term. I use it here simply to refer to the governance of the financial structure as a whole, described by Susan Strange as, 'the sum of all arrangements governing the availability of credit plus all the factors determining the terms on which currencies are exchanged for one another'.[6] Today, the interactions of a multiplicity of actors in a range of settings determine the governance of currencies and the availability of credit. Global financial governance might be viewed as the totality of these interactions, including various borrower and lender practices at the level of the individual citizen.[7] What we are concerned with in this chapter however, is how the G7 process fits into the complex pattern of governance that results from these interactions, and in particular, with identifying and developing an analytical framework that can help us locate the G7 in such a complex governance pattern.

First, it is necessary to say something about the contemporary financial context in which the G7 operates. The contemporary financial order is perhaps best characterized by Randall Germain's term 'decentralized globalization'.[8] Decentralized financial globalization involves both interconnectedness and decentralization. The most prominent feature of 'decentralized globalization' is the increased size and scope of financial markets, which now dwarf, and have become divorced from, the production of and trade in goods and services. New innovative financial products have been initiated to hedge against exchange rate risk, interest rate risk, or commodity price changes, but these disintermediated financial markets have become great sources of profit and speculative trading in their own right.[9] Barriers between different national and sectoral financial markets have also become less relevant and there is a situation of increasing interconnectedness and interpenetration between previously separate financial markets due to advanced telecommunications, which means that developments in one market can rapidly spill over into another, creating a situation of mutual vulnerability to financial disruption.

The mutual vulnerability that results from the interconnectedness of the contemporary global financial system also gives the system a distinct decentralized character. Today, there is no single principal financial centre in the world economy. London, New York, Frankfurt, Hong Kong, Tokyo and a host of other financial centres, compete with one another as sources and destinations for capital and credit.[10] Governance of this decentralized but interconnected system cannot be conducted solely from any one of these centres, and as a consequence there is no single locus of authority and decision making in the contemporary global financial system.

In this context, some degree of consensual decision making is an essential component of global financial governance because of the need for a variety of states and bodies to implement shared initiatives if the omnipresent threat of systemic contagion is to be minimized in an open financial system.[11] Consensus, as we shall see, is also important in global financial governance because of the diffused nature of decision making across a number of specialist bodies. Possibly most crucial to the analysis here however, is the fact that the technically specialist nature of finance as an emerging technical system has seen technocrats from finance ministries and central banks use argument and reason as guiding precepts of debate and deliberation out of respect for one another's professional expertise and this in turn engenders collegiality.[12]

Despite a loose consensual mode of operation, the pursuit of self-interest and the exercise of power are not entirely absent from global financial governance. On the contrary, the United States remains the world's most important financial power and this is reflected in financial governance structures in a variety of ways, and most tellingly in the fact that any financial governance initiative is doomed to fail without US support because its financial markets are still the most liquid and significant for the world financial structure as a whole. In other words, the United States still has the capacity to determine what is acceptable in financial governance and effectively defines the parameters of debate, which gives the US an enormous power of veto. At the same time however, because of the decentralized nature of the contemporary financial system, as well as its interconnectedness and the mutual vulnerability that results from this, the United States cannot simply impose its preferences on other states and authorities. The result is that financial governance is characterized by the uneasy co-existence of consensual deliberations and debates, and the long-standing exercise of what Susan Strange called US structural power, stemming primarily from large and liquid US capital markets and the importance of the dollar for international trading and monetary systems.[13] The dynamics of this uneasy tension will be investigated throughout the rest of this book.

Finally, the terrain of global financial governance is further defined and shaped by the presence of a multiplicity of actors and a complex specialized division of labour, which further adds to the decentralized and the diffused nature of decision making governing the global financial system. For example, perhaps the central institution in global financial governance is essentially a suprastate bureaucracy – the IMF, whose permanent staff conduct continuous analyses of countries' balance of payments and macroeconomic positions and on this basis negotiate loan agreements with debtor countries, at the instigation and instruction of their major shareholder countries.[14] There are also a collection of specialized regulatory agencies which act to facilitate collaboration between national regulators including IOSCO (the international securities regulator) and the International Association of Insurance Supervisors (IAIS).[15] Central banks have responsibility for the soundness of domestic financial systems and collaborate through the Basle Committee on Banking Supervision (BCBS) and through the Financial Stability Forum (FSF), which also brings a whole host of specialist regulators to the table.[16] Furthermore, private market agents and financial institutions develop collective positions through mechanisms such as the G30, or through international trade associations such as the International Securities Market Association, or the International Accounting Standards Board.[17] The operation of private markets is further facilitated by the activities of private credit rating agencies, who reach judgements on the creditworthiness of governments and corporations and consequently influence the market decision-making process as a whole.[18] And finally of course, we also have the joint meetings of national finance ministries and central banks, both as a Group of Twenty (G20) and as a Group of Seven (G7). These meetings discuss a range of financial and monetary governance issues and attempt to set priorities and agendas for this decision-making complex as a whole.[19]

In the context of such a diverse range of actors and such a diffused decision-making structure, no one single actor is in a position to dominate or control the entire complex of global financial governance. What is urgently required, if we are to have a better understanding of the topography of global financial governance, is improved understanding of the complex inter-relationships and interactions between some of the different actors identified above. This book sets out to enhance our understanding of the terrain of global financial governance by working outwards from the meetings of the Group of Seven finance ministries and central banks, because the group has a relatively broad mandate and deals with a broad range of issues that have implications for the work of, and simultaneously links, a whole host of the actors and agencies mentioned.

Transgovernmentalism

However, before we examine and explain the relations and interactions the G7 have with the broader array of institutions and bodies involved in global financial governance, we first need to obtain an understanding of the dynamics of the interactions between the finance ministries and central banks and how these interactions inform their relationships with other actors and agencies. From the outset, it is important to have an awareness of the dangers of viewing G7 interactions simply in terms of conventional inter-state relations, particularly if we base this on a realist or neo-realist understanding of states as unitary rational actors seeking to maximize a pre-defined self-interest.[20] In this regard, we should at least allow for the possibility that finance ministries and central banks collaborate so as to arrive at shared positions and collectively maximize their interests and influence in the wider global system, particularly in a context of decentralized globalization.[21] Indeed, acknowledging the above also implies that finance ministries and central banks may have their own sets of interests, preferences and agendas that are distinguishable from those of other national bureaucracies and interests. Once we move away from the notion that states act as unitary actors in international affairs, and accept that different bureaucracies have different interests and agendas, we also have to acknowledge that relations between states and like-minded bureaucracies can be a great deal more consensual and co-operative than realists and neo-realists would have us believe.

In attempting to decipher the question of why the G7 collaborate, in the context of decentralized globalization described above, we are immediately forced to grapple with the structure–agency dilemma that has long faced International Relations scholars. On the one hand, the wider environment, such as the diffuse, diverse decision-making structure that characterizes global financial governance, will influence and inform G7 interactions and strategies. On the other hand, the nature of G7 interactions will be instrumental in shaping G7 relations with, and the group's strategic position and role within, the wider decision-making structures of global financial governance. While acknowledging that G7 interactions do not take place in a vacuum (an issue that will be further explored later in this chapter) but functionally entwine with other social spaces and decision-making arenas in complex ways, we nevertheless require some conceptual tools that enable us to better understand and interpret the interactions of the G7 finance ministries and central banks.

One such conceptual tool is Keohane and Nye's concept of transgovernmentalism, first introduced to the study of International Relations some thirty years ago, but which has since been somewhat neglected, and has rarely been systematically applied to sets of inter-state relations. The importance of Keohane and Nye's concept of transgovernmental relations was that it managed to achieve what numerous other theories had claimed to do, but had rarely managed, and that was to disaggregate the state and treat states as something other than unitary rational actors in international affairs. Keohane and Nye define transgovernmentalism as direct interactions among sub-units of different governments that are not controlled or closely guided by the policies of the cabinets or chief executives of those governments. Their aim was to focus attention on bureaucratic contacts that take place below the apex of the organizational hierarchy of states. They identified two principal forms of transgovernmental activity – transgovernmental policy co-ordination and transgovernmental coalition building, which overlap, with the former often providing the prelude to the latter.[22]

Transgovernmental policy co-ordination, in its most basic form, consists of simple informal communication among working-level officials of different bureaucracies. Face-to-face communications, Keohane and Nye pointed out, can often affect policy expectations and preferences. Moreover, when the same officials meet recurrently, they sometimes develop a sense of collegiality, which may be reinforced by their membership in a common profession, such as economics. Certainly there is some evidence of this, as we shall see, in the case of the G7 deputies. In such instances officials even begin to define themselves in relation to their transgovernmental reference group as well as in national terms. Regularised patterns of communication and interaction can create attitudes and relationships that will at least marginally change policy or affect its implementation. Transgovernmental elite networks are created when officials in different governments become linked to one another through ties of common interest, professional orientation and personal friendship. The existence of such a network will not always result in major deviations from central policy positions, but it will allow for flexible bargaining behaviour in which concessions need not be requited immediately on an issue-by-issue basis, because political bank accounts involving a mental scorecard of credits and debits, which are in turn dependent on small group collegiality, can operate, relaxing the need for immediate pay-offs.

Transgovernmental policy co-ordination can shade over into transgovernmental coalition building. In most cases, regular contacts, shared reference points and some sense of collegiality are preconditions for transgovernmental coalition building. Transgovernmental coalitions occur when sub-units of different governments jointly use resources to influence national governmental decisions. According to Keohane and Nye, transgovernmental coalitions are most likely when there is a high degree of conflict of interest between sub-units, or between sub-units and central foreign policy-makers, and relatively low executive capacity to control subordinates' behaviour and deter such coalition building.[23]

The resultant model Keohane and Nye propose is a simplified and slightly mechanical two-by-two matrix. If we take the view that the finance ministries and central banks retain a degree of autonomy from central decision makers given a) their technical expertise, and b) the rise of constitutional and institutional features such as fiscal rules and independent central banks, then we have to accept that in Keohane and Nye's terms, transgovernmental coalition building is certainly something the G7 finance ministries and central banks are capable of. Yet at the same time, there would also appear to be little incentive for finance ministries and central banks to build transgovernmental coalitions given their increasing dominance over other government agencies, at least as far as macroeconomic policy is concerned, and for low levels of conflict with other agencies in the context of the general embrace of neo-liberal and neo-classical economic ideas.[24] Of course, the extent to which neo-liberalism has been embraced varies across the G7 and across institutions and state bureaucracies. Consequently, so too the incentives G7 finance ministries and central banks face to build transgovernmental coalitions and their willingness to engage in such activities will vary across the G7 in accordance with the degree to which competing ideas and interests are represented in a range of key state bureaucracies across the G7.

More significantly, simply considering domestic factors as a measure of the incentives bureaucracies face to build transgovernmental coalitions, as is the case in Keohane and Nye's model, is simplistic and misleading. In the context of decentralized globalization, authority and power in the global political economy has diffused away from states, to both transnational markets and multilateral institutions and bodies, while resistance to financial globalization in civil society has been growing.[25] Our understanding of transgovernmentalism should be sensitive to this context. State agencies do not engage in transgovernmental coalition building simply to maximize their influence in domestic politics, but crucially are increasingly concerned with collectively directing and steering a whole host of other sites and settings in the global political economy. In other words, in a context of decentralized financial globalization, the incentives for finance ministries and central banks to act collectively and build transgovernmental coalitions are multiple and might even be said to have increased. We should also note that finance ministries and central banks may also seek to reinforce or buttress their domestic supremacy, particularly in the context of growing criticism from transnational civil society groupings. In other words, national bureaucracies will come together and construct transgovernmental coalitions not simply to influence domestic decisions, but to maximize their influence in a whole host of other spatial settings. Indeed, we should at least concede that in contrast to Keohane and Nye's formulation, it is a possibility that influencing the domestic setting may have become the least significant concern for finance ministries and central banks and consequently the specifics of a domestic setting may not be a particularly good indicator of the incentives state agencies face to engage in transgovernmental coalition building.

It is of course possible to argue that a discussion of transgovernmentalism is irrelevant in the case of finance ministries precisely because they are part of the central state core executive machinery and should not be considered as a sub-unit of governments. However, finance ministries enjoy considerable autonomy in national policy processes, largely because together with central banks they act as the state's principal source of technical expertise on financial and monetary matters, and they exploit this expertise as a resource to monopolize international financial policy debates and act largely independently of central direction or co-ordination. Leaders' offices largely remain dependent on the qualified judgements of finance ministries and their officials on international financial questions and even the detailure of fiscal policy. Likewise, central banks' participation in the G7 process enhances the autonomy of this particular series of interactions and exchanges. As one former G7 deputy has pointed out, there is a clear understanding that 'nothing the heads of state and government say at the G8 summits ties the central bank governors, particularly on monetary and exchange rate questions'.[26] We have to at least allow for the possibility that the preferences and views of finance ministries and central banks can both exist independently of, and differ from, those of chief executives, and that both agencies possess sufficient resources and capacities to pursue these preferences with limited central direction.

As we have established, in a context of decentralized financial globalization, finance ministries and central banks have multiple incentives to engage in transgovernmental coalition building. Keohane and Nye's view that a high level of conflict of interest among sub-units is a necessary pre-condition for transgovernmentalism, is consequently a narrow and overly mechanistic one. In particular, it is a view that rests on the assumption that the principal reason for engaging in transgovernmental coalition building is to reinforce or to pursue particular policy positions in relation to other domestic agencies. Despite their best intentions and claims to the contrary therefore, Keohane and Nye were still guilty of acute state centrism. The audiences finance ministries and central banks may wish to influence are not just other domestic state bureaucracies and policy-making organs, but also domestic electorates and societal interests, whose expectations and perceptions they might seek to shape. Likewise, in a quite different dynamic the finance ministries and central banks may also, given transgovernmentalism's overriding characteristic of small group collegiality, seek to create an internal consensual position, prior to collectively promoting that position in wider multilateral institutional settings, or to influence the priorities, mandates and agendas of a whole host of other bodies involved in global and international financial governance. Finally, the emergence of transnationalized financial markets and the risk of contagious financial crises that spread quickly, often sees finance ministries and central banks seeking to communicate collectively with financial markets as transborder spaces, to provide them with reassurance and collective messages concerning future policy intentions. Consequently, transgovernmentalism is an increasingly multi-spatial phenomenon that needs to be understood in multi-spatial terms, rather than in simply domestic terms. If it is to have relevance today therefore, we must move beyond Keohane and Nye's restrictive and static conceptualization of transgovernmentalism, as a device by which national bureaucracies can initiate domestic policy shifts or enhance their domestic standing. Rather we need to view transgovernmentalism as a mechanism through which state bureaucracies can attempt to influence world order more generally by acting collectively and seeking to carve out a strategic position for themselves in the increasingly complex and specialized, but fragmented field of global financial governance.

Because it is based predominantly on informal exchanges and deliberations between a community of like-minded professionals from bureaucracies and agencies with a reputation for considerable autonomy and independence from central direction, which in turn leads to a strong sense of collegiality and often the cultivation of personal friendships, G7 interactions would appear to be well suited to the application of transgovernmental insights.[27] In the 1960s, Robert Russell found the opposite to be the case in his study of interaction in the international monetary system. Russell argued that intergovernmental type bargaining, of the sort envisaged by neo-realists, was a more accurate characterization of relations between G10 finance ministries and central banks, although it should be noted that the G10 were more concerned with fine tuning balance of payments financing and exchanging information on national policies during the 1960s.[28]

Exchanging information on national policies is still a concern for the G7, but the emergence of a complex process of global financial governance has created a wider range of activities that the finance ministries and central banks are concerned with and a wider range of incentives to engage in transgovernmental coalition building. By the same token, efforts to co-ordinate national macroeconomic policies, or target and fine tune payments imbalances, have pretty much been abandoned by the G7, suggesting that intergovernmental bargaining may be a much less significant aspect of G7 interactions than was previously the case. Nevertheless, the extent to which the G7 finance ministries engage in collective transgovernmental activities as opposed to more conventional intergovernmental exchanges or bargaining over national policies, remains something to be determined. This requires a discussion of the incentives the G7 finance ministries and central banks have to engage in transgovernmental coalition building, the resources they possess that facilitate such activities, the obstacles that impede and constrain transgovernmentalism, the strategic reasons for engaging in transgovernmentalism, the extent to which they attempt to collectively influence different decision-making arenas and the success they have.[29]

Transgovernmentalism has often been viewed as primarily a technical problem-solving activity, based on a mutually advantageous exchange of information and resources.[30] However, when we pose questions such as those above, we can begin to appreciate that transgovernmentalism can also have a very clear political purpose and very definitely serve and advance certain political interests or positions. Questions such as those above need to be asked if we are to obtain a sense of the political as well as the technical purpose of transgovernmental activities amongst finance ministries and central banks.

Power and authority in global financial governance

One of the principal themes of this book is the power and authority the Group of Seven enjoy collectively, as well as the patterns of power and authority that characterize relations and interactions between the finance ministries and central banks. Before discussing a suitable analytical framework that will enable us to analyse those interactions and most crucially to situate them in the wider complex of global financial governance and the structural context of decentralized financial globalization, it is first necessary to briefly discuss what we mean by power and authority in the field of global financial governance.

The structural power of the United States

Perhaps the biggest single contribution any scholar has made to the study of power in the international monetary system is Susan Strange's concept of structural power. Structural power refers to the possession of resources that enable actors to change the range of choices open to others without appearing to put active pressure on them to make a particular decision or choice, because these actors shape or control the frameworks within which all actors have to operate.[31] Thinking in terms of structural power enables the researcher to recognize that power over outcomes can be exercised impersonally, often unintentionally but also intentionally, by those buying, selling and dealing in markets. For example, George Soros has argued that financial markets respond to the perceptions of market watchers and these perceptions in turn affect market outcomes, and ultimately the choices of policy-makers, giving these market watchers immense influence.[32]

In the international monetary sphere, markets and other states are most interested in the value of the dollar because of its international reserve status and because it is the currency of the world's largest economy. In this respect, the US has power in international monetary relations because it can get the subject of its own economic performance and the value of its currency to feature on international agendas, in a way lesser G7 powers such as Canada and the UK cannot. Every country has an interest in the dollar and US economic performance. This raises the issue of the capacity of the United States to engage in what Jonathon Kirshner refers to as currency manipulation, and influence the value of the dollar.[33] As the last chapter indicated, the history of the G7 process has been bound up with discussions of the value of the dollar and the United States has at various points over the last thirty years used its participation in the G7 to influence the dollar.[34] What is at question however, is its continuing discretion and capacity to manipulate the dollar at will. Surprisingly little research has been conducted into this aspect of US monetary power, although Peter Gowan has somewhat controversially argued that US Treasury Secretaries can talk the value of the dollar up or down at will.[35]

As the principal multilateral setting for the discussion of the exchange rates of the major currencies, a study of the G7 process provides an opportunity to test this proposition. Despite some doubt over US capacity to manipulate the dollar, what is clear is that the US has a huge agenda-setting role in international monetary and financial governance stemming from the importance of the dollar and its financial markets for the functioning of the system as a whole. Without US approval, and the endorsement of the authorities overseeing the world's most important currency and the world's most important financial markets, no international financial governance initiative has much chance of successful implementation. This translates into an enormous power of veto that sets the parameters for debates on global financial governance more generally.

A second aspect of US monetary power is a direct product of its liquid capital markets and the reputation of the dollar as the currency of the world's largest and most successful economy. The United States is regarded as an investment safe haven as a consequence of these features and has the capacity to attract foreign investments in a fashion that other states cannot. This gives the US government what Benjamin Cohen calls, the 'power to delay' macroeconomic adjustment, meaning that the US can run budget deficits and trade deficits without experiencing a sharp decline in the value of the dollar or the value of US assets on world markets, because these deficits can continue to be financed with foreign money and continuous inflows of foreign investment.[36] The power to delay gives the United States greater domestic macroeconomic policy autonomy than any other state on the planet and limits the external constraints the United States government faces. This is power in the form of freedom from the constraints of external forces.

Connected to this is a third form of US power. The US has to pay much less attention to other economies' performance when setting domestic monetary policies, while all other states have to keep at least one eye on economic developments in the US and the decisions of the US Federal Reserve.[37] The fact that changes in US interest rates and movements in the dollar can force other countries to respond with policy action, also gives the US a 'power to deflect' adjustment costs onto other states, although this can be exercised quite unintentionally.[38] In other words, the US has a privileged position in the international monetary system that constitutes a degree of structural power, which enables the US to shape agendas in international monetary relations and has resulted in a long-standing asymmetry in international monetary affairs. This structural power, and the series of privileges it entails, is the consequence of certain systemic properties, resources and privileges that enable one country to influence and shape agendas in international monetary relations to a greater extent than its G7 partners, because of its central position in the international monetary system itself.

Authority

Authority is a quite distinct form of power. It rests on obedience based on a recognition of legitimately held titles or offices, or the possession of critical expertise.[39] In this respect, while the exercise of structural power is not always deliberate, the exercise of authority always is. Unfortunately, authority is a concept that remains shrouded in confusion and ambiguity and its application to international politics is far from straightforward. According to Arrendt's seminal work, authority is considered to require obedience and a recognition or acceptance of some form of hierarchy.[40] In the case of the US's capacity to set agendas in international monetary relations this is not a consequence of other states accepting or obeying US authority, but merely a product of material realities that give the United States structural power.

Due to its reliance on hierarchy and obedience, authority is a concept that has most resonance in the domestic sphere, because domestic responsibilities and functions are often clearly demarcated by domestic legal frameworks. In the monetary and financial field therefore, other domestic actors are willing to accept the authority of finance ministries and central banks for example, because they have legally enshrined responsibilities and because they have expertise and experience in dealing with financial and monetary affairs. In the international sphere the situation is less clear. Finance ministries and central banks who meet with one another may have similar domestic responsibilities, but no clearly defined international responsibility or authority. Moreover, they are likely to share similar levels of technical expertise, although this will vary in accordance with incumbent individuals and their reputation for producing sound policy and their credibility with their counterparts. Long-serving successful individuals such as the current Chairman of the Federal Reserve Alan Greenspan, can build up the cult of personality and will therefore have a greater degree of authority at international meetings than individuals who are newly in post. The authority of individual finance ministries and central banks relative to their counterparts is therefore far from clear cut and is likely to vary over time, meaning that authority is a matter that can only be assessed through case-by-case empirical investigations.

The issue of the authority of individual actors at international meetings is further complicated by the contention that authority is incompatible with argumentation or persuasion, which presupposes some degree of equality rather than the hierarchy on which authority is based.[41] However, a crucial source of authority is often the critical expertise of a particular office or title holder. The articulation of critical expertise often requires the presentation of convincing arguments, which persuades actors to accept the expertise of other actors and therefore establishes their authority. Therefore, arguing may not be as incompatible with authority as is often suggested, precisely because an argument forwarded may be authoritative and convincing. The track record of individuals and actors in forwarding convincing interpretations and arguments is in fact a key element in determining the levels of authority they enjoy in multilateral settings. In other words, argumentation can be viewed as a constituent property of authority. Applying these conceptual points to a multilateral process with deliberative characteristics such as the G7 would suggest that examining the track record of states in influencing G7 debates will give us some sense of the patterns of authority within the coalition. For this reason, acceptance that arguing takes place among the G7 finance ministries and central banks should not be seen as admission that there is an equality of capability or authority among the G7, or as an affirmation of the Kirton 'concert of powers' thesis mentioned in Chapter 1. As noted above, authority not only varies from state to state, but the authority of individual states varies over time in accordance with factors such as incumbency, length of tenure, track record and reputation of key personnel. Moreover, sensitivity to the issue of authority and its variations also needs to be combined with an awareness of states' power or their ability to set and veto agendas, because processes of deliberation and arguing take place within certain parameters which will reflect underlying structural power relations, and in this regard G7 states clearly have quite different structural resources and properties, most evident in the form of continued US structural power.[42]

The issue of the collective authority of G7 actors with external audiences is similarly complicated. It is most straightforward in relation to the acceptance of collective G7 arguments or initiatives by other domestic actors, due to a recognition of the expertise that finance ministries and central banks possess on financial and monetary matters, or because these other domestic actors lack the expertise to effectively challenge the finance ministries and central banks, and because they are not recognized as legitimate authorities on such matters by the finance ministries and central banks themselves, or by other key domestic actors.

In regard to relations with other governments outside of the G7 and wider institutions such as the IMF, there is often a circularity and complementarity to G7 and IMF analyses, as the two frequently feed into and influence one another, while it is rare for there to be substantial analytical and policy differences between the G7 and the IMF.[43] Certainly, the IMF and the G7 finance ministries and central banks share certain analytical assumptions and ideas about the importance of financial markets and how the economy functions, but the G7 are also in a position to win votes in the IMF due to a weighted voting system based on quotas – the system of financial contributions to the Fund. Furthermore, it is also often difficult to decipher whether authorities in emerging markets accept IMF/G7 policies because they accept the wisdom of those policies and the analyses on which they are based, or whether a more coercive pattern of influence is at work, in which states have to accept IMF conditionality in return for desperately required funds, so as to appease private creditors and investors. Complicating this is the fact that local elites in finance ministries and central banks, who are charged with the task of implementing IMF programmes, are often secretly convinced of the correctness of, or are at least sympathetic towards such policies, despite opposition from across the political spectrum.[44] Authority is therefore a slippery and elusive concept, particularly in a technical area such as financial and monetary governance.

Ultimately however, individuals' track record in advancing convincing interpretations and explanations over time, whether those individuals reside in the private or public sector, is the key to authority in monetary and financial affairs. Individuals with a good reputation can cause others to suspend their own judgement, by advancing a particularly convincing interpretation or argument of their own, which in turn becomes accepted conventional wisdom.[45] The rise in market-generated analysis of currency valuations and interpretations of economic events more generally is therefore an interesting phenomenon to chart and would point to a possible rise in market authority at the expense of public authority. Once again this observation emphasizes the importance of situating any analysis of G7 authority in a wider context and that wider context is the diffusion of authority and power represented by the structures of decentralized globalization.

G7 transgovernmentalism in a context of decentralized globalization: from two-level games to multi-dimensional diplomacy

The diffused and polycentric decision-making complex that characterizes decentralized financial globalization means that there are very real empirical reasons for conducting a multi-spatial analysis of G7 interactions, in the sense that such an analytical framework reflects and represents the multi-spatial reality of contemporary global financial governance.[46] However, there is also a very good theoretical rationale for conducting such a multi-spatial analysis.

Structure, agency and the theoretical rationale for multi-spatial analysis

John Hobson has recently made the telling observation that a great deal of International Relations (IR) theory has been parsimonious, or has been a modified form of parsimony.[47] That is to say it either explains outcomes through one exclusive independent variable such as liberalism, realism and neo-realism, or a basic causal variable is primary but is also supplanted by a set of intervening variables as in the case of modified neo-realism or new liberalism. Traditional IR theory has therefore suffered from some quite fundamental limitations based on reductionism or one-way determinism.[48] Theoretical complexity on the other hand seeks to explain outcomes through the operation of two or more independent variables. Rather than distorting analyses by focusing on one particular variable at the expense of another, which often inevitably confirms the significance of the particular variable given explanatory status, theoretical complexity rests on the view that there is no single source of power in a society, or that no one particular spatial dimension, be it domestic or international, dominates or determines the form of others. No single social space is self-constituting but national, international, global/transnational all affect and structure one another and cannot exist without the others, as different realms are embedded in one another and functionally entwine in complex ways, while their interactions change one another's inner shape as well as their outward trajectories.[49] Of course, empirical analysis may reveal that such an assumption is erroneous in a particular issue area, but unless we start from a position that avoids preconceptions concerning causal relationships and at least acknowledges the possibility of mutual interdependence between different spatial settings, we risk distorting empirical findings and missing part of the picture.

What is to be aimed for in studies of inter-state activities in the global political economy is a synthesis of structure and agency, in which there is an acknowledgement that structures constitute states and that states as agents also constitute structures, or what John Hobson calls a complex approach that 'reintegrates a partially autonomous state alongside partially autonomous non-state actors/structures within a complex social universe'.[50] Such an approach is beginning to gain ground in IPE and is evident in Geoffrey Underhill's concept of an integrated ensemble of state–market governance, or a state–market condominium.[51] In this respect, agents are constrained by structures that they themselves have cumulatively created.[52] More generally, this kind of approach represents a structuration tradition which sees structure and agency as being mutually constituted, involving uneven interactions in an ongoing historical process.[53] A structuration approach allow us to escape the binary logic of much IR theory and move away from the position that strong states and strong non-state actors or social forces are mutually exclusive. A basic knowledge of political economy would tell us that this is not so, and that strong state and non-state actors can and do reside together in global and domestic space.[54]

In what follows, I take my lead from John Hobson and his neo-integrationist second-wave Weberian historical sociology approach and use the assumptions underpinning this approach to develop an analytical framework that is specific to the G7 process, but within this framework I utilize insights from a range of authors and perspectives including the work of Robert Cox, a modified version of Keohane and Nye's transgovernmentalism, some work in the social constructivist tradition and Tony Porter's recent neo-functionalist derived work on technical systems. Hobson begins with the assumption that international/global realms both shape and are shaped by national and sub-national realms and that international, global and domestic realms are not discrete and self-constituting, but only have partial autonomy and functionally entwine in complex ways.[55] In other words, there is no single outside-in, or inside-out relationship that can simply be assumed because the state resides within the vortex of the internal and external realms.[56] I am most concerned with illuminating the linkages between the state, the domestic, international and global realms, rather than reifying the power of either global structures or the state. As Hobson concludes, developing a neo-integrationist position requires giving 'equal ontological status to international and global social, normative, economic and political structures on the one hand, but also the state and state–society relations on the other'.[57]

Domestic politics and two-level games

One of the most frequently made arguments in IR is that domestic politics and inter-state relations are mutually entwined. Liberal intergovernmentalism for example, sees that inter-state bargaining is one of the principal activities in the international system, which is in turn viewed as a response to the need to manage a condition of interdependence among states. Unlike John Hobson's approach discussed above however, the basic premise of liberal IR theory is that societal preferences and the way these are mediated through national institutional arrangements are the key independent variables explaining state behaviour in multilateral processes. States develop preferences and positions as a consequence of the preferences of certain societal groupings and then have to adjust these in accordance with the preferences of other states (as the intervening variable), leading to trade-offs between societal demands and the demands of other states.[58]

On the basis of these liberal premises, the concept of two-level games has been advanced as an analytical framework for examining intergovernmental bargaining. The two-level game concept is of particular relevance and interest in studies of G7 diplomacy, because it was first developed on the basis of a case study of the Bonn Summit of 1978, and has subsequently been indelibly associated with, and even become a metaphor for, G7 co-operation.[59] More generally, international monetary relations and forms of monetary co-operation have often been presented as a form of two-level game.[60] However, contemporary international monetary relations today involve a more complex pattern of governance than a simple two-level game and the concept of two-level games is not without analytical problems.

Two-level games divide multilateral co-operation into two levels.[61] Level I involves negotiations between national delegates in multilateral settings. Level II involves the domestic ratification and implementation of the subsequent international agreement. The approach acknowledges that the relationship between the two levels is characterized by reciprocity because prior consultations and bargaining at level II will determine an initial position for level I negotiations. Three critical variables are cited as affecting the potential for co-operation between states. First, domestic preferences and the possible range of domestic coalitions affect the potential for co-operation. Advocates of the two-level game approach expect the potential for co-operation to be determined by the balance of internationalist social forces, those who stand to benefit from an international agreement in a particular issue area, relative to isolationists, those who stand to lose from such an agreement. Second, the possibility of co-operation depends on domestic political institutions and their role in the ratification process. In particular, two-level games would appear to confirm the hypothesis that the greater the autonomy of central decision makers from their domestic constituents, as a consequence of national institutional arrangements, the greater the likelihood of achieving an international agreement. The reasoning here is that the more removed decision makers are from their constituents, the more leeway they will have to implement an agreement without making recourse to various societal interests. Stemming from this argument is the hypothesis that independent central banks increase the potential for international monetary co-operation, because under such arrangements policy-makers have more autonomy to act in accordance with international, rather than domestic imperatives.[62] Third, the potential for inter-state co-operation depends on level I negotiators' strategies. For example, negotiators can more easily conclude an agreement if their domestic situation is favourable, but this weakens their position *vis-à-vis* other negotiators. In contrast, unfavourable domestic circumstances might increase a negotiator's capacity to obtain concessions from other negotiators. Domestic difficulties can be presented as something that could potentially stall an international agreement and they can therefore be used as bargaining collateral so as to obtain further concessions from level I counterparts.

In other words, the two-level game concept attempts to provide a basis for a formal aggregation of preferences across the two 'levels'. The two levels are defined by 'ratification' and by the potential for the application of 'win-set' analysis based on the variables highlighted.[63] The aim of the two-level game approach is to generate testable propositions concerning the prospects for negotiating inter-governmental agreements. In this respect, two-level games are most suited to analysing what Robert Keohane has referred to as 'hard bargaining' or policy co-ordination between states, defined by Henry Wallich as 'a significant modification of national policy in recognition of international interdependence'.[64] However, as an analytical tool, the two-level games concept has a narrow focus and two principal weaknesses.

The first of these weaknesses is that if we are concerned with the specific contribution of a particular forum to a wider process of global governance, the authority of that forum in the wider global political economy and the social basis of that authority, two-level games are of limited use. For example in the earlier discussion of decentralized globalization, it was established that market structures are integral to the process of global financial governance. At the same time, assorted non-state actors and various bureaucracies all co-exist and have various roles in international financial governance. On financial matters therefore, governments have relations with a wider range of actors in a wider range of locations than those covered by Putnam's two levels. In other words, the two-level game concept ultimately neglects to locate multilateral processes in a wider context.

The second weakness is the assumption that intergovernmental bargaining is the principal activity that takes place between states in multilateral settings. Interstate co-operation can take forms other than hard bargaining or policy co-ordination. This can include activities such as suasion, peer review, information exchange, deliberation and consultation. These forms of interaction can lead to the socialization of elites and the formation of common beliefs and shared understandings that are less conducive to the formal application of two-level analysis or game theory, because the absence of a specific agreement or precise bargain means there is no clearly identifiable domestic ratification process, while shared elite understandings and beliefs can also diverge from wider domestic societal preferences.[65] In studies of multilateralism more attention needs to be paid to the black box of elite interactions and in particular the norms, beliefs and shared social practices that shape those interactions and the resulting outcomes. In this chapter it has been suggested that we need to allow for the possibility that the G7 finance ministries and central banks engage in transgovernmentalism as well as more traditional intergovernmentalism.

The four-dimensional framework developed in the rest of this chapter attempts to overcome two-level games' shortcomings by considering G7 relations with a wider range of settings, thus locating the G7 in a wider world context and by drawing attention to the shared beliefs, understandings and social practices of elites involved in the G7 process. The aim of the framework is to facilitate examination of the inter-relationships and interactions between elites' shared beliefs and understandings, the domestic political environment, market structures and behaviour and wider international institutions and bodies. In this respect, it builds upon some of Robert Cox's pioneering work that advocated examining and traces the interconnections between ideas, material structures, and between social forces, states and world orders in international politics.[66]

Multilateralism and multi-dimensional diplomacy

The rise of what Robert Cox and others have called complex multilateralism, involving complex interactions between both state and non-state actors, makes the analysis of multilateral or transgovernmental processes, such as the G7, far from straightforward.[67] The task can be made manageable by identifying the discrete but intertwined social spaces, or spatial dimensions relevant to a particular policy area. Distinct socially constructed spatial dimensions are constituted by an identifiable series of interactions, deliberations and communications between actors that are clustered around specific locational 'focal points' or co-ordinating mechanisms, such as the nation state, a specific multilateral process, or even a particular marketplace. Spatial dimensions can therefore be viewed as 'systems' of social interaction, or as 'a series of social relations between individuals and collectivities that are stably reproduced over time and space to create "patterns" of interaction'.[68] A spatial dimension, while displaying an interdependent relationship with other dimensions, is therefore characterized by its own distinct logic, or dynamics. Crucially however, we cannot assume that any single spatial dimension enjoys independent status. Each dimension may have its own form, shape and trajectory, partially determined by the features and characteristics of other spatial dimensions. It is the relationships and linkages a dimension has with other dimensions or settings that will be all important in determining broader patterns of governance and it is these relationships and linkages which remain to be deciphered and which the multi-dimensional approach advanced here can help to illuminate.

The starting point for what I refer to as multi-dimensional analysis is to identify the relevant discrete social spaces, whose inter-relationships will shape the dynamics of governance in a particular policy area. Understanding the patterns of interaction and the linkages between different spatial dimensions also requires that the variables and interactions specific to each spatial dimension are identified. Such an approach helps us to understand how different variables specific to particular locations such as the shared beliefs and practices of elite participants in multilateral processes, particular domestic institutional arrangements, political interests, and the preferences and decision-making processes of participants in a particular transnational marketplace, come together and interact to produce particular patterns of governance. Multi-dimensional frameworks facilitate a multi-spatial form of analysis that fits with Hobson's neo-integrationist approach.

Of course, the notion of dimensions is not without controversy. As with two level-games and multi-level governance, the most notable problem with the concept of a dimension is one of boundaries. In particular, the whole notion of a dimension is susceptible to the allegation that it simply divides subject matter into 'convenient boxes'.[69] For example, the literature on globalization suggests that relationships between national, international, and transnational arenas are becoming highly fluid and porous because of global processes and global flows.[70] In other words, old 'spaces of places' models are being thoroughly complicated by new 'spaces of flows' models.[71] However, it is not the intention of the dimension concept, as advanced here, to deny such complexity. On the contrary, it merely allows for the existence of distinct settings, with their own distinguishable logics. It is not to say that these settings and logics do not cut across and interlock with one another. Rather, the dimensional concept is designed simply to enable some of these interlocking and cross-cutting relationships to be examined in closer detail and to be brought into sharper relief.

The four-dimensional framework and the Group of Seven

Clearly, while the G7 process can be considered to represent a classic example of multilateralism, the process involves a whole series of more complex interactions than the conspicuous and immediately identifiable state–state diplomacy that takes place at G7 meetings. The framework advanced here identifies four spatial dimensions that are of relevance to the G7 process. These four dimensions help us to locate the G7 process in a wider political, economic and structural context and to understand some of the variables and inter-relationships that determine how the G7 process operates, its function and ultimately its authority and influence.

Dimension I: interactions between the G7 finance ministries and central banks

Like level I in Putnam's two-level game concept, the first dimension in this four-dimensional framework is comprised of the series of interactions that take place between national representatives at G7 meetings, at both official and ministerial level. What has been absent from many existing accounts of multilateral processes is a sense of the routine practices and shared social understandings that shape and influence elite interactions. These are particularly important in the context of the interactions between G7 finance ministries and central banks, which are regularised and semi-institutionalized, but are also based on a high degree of informality and personal relationships between individuals. A shared sense of professionalism as economists and financial analysts creates a pronounced sense of collegiality amongst the finance ministries and central banks and consequently we need to relax assumptions that inter-state diplomacy simply involves governments bargaining with states simply trying to realize national preferences. While there is an obvious need to accept that intergovernmental bargaining continues to take place to a certain extent, we have to look at how and why the finance ministries and central banks attempt to construct consensus, including the ideational, social and political foundations of this consensus. In other words, we need to assess the extent to which the G7 finance ministries and central banks collaborate so as to construct a *de facto* transgovernmental coalition, in order to maximize their influence in a context of decentralized globalization, by speaking with a collective voice, combining their expertise and magnifying their authority through collective action.[72] We also need to obtain a sense of the differing circumstances in which the G7 will behave in that fashion or in a more conventional and potentially conflictual intergovernmental fashion. In doing this we need to accept that transgovernmental coalitions may attempt to influence developments in settings other than the domestic one as originally proposed by Keohane and Nye.

Robert Cox has referred to how an inter-state process of consensus formation amongst the leading capitalist states takes place through a series of elite networks, or a *nébuleuse*, with the resulting consensus being transmitted into agencies such as finance ministries and central banks, promoting the transformation of the state in a neo-liberal direction and institutionalizing the interests and priorities of transnational capital in an effective 'internationalization of the state'. What is required however, is a better sense of how elite consensus formation among finance ministries and central banks proceeds and the extent to which the finance ministries and central banks operate as a transgovernmental coalition, in relation to a variety of domestic, international and transnational arenas, of their success in influencing developments in these other arenas and of the constraints and differences that undermine their ability to act collectively.

Obviously, the first part of such an analysis is to come to a better understanding of how the finance ministries and central banks interact with one another, including the social practices, conventions and routines that shape those interactions. It is important here to trace the competing and complementary ideas the finance ministries and central banks hold about financial and monetary governance and examine how these ideas affect their interactions. For this reason the next chapter traces the contours of conflict and consensus amongst the finance ministries and central banks.

Two concepts from within social constructivist literature stand out as being of use in analysis of an essentially deliberative forum like the G7 process. The first of these forms of interaction is what Thomas Risse calls the 'logic of arguing'. Arguing involves actors engaging in truth-seeking activities so as to arrive at mutual understandings and a reasoned consensus.[73] The logic of arguing implies that actors are willing to revise their perceptions if they can be persuaded by a better argument. This would suggest that actors are prepared to change their views of the world, and therefore their interests, in the light of the emergence of better arguments. Where arguing and deliberation are present, convincing ideas and arguments become a more important consideration in determining actors' responses than simple power or interest motivations. In technical policy areas such as monetary and financial governance, arguing is likely to be a particularly prominent form of interaction because they are dependent on analyses of the complex relationships that make up the economy.[74]

However, what is to be argued over in multilateral settings, in terms of policy beliefs and objectives, can often prove to be highly restricted, as an existing consensus and the social practices surrounding that consensus, and by association, the interests supportive of that consensus, determine what is open for debate. When the potential for debate and deliberation is constrained it is likely that only marginal adjustments and gradual refinements to an existing consensus can be achieved. In other words, actors' responses in multilateral settings can be determined by a shared understanding of what is acceptable, permissible or appropriate in that particular multilateral context. On the one hand, actors will know there is no point in pushing a certain proposal if another actor, or interests connected to that other actor, are likely to veto the proposal. Actors are constrained by a logic of the possible. In this respect, actors may invoke a specific identity, matching it to the particular context they find themselves in, out of a sense of obligation and 'appropriateness', and thus develop codes of meaning and ways of reasoning that will determine and influence their actions. Consequently, actors act in accordance with practices and routines that are socially constructed, and are learnt and accepted over time. State delegates in multilateral settings therefore might be expected to become role-players basing their actions on shared intersubjective understandings, which in turn could be the product of shared normative and causal beliefs, or previous instances of arguing and deliberation. This kind of interaction resembles what March and Olsen call a logic of appropriateness.[75] Logics of appropriateness, arguing, and of the possible can co-exist and overlap with one another. For example, we might expect arguing to take place in the context of an understanding of what it is appropriate and possible for participants to argue over.

Other additional important variables contribute to the character of a first-dimensional multilateral process including the regularity of contact between participating actors, the type of contact/interaction that takes place between participants, any routine or procedures for chairing meetings, the seniority/resources and background of participants in terms of national hierarchies, the timing of meetings relative to other significant gatherings and the methods of communicating, recording and enforcing the outcomes of meetings. All of these variables make an important contribution to the particular character of a multilateral process, as the discussion in Chapter 5 will demonstrate.

While multilateral interactions are not simply reducible to hard bargaining, it would also be mistaken to consider that bargaining or negotiation based on states' material interests have disappeared from view altogether in international monetary and financial relations. Both states and their domestic constituencies continue to have specific material interests in relation to issues such as whether the dollar rises or falls, IMF lending policies and the openness of financial markets. It is clearly necessary in analyses of multilateral processes to assess the capabilities of different states in terms of their ability to realize their preferences and the methods and means used to achieve those preferences over time. Clearly these questions concerning the power and authority of individual G7 states are something that need to be assessed on the basis of case-by-case analyses of G7 discussions. The way in which Canada achieves objectives in the G7 may, for example, differ from the methods employed by the United States to realize its preferences or objectives. Certainly this is something that needs to be examined and different types of interaction based on: notions of appropriateness or shared social practices; consensus, truth seeking, or problem-solving activities such as deliberative arguing; and interest or power-based bargaining, can all co-exist and interact in the operation of the same multilateral process. Most importantly, recognition of these different types of interaction can help in contributing to a more sophisticated understanding of the dynamics of first-dimensional G7 diplomacy, including the resources, opportunities and constraints faced by individual states. Using these different analytical approaches, while avoiding the blanket application of any one of them, should also enhance our ability to determine whether the G7 acts as a genuine modern concert of international powers, as John Kirton insists, or whether the G7 are in fact closer to an asymmetrical US-led transgovernmental coalition, most often, but not always, mobilized for US purposes.[76]

Dimension II

Dimension II in this four-dimensional analytical framework, like level II in the two-level games concept, refers to domestic politics. Finance ministries and central banks are constrained and partially defined by their domestic institutional mandates and the domestic decision-making processes and frameworks they operate within.

Quite simply, understanding the institutional origins and loyalties of participants is essential to an appreciation of the pattern of interactions that characterize a multilateral process.[77] Institutional mandates and decision-making procedures determine what state agencies and therefore multilateral processes are capable of. The deployment of win-set analysis, as advocated by proponents of the two-level game approach, would suggest that the more autonomy an institution enjoys *vis-à-vis* other political and societal actors, the more likelihood there is of an international agreement being reached. However, if increased institutional autonomy from societal interests is accompanied by institutional mandates which pre-commit state agencies to specific objectives, as is increasingly the case for finance ministries and central banks in the form of fiscal rules and inflation targets, then the capacity of the representatives of these agencies to offer commitments in negotiations with overseas counterparts will be restricted. Similarly multilateral commitments become difficult if national decision making is dependent on collective voting or consent, as is the case with a number of independent central banks. The fact that central banks are independent is an insufficient consideration on its own. Close attention has to be paid to the institutional mandates of finance ministries and central banks, as well as the processes through which they arrive at decisions on national policy matters.

While domestic institutional arrangements need to receive closer scrutiny in second-dimensional analysis, domestic societal preferences cannot be written out of the equation altogether. Patterns of domestic interest representation and wider societal preferences remain key second-dimensional variables, but their significance for multilateral outcomes cannot be simply assumed. For example, domestic interests will attempt to influence exchange rate, macroeconomic and financial regulatory policies through the domestic political process, although McNamara has noted how finance ministries and central banks remain relatively insulated from political pressures.[78] Furthermore, finance ministry and central bank officials will have informal contacts with social groupings, primarily the financial sector. This can lead to the evolution of a shared professional ethos and a tendency to view matters through the eyes of the financial sector, rather than other sectors of the economy. The educational background and social networks of officials are also pivotal where the acquisition of causal and normative beliefs are concerned. The key point here is that despite efforts to insulate policy areas by making claims to technical specialist knowledge, policy agendas in multilateral settings will to some extent be affected by patterns of interest representation within key domestic state agencies and departments.

Wider societal preferences and relationships clearly affect the calculated strategies of state agencies. For example, if domestic banks enjoy shareholdings in a nation's manufacturing sector, this is liable to generate strong societal preferences for a competitively valued exchange rate, which in turn may make particular finance ministries more favourably predisposed to multilateral exchange rate co-operation.[79] Moreover, a greater proportion of activities within a financial system being based on traditional credit banking, rather than equity-based investment finance, and a prioritization of long-term investment ahead of shareholder value, will create a different set of societal preferences concerning global financial governance arrangements. Second-dimensional analysis needs to take into account the different balance of social forces within the different domestic settings within the G7 countries and examine how these social forces and preferences are represented by the finance ministries and central banks.[80]

However, the influence of societal preferences needs to be offset against prevailing institutional intellectual orthodoxies, particularly orthodoxies that advocate an opposite course of action to that favoured by wider societal interests, such as policy-makers' rejection of proactive exchange rate policies on technical grounds, when societal coalitions favour a competitively valued exchange rate. In such an event, a combination of state bureaucracies' technical expertise appeals to a multilateral consensus and control over key policy instruments can circumvent strong societal pressures in favour of a different course of action such as a more proactive exchange rate stance. As well as discussing domestic institutional mandates and decision-making procedures therefore, second-dimensional analysis needs to examine domestic institutional cultures, societal preferences and trace the contours of any intellectual orthodoxies that characterize particular state agencies, while examining the linkages between all three.

Dimension III

Dimension III is the foreign exchange market and financial markets more generally as cross-border networked spaces characterized by transaction relationships. As a discipline, IR has tended to delineate political space and political authority in purely territorial terms, predominantly revolving around the state.[81] The possibility that the structures of authority in the global political economy have become de-territorialized is rarely entertained. A notable exception is evident in Benjamin Cohen's spaces of flows model.[82]The spaces of flows approach refers to de-territorialized sites and authority structures based upon functional notions of space characterized by networks or transaction relationships. These sites or spaces are not compatible with Westphalian traditions of much IR scholarship. Third-dimensional spaces transcend political frontiers and are defined by the extensity of the transactions and relationships involved. This reflects the reality that whilst the state remains a vital source of authority it is not the only source of authority in the contemporary global political economy and that territoriality is overlain by functional, sectional and socially oriented spatial forms. In other words, states may be constitutive but they are not definitive of spatial frameworks of analysis.[83]

In his plurilateral model of the international system, Philip Cerny notes how what he calls structural levels such as the international and the domestic are cut across by functional categories, as a distinct type of interaction. Transnationalized financial markets can be viewed as such a 'functional category'. In this sense, despite being located in particular financial centres, foreign exchange traders and investors more generally tend to operate in the context of 'spaces of flows' rather than places, as trades take place across national borders through a series of interconnected computer terminals.[84] Dimension III variables in this instance include the interactions between and the social practices and norms of traders, the process through which traders reach decisions on what to buy and sell, the role of any particular reserve currency, the infrastructure that enables the market to function, the volume of trades taking place in a market, the speed at which trades take place, the way in which this affects prices in a given market, and most significantly the channels of communication which enable the market to function and exert influence. What is noticeable about monetary and exchange rate policy for example, is that increasingly, policy-makers formulate decisions and adjust strategies as a consequence of their informal communications and dialogue with private analysts in the foreign exchange market. An on-going public but sometimes-coded series of communications are played out on the pages of global newspapers such as the *Financial Times*, which have become central intermediary mechanisms for the conduct of contemporary international monetary relations. Generally, market spokespeople attempt to articulate the mood of the market as a whole and express views on the implications of this for national policy in a variety of locations, while policy-makers attempt to pre-empt market movements by giving an analysis of prevailing economic conditions and how they think market movements should respond. This is third-dimensional diplomacy – an emerging form of diplomacy that is being played out between the market and national authorities, often to a global audience, with profound effects for macroeconomic and exchange rate governance and I would argue patterns of power and authority in the global political economy.[85] The words, analyses and discourses of those market watchers (private and public sector) who have over time offered the most convincing interpretations, can trigger market movements, giving them a real form of communicative or discursive authority.[86] As Walter Wriston has pointed out, financial markets can be viewed as 'a giant voting machine that records in real time, real world evaluations of policy'.[87] Consequently, operators in financial markets are engaged in a kind of perpetual opinion poll on the viability of a range of national policies.[88] They are further assisted in this activity by credit-rating agencies that arrive at ratings and scores for national governments as a guide for market decision making.[89]

A high degree of capital mobility appears to be systematically circumscribing the policy options available to states by rewarding some actions and punishing others.[90] A convergence on the targeting of low inflation and fiscal balance as macroeconomic objectives throughout the industrialized world and a general shift away from Keynesian economics appears to provide evidence to support the argument that the rise of international capital mobility has had a structural affect on states.[91] Generally, states have found that the rise in international capital mobility has increased the threat of capital flight, exchange rate depreciation and balance of payments crises. Moreover, according to Andrews, socialization processes cause governments to perceive that the current situation is irreversible. This perception becomes a self-fulfilling prophecy as states come to believe there is no alternative to macroeconomic austerity, reinforcing the structural characteristics of international capital mobility.[92] Whether the constraints of rising international capital mobility are real or imagined is not to be considered at any length here, rather it is the fashion in which constraints are invoked and constructed that is of most interest, and the ongoing communications and signals exchanged between policy-makers and financial markets as transborder spaces, or third-dimensional diplomacy, is key in this regard.

One way to conceive of these interactions is to view global finance as an evolving technical system consisting of a spatially extended and functionally integrated socio-technical network, comprised of electronic networks such as the Clearing House Inter Banks Payments System (CHIPS) in New York and characterized by the evolution of complex financial instruments and products which build upon earlier instruments, such as the way in which derivatives markets shadow existing assets.[93] Highly complex models of assessing risk are often employed, determining decision making in finance in ways which are impenetrable to the wider public. On these grounds, finance clearly has many of the features of a highly technical system. The basic premise of the technical system approach is that the evolution of agreements, organizations and regimes, such as those in the area of global finance, are better understood not as the outcome of a series of bargains, but as a consequence of their relationships and interactions with the evolving technical system they are designed to regulate.[94] In other words, 'a technical systems approach would suggest that there are some issue areas, or industries, in which the institutional character of the technical system is sufficiently well developed that it interacts with and modifies inter-state institutions in significant ways'.[95] These are interesting and potentially useful insights to apply in a study of the G7 simply because the G7 have spent the last ten years responding to global financial crises by instigating new institutional mechanisms and procedures designed to prevent and more effectively manage financial crises, in response to the continuing evolution of an increasing complex, interconnected and global financial system. This has implications for the way the G7 interact with one another and discuss proposals and issues, but also for their relations with the range of specialist technical bodies that characterize global financial governance in an era of decentralized globalization. Most significantly, we would expect the technical system of finance to act as a very real constraining influence on the entire field of global financial governance, with inherited technical institutional legacies and previous technical work exerting a very real determining influence on global financial governance and institutionalizing a modest and incremental reform trajectory based on a prior history of technical collaboration.

The introduction of a third dimension to this analytical framework allows the continuous ongoing three-way interactions between multilateral activities including elite cognitive processes, domestic policy-making and developments, trends and moods in increasingly global financial markets to be examined in closer detail. This is an important component of contemporary financial governance because policy-makers at G7 meetings deliberately attempt to influence and communicate with financial markets as de-territorialized transborder spaces through collective statements, while at the same time facilitating enhanced market scrutiny of national policies and governance structures. The highly technical nature of financial markets also shapes the discourse of, interactions involved in, access to and outcomes of global financial governance, while trends within those markets also help to determine international agendas, as interactions with the technical system of global finance appear to be having a critical impact upon the evolution of the inter-state regime of global financial governance.

Dimension IV

Dimension IV in this framework is comprised of all those other states outside of the multilateral process under immediate consideration (the G7), together with all other actors involved in the relevant policy area. This fourth dimension is obviously a somewhat generic category. Certainly, it is the most problematic in terms of its dimensional qualities, or whether or not it constitutes a series of stable social relations that resemble a pattern of interaction. However, it is a category well suited to analysis of the G7 process. As newly industrialized and developing countries become increasingly significant for systemic financial stability, the G7 have been attempting to communicate with them, both directly and through intermediate agencies, to an ever-increasing extent. At the same time, specialist international bodies, groupings and secretariats such as the IMF and World Bank, IOSCO, the Basle Committee, G20 and the Financial Stability Forum, perform particular niche roles in global financial governance. As Andrew Crockett of the Bank for International Settlements and the first chair of the Financial Stability Forum pointed out, 'it is important that there be both a forum where a limited number of large countries can make politically sensitive "bargains" (the G7) and a forum in which the rest of the world can effectively communicate its views and concerns to the large countries (G20, IMF)'.[96] It is these vitally important latter communications that form the fourth dimension in this analytical framework.

There can be little doubt that the G7's relations with the rest of the world have become more important as financial integration and innovation have progressed in the context of decentralized globalization. In this respect, the extent of international capital mobility, a third-dimensional variable, is pivotal in determining the interest the G7 take in fourth-dimensional actors. As financial globalization has proceeded, various previously peripheral countries have become more significant for the stability of the international financial system as a whole and fourth-dimensional relations have become more central to the G7's activities. It is in the context of 'decentralized globalization' and recurring financial crises that the issue of the global financial architecture, which brings the G7 into direct contact with fourth-dimensional actors, has been put on to the international agenda in a more prominent way.

Most notably, the G7 cannot simply impose themselves on existing international institutions and bodies, or on monetary and economic authorities in developing countries, but rather they have to engage in a continuous process of persuasion.[97] The key to understanding fourth-dimensional diplomacy therefore, is to examine the relationships national G7 finance ministries and central banks have with institutions such as the IMF, the Basle Committee and IOSCO, the degree of independence these agencies have from G7 authorities, the functions of these bodies, their role and powers in countries outside of the G7 and the manner in which the

G7 seek to promote collective shared preferences and beliefs. Again the application of the insights of a technical systems approach can help us to locate the G7 in the decision-making complex of global financial governance, and enhance understanding of how that complex has evolved historically and the series of relationships and the impact of the various legacies that historical evolution has involved.

Finally, it is worth noting that a fifth category of communication with trans-national civil society groupings may have been considered as a fifth spatial dimension to G7 diplomacy. Unfortunately outside of interactions at a national level, communications between central banks, finance ministries and civil society groupings have been sporadic, ad hoc and infrequent, although in time they may become a more regular and institutionalized form of interaction.

Conclusion

This chapter has looked at how the G7 process might be examined in terms of a range of 'spatial dimensions' that shape and influence the collective functions, purpose and authority of the meetings of the finance ministries and central banks. The chapter began by outlining the context of 'decentralized globalization' in which different social and territorial spaces are becoming increasingly interconnected and inter-penetrated and in which no one single actor is dominant. The framework that has been forwarded here is based on neo-integrationist second-wave Weberian historical sociology and is an open-ended framework of analysis that is sceptical of parsimonious approaches that attempt to identify one single causal variable. Rather it aspires to theoretical complexity and rests on the view that there is no single source of power in society, or that no one particular spatial dimension, be it domestic or international, dominates or determines the form of others. National, international, global/transnational all affect and structure one another and cannot exist without the others and none of these spatial dimensions are self-constituting. The framework seeks to integrate a partially autonomous state alongside partially autonomous non-state actors/structures within a complex social universe and equal ontological status is given to international and global social, normative, economic and political structures on the one hand, but also to the state and state–society relations on the other. The aim of the framework is to illuminate the linkages between the state, the domestic, international and global realms, rather than reifying the power of either global structures or of the state. Within the framework, I draw on insights from a range of authors and perspectives including the work of Robert Cox, a modified version of Keohane and Nye's transgovernmentalism, some work in the social constructivist tradition and Tony Porter's recent neo-functionalist derived work on technical systems.

In the last part of the chapter, I have argued that understanding the G7 process and the patterns of authority and power surrounding it requires multi-spatial analysis. Four spatial dimensions, or series of social interactions that are significant to the G7 process, but which also overlap and interact, are identified: i) interactions between participants at G7 meetings/preparations; ii) domestic decision making and inter-relationships between domestic institutions and social forces; iii) interactions with global financial markets which resemble an emerging technical system; and iv) interactions with non-G7 states and wider international institutions and specialist bodies that comprise the wider decision-making complex of global financial governance. Thinking in terms of these four spatial categories or dimensions provides a means of analysing the contribution of the G7 to global financial governance.

Throughout the chapter it was argued that it is important to locate multilateral processes in a wider structural context and the current context where the G7 finance ministries and central banks are concerned is a context of 'decentralized globalization'. In this context finance ministries and central banks face multiple incentives to engage in what Keohane and Nye referred to as transgovernmental coalition building. What we need to evaluate is the extent to which finance ministries and central banks have developed their own ways of reasoning, deliberating and interacting based on the emergence of global finance as a technical, but interconnected and decentralized system, and as a consequence do not merely act as functionaries of wider social and political forces, but have shared professional norms that need to be examined in more detail if we are to understand how and why the finance ministries and central banks collaborate, and for what purpose. This is not to say that we can disconnect finance ministries and central banks from wider social forces, but we must not assume their determining influence. Rather we have to seek to establish how social forces relate to the distinct social practices of finance ministries and central banks and how these social practices relate to and interact with wider structures including the technical system or transborder network of global finance and the diffused decision-making complex of the wider global financial architecture. These are essential analytical challenges that need to be addressed if we are to adequately situate the Group of Seven in a context of decentralized globalization. The four-dimensional framework developed makes that undertaking manageable.

4 The Group of Seven and the politics of financial ideas

The durability of the economic consensus of the 1990s

During the course of their exchanges and deliberations over the last three decades, the G7 finance ministries and central banks have developed a loose and somewhat uneasy consensus on the principles informing the design of the global financial system and the implications of this for macroeconomic policy. In this chapter the contours of this consensus are traced. The inconsistencies of its constituent ideas are explored and the interests that underpin the consensus are identified. Likewise, the tensions and different national emphases and interpretations that accompany the broad consensus are also discussed. Yet despite a series of modest adjustments and refinements to the existing consensus and a growing number of challenges to it, the extent to which the G7 finance ministries and central banks share this basic consensus is often underestimated, while the extent to which a qualitatively different set of beliefs and principles have emerged in its place is often overstated. In short, the problematic economic consensus of the 1990s has not been displaced by something else, but persists, albeit in a modified form and has displayed a remarkable durability. Of course, if we presented a stylized and caricatured picture of the consensus of the 1990s as extreme free market fundamentalism we can arrive at a quite different conclusion, but in reality the finance ministries and central banks have always had a rather more pragmatic, qualified and nuanced, but also more intellectually inconsistent approach to financial governance than that of extreme free market fundamentalism.

The importance of ideas in the field of financial governance is well established in the literature, given the increasingly technical nature of financial markets and the importance of economists in devising technical policy solutions to financial and monetary matters.[1] However, it has also been widely recognized that ideas are political and serve political purposes, because the accompanying intellectual case and supporting evidence is often disputed or far from clear cut.[2] Here some of the inconsistencies that characterize prevailing ideas about financial governance are identified, yet these ideas continue to inform shared G7 proposals and approaches, which would indicate that they may be being promoted for political reasons as much as for intellectual ones.

The rest of this chapter is divided into four sections. The first section identifies the consensus of the 1990s and its inconsistencies. The second section examines how these ideas dovetail with certain political interests. In the third section some of the traditional national differences that exist between the G7 countries are discussed. Therefore, although the G7 may have developed a loose consensus consisting of certain shared fundamental beliefs and principles, within that consensus certain tensions based on national distinctiveness and differences continue to simmer below the surface. The current consensus is consequently an uneasy, if well-established one and serves to mask some of the differences between G7 countries. The fourth section examines some of the supposed challenges and changes to the consensus of the 1990s. Some of the existing interpretations of these challenges and changes are questioned. The overriding objective of the chapter is to argue that a loose G7 consensus based on the principles of sound money and open markets continues to exist. Later chapters will look at how this shared consensus and the social practices and understandings surrounding it have influenced G7 interactions and outcomes and how the consensus relates to different interests and institutions across the G7.

The open market sound money consensus

Two fundamental organizing principles – sound money and open markets – defined the economic consensus of the 1990s and these two principles continue to dominate contemporary financial and monetary governance. The consensus itself was the major industrialized states' protracted response to the collapse of Bretton Woods in the 1970s. Indeed, what is seldom recognized is just how long it took the G7 countries to develop the consensus in the form it took during the 1990s.[3] The breakdown of Bretton Woods, and the US and the UK's decisions to liberalize capital controls and de-regulate financial markets in New York and the City of London, were pivotal moments in the movement towards the consensus of the 1990s giving it a distinctly Anglo-Saxon character.[4] Following the Anglo-Saxon lead, continental European countries and Japan also embraced capital liberalization to varying degrees during the second half of the 1980s,[5] and increasingly began to advocate macroeconomic austerity. I will argue that the longevity of the construction of the current consensus (it has been evolving and developing for over thirty years) means that claims that the financial crises of the late 1990s resulted in the reversal of the consensus are overstated. The current consensus may appear to be an uneasy one, but it remains in place, at least for the time being. It has continued to evolve and it has been repeatedly refined and adjusted, but it has neither disappeared, nor been qualitatively transformed, because ultimately the fundamental principles of sound money and open markets continue to inform the basic design of the international financial system and have provided the rationale for group collaboration between the G7 finance ministries and central banks.

The international policy consensus of the 1990s was often referred to as the Washington consensus, although this term was initially used to refer to a magic formula for economic growth in the developing world, based on the experience of Latin American countries in the 1980s.[6] The Washington consensus itself goes beyond the consensus that has shaped the interactions of the G7 finance ministries and central banks and includes ten prescriptions or commandments. Where the

G7 finance ministries and central banks are concerned, we are really talking about a shared belief in the virtues of sound money and open markets, as the normative principles that above all others should inform the design of the international financial and monetary system.[7]

Open markets

Support for capital account liberalization and open integrated financial markets is justified on the basis of a particular view of how financial markets function. These views of financial markets together with the perceived advantages of capital account liberalization also inform understandings of what constitutes good practice in macroeconomic policy. Since the 1980s, the G7 finance ministries and central banks have started from the position that 'greater capital mobility and increasing integration of world capital markets, are good for the world economy and increase overall global welfare'.[8] Both are believed to lead to a greater realization of the efficiencies available from specialization, from more rapid technology transfer and more productive allocation of resources, from comparative advantage, and from the spur of competition. Benefits are believed to show up in higher rates of economic growth, leading to higher wages and higher returns to capital, leading to higher standards of living.[9] These beliefs have become conventional wisdom among the G7 finance ministries and central banks.[10]

At the root of these views is neo-classical economic theory and its two principal assumptions, that individuals are self-interested maximizers and that markets always clear. In the absence of informational asymmetries neo-classical economists expect agents' expectations about the future state of an economy to converge, promoting a self-perpetuating equilibrium.[11] Consequently, it is not possible for markets to make systematic mistakes on prices because any informational advantages would be revealed in an agent's market decision making, driving prices into equilibrium through competition.[12] What Mark Blyth calls the 'modern theory of markets', therefore creates a case for minimal levels of regulation as a root to efficiency, including free markets for goods, labour and capital and a minimal state, because intervention produces inefficient market distortions.[13] Disequilibrium can therefore only occur when there are informational imperfections, making better information and greater transparency the only possible solution to market distortions. In short, the modern theory of markets reverses Keynes' insight that financial outcomes are the result of expectations, which are non-rational and myopic, based on interpretations of market trends and the behaviour of other traders, rather than economic fundamentals, which in turn makes financial markets prone to speculative herd-like behaviour.[14]

In the 1990s, it wasn't just the UK and the US who were making the case for capital account liberalization even if they were its most enthusiastic advocates. Former French socialist finance minister Dominique Strauss-Khan outlined a three-fold rationale for capital account liberalization, including a better allocation of world savings, an increased capacity to absorb temporary shocks, and an enhancement of the quality of investment.[15] In short, the political and intellectual commitment to capital account liberalization among the G7 has gone beyond the Anglo-Saxon countries to include European countries that have often been portrayed as being more sceptical.[16] Likewise although being more circumspect and less enthusiastic than the Anglo-Saxon countries, representatives of the Japanese Ministry of Finance have repeatedly advocated a liberalized financial order and have argued in favour of the principle of capital account liberalization.[17]

According to the G7 finance ministers and central bank governors, 'financial markets consider all the information available to them and then use that information to maximize expected returns, whilst taking account of risk'.[18] On this basis, G7 policy-makers expect markets to punish 'bad' policies and reward 'good' domestic policies. 'Therefore, if markets conclude that a country is pursuing poor economic policy they are likely to take their money elsewhere.'[19] Policy-makers also expect markets to 'react to news in a more rational fashion and revise prices accordingly if the information they receive is more accurate, timely and frequent'.[20] Moreover, 'countries prepared to provide more information about themselves are expected to have a lower risk premium and therefore cheaper access to world capital markets'.[21] Better information is thought to help reduce the risk that wishful thinking and bandwagon enthusiasm might sustain the unsustainable. This in turn will minimize the intensity and scope of potential crises.[22] It is this kind of thinking that was at the root of recent G7 efforts to improve the quality of information available to market participants on countries' macroeconomic policies and the state of their financial sectors under the auspices of the banner 'transparency'. At the root of these beliefs though, has been a fundamental faith in the capacity of markets to make decisions rationally and efficiently.

However, this faith in markets, particularly in relation to their supposed rational behaviour, is far from unqualified, suggesting that the G7 finance ministries and central banks do not accept the tenets of neo-classical economics without reservation, or have at least been pragmatic in their application of the theory. Despite repeated endorsement of fully liberalized capital markets as the most efficient form of economic organization, the G7 finance ministries and central banks have since the mid-1990s also accepted that liberalized financial markets carry with them a greater risk of disruption and crisis.[23] Yet the intellectual case for liberalized capital markets, as outlined above, rejects the prospects for market failure unless there are information shortfalls. The intellectual inconsistency of the finance ministries and central banks has been most apparent in their collective exchange rate policy where they have sporadically attempted to temper what they have deemed to be excessive movements in the major currencies that could not be justified in terms of underlying fundamentals, by releasing statements calling for market corrections or stabilization (see Chapter 6). At the very least such behaviour indicates that finance ministries and central banks accept that markets can interpret data incorrectly, or that traders in the market have ignored the data and based their decision on market trends rather than economic fundamentals, producing perverse extreme movements that authorities need to persuade the market to correct. Either way it is an acknowledgement that left to their own devices, financial markets are prone to volatility and require guidance from public authorities. This acknowledgement would appear to be inconsistent with the case for self-equilibrating liberalized financial markets as developed by neo-classical economic theory. While there are grounds for claiming that the finance ministries and central banks have accepted the efficiency arguments of neo-classical theory in relation to financial liberalization, there is equally a case for saying they appear far from wholly convinced that markets tend towards equilibrium and always react rationally in response to fundamentals. In other words, their approach appears to be less than intellectually consistent.

Once we begin to question the intellectual consistency of the finance ministries and central banks' support for liberalized financial markets, we also have to factor in pragmatism and political calculation as part of the equation. Their actions do not appear to be entirely based on a commitment to theory, despite their claims to the contrary. Rather, economic ideas appear to have been invoked as a convenient legitimating device. This line of argument will be further developed in the next section.

In other ways however, neo-classical theories of markets appear particularly compatible with the proposals and actions of the G7 finance ministries and central banks. For example, during the 1990s, the finance ministries and central banks attempted to outline a common approach or set of principles on how to prevent financial crises and how to respond to them should they occur. This involved affected countries moving as rapidly as possible to put in place sound policies.[24] In cases of financial crisis where a currency's value was falling, the consensual G7 view was that it was incumbent on national authorities to reduce the supply of the currency, or at least the growth in the supply of the currency, if they wanted to achieve stability.[25] The view was that efforts to implement policies that supported a national currency, instead of dashing for growth with expansionary macroeconomic measures, would have beneficial long-term effects. The result would be less of a decline in the value of a currency, which would in turn feed through into lower long-term interest rates. A strong currency was seen to be in any country's interest because it reduced the prices of imports, held capital costs down, spurred increased productivity and competitiveness, and acted to reduce inflation, making more economic expansion possible.[26] Such orthodoxy was certainly evident in G7-supported IMF packages for emerging markets throughout the 1980s and 1990s.[27] At the same time, and fitting with the neo-classical perspective, there was a view that 'blaming speculators in the event of a crisis was almost always the wrong response'. Speculative flows were seen to respond to 'deeper factors', while blaming investors tended to be 'counter-productive in terms of attracting future capital inflows'.[28] The primary onus in the G7 approach to crisis resolution then was on authorities in affected countries assuming responsibility and taking action to put things right. What the G7 approach illustrates is that financial ideas generate solutions to problems and these solutions require different degrees of action from different actors. Financial ideas therefore give expression to and produce specific sets of power relations. The approach to crisis resolution developed in the 1990s therefore seemed to favour private financial actors and to shift primary responsibility on to authorities and citizens in crisis-affected countries.

However, the pattern is not quite as clear cut as the discussion above would suggest. An approach based on a transfer of responsibility for crisis management to domestic policy adjustment, particularly in emerging markets, has also been accompanied by a growing recognition of the importance of private sector involvement and co-ordination in financial crisis resolution. Often this is highlighted as a new post-Asian development, but it was first referred to and promoted in a G10 deputies report in 1996.[29] Growing private sector involvement in crisis resolution is seen as a countervailing force to the threat of 'moral hazard', where private investors and institutions invest in a reckless fashion because of a belief that the official community will bail them out. Private sector involvement is increasingly being referred to in G7 statements, and a range of initiatives are being pursued, but their origins precede the Asian financial crisis.[30]

Implicit in the concept of private sector burden sharing is the view that market actors have to bear some of the burden for resolving a crisis because they have participated in the crisis in the first place, although it should be noted that as a principle, private sector burden sharing has relatively little to say about questions of causation where financial crises are concerned. Private sector burden sharing is also part of a pragmatic political balancing act designed to produce negotiated solutions to financial crises, even if the majority of the burden and responsibility for resolving the crisis continues to lie with actors in the crisis-affected country rather than with foreign investors. Nevertheless, private sector burden sharing is not an outcome, or approach, that can be justified in terms of, or derived from, neo-classical theory. It is a concept that recognizes financial crises involve multiple actors[31] and it is designed to discourage reckless market investment and unnecessary risk taking by indicating that private actors will have to take some responsibility for their actions. Through its existence as a principle informing crisis resolution, private sector burden sharing effectively concedes that it is possible for markets to overreact and behave recklessly, and moreover that there is a need to create disincentives that discourage this kind of behaviour. This is a position that most certainly does not sit comfortably with the central tenets of neo-classical theories of markets. Consequently, we can see that even in the mid-1990s when the Washington consensus was supposedly at its height, the finance ministries and central banks' commitment to neo-classical theory was somewhat inconsistent and at best pragmatic, while its application has always been somewhat cautious and selective. Yet despite all of these caveats there has still been a marked reluctance to consider the possibility that crises may be a consequence of the very nature of liberalized markets and the way they behave, which would constitute the ultimate rejection of neo-classical equilibrium theory. The influence of neo-classical theory has consequently been somewhat mixed and it has been invoked in a politically convenient fashion.

Capital controls became a controversial topic after the Asian financial crisis, with several commentators making a case for them.[32] Despite this the G7 position on their use has remained markedly similar. Essentially the general G7 belief on capital controls is that in a world of capital mobility, governments' capacity to tax capital or to regulate industry is eroded as jurisdictions are pitted against one another.[33] In this respect, it is believed that capital controls cannot substitute for good policies. The economic distortions and macroeconomic costs induced by controls are on the whole seen to be far more costly than the potential benefits. However, this position is also not as straightforward as it seems and the qualification is that the exception to the norm of free capital mobility are cases where inadequate prudential regulation of the banking system may justify for a transitional period, for prudential reasons, the maintenance of capital controls on short-term inflows into banks – so-called Chilean-style controls.[34] Notably, this was a position the US G7 deputy was happy to publicly outline as early as 1996. Moreover, support for controls on capital inflows would suggest that authorities are prepared to acknowledge that short-term market movements can be excessive and based on market trends rather than fundamentals. Again this is a position that does not sit comfortably with the neo-classical equilibrium theory of markets.

More generally, enthusiasm for the principle of capital account liberalization reached its peak in the mid-1990s with a proposal from the British Treasury, strongly supported by the US Treasury, to amend the IMF's articles of agreement to encourage capital account liberalization. This measure was designed to signal the direction all IMF members were expected to proceed in if they were to retain the benefits of membership of the organization, to discourage backsliding, including the resort to stringent capital controls in the event of a crisis and to give the IMF a legitimate role in supervising an orderly process of capital account liberalization world wide.[35] At around the same time, increased international capital mobility was being cited as the principal reason for growth in emerging market economies in South East Asia as net capital flows to developing countries increased from $25 billion in 1986 to over $165 billion in 1995. However, the Asian financial crisis subsequently served to highlight some of the pre-conditions and qualifications that needed to accompany capital account liberalization, such as adequate sequencing and necessary regulatory provisions. Consequently, capital account liberalization as a standard prescription to be supervised by the Fund was rejected at the end of the 1990s.[36] Nevertheless, the G7 finance ministries and central banks continue to favour open markets and advocate capital liberalization as the ultimate goal and objective of many of their joint initiatives in accordance with the neo-classical position, even if their application of the theory in practice has always been pragmatic, selective and accompanied by caveats and qualifications.

Sound money

The second principle of sound money is essentially based on the belief that both stable public finances and low inflation are essential pre-requisites for sustainable and stable levels of growth and employment, and is most crucially necessary for wider systemic financial stability.[37] Concerted efforts to bring down inflation across the industrialized world began in principle at the end of the 1970s, when economic policy-makers identified inflation as the number one economic problem they faced. Such efforts were the direct consequence of national experiences, and in particular the failure of Keynesian reflation, most notably in Britain in 1976 and in France in 1983.[38] The subsequent macroeconomic focus on low inflation had its intellectual roots in the work of Milton Friedman and his argument that an expansionary monetary and fiscal policy mix cannot, in and of itself, deliver, let alone sustain, full employment.[39] Excessive macroeconomic expansions are believed to lead to inflation, which then has to be forcibly controlled and can lead to higher long-term unemployment.[40] Furthermore, today economic growth is increasingly seen as a product of endogenous factors such as technology, labour market skills, infrastructure, tax regimes and corporate governance, while it is believed that unemployment often owes more to poor performance in these areas than demand deficiency that can be tackled through macroeconomic expansion.[41] Clearly if policy-makers take theories which hold that there are limits to the extent to which macroeconomic policy can be used to generate growth and employment, at face value, then the obvious target for macroeconomic policy is low inflation. The danger with such orthodoxy however, is that it can lead to a confusion of ends and means, because rather than being prioritized for its own sake, low inflation is only positive if it is contributing to growth and low unemployment.[42]

Despite the focus on bringing down inflation in the 1980s, in practice the US and other G7 countries continued to follow expansionary fiscal policy throughout this decade, albeit to varying degrees. For example, average G7 annual fiscal deficits rose from an average of 2.9 per cent in 1982 to an average of 3.4 per cent of GDP in 1992.[43] After this date the pattern reversed and by 1997 average deficits had fallen to 1.9 per cent. In other words, deficit reduction and fiscal consolidation took on a more tangible element across the G7 after 1992, as the commitment to fiscal austerity seemed to strengthen in the 1990s. During the 1980s, several centre-right governments used taxation cuts to inspire electoral success and the resulting fiscal deficits were funded by the new sources opened up by financial liberalization, although public expenditure also came under increasing pressure in all G7 countries to varying degrees as a consequence of tax cuts.[44] In the 1990s, there was a recognition that sustained deficits could cause exchange rate volatility, but that most importantly these growing deficits also had to be financed, wasting public funds that were increasingly scarce following the tax cuts of the 1980s. Large budget deficits also tended to result in higher long-term interest rates impeding economies' growth prospects. On the other hand, it was reasoned that lower deficits would translate into lower interest rates and higher rates of growth. Such a calculation was certainly evident in the Clintonomics of the United States in the 1990s and efforts to turn the US from being the world's biggest sovereign debtor to a position whereby in early 1998 the US was running a small fiscal surplus for the first time since the 1960s.[45]

However, the 1990s was also a decade in which the Japanese economy was beset by stagnation. Devoid of other options, the Japanese resorted to fiscal stimulus and were even encouraged to follow this course by G7 partners at G7 meetings in 1997–8. On this basis, the notion of any consensus among the G7 on fiscal consolidation might look rather flimsy, but the unique and desperate circumstances of the Japanese economy proved to be the exception rather than the rule. Fiscal rules were introduced in Europe, debated in the US, while all G7 states with the exception of Japan reduced the size of their deficits during the 1990s. A belief in fiscal austerity was also repeatedly reflected in numerous G7-backed IMF financial packages to developing countries affected by currency depreciation and liquidity problems throughout the 1980s and 1990s.[46]

The principle of sound money has also informed monetary policy. Low inflation has been the objective of monetary policy across the industrialized world since the 1980s and in some cases the 1970s. During the 1980s, G7 states experimented with several methods of controlling inflation including money supply targets and exchange rate targeting. By the 1990s, the expansion of sources of credit, financial innovation and an exponential expansion in the extent, scope and speed of international capital flows had led to both methods being rejected for implying perverse policy mixes. Exchange rate targeting, it was even suggested by a considerable number of G7 finance ministry and central bank officials, could actually encourage volatility and acted as a direct target for the markets, as market operators would challenge specific exchange rate ranges in the belief they could force abandonment of the policy and make huge profits when governments inevitably moved, albeit vainly, to protect a specified exchange rate target.[47]

As a consequence of the experiences of the turbulence in the European Monetary System in 1992–3 and the problems that beset the Mexican peso during 1994–5, the G7 countries abandoned any pretence of exchange rate targeting and began actively discouraging it in public statements. In the words of former US Treasury Secretary Larry Summers:

> What we've learnt is that the idea that you can have a monetary policy, a fiscal policy and an exchange rate policy is a profound confusion. There is no enduring exchange rate policy that is independent of monetary or fiscal policy. I think that there are very real costs when monetary policies are directed at exchange rate objectives rather than at growth or price stability objectives. Without monetary policy changes there are real limits to how much governments can affect exchange rates – I think that's the lesson of the EMS period, that's the lesson of the bubble period in Japan.[48]

Summers also argued that in an era of international capital mobility fixed or pegged exchange rates were like coiled springs because they made market volatility greater. This view was echoed by former German deputy Jurgen Stark who believed that explicit exchange rate arrangements involved treating the symptoms rather than the cause and that 'each country must accept its responsibility and put its own house in order'.[49] In other words, exchange rate stability was believed to be a product of sound national macroeconomic policies, which in turn should be focused on national price stability.

These beliefs obviously placed limitations on the extent to which the G7 finance ministries and central banks could collaborate on exchange rate matters. Unlike in the 1980s, the finance ministries and central banks denied the value of targeting specific reference ranges for exchange rates, despite the fact that the IMF continued to advocate that certain developing countries maintain exchange rate pegs of various sorts, often with disastrous consequences. The G7 approach in the 1990s emphasized that exchange rates should reflect underlying fundamentals. Consequently, the G7's multilateral surveillance exercise focused on a thorough examination of various domestic indices of their own economies such as growth rates, inflation and fiscal deficits, and increasing attempts to export similar surveillance exercises to emerging markets. On the basis of surveillance there were occasional attempts to correct what the G7 identified as 'sustained and pronounced' market-induced exchange rate misalignments. Ultimately therefore, despite an acceptance that markets can be prone to volatility, the G7 approach to exchange rates during the 1990s reflected a belief that market-determined outcomes were superior and that markets themselves were on the whole efficient and rational, provided timely information and data were made available. While a neo-classical orientation is evident, the finance ministries and central banks' position on exchange rates is not entirely derived from neo-classical theory, precisely because it seems to contain an acceptance that financial markets can overshoot and behave in a volatile fashion, and that market decision-making processes are not always flawless.

The finance ministries and central banks also became increasingly selective in their use of the tool of exchange market intervention throughout the 1990s.[50] The view was that the utility of exchange market intervention as a policy instrument had diminished as a consequence of the expansion in private international capital flows. Officials referred to their 'immense humility' in their dealings with the markets[51] although critics have deemed this 'abstention'.[52] Exchange market intervention was believed to be most effective when it was used in the context of supportive monetary and other economic policy actions, because it could convey a signal of a strong common approach among the G7 countries.[53] When it was widely anticipated and perceived as a substitute for action on fundamentals, in the face of strong market pressure in the opposite direction, such intervention was seen to be less effective.[54] The question of the most appropriate exchange rate was seen to be changing on a daily or even hourly basis.[55] Exchange rates are nevertheless viewed as the markets' verdict on the performance of a particular national economy and the success of domestic monetary and fiscal policies. In other words, the G7 approach to exchange rates is an effective invitation for markets to judge domestic economic performance. Again we can see here how financial ideas give expression to and produce specific sets of power relations with markets being encouraged to engage in an effective continuous opinion poll on national policies, as the finance ministries and central bankers' world view facilitates a continuous process of market scrutiny that sustains market ascendancy, or what was referred to in the previous chapter as third-dimensional diplomacy.

Ideas have also produced a specific set of similar power relations in the field of monetary and interest rate policy. Market judgement of national policies has received expression in monetary policy via the notion of 'credibility', which involves policy-makers demonstrating their commitment to deliver a stated objective so as to influence market expectations and convince investors that stated policy targets are believable.[56] An increasing number of G7 central banks have adopted national inflation targets to which they are 'pre-committed' and have justified this on the grounds of enhancing their credibility.[57] The commitment to deliver low inflation has also been thought to be more 'credible' where central bankers are free to set interest rates without government interference. Numerous continental European states, the UK, and Japan all moved towards central bank independence, and by the end of the 1990s all G7 central banks with the exception of the Bank of Canada were operationally independent. At the beginning of the decade only the US and Germany had independent central banks, suggesting that central bank independence was very much a product of the intellectual and political climate of the 1990s.[58] The principal logic behind central bank independence was to place the setting of interest rates outside of the political process and insulate it from societal demands and pressures, so that decisions could be made on supposedly technical and economic grounds rather than political ones.[59] Unelected central bankers are believed to face less temptation to deliver pre-election gifts to voters in the form of interest rate cuts. Stephen Gill has referred to these developments as a form of new constitutionalism – a legal and political strategy for separating economic forces and policies from broad political accountability, securing management of the economy in the hands of central bankers and technocrats responsive to transnational capital.[60] In this regard, it is not coincidental that the two most monitored indictors in foreign exchange markets – current rates of inflation and fiscal deficits, are increasingly prioritized in the targets of G7 finance ministries and central banks, so as to convince financial investors of their good intentions. In many respects, these practices are indicative of the structural power of speculative finance, as the preferences of international financial investors are prioritized in macroeconomic policy-making, over the interests of groupings such as export-based manufacturing, SMEs, trade unions, and the unemployed.[61] Central bank independence and fiscal rules therefore represent the endogenizaton of the global agendas of financial markets in domestic institutional orders in an effective denationalization of macroeconomic policy.[62]

Low inflation mandates for independent central banks and fiscal policy frameworks that set limits to budget deficits, represent policy-makers' attempts to communicate symbolically with financial markets and indicate their commitment to following finance-friendly macroeconomic policies, so as to inspire confidence and credibility in the world of finance – in an implicit form of third-dimensional diplomacy.[63] The importance of this is emphasized by one policy-maker who makes the point that 'global capital markets immediately punish any government which strays from the macroeconomic straight and narrow' and goes on to make the case that financial investors therefore require reassurance.[64] Financial markets consequently effectively dictate the long-term objectives and suitable frameworks for the conduct of macroeconomic policy as a consequence of the ascendancy of certain financial and monetary ideas, which have in turn provided a rationale and a justification for the institutionalization of certain sets of social and power relations.

The dovetailing of financial ideas, interests and institutions

As the discussion above illustrates, financial ideas clearly influence policy-makers, but as a stand-alone explanation of the politics of financial governance they are insufficient. Ideas have informed the finance ministries and central banks' consensus, but at the same time that consensus has been far from intellectually consistent and it has not been entirely derived from neo-classical economic theory and models. Rather, the consensus appears to have been accompanied by a practical pragmatism and a number of minor qualifications and deviations from neo-classical logic. In this regard, the G7 consensus has been a broad approach, rather than a coherent set of intellectual premises and ideas. Moreover, a growing number of economists and commentators are beginning to question the intellectual merits of the case for capital account liberalization and fully liberalized financial markets.[65] In the context of increasing questions about the wisdom of financial liberalization, the apparent intellectual inconsistency of the G7 approach and the extent to which it is true to neo-classical theoretical premises, we need to search for alternative explanations for the G7's commitment to the consensus of the 1990s. An emphasis on ideational factors alone would appear not to suffice. Here I will suggest that ideas, institutions and interests have dovetailed, as an effective transnational state–society coalition comprised of the finance ministries and central banks, and financial interests in G7 countries have combined to create a very real political motivation for the G7's continued commitment to the principles of sound money and open markets.

Several important academic voices on international monetary affairs have identified a remarkable congruence between ideas, institutions and interests, particularly where capital account liberalization is concerned.[66] Most obviously, financial interests engaged in wide-scale foreign borrowing and lending can make more profits the more integration and liberalization proceed, and therefore have a lot to gain from capital account liberalization and a lot to lose from capital controls. However, the relationship between financial interests and salient neo-classical ideas goes beyond this rather simple calculation. By invoking a neo-classical view of markets it is possible to represent the current method of organizing the international monetary and financial system as the only feasible alternative, because the neo-classical approach is not only an explanatory theory that makes causal claims, but also a series of prescriptions that constitute a specific normative vision of how and why an ideal market-based financial system should be constructed.[67] Indeed, increasingly the normative elements of neo-classical theory are more likely to be invoked by policy-makers than the explanatory elements, with certain neo-classical assumptions being elevated to the status of 'singular truths', demanding to be taken as faith on the basis of inconclusive evidence.[68] In this context, neo-classical ideas come to resemble an ideology, as policy-makers' commitment to their beliefs often runs ahead of the facts.[69] Ideology can in turn act as a 'filtering device', setting the parameters of debate within which interested parties have to operate, determining policy-makers' responses and ultimately providing a barrier to change even in the light of new evidence.[70]

When ideas come to resemble an ideology more closely than they do an explanatory theory, we can be sure that important political interests are at work. For example, neo-classical theory's claim that markets only malfunction in the presence of imperfect information is a particularly convenient cloak for financial interests, because any disruption cannot by definition be the fault of the markets. In the event of a financial crisis, neo-classical premises immediately shift the emphasis and blame onto authorities in affected countries, domestic cronyism and local banks. The financial sector is consequently largely immune from criticism, or fundamental reform for as long as neo-classical theory is ascendant, providing a *de facto* ideational shield for financial interests. Financial interests therefore clearly have a strong incentive to promote neo-classical beliefs and ideas, because these ideas enable them to define and re-define society in their own image. In the words of Mark Blyth, 'the political power of such ideas is to allow market participants to blame the victim, to take the reward and disavow responsibility for generating any of the costs'.[71]

Financiers also have a clear interest in the sound money aspect of the current G7 consensus. Low inflation is not a neutral value-free policy objective. It involves the protection of the value of money and existing wealth, and sometimes this objective has been pursued to the detriment of those at the lower end of the income scale and often at the expense of growth and employment, even in the industrialized world, as well as more noticeably in the case of the developing world through IMF prescriptions.[72] Prioritizing low inflation ensures that creditors can reclaim the full value of their investments, but it can also exacerbate the costs of debtors, leading to bankruptcies and rising unemployment, yet little macroeconomic research pays attention to the societal distributional and income differential consequences of the dogged pursuit of low inflation.[73] At the same time, neither is the contemporary notion of macroeconomic credibility an impartial concept. This becomes particularly apparent if we pose the question of credibility for whom. Contemporary macroeconomic credibility is a direct response to and attempt to communicate with market sentiment, based on a fear that market actors will abandon the national currency in the absence of symbolic anti-inflationary institutional reassurance.[74] Consequently, contemporary macroeconomic credibility effectively involves market sentiment defining current notions of macroeconomic best practice. With even those who view it positively conceding that there is little evidence to connect central bank independence to improvements in economic growth,[75] we have to accept that the current macroeconomic regime is largely politically and socially constructed. In short, institutionalizing low inflation as the principle objective in macroeconomic policy is a signal that a government will defend a social structure of accumulation based on monetary orthodoxy (the prioritization of the interests of lenders through policies designed to provide the optimum conditions for the operation of the financial sector, with limited regard for other sectors) and that this particular way of organizing society is being simultaneously constructed and defended against possible redefinition.[76]

Unsurprisingly, financial interests have found willing accomplices in the promotion of neo-classical visions of financial markets within the state in the form of finance ministries and central banks. Advancing the efficiency equilibrium view of financial markets and promoting capital account liberalization has created a ready-made justification for central bank independence and fiscal deficit frameworks as the only credible institutional arrangements that will appease powerful, but rational and efficient financial markets. Consequently, finance ministries and central banks have been able to use neo-classical theories to enhance their own institutional standing in domestic terms, relative to other state agencies. Increasingly, central banks are able to set monetary policy independently of other actors in accordance with narrow anti-inflationary and financial objectives, while excluding other concerns and alternative voices. Likewise, finance ministries have seen their power to police public expenditure processes increase, along with their capacity to set pre-defined limits to spending and deficits, which has enhanced their negotiating capacity with spending departments. Arguments in the direction of sound money, central bank independence and fiscal rules begin however with justifications for capital account liberalization and the neo-classical view of financial markets. With the vacuum left by the failure of Keynesian macroeconomics and the increasing lack of success of industrial policies, financial interests and elites in finance ministries and central banks were able to make their case, as the effects of financial liberalization and the dangers of disruption unfolded from the 1980s onwards.

However, finance ministries and central banks' connection to financial interests also goes beyond this rather simple rational interest calculation. There is a long-standing traditional social bond between financiers and central banks and finance ministries, borne out of the traditional functions of finance ministries and central banks. Finance ministries have traditionally been charged with managing the nation's debt, which results in them engaging in financial market activity and creates contact with and appreciation of the concerns of financial market actors. At the same time, capital account liberalization expands the range of methods for managing and financing government debt. Central banks, on the other hand, have had a responsibility for guaranteeing the stability and soundness of the financial system as a whole, most evident in their concern with delivering a stable currency. Again this has required financial market operations and the managing of foreign currency reserves, while capital account liberalization has increased the options and strategies open to central banks and the financial sector in general, particularly with regard to how to finance current account deficits.

In the process of performing the functions and activities described above, finance ministries and central banks develop social networks that link them to their finance sectors, which in turn facilitate conversations, mutual learning, the sharing of ideas, expertise and personnel. These repeated social interactions create a sensitivity to one another's views and to some extent a shared but ultimately quite restricted way of viewing the world.

It is worth noting at this point that all of the G7 countries have internationally active financial sectors, although this is most evident in the cases of the US and the UK. Those officials working in the international divisions of finance ministries and central banks who are charged with the task of preparing agendas and briefings for G7 meetings, are acutely aware of the concerns of these internationally active institutions. It is the activities of these institutions that are most directly affected by the outcomes of the international financial system and of international financial governance, which means that officials preparing for G7 meetings have continuous direct exposure to the concerns of internationally active private financial institutions. Furthermore, regular exchanges and interactions with other officials, particularly British and American officials, has further augmented shared neo-classical assumptions, particularly concerning capital liberalization and sound money. Political socialization of this sort serves to reinforce the formal neo-classical economics training of many finance ministry and central bank officials, as this branch of economics continues to determine the norms of the economics profession and is particularly influential in the most prestigious and 'conservative' US graduate schools. In other words, shared social networks throughout the G7 countries help to reinforce and maintain the shared consensus described earlier and further tighten the congruent fit or dovetailing of ideas, interests and institutions in the domain of financial governance. In this context, shared assumptions and views reign, while alternative voices go largely unheard or are ignored.[77]

Therefore there are undoubtedly elites in French, German, Italian, Canadian and Japanese finance ministries and central banks who are sympathetic to the neo-classical position, as a consequence of a combination of formal training, their strategic calculation of their own institution's position in domestic policy-making relative to other agencies, their awareness of the needs of internationally active institutions in their own financial sectors, and the socialization processes that result from their exposure to these interests, as well as from their interactions with G7 colleagues and the personnel of multilateral financial institutions. However, despite the existence of a number of technocrats who are sympathetic to the neo-classical position, none of the above states can be said to have the same strategic national interest in capital account liberalization as the United States and the United Kingdom. In both of these countries an overriding national interest in capital account liberalization is deeply embedded in socio-economic structures. This is not replicated to anywhere near the same degree in any of the other G7 countries. The commitment to capital account liberalization goes far beyond treasuries and central banks in the US and the UK, which possibly accounts for the fact that support for the G7 consensus is most pronounced in the US and the UK and is often more qualified and circumspect in the rest of the G7.

It is possible to make sense of the US and the UK's commitment to capital account liberalization in the context of an appreciation of the relative financialization of the political economies of each state. Financialization in this case refers to the political influence of financial centres, Wall Street and the City of London, over domestic policy-making.[78] However, it also refers to the increasing dominance of the finance industry in the sum total of economic activity, of financial controllers in the management of corporations, of financial assets among total assets, of the stock market as a market for determining corporate strategies and as a determinant of business cycles.[79] In terms of the performance of the UK and US economies the health of the financial sector is a crucial ingredient in the act of wealth creation.[80] Traditionally, the financial sector in both countries has also had an arms-length relationship with the manufacturing sector, preferring to accumulate profit as quickly as possible, rather than investing and building close relationships with manufacturing clients. This arms-length relationship has also translated into a strong preference from the financial sector for a strong currency as a means of protecting the value of investments abroad and attracting inward investments.[81] Since the unravelling, or dismantling, of the post-war embedded liberal compromise, evident in the demise of the fixed exchange rate system and increasing financial liberalization, this preference has become even more pronounced. One of the principal outcomes of having little concern with a competitively valued currency, together with the financial sector's general neglect of domestic manufacturing, has been the chronic long-run balance of payments deficits the US and the UK have experienced, partly as a result of financialization.

However, financialization has also provided a solution to these long-run chronic structural deficits for both countries. The large well-developed financial sectors of both the US and the UK, Wall Street and the City of London, have enabled both states to finance their deficits by running a capital account surplus, that is to say by attracting capital inflows from the rest of the world. As a consequence of their structural position in the world economy as states with chronic balance of payments problems, and as the countries most integrated into contemporary international financial markets, the US and the UK are the two states most in favour of capital account liberalization and the current regime. These three facts are not unrelated. Rather the first two provide an incentive for the US and the UK to reinforce, promote and maintain the current liberalized regime.[82]

Therefore, under the current regime, states with large financial sectors can avoid hard choices over their structural deficits and can exercise a 'power to delay' macroeconomic adjustment.[83] The promotion of the current regime and the downplaying of its risks and hazards are therefore essential for these states and their financial allies to reap the rewards of the system and this in turn creates a strong and very real political motivation for the US and the UK to promote neo-classical economic theories and assumptions. Consequently, a *de facto* transnational coalition between financial interests and finance ministries and central banks with a shared mutual interest in promoting the current system, what is sometimes referred to as the US Treasury, Wall Street, UK Treasury, Bank of England, City of London axis, has supported and advocated a predominantly neo-classical reading of financial markets.

Of course, this coalition is most powerful and most well developed in the US and the UK. However, a further feature of the current system is that recent financial crises, particularly the East Asian crisis, have been characterized by a 'flight to quality', most especially inflows of capital into the City of London and Wall Street, which pushed up the value of equities and bonds in both locations, but also into European, Japanese and Canadian financial markets. While it is clear that the more the current system is extended, the more the US and the UK asymmetrically benefit, the same is also true of other states with well-developed financial sectors. As the financial sectors of other G7 states expand and develop, so too they develop a greater stake in the continuation and extension of the current financial system. As Blyth has argued, states with large financial interests can attract more resources from a larger available pool of capital, avoiding domestic trade-offs by rent seeking from the rest of the world and deflecting risks and adjustments costs on to other states.[84] Moreover, they can do all of this while justifying and rationalizing the current system by invoking a neo-classical theory of financial markets as rational decision-making entities that produce efficient outcomes, thus ring-fencing debates on global financial governance and minimizing the possibility of fundamental reform. In short, the development of a country's financial sector and the degree of financialization, determine a state's interest in the current financial regime. Creeping financialization in states such as Japan and Germany (which in part is being cultivated by finance ministries and central banks) helps to explain these states' continuing commitment to the current regime and to the G7 consensus, even though they continue to run current account surpluses and are not financially dependent on capital account liberalization in the way deficit states like the US and the UK are. Should these countries see balance of payments surpluses eroded by increased export competition from emerging markets and developing countries, we can then expect the commitment of the rest of the G7 to neo-classical ideas, capital account liberalization and the current regime to strengthen further.

Traditional national positions and conflict at G7 meetings

While the G7 finance ministries and central banks share a loose, broad consensus on the benefits and virtues of sound money and open markets, there have also been some quite distinct traditional national positions adopted at G7 meetings. The key point however, is that disputes and differences take place and exist within the parameters set by the broad overarching consensus described above. One notable difference is how the Anglo-Saxon approach to labour market governance differs markedly from the notion of some form of continental European social model. While this is an example of a clear difference that exists between the G7 countries, in this book we are concerned with the approach to financial and monetary issues and threats to the basic sound money–open markets consensus, rather than a broader range of economic governance issues, although this is not to deny that there are obvious linkages between the two.

Traditional macroeconomic differences

One of the main differences between G7 countries has been rooted in the quite different historical economic experiences of G7 states. Due to the traumatic economic experience of the great depression of the 1930s, the US has traditionally been concerned with the maintenance of economic growth and this has been reflected in national macroeconomic priorities and positions at G7 meetings. For example, unusually for a central bank, a concern with growth and employment has even been evident in the mandate of the Federal Reserve as established by the Humphrey Hawkins Act of 1978. Moreover, this concern with growth was evident in a US tendency to urge the Germans and the Japanese to assume a greater responsibility for world growth at G7 meetings, particularly in the 1970s and at times in the 1980s. Germany on the other hand reacted to the legacy of the hyper-inflation experienced by Weimar Germany in the 1920s by creating a central bank obsessed with tackling inflation and by demonstrating a commitment to fiscal discipline. The inflationary outcome of the Bonn agreement of 1978, when the US persuaded the Germans to adopt expansionary fiscal measures, has further contributed to antipathy amongst German policy-makers and academics towards US proposals for international economic policy co-ordination designed to deliver growth objectives.[85]

The current account deficit–surplus divide

Another difference between G7 countries has been rooted in the current account positions of the various countries. The US has run a persistent current account deficit for nearly four decades, while Germany and Japan have tended to run surpluses. Traditionally, this has resulted in Germany and Japan urging the deficit country, the United States, to initiate adjustment. In contrast, the US has called for surplus countries to take parallel initiatives and even lead the process. Most economic analyses suggest this is dependent upon the overall global economic outlook. For example, it is commonly argued that if recession and unemployment is the principal risk, then surplus countries should adjust by expanding demand, whilst deficit countries should devalue. On the other hand if inflation is the main international concern deficit countries should contract and surplus countries should re-value.[86]

The declining importance of traditional national macroeconomic positions in the 1990s and the consolidation of consensus

During the second half of the 1980s and the 1990s the international consensus gravitated towards the German position and that of surplus countries as the fight against inflation pre-occupied policy-makers.[87] Consequently, disagreements between the US as a deficit country and Germany as a surplus country, lessened in accordance with the acceptance of the consensus described above.[88] In particular, two principal features of Clintonomics reflected the evolving consensus on sound money and were at the heart of the improved relations between surplus and deficit countries. First, there was a fiscal consolidation programme in the US, which in 1998 saw the United States record its first small budgetary surplus since the 1960s. With a vital source of inflation removed from the US economy, the Fed was able to adopt lower interest rates, which in turn gave a boost to stock market performance and the wealth and earnings of the 53 per cent of the US population who owned stocks and shares.[89] Second, by actively pursuing a high dollar policy from 1995 onwards, the Clinton Treasury appeared to be much less concerned about the size of the US trade deficit. Instead they accepted the benefits of improved stock market performance that came from lower interest rates, which were in turn partly facilitated by the anti-inflationary impact of a higher dollar.

Differences on exchange rates

Differences on exchange rates have traditionally involved Japan and Germany placing a much higher value on competitively valued currencies than the Anglo-Saxon countries, with the US and the UK being less concerned about the negative affects of currency appreciation, and the French having a general distrust of floating market determined rates. These differences are rooted in the financial and banking sectors of the different countries. The Japanese and German financial sectors have been dominated by credit and commercial banking practices rooted in the 'real' economy.[90] The political economy of Japan and Germany has also been characterized by a traditionally close relationship between manufacturing concerns and credit banks, with the banks often having seats on the boards of large industrial firms.[91] As Randall Henning's impressive study of currency politics in the US, Japan and Germany demonstrated, this created strong societal preferences in favour of competitively valued exchange rates in Japan and Germany, as both the banking and manufacturing sectors identified the export-related benefits that could be derived from a competitively valued exchange rate.[92] Such strong societal coalitions meant that Japanese and German authorities intervened in foreign markets far more often than their counterparts in the US and the UK, and also maintained capital controls for a longer period of time due to a stronger societal preference for a modest exchange rate. Japan and Germany have also tended to be less critical of the use of some forms of capital controls.

In contrast, the financial sectors in the US and the UK have had a more arms-length relationship with manufacturing industry. Both London and New York have specialized in international investment banking practices and the servicing of internationally mobile capital.[93] Industrial firms display a greater reliance on equity capital and raising finance through the stock market than in either Germany or Japan. This has resulted in weak and discordant societal preferences in favour of competitively valued exchange rates in the Anglo-Saxon countries, because the financial sectors in these countries have valued a strong currency so as to protect the value of investments and have been largely indifferent to the detrimental effects of this on the manufacturing sector. The US and the UK were the first countries to abolish capital controls following Bretton Woods and engage in foreign exchange market interventions so as to affect the value of their currencies far less than was the case in either Japan or Germany.[94] Clearly this has affected national positions at G7 meetings, with the Germans and Japanese being far keener on proactive co-operative efforts to manage exchange rates than either the US or the UK.

However, these traditional national differences on exchange rates also became less apparent during the 1990s. Authorities became more sceptical about the extent to which exchange market interventions could deliver exchange rate objectives as a direct result of rising international capital mobility, which saw daily private foreign exchange transactions dwarf the collective resources of G7 central banks.[95] This was a direct example of ideational adjustment responding to changing material circumstances, although changing consensual multilateral beliefs were serving to reinforce and accentuate that material change and were in turn leading to domestic institutional reform in the direction of independent central banks and fiscal rules, illustrating a mutually reinforcing relationship between multilateral consensual ideas, domestic policy-making arrangements and market structures, or at least the perception of market structures. At the same time, central bank mandates (the European Central Bank (ECB), the Bank of England and the Bank of Canada all had inflation targets, while the Bank of Japan had a mandate of domestic price stability)[96] made it difficult to use interest rate policy to support any exchange rate objectives. This difficulty corresponded with the Mundell–Flemming dilemma, which holds that it is not possible to have a national interest rate objective and an exchange rate policy simultaneously under conditions of international capital mobility except on an episodic basis.[97] Moreover, as discussed earlier in this chapter, exchange rate targeting was more or less rejected on the grounds that it often implied perverse policy mixes. Consequently, in the context of shared beliefs, domestic institutional arrangements and increased international capital mobility, joint G7 policy on exchange rates increasingly came to rely on declaratory policy and the issuing of shared public statements. This reliance on communication, statements and argumentation, as we shall see, had significant implications for patterns of authority in international monetary affairs.

Of course, in Europe, exchange rate co-operation continued to take a more explicit form in the European monetary system and the movement towards a single currency. European monetary co-operation appeared in part to be motivated by a collective European desire for shielding the continent from the negative affects of the US's neglect of the dollar, but after 1993 the introduction of wider margins of fluctuation to the European Monetary System and the increasing focus by European states on domestic fundamentals in order to meet the Maastricht convergence criteria on national inflation rates and budget deficits, meant that rigid exchange rate targeting was less explicit even in Europe. Moreover, exchange rate collaboration was seen as a distinctly European, rather than global enterprise, viable only in a specific regional context. Any wider collaboration linking the major currencies of Europe, North America and Asia was rejected, presumably because it would have distracted from the European Monetary Union project and because officials seemed to have no faith that a wider system of global target zones was workable.[98] The notable exception to this came in 1998, during the brief period that Oskar Lafontaine was German Finance Minister, when he pushed the idea of a system of global target zones. However, his term of office was ill fated and short lived, and his ideas were roundly rejected and scorned both by those close to the German Chancellor and by French and US officials.[99]

Finally, it is also worth noting that we might expect the ability of key German interests to influence exchange rate policy to recede as European monetary and exchange rate policy has been centralized under the terms of a monetary union. At the same time, reforms such as changes to clearing banks and a financial 'Big Bang' in Japan, the abolition of capital gains tax in Germany (which may remove domestic credit banks' incentive to retain shareholding in German manufacturers), the adoption of riskier Anglo-Saxon financial practices in the German financial sector,[100] and the simple fact that large German and Japanese firms and banks are becoming more involved in overseas activities, are all serving to loosen the bonds between finance and industry in these two countries. Such close social ties were at the root of societal preferences for competitively valued stable exchange rates, so we might reasonably expect these societal preferences to become less pronounced.[101] In this context we might also expect Japanese and German authorities' preferences at G7 meetings for exchange rate attentive policies to weaken, and indeed this appears to have been the case during the 1990s. At the very least, finance ministries and central banks certainly believe they have less capacity to pursue such policies, because of a combination of shared beliefs, prevailing domestic institutional arrangements and an increase in the size and speed of international capital flows.[102]

Financial sectors and financial regulation

Occasional G7 conflict also emerges from basic philosophical differences between the G7 countries concerning the fundamental social and economic purpose of the financial and banking sector. In the Anglo-Saxon countries, particularly the US and the UK, the financial sector's rationale is to maximize profit and return, while taking account of the risk this entails. In Japan and Germany, the financial sector has more of an obligation to assume a social role, providing finance for and supporting domestic industries and small and medium sized enterprises (SMEs), which are often viewed as social institutions in their own right.[103] Occasionally these basic philosophical differences can translate into conflict on important international regulatory questions. One of the most recent examples of this came in the recent Basle II negotiations, which were characterized by disputes between German and US regulators over the issues of external credit rating agencies and loans to SMEs. Basle II proposals translated into higher capital charges set against SME loans to cover risk. This threatened to divert credit away from SMEs and led to higher borrowing costs for this sector. Banks in both Japan and Germany were more dependent on SME loans than banks in the US. Eventually, the Germans were able to extract a concession in Basle II allowing banks to distinguish SME borrowers from other corporate clients.

Another dispute involved the use of external ratings agencies in risk assessment. The relative scarcity of ratings agencies in Germany compared with the US was an issue of considerable tension. Despite the fact that these disputes were largely handled as technicalities at Basle Committee meetings, and the G7 finance ministers and central bank governors' interventions were limited and restricted to points of principle, it demonstrated the gap between the US and Germany on important financial regulatory issues. Differences rooted in the national distinctiveness of financial sectors remain among the G7, although one identifiable trend that has resulted from Basle II is that a greater emphasis is being placed on internal bank models as risk measurement tools, with banks themselves shouldering more of the burden in determining how much regulatory capital is appropriate. In other words, there is a shift in responsibility for regulation to the market itself, and a general Anglo-Saxon perspective. The Anglo-Saxon position on the question of the regulation of hedge funds also appeared to prevail in the early conclusions of the new Financial Stability Forum in 1999 and 2000. Germany favoured a much more active interventionist stance, while the US rejected such a stance on the grounds that by their very nature it was not possible to actively regulate hedge funds. The FSF reports rejected any new regulation of hedge funds, but did call for enhanced surveillance of their activities.

Different attitudes towards the IMF

A final tension between G7 powers has related to attitudes towards the IMF and German distrust of the institution. The Germans have resented the fact that increases in Fund financial contributions have not been accompanied by a corresponding increase in political influence. There is a sense that the US have used Germany as a reliable paymaster, enabling them to run the world with other people's money.[104] In terms of the share of IMF personnel, Germany's portion remains well below its capital allocation, while both France and the UK have exceeded their capital contribution. The two most recent Managing Directors of the IMF were also French, adding to the German perception that the IMF operates as a US–French kitchen cabinet.[105] However, the arrival of Horst Kohler, a former G7 deputy and summit sherpa, as the Managing Director of the Fund lessened German antagonism towards the institution.

Recent challenges to the open markets sound money consensus

It should be clear from the discussion above that while there is a broad agreement among the G7 finance ministries and central banks that open markets and sound money should be the core normative principles underpinning the organization of the international financial system, there are also a number of national tensions and differences that exist within the parameters of this broad consensus. However, since the financial crises of 1997–8 the viability of the open markets – sound money consensus has not only been questioned,[106] but also some have even gone as far as to suggest that the neo-liberal (sound money open market) consensus of the 1990s has been abandoned and been replaced by a new more socially responsible G7 consensus.[107] According to John Kirton at first the G7 were constrained by 'a Washington consensus with neo-liberal values at its core', but the financial crises of 1997–8 then caused the G7 'to change significantly to a quite different policy model'.[108] The problem with such an interpretation is the emphasis on the switch to a 'quite different policy model'. When we begin to scrutinize the substance of such a change it is considerably less significant and substantial than it first appears. While there is no doubt that reigning G7 ideas and beliefs continued to be modified and adjusted after the crises of 1997–8, as indeed they had been over the previous thirty years, Kirton's interpretation overstates the extent of the change and ignores the fact that the fundamental organizing principles of sound money and open markets have not been challenged or overturned, let alone replaced by something quite different. Indeed, in many respects sound money and open markets have been further institutionalized as the organizational basis for the global financial order following the financial crises of 1997–8 (see Chapter 7), as the G7 finance ministries and central banks used the experience of the crises to push their agenda further.[109]

Challenges to the principle of sound money: what has really changed?

For Kirton, the G7 response to liquidity shortages which brought about the financial crises of 1997–8 in the form of collective calls for interest rate cuts, marked a 'historic shift in the G7's decade-long macroeconomic focus on fighting inflation'.[110] However, while all G7 central banks did move towards interest rate cuts and noted that slow growth was more of a threat to world economic performance than inflation, whether this constituted a 'historic shift' is more debatable. For example, interest rate cuts alone are not indicative of a fundamental or historic shift in economic policy objectives. At several times during the previous decades various central banks had moved to cut interest rates, and while growth was a more immediate concern than inflation for central banks, this did not mean that central banks had abandoned low inflation as their principal economic objective. This last point becomes clearer if we take Peter Hall's distinction between first-, second- and third-order policy objectives. For Hall, first-order policy matters are those day-to-day operational decisions on public expenditure levels; second-order policy matters are the frameworks, methods and policy instruments employed to achieve certain policy objectives; while third-order policy matters include the fundamental objectives, overarching assumptions and causal beliefs that inform policy. On this basis we can appreciate that the 1998 movement towards interest rate cuts should be interpreted as an example of a first-order policy change, but because central banks did not reform their mandates, denounce their focus on low inflation, or abandon this as a medium/long-term objective, it is not possible to interpret this as a more fundamental third-order policy change, or historic ideational shift in the overarching assumptions informing monetary policy. In other words, interest rate cuts in 1998 did not constitute either a challenge to, or a reversal of, the sound money element of the G7 consensus.

A more significant development involved calls from the G7, particularly Canada, for the IMF to prescribe less restrictive fiscal policy in some Asian countries on the basis of the circumstances of individual countries. Such moves were more about adjusting and refining an existing orthodoxy, rather than replacing it with something quite different. The G7 began to offer a more cautious, qualified and circumspect form of support for fiscal consolidation than had previously been the case. This did not mean that the idea of limiting the size of government deficits, and even aiming for fiscal surpluses where possible, had been abandoned, merely that increases in government spending could play a role in stabilizing situations in certain countries at certain times depending on the circumstances prevailing. Fiscal austerity has certainly not been abandoned altogether. Indeed it was a central part of the IMF package to crisis-ridden Argentina in 2002.

Those claiming that the G7's focus on tackling inflation has shifted are on stronger ground when considering the record of the Bush administration on macroeconomic policy for two principal reasons. The Bush administration has reversed the two central elements of Clinton's macroeconomic strategy. First, in true Republican fashion they have abandoned Clinton's fiscal consolidation strategy and introduced tax cuts that are of particular benefit to higher earners, while expanding military spending, returning the US to a position of fiscal deficit. This has been an effort to stimulate the economy by administering a fiscal stimulus, following the fall in US equity prices and slowing growth figures. In the long term, these policies may spell difficulties in terms of the sustainability of the US fiscal position, but they have been very much a short-term effort to restore growth. Second, the Bush administration has been happy to accept the export-related benefits of a lower dollar and a lower US trade deficit. One of the reasons for the lower dollar has been a series of enthusiastic interest rate cuts from Alan Greenspan at the Federal Reserve, in an effort to restore growth and give a boost to a floundering US stock market. Greenspan even referred to the dangers of deflation in Congressional testimonies in May 2003, so there has been a definite recognition of the receding threat of inflation and the growing threat of disinflation. These developments point to the fact that the focus on tackling inflation across the industrialized world since the 1980s has been quite successful, but low inflation has been achieved at the expense of lower growth. Increasingly, US policy-makers came to the recognition that the biggest macroeconomic problem faced by the world at the start of the twenty-first century was not inflation, but slow growth and low employment. However, this recognition is only leading to a re-prioritization in macroeconomic policy on an ad hoc basis evident in interest rate cuts and a variety of experiments with varying degrees of fiscal stimulus. Central banks remain vigilant where inflation is concerned and have even been criticized in both the US and Europe for failing to move sufficiently swiftly or decisively enough to lower interest rates.

The key question and one side-stepped by Kirton, is whether experiments with varying degrees of macroeconomic stimulus are simply a short-term response to current economic circumstances, or whether they constitute an abandonment of the long-term commitment to fighting inflation as the principal objective of macroeconomic policy, and whether this is comparable to the intellectual revolution of the late 1970s and early 1980s that saw the displacement of the Keynesian paradigm and notions of full employment with various forms of neo-monetarism. At the very least any assessment in favour of the latter scenario would currently seem premature. Certainly, US policy-makers have been able to exploit the greater flexibility and latitude evident in the institutional framework for US macroeconomic policy. Unlike their counterparts in Europe, US policy-makers have not been constrained by fiscal rules, or a tightly defined inflation target. In contrast, the ECB, the Bank of England, and the Bank of Canada all have inflation targets, while the growth and stability pact limits the size of deficits that can emerge in Europe. In other words, while the US has a degree of flexibility in the field of macroeconomic policy, institutional arrangements in the rest of the G7 countries continue to prioritize sound money.

In the United States, the language and rhetoric of the Bush administration has differed from that of the Clinton administration. While structural reform of European labour markets to restore growth in Europe was the favoured message of the Clinton Treasury, current US Treasury secretary, John Snow, has been keen to point out to the Europeans that a healthy global economy needs several engines and they ought to take steps to restore growth and jobs, including less restrictive monetary and fiscal policies. In other words, the current US focus is on using macroeconomic policy as well as structural reform to boost growth in Europe, at least for the time being.[111] This has been accompanied by increasing US disquiet about the restrictive nature of the ECB's mandate and the terms of the growth and stability pact. In short, we might be witnessing the start of a process of substantive ideational change, which in turn may lead to the start of a process of institutional reform, but until we see such tangible institutional reform it is not possible to say that the G7 have abandoned their commitment to low inflation and sound money, precisely because formally most G7 finance ministries and central banks continue to prioritize these objectives.

Ultimately, while the US have used the flexibility evident in their own policy-making frameworks to pursue more growth-orientated macroeconomic policies through tax cuts and interest rate cuts, on its own this does not constitute a fundamental reversal of the principled commitment to the fight against inflation across the G7. Until US, IMF and other G7 policy-makers actively state that the war on inflation has been successful, is effectively over and that this necessitates domestic reform of the institutional macroeconomic frameworks that exist in G7 countries, such a verdict is premature.

Furthermore, until we see such institutional reform, the US will face difficulties in encouraging Europe to adopt growth-orientated policies, because of restrictive institutional frameworks such as the growth and stability pact and the price stability mandate of the ECB. The US Treasury has also spent the last ten years applauding and promoting the virtues of the targeting of inflation by independent central banks and fiscal rules that encourage balanced budgets, both in the developed and developing worlds. A reversal of this position would require at least a tacit acceptance that these institutional fixes were not the answer and that the IMF and the G7 finance ministry and central banking community have in fact been misplaced in their macroeconomic diagnoses and prescriptions. Such an acceptance has not been forthcoming, nor is it likely to be. Moreover, the degree of commitment to the terms of the growth and stability pact and the general principle of fiscal consolidation that exists among European finance ministry officials is often underestimated. Eurozone finance ministry officials share a consensus on the desirability of the principle of fiscal consolidation. Recent reform efforts indicate a belief that the growth and stability pact and its fiscal rules are workable and are not in need of wholesale reform. Debates have revolved around a relaxation of the uniform 3 per cent of GDP criteria and its replacement with an individual calculation of the deficit limits of different governments in accordance with the total size of their public debt, while steps have been taken to relax the corrective arm and enhance the preventative arm of the stability pact, but reform has been modest.

Institutional reform of central banks is also problematic. As Matthew Watson has pointed out, the effects of moving to a regime dominated by central bank independence are likely to persist long after the conditions (in this case the threat of inflation in the 1980s and more specifically the 1990s) which were thought to necessitate independent central banks with inflation targets in the first place, have long disappeared.[112] Problems arise because central bankers are cautious by nature and their sound money instincts often make them reluctant to move decisively in the direction of interest rate cuts. For example, some critics have argued that the history of central bank independence has revealed that interest rates have tended to be higher than they needed to be when central bankers have been free to set rates. The natural caution of central bankers has been compounded by mandates such as specific inflation targets, which provide incentives for central bankers to ensure that they meet the inflation target, regardless of the consequences of this for the economy as a whole. Unfortunately, while the favoured quick institutional fix to tackle inflation in the 1990s – central bank independence – was relatively quick and easy to implement, overturning that institutional fix to reflect new conditions and circumstances (in this case the growing threat of prolonged and persistent disinflation) will not be as easy or as quick. Many within the central bank community would deny that institutional reform is necessary on the grounds that they are perfectly capable of taking adequate action in sufficient time to avoid deflation. The experience of the 1920s and 1930s might suggest that this is debateable. Furthermore, institutional arrangements lock in patterns of behaviour and institutional norms, which in turn filter out alternative prescriptions. At the same time, monetary economists tend to gravitate towards the central banking community, providing that community with a monopoly of intellectual expertise and a control over the technocratic discourse, which surrounds monetary politics. This monopoly of expertise creates barriers to the possibilities of institutional reform, because precious few voices from within the central banking community are likely to begin advocating the reversal of hard-won central bank independence, on the basis of what they view as only a temporary receding of the threat of inflation. It would consequently be a mistake to expect a consensus that has been built up over a period of thirty years, and most crucially one that has been embedded in national institutional arrangements during the 1990s, to be overturned in a short space of time.

Currently, the viability of sound money as a fundamental organizing principle of the international monetary system is being questioned, but it will take a stronger and more encompassing coalition of public–private actors to overturn the current consensus and replace it with something qualitatively different.[113] In particular, it will require academic economists, central bankers, the IMF and private sector financial analysts to admit that their analyses have been misplaced and that central bank independence and the strict targeting of inflation are not the institutional panaceas that they have been presented as. Pressure from politicians, manufacturing interests, environmental lobbyists and trade unionists alone will be insufficient. Those at the heart of the broad technocratic policy community that have come to dominate financial and monetary policies and have gained in influence as a consequence of monetary orthodoxy, will have to back track and admit mistakes. These individuals may have toned down their message. There may be signs of marginally more flexibility and less rigidity in their views and prescriptions, but we have seen no U-turn as such, yet.

Challenges to the principle of open markets: what has really changed?

Several authors have pointed to an intellectual sea change towards the principle of capital account liberalization and a growing scepticism among a number of G7 countries towards unrestricted capital flows, most notably Japan and Canada, yet it is worth asking what either country has actually done to pursue the agenda of controlling international capital flows. On this basis the extent of any intellectual sea change on capital liberalization has to be questioned.[114] John Kirton has made the point that the statement from G7 finance ministries and central banks on 30 October 1998 contained carefully crafted language that amounted to a tacit acceptance of the concept of capital controls. But as Kirton concedes the statement only made reference to the need to 'minimize the risk of disruption' and 'an orderly and progressive approach to capital account liberalization'.[115] In other words, capital account liberalization was still an ultimate G7 policy objective. It was just that now it was accompanied by some degree of qualification.

Significantly, no G7 country has used capital controls over the last decade and no G7 country has strongly advocated them without considerable qualification. Even after the financial crises of 1997–8, with the notable exception of Malaysia, emerging markets did not rush to implement wholesale capital controls.[116] The G7 and the IMF have talked about adequate sequencing and regulatory reform prior to capital account liberalization. They have also highlighted the merits of Chilean-style controls on short-term capital in-flows. Some have suggested that this is a major post-Asian U-turn, but those who have followed the debate for longer will appreciate that even officials from the most enthusiastic pro-liberalization country – the US – were accepting this caveat as early as 1996 (see earlier in this chapter).[117] The principal points of difference among the G7 finance ministries and central banks continue to revolve around the circumstances in which Chilean-style controls are justified, but generally it is agreed that this should be judged on a case-by-case basis.[118] In other words, the G7 consensus has not been fundamentally shaken by recent financial crises, although it does leave scope for dispute and differences of interpretation and emphasis.

Kirton also cites discussion of a Canadian proposal for a standstill mechanism,[119] a temporary interruption of payments to creditors, which would give countries time to restart their stalled economies, as evidence of an intellectual shift away from a commitment to capital account liberalization. Proposals were discussed by the G7, and an endorsement of modest collective action clauses followed, but a more ambitious standstill mechanism was rejected (see Chapter 7 and the discussion of the SDRM).

As Chapter 7 will demonstrate, G7 proposals on the global financial architecture were so modest and incremental, it's difficult to even say that the enthusiasm for capital account liberalization has dimmed, because many G7 reform proposals have been designed to facilitate further capital liberalization by preparing the domestic structures of emerging markets for such an eventuality, improving the (official and private sector) international community's ability to respond to crises and improving the advice and flow of information to both policy-makers and markets ahead of liberalization (transparency). In short, capital account liberalization appears to be the ultimate objective and the overriding principle informing recent reform proposals.[120]

Of course, a formal proposal to change the mandate of the IMF to encourage members to liberalize their capital accounts stalled following the Asian financial crisis. The stalling of this proposal was the result of a recognition that some emerging markets had been hasty in liberalizing their capital accounts and that the IMF needed to provide more advice on regulatory and supervisory matters and adequate sequencing for developing countries moving towards capital account liberalization. There was a fear that a formal institutional mandate might lead to hasty liberalization and a backlash against the entire principle of capital account liberalization. However, it should also be noted that officials at the Federal Reserve had expressed reservations at the annual autumn meetings of the IMF in 1997, prior to the emergence of the full affects of the Asian financial crisis, that a formal IMF mandate change might create a formulaic bureaucratic process run by the Fund, resulting in automatic capital account liberalization irrespective of national circumstance.[121] There is no doubt therefore that the G7 have become more circumspect in their support for the principle of capital account liberalization, but they do nevertheless continue to support it in principle and even see it as the ultimate and fundamental objective of their collective efforts. These changes have not constituted wholesale change to the G7 consensus, but a process of adjusting, refining, elaborating and qualifying existing beliefs.[122]

In support of this view, we can cite Joseph Stiglitz's insider view of the Asian crisis, its aftermath and the role of the IMF and G7 governments in handling the crisis. As Stiglitz points out, the IMF reflects the mindsets of those to whom it is accountable,[123] in this case the finance ministries and central banks of the leading industrialized nations, whose views are most commonly articulated collectively through the G7 process, but who also represent their countries at IMF meetings and tend to view matters through the eyes of their own financial sectors. For financiers who have lent money, devices that prevent them from accessing that money, such as capital controls, are a real threat, as is the danger of inflation which reduces the value of repayments on loans, resulting in losses for creditors. It is not surprising therefore that the G7 finance ministries have prioritized sound money and open markets above all other concerns. Following this logic we would expect the IMF to reflect the views of its majority shareholders (collectively, the G7 have around 45 per cent of voting rights). According to Stiglitz, amongst the IMF, the US Treasury and ultimately the G7 finance ministries and central banks, there was a sense that only minor changes were needed in response to Asia, and the IMF and the G7 did everything to shift the blame to others, most notably emerging markets and their lack of transparency. Certainly, this is a view that is supported by the research for this book. Today, even senior IMF officials acknowledge that premature capital account liberalization can be dangerous, and while Stiglitz accepts that this constitutes a change in the official stance of the IMF, his assessment concurs with the one reached in this chapter that it is too soon to see how this adjustment in rhetoric and tone will be reflected in the policies implemented in crisis-hit countries.[124] We should note however, that despite the shelving of the proposal for changing the IMF article of agreement so that it advocated capital account liberalization, the purposes of the IMF as listed under point iv of article 1 of its constitution is to 'assist in the elimination of foreign exchange restrictions which hamper the growth of world trade'. Furthermore, one of the last speeches of the former Managing Director of the IMF reveals that 'promoting further liberalization of capital flows remains an appropriate and important objective' because 'free movement of capital provides developing and emerging market economies with access to technology, investment, and also financial expertise' and 'these are important pre-requisites for economic growth and employment'.[125] Similarly, the IMF's director of research has outlined how he sees the move to greater capital mobility as an 'emerging global norm', and while this message was accompanied by the usual proviso that Chilean-style controls on short-term inflows can be useful in dealing with crises, he also warned that temporary controls can easily become ensconced and should be approached with caution.[126] Such statements would be inconceivable without the support of major shareholders. In the light of this, one is entitled to ask what has really changed in the fundamental beliefs of the IMF and their major shareholders, because they appear remarkably similar to those being advocated prior to the Asian financial crisis.

Certainly, some G7 finance ministers remain more sceptical of financial liberalization than others. Canada's Paul Martin, in particular, initiated some interesting discussions at G7 meetings, but ultimately he felt bound by the collegiate nature of the G7 process and the tradition of seeking consensus. Consequently, no individual has felt it appropriate to openly question or fundamentally challenge the G7 beliefs and principles of sound money and open markets, or even talk directly of abandoning them as the basic normative principles underpinning the international financial system.

It is perhaps unsurprising that the most notable shift in the G7 stance has not resulted from crises in distant emerging markets, but a terrorist strike at the heart of the G7's leading power. After 11 September 2001, the G7's attitude to offshore banking centres shifted markedly. Prior to this, offshore centre's such as the Caymen Islands were rarely criticized directly. Post-September 11, it was recognized that billions of dollars are in such centres because secrecy allows them to engage in tax evasion, money laundering and other nefarious activities including the financing of terrorism. While, prior to September 11 such issues were pursued by the long-standing Financial Action Task Force, they have now moved centre stage onto the G7 agenda and the financing of terrorism is leading to a variety of interventionist measures and monitoring initiatives. What this will mean for key issues such as the tighter regulation of hedge funds remains to be seen.

Ultimately, capital account liberalization, albeit 'cautiously and in an orderly fashion', has remained a key element of the G7 policy agenda.[127] Nowhere in G7 statements is the principle of open capital accounts challenged. Given the repeated financial crises of the last decade, the wisdom of capital account liberalization in principle is a quite fundamental question that the G7 finance ministries and central banks seem reluctant to ask. Capital account liberalization appears to be seen as something incontrovertibly good, something to be maintained and protected, regardless of the difficulties, distress and costs it brings, and where it is restricted or not in evidence it is something to be aspired to. The refusal to ask fundamental questions about capital account liberalization, and the fact that G7 proposals are driven by a desire to cope with a world in which capital account liberalization is an accepted and indeed defining feature of the international financial system, suggest that capital account liberalization is a sacrosanct principle. Other ideas and beliefs have evolved and been adjusted and refined, but at the root of the shared beliefs and ideas sketched earlier in this chapter is the fundamental belief that an open liberalized financial system maximizes efficiency and wealth.

Cologne consensus? Montreal consensus? Plus ça change?

The idea that shared G7 beliefs have undergone a qualitative change is given some credence by increasing references to a new post-Washington consensus, a Cologne consensus and a new Montreal consensus. When these new forms of consensus are scrutinized however, it becomes less clear that they involve a fundamental transformation or reversal of the Washington consensus. There is no doubt that the G7's tone and rhetoric have changed following the Asian financial crisis. Recent G7 statements have referred to global cohesion, strong and sustainable economic growth in developing countries, and meeting the challenge of poverty in developing countries, but the policy implications of this change in tone are less than clear. What has been labelled the Cologne consensus refers to the need to establish links between finance and the environment, reduce ecologically wasteful subsidies, mobilize international financial institutions to promote sustainable development, and account for ecological capital in the ongoing surveillance activities of the IMF and World Bank.[128] Yet it is not clear how such a wish-list will translate into concrete policy proposals, or whether it constitutes anything more than rhetoric or discourse.

Moreover, to refer to a new Cologne consensus replacing the old Washington consensus, after a series of discussions at one summit, rather misses the point of what the label Washington consensus referred to. Washington consensus was a term that reflected the exercise of structural power in international monetary relations as much as it was a reference to a series of shared ideas and beliefs. Those power relationships – the Treasury, IMF, Wall Street axis – have not changed noticeably.[129] The US Treasury, together with other G7 finance ministries and IMF staff, take the lead in IMF work-out programmes, and first and foremost they consider the interests of their own financial sectors and Wall Street when framing their proposals, even if there are more qualifications surrounding the basic message of sound money and open markets, and the IMF has increased the extent to which it engages with civil society.[130] These pivotal social relations and the fundamental principles and beliefs they give rise to remain unchanged. A series of discussions and statements emanating from one summit meeting cannot realistically be compared with these deep underlying structural features of the international monetary system, especially as the Cologne statements appear to have been in part an exercise in rhetoric.

The so-called Montreal consensus was the outcome of one of the first meetings of the new G20. It contained an important acknowledgement that economic growth needed to be accompanied by social developments including solid health care and education, which in turn were acknowledged as areas that needed to be targeted by foreign aid. Unfortunately, G7-supported IMF programmes frequently involved fiscal austerity, which often required cuts in public expenditure, reducing the levels of funding available for crucial public services. It remains unclear how much of the G7's change in tone is rhetoric and how much of it will translate into concrete policy outcomes. Moreover, there was no universal agreement among the G7 on the extent to which markets required guidance and oversight at Montreal. Some G7 members maintained that good things would emerge from freer markets, while others, most notably Canada, maintained that carefully channelled public expenditure and aid could play a role.[131] The Montreal consensus is therefore little more than a loose recognition that tackling poverty and deprivation in the developing world is a priority, but the way forward is uncertain and doubts remain as to whether this meagre but important recognition represents another false dawn. More generally, the debate and consensus on global financial governance issues has shifted in tone, both within the G7 and beyond. It is the degree of that shift and its practical significance that remains to be debated by both policy-makers and commentators. These debates offer the opportunity to revitalize the regulatory role of governments and give greater attention to social issues. Crucially however, as Richard Higgott and Nicola Phillips have pointed out, the post-Washington consensus in its various hues does not reject open markets, rather it represents 'an attempt to institutionally embed and even humanise earlier elements of the WC'.[132] Possibly most notably, the question for the G7 finance ministries and central banks is how to enable poor countries to participate in markets as they are opened.[133] In this light, the G7 appear as determined as ever to pursue the agenda of capital liberalization and are reluctant to question the rationality of open financial markets, or entertain the possibility that they are inherently speculative and unstable.

Conclusion

This chapter has made three main points. First, the G7 finance ministries and central banks have developed a loose consensus based on a belief in the value of and a normative preference for the basic principles of sound money and open markets. These basic shared beliefs inform and provide a frame of reference for the G7 finance ministries and central banks' interactions, set the parameters for their collaboration on financial and monetary issues, and provide the common ground that enables the finance ministries and central banks to operate as a transgovernmental coalition. The consensus on the basic principles of sound money and open markets has been developed, refined and adjusted over the last two to three decades. These basic beliefs have developed a technocratic character as the finance ministries and central banks have sought to justify their normative preferences. In its current form the consensus involves a faith in independent central banks that target national inflation; a growing scepticism of the benefits of pegged exchange rates; a belief in long-term fiscal consolidation; a view that capital account liberalization is beneficial but that it needs to be accompanied by appropriate sequencing and adequate regulatory provision; recognition of the need for financial crisis-prevention mechanisms such as multilateral surveillance and data transparency that facilitate a liberal financial order and further financial liberalization; a growing commitment to private sector involvement in the international community's responses to financial crises; and a basic approach to financial crises that involves debtors taking steps to put the right measures in place, which on the whole involves keeping financial markets open, macroeconomic policies designed to support national currencies and the initiation of negotiations with creditors.

Second, despite this basic broad consensus, several national differences continue to characterize relations between the G7 countries. The United States has traditionally been the state least committed to macroeconomic austerity, at least in relation to its own policies and even those of other developed countries, although this has varied in accordance with the preferences of different administrations. The US and the UK have also been the states least concerned with exchange rate valuations, reflecting the distance between their manufacturing and financial sectors. However, this difference between the Anglo-Saxon countries and the rest of the G7 is lessening as proactive exchange rate management has been collectively eschewed because of a combination of ideational, institutional and material factors. Japan remains the most notable exception to this. The greater emphasis on intervention, management and social aspects in the economies of Japan and Germany have also meant there has been a gap between the Anglo-Saxon countries and the rest of the G7 on financial regulatory and supervisory issues. Both Japan and Germany were, for example, keen to protect SMEs' privileged source of financing in Basle II negotiations, while the US and the UK displayed no such sensitivities. Germany has also been keen to investigate ways of regulating hedge funds, an enthusiasm which has not been shared by the US. In other words, identifying a shared G7 consensus should not be equated with a process of convergence. National distinctiveness can still be identified among the G7 countries and differences of opinion and even conflict can arise at G7 meetings, particularly on financial regulatory questions and the role the financial sector can play in the economy, but these differences exist within certain parameters and a general belief in the virtues of capital liberalization and the prioritization of price stability above other considerations in macroeconomic policy. Moreover, rentier and speculative interests appear to be becoming more prominent in both Germany and Japan.

Third, despite the claims of some observers, the faith in sound money and open markets, which provided the mainstay of the Washington consensus, has not been reversed or overturned. Furthermore, talk of a qualitatively new consensus based on very different policies to those of the Washington consensus is premature.

Any new consensus is heavily derivative of the Washington consensus and continues to be based on the core defining principles of sound money and open markets. Certainly the consensus has been adjusted and refined and its tone has changed, as the triumphalism of the mid-1990s has been dropped and replaced with a more circumspect and qualified version, but sound money and more especially open markets continue to act as the defining principles informing the design of the international financial system. Moreover, further capital account liberalization has become more, not less likely as a consequence of recent reform efforts, as the net result of such efforts is the institutionalization of capital liberalization as a 'global norm'.

The G7 consensus described and discussed in this chapter is the lens through which the G7 finance ministries and central banks view problems and issues in the international financial system. It is the starting point for their discussions and sets the parameters for those discussions. The fundamental principles of sound money and open markets are the root cause of one of the principal asymmetries in global financial governance. These principles, particularly the sacrosanct principle of capital account liberalization, mean that in instances of financial crisis, the onus is on emerging markets to adjust and reform their domestic structures. The integrity of liberalized financial markets is rarely questioned, although it is acknowledged that this liberalization can be hasty, requires adequate sequencing, appropriate regulatory arrangements and sometimes crises require some temporary controls on short-term capital inflows, but only when this is agreed by the IMF and the G7 finance ministries and central banks. Joseph Stiglitz has perceptively referred to the current G7 consensus and its application by the IMF as a mind-set:

> A set of beliefs so strongly held that one hardly needs empirical confirmation. Evidence that contradicts those beliefs is summarily dismissed. For the believers in free and unfettered markets, capital market liberalization was so obviously desirable; one didn't need evidence that it promoted growth. Evidence that it caused instability would be dismissed as one of the adjustment costs, part of the pain that had to be accepted in the transition to a market economy.[134]

Economic science has been used to justify the current consensus, but as Stiglitz points out the difference between science and ideology, or a mind-set, is that science always accepts the limitations of what is known. There is always uncertainty. In contrast, the finance ministries and central banks have been reluctant to discuss uncertainty or admit mistakes. Their statements are reiterated year after year. There may be some rephrasing and some added qualifications, but at the core of these statements are the same basic analytical principles, an assuredness that they are correct and a refusal to question these principles. Even when the finance ministries and central banks have admitted failures in their strategies, particularly after the Asian crisis, there has been a reluctance to discuss those mistakes with outsiders. Staff at the IMF, officials from finance ministries and central banks, together with the finance ministers and central bank governors themselves, have dominated discussions on global financial governance and have seen little point in talking with other groups who do not share or understand their basic beliefs. The next chapter discusses why this was so, as well as the source of the G7 mind-set and some of its implications for the G7's behaviour by applying the framework of four-dimensional diplomacy developed in the previous chapter.

5 The Group of Seven as a multi-spatial transgovernmental actor in world politics

Four-dimensional diplomacy in practice

In Chapter 3, four spatial dimensions relevant to G7 interactions were identified: i) multilateral interactions between the G7 finance ministries and central banks; ii) domestic politics; iii) financial markets as globally networked extra-territorial spaces; iv) the wider sets of institutions concerned with global financial governance and states outside of the G7. This chapter will argue that looking at the G7 in terms of these spatial dimensions enhances our understanding of how and why the G7 finance ministries and central banks collaborate. Moreover, such multi-spatial analysis is essential if we are to appreciate the role and purpose of small group, or K-group, diplomacy in world politics.[1] Obviously, each of the four spatial dimensions is in large part an arbitrary abstract construction designed to enhance and facilitate analysis of the collective activities and the interactions of the G7 finance ministries and central banks, but thinking in terms of these four spatial dimensions provides us with a way of visualizing the series of interactions that constitute the Group of Seven as an ongoing interactive process. It also enhances appreciation of the incentives and rationale for small groups of finance ministries and central banks to act collectively. This chapter looks at the series of interactions, routines, practices and relations that constitute the G7 process in terms of these four spatial dimensions.

The most prominent scholarly voice on the G7/G8 has argued that the G7 represents a centre of global governance.[2] According to John Kirton, a thriving system of working groups, various ministerial fora with the annual leaders' summit at its apex, a range of innovative links with the rest of the world, together with the incorporation of more ministries into the work of the G7, have led to the G7 emerging as an international centre of domestic governance.[3] Furthermore, an expanding G7 agenda and the establishment of a rhythm of follow-up procedures have enabled the G7 to become an ongoing annual system of governance, with the result that commitments are less likely to be forgotten because the institutional machinery below visible meetings reinforces the G7's capacity to act as a reliable system of global governance. Kirton is not alone in pointing to the significance of the G7 coalition of states for global governance. From a more critical perspective than Kirton's optimistic liberal institutionalist view of the G7, Stephen Gill refers to the G7 sitting at the apex of an ongoing and differentiated policy process consisting of neo-liberal elite consensus formation – a G7 nexus,[4] while Robert Cox has referred to a *nébuleuse*, or process of consensus formation that is transmitted into the policy channels of leading governments, particularly finance ministries and central banks, resulting in a discourse that defines policies and circumscribes what can be thought and done.[5]

As the principal mechanism for exchanges between leading finance ministries and central banks, the G7 process is certainly of some significance, although how it does some of the things frequently attributed to it is less clear. What has been absent from the existing literature until now, is a detailed account of the dynamics of the G7's oldest and most active ministerial forum, the politics, beliefs and norms that influence the interactions between finance ministries and central banks, and the G7's relationships with other domestic actors, markets and wider multilateral institutions and bureaucracies. This chapter looks at these issues by looking at the G7 process as a series of interactions between finance ministries and central banks, rather than looking at the G7 as a coherent actor, or coalition of states, in its own right. The centre of global governance interpretation I will suggest is based on an insufficiently disaggregated view of the state and the social forces and institutions that make up each of the G7 states. I will suggest that the G7 finance ministries and central banks display many of the features of a transgovernmental coalition and are often resistant to central co-ordination. Global financial governance more generally is a technically specialist policy area and has a predominantly transgovernmental character, as technocrats have dominated and enjoyed considerable autonomy from politicians and heads of government, while at the same time they have had to try to act on the basis of consensus simply because of the fluid, fungible and interconnected nature of finance and because monetary transactions rely on mutual and reciprocal trust.[6]

The chapter applies the four-dimensional framework developed in Chapter 3 to the G7 process in an effort to illuminate some of the distinctive characteristics of finance ministries–central banks interactions, the inter-relationships the G7 have with a variety of other spatial dimensions, and the resources, power and authority individual states and the G7 process collectively possess. There are four sections to the chapter as each spatial dimension is considered in turn.

The first dimension: multilateral interactions between G7 finance ministries and central banks

In first-dimensional analysis we are concerned with patterns of interaction that characterize relations between G7 finance ministries and central banks at G7 meetings. The task here is to scrutinize the black box of elite interactions and the influences on them. All too often in studies of multilateralism and inter-state relations the nature of these interactions are ignored, or are simply assumed to involve rational unitary actors seeking to maximize their utility in accordance with a pre-defined national interest. These realist and neo-realist assumptions have been challenged often enough by a wide range of IR scholars, but still it is assumed that if states come together, their principal activity will be bargaining and negotiation so as to maximize national preferences. I will argue however that the G7 finance ministries and central banks' interactions are not that simple and that their collaboration is increasingly motivated by a desire to collectively maximize their influence in relation to the wider decision-making complex of global financial governance referred to in Chapter 3.

First however, I engage with the principal conceptualization of the G7 as an actor in world politics that is advanced in the existing literature – John Kirton's concert equality model.

The limitations and drawbacks of the concert equality model

John Kirton, director of the world's only specialist G7 (now G8) research centre, has argued that the Group of Seven represent a modern international concert of powers.[7] A concert of powers has four criteria. It should consist of all the great powers in an interdependent system, contain only great powers as core members, maintain a predominance of capability *vis-à-vis* the remainder of the system, and there should be an effective equality of capability among concert members.[8] Kirton's argument is that the G7 have succeeded in meeting the four requisite concert criteria to a minimum extent.[9] Possibly the most interesting issue in relation to these 'concert criteria' however, and the one that will be focused on here is the issue of measurement. Most notably, what is meant by capability and how do we measure and define equality?[10]

Kirton has alluded to GDP, arguing that the criteria of equality applies to the G7 because the US commands less than half of the capability (in GDP terms) in the group and even Italy could prevent the US from reaching the margin of dominance set at a 50 per cent threshold.[11] More recently, discussing the important role played by Canada and the UK in steering G7 architecture debates in the aftermath of the Asian financial crisis, Kirton has argued that 'the institutional character of the G7, as a concert of effective equals, allowed even the least capable country to play a consequential leadership role'.[12] According to Kirton, any single power is capable of exercising leadership within the G7 at any given time.[13] In this respect, Kirton has used the concert equality model to explain G7 outcomes and argue that the G7 is a flexible, effective governance institution that has shown itself to be capable of dealing successfully with the challenges of financial globalization.

However, this is a very optimistic reading of the G7 process, particularly in the financial and monetary domain. In particular, it is an analysis that fails to identify the constraints and parameters within which the G7 finance ministries and central banks operate, and therefore tends to overestimate the significance of, or misrepresent, what are often ambiguous G7 statements.[14] A closer reading of the interactions of the G7 finance ministries and central banks reveals an inherently conservative process, in which actors are constrained by norms and a prevailing mind-set, as well as underlying market dynamics, the rise of international capital mobility and the structural power of the United States

When attending G7 meetings, finance ministries and central banks operate in the context of existing social practices, routines, norms and shared understandings that impose considerable constraints on the capacity of any one state to exercise leadership and instigate changes in prevailing assumptions and conventions. While it is certainly true that lesser powers can exercise intellectual leadership in the G7, it is for quite different reasons, in different ways and with quite different effects, than Kirton suggests. Most significantly, the concert equality model dangerously underestimates the notable asymmetries of power that characterize international monetary affairs by simply ignoring them, and as a consequence analytical studies using the concert lens tend to distort empirical findings because of the prior assumption of equality. What is required is a more detailed analysis of the procedures, norms and social practices that characterize G7 meetings, combined with an appreciation that G7 interactions take place in the context of the structural power relations that typify the international monetary and financial system.

Crucially, the concert equality model misreads why lesser powers, such as the UK and Canada, can crucially influence G7 debates in the field of financial governance. This issue of why lesser powers can exercise leadership within the G7 on financial issues would not be so important if it were simply an issue of causation. However, a failure to acknowledge why lesser powers can exercise leadership within the finance ministries and central bankers' process has also led to an exaggeration of the extent to which countries such as the UK and Canada can exert influence, and this in turn results in a distorted view of global financial governance more generally. At the root of this shortcoming is definitional imprecision and the failure of the concert equality model to distinguish between the concepts of structural power and technical authority in international financial relations, condensing both under the vague and conceptually ambiguous heading 'capability'. At the same time, the concert equality model also pays too little attention to the micro-politics that are specific to the interactions of the G7 finance ministries and central banks, viewing the Group of Seven as a coherent coalition of states, rather than as a series of sectoral transgovernmental networks, that may on occasion have conflicting priorities and objectives.

As Chapter 3 established, authority can be conceived as something emanating from expertise or technical capability. The meetings of G7 finance ministers and central bank governors bring together individuals of considerable expertise and technical capability. As we will see, this gives G7 meetings a deliberative character, as participants involve themselves in a process of discussion and argumentation. Often, it is the personal reputation and expertise of incumbent officials, governors and ministers, rather than the country they represent, which is key in determining the course of G7 debates and deliberations. The valuing of expertise and a mode of interaction based on argumentation certainly means that lesser states such as the UK and Canada can steer G7 debates in a critical fashion, because the individuals who advance the most persuasive and authoritative case are often able to exert the most decisive influence on any resulting G7 consensus. In other words, it is the expertise, knowledge, ideas and personal reputation of individuals that enable states such as Canada, Italy or the UK to critically influence the course of G7 discussions, rather than just the capabilities these states have more generally, or any inherent qualities the G7 as a group of states possess.

Yet, despite the fact that exchanges between the G7 finance ministries and central banks have a deliberative quality and are based on a mutual recognition of expertise and a willingness amongst participants to view one another as equals,[15] international monetary affairs continue to be characterized by some notable asymmetries of power. The UK and Canada, for example, can influence G7 debates providing they operate within the parameters of the sound money and open markets consensus referred to in the previous chapter and the shared understandings that flow from this. As recent experiences demonstrate they are able to refine and adjust the existing consensus, but a fundamental revision of the consensus is something that is not open for debate. The sound money and open market consensus is embedded in a key societal axis between the G7 finance ministries and central banks and their financial sectors, and most crucially between Wall Street and the US Treasury.[16] In Chapter 3 it was established that the US's position as the world's most significant financial market, the role of the dollar as a reserve currency, the position of the US as the leading share holder in the IMF, and the Treasury Department's close relationship and well-cultivated linkages with Wall Street as the world's leading financial centre whose health is essential for global prosperity, give the United States government powers to delay and to deflect in relation to their own macro-economic policies.[17] In terms of G7 deliberations, while it is true that other G7 powers can restrain and curb the US Treasury, the above resources also amount to an effective veto for the United States in international monetary and financial affairs. Quite simply, nothing happens in global financial governance unless the US government agrees. This power of veto is not shared by any other G7 power. It is the failure to recognize this fundamental and pivotal asymmetry at the heart of international monetary affairs that has resulted in the concert equality model misreading the G7's response to the Asian financial crisis and subsequently overestimating the extent of the ideational or policy shift among the G7 finance ministries and central banks.[18]

The relative sense of equality that surrounds exchanges at G7 meetings means that the finance ministries and central banks' deliberations are far from irrelevant in adjusting and refining consensus among the industrialized powers on global financial issues. Those exchanges do influence global financial and monetary outcomes and the international consensus in quite meaningful ways. In this respect, the politics of G7 interactions represent more than the US simply trying to get the other main capitalist powers do what the US wants,[19] and while US policy-makers enjoy a number of advantages and privileges in international monetary politics, in other ways they face some very real constraints. Both the concert equality model and strong versions of the American hegemony thesis represent caricatures of international monetary and financial affairs that are not strictly representative of reality. The former overestimates the significance and influence of G7 exchanges, or at least the equality that exists among G7 powers and fails to acknowledge that underlying features of the international monetary system mean that G7 interactions do not take place on a level playing field. Meanwhile, the view that the US is all powerful and that G7 outcomes simply reflect and are an expression of US power, underestimates the constraints the US face and the ability of the rest of the G7 to restrain, or at least modify US positions. Ultimately, G7 outcomes need to be looked at on a case-by-case basis without prior assumptions, but with a full understanding of the norms and social practices that characterize G7 meetings, as well as the structural power relations underpinning the global financial order. The rest of this chapter examines the dynamic relationships between G7 norms and US structural power, between notions of equality based on technical expertise and the underlying inequalities of power, or capability, that define acceptable G7 norms and ideas in the first place.

The last chapter outlined the basic consensual beliefs and fundamental principles shared by the G7 finance ministries and central banks. The discussion that follows will look at how this 'mind-set' sets the parameters for and influences procedures, routines and social practices at G7 meetings, creating a series of norms that structure G7 interactions

Technical expertise and processes of arguing and deliberating

One of the key characteristics of the G7 process is the degree of shared technical expertise amongst finance ministries and central banks. Officials tend to advance their position and make key points at G7 meetings in technical terms. It is commonly accepted and understood that the language of debate at G7 meetings is as much the language of economics and finance as it is of politics. Political points are occasionally made but this is usually done within the terms of economic language.[20] In this respect, a lot of G7 discussion follows what Thomas Risse has called the 'logic of arguing', as the aim of discussion is often not to achieve the pre-ordained fixed preferences of each individual G7 state, but to seek a reasoned consensus that sits comfortably with the technical ideas and causal beliefs the various protagonists hold about monetary and financial governance, while avoiding any serious breach of key domestic or national interests. The logic of arguing therefore acknowledges the possibility that ideas and interests can change in the course of discussions, with participants modifying their position as they learn and listen to others, although as the last chapter demonstrated the room for manoeuvre and the scope for change can be informed by some fundamental defining principles, setting limits to the extent of any movement to be expected by participants around the table (in the case of the G7 – sound money and open markets).

Bargaining power, while not departing the scene entirely, becomes less relevant in this context, as the G7 finance ministries and central banks largely engage in a process of deliberation and argumentation. At the very least, it is the individual authoritative expertise of G7 participants that determines national delegations' bargaining power, albeit within the terms of a pre-existing consensus. Arguing and persuasion presupposes some basic level of equality of knowledge and technical capability among participating individuals, even if over time the reputation and authority of individuals varies in accordance with the extent to which they are able to forward convincing interpretations and diagnoses of events. Kirton appears to mistake this socially constructed mode of arguing, including a respect for and a valuing of expertise and intellect amongst the finance ministries and central banks, with a more general and less transient equality of capability amongst the G7 powers, when he refers to the examples of Canada and the UK exercising intellectual leadership in the G7 on the post-Asian debate on the global financial architecture, and how they demonstrate that the G7 operate a form of concert governance.[21] The accepted mode of interaction among finance ministries and central banks means that all G7 finance ministries and central banks can influence G7 debates in decisive ways, providing they operate within certain parameters and suggest modest, rather than wholesale changes to the status quo. Generally, capability, in terms of some measure of economic significance, has been a less important consideration in influencing the detail and tone of debates among G7 finance ministries and central banks, although it is admittedly crucial in defining the parameters within which debates take place and what remains out of bounds at G7 meetings. For example, an individual Canadian minister might believe in the implementation of some comprehensive form of capital controls, but would be unlikely to be able to push that agenda at G7 meetings. First, officials who had worked in international financial networks for some time would in all likelihood be intellectually sceptical of such proposals. Second, the same officials would appreciate that strong US opposition, as a consequence of the advantages the US gains from a liberalized international financial order (see Chapter 4), would ensure that there would be very little chance of such controls being received favourably in the G7 setting, and even less chance of them working without US support. In other words, strong US preferences define the parameters of G7 discussions, but within those broad parameters there is a great deal of significant detail to be argued over. Clearly, however, in this context it is an overstatement to refer to the G7 as a concert of equal powers.

Where the process of arguing is concerned, Risse has pointed out that it requires that the actors involved need to recognize each other as equals and have equal access to a discourse.[22] As we have already seen, at the meetings of G7 finance ministries and central banks equality is not absolute. However, some degree of equality does come from a shared sense of professionalism and expertise, which in turn means that the deep underlying asymmetries of power that characterize international monetary relations are not always immediately evident around the table at G7 meetings, in what is generally a collegiate and discursive environment. Finance ministries and central bank governors' interactions are therefore not really characterized by the same clear-cut notion of national interest and power politics as other diplomatic settings. Finance ministries and central banks willingly acknowledge that even in wider settings such as the G20, they are dealing with 'very competent people who have lots of expertise'.[23] This mutual respect and recognition of expertise applies in equal measure to the G7 finance ministers and central bank governors' own meetings. Insights into this have come from the Governor of the Bank of Canada, David Dodge. 'We talk to each other on very much equal terms, because a lot of our backgrounds are similar and certainly we understand the issues in a similar way.'[24] As Paul Martin, the Canadian Minister of Finance, has explained to members of the

University of Toronto's own G8 Research Group as part of an aural history project:

> Really very little negotiating takes place at these meetings. What really happens at G7, G20 or IMF meetings is that essentially ministers come together. There will be a lot of corridor discussion. Consensus will begin to develop on a certain set of issues. Officials may be pushing for a certain set of issues, or individual ministers may have very strong views. Then they have their committee meeting. They will basically establish the agenda and the officials will then go away, and in the interim months work on that agenda and come back and report. At the reporting stage, it would either be this is the progress we've made, or this is the progress we haven't made. So it's an ongoing process all the time. But the detailed work is done by officials in between meetings.[25]

In the same interview, Martin goes on to explain how the real strength of the G7 is that 'it is small enough that participants are able to argue back and forth across the table, with the great advantage that there is a genuine interchange of views rather than a reading of set piece statements, which can arise in larger IMF meetings'. The real significance of this is that there is a genuine potential for exchange, argument and some degree of learning on the basis of the emergence of convincing technical arguments.

The technical nature of debates at G7 meetings will of course vary, depending on which individuals occupy key positions. For example, during the 1990s, the presence at G7 meetings of Lawrence Summers, a former award-winning Harvard economist, was reported to have meant that G7 officials' discussions increasingly focused on substance rather than politics.[26] Similarly, the leading British Treasury official, Nigel Wicks, was accorded great respect and older statesman-like status because he had been taking the lead in the UK's G7 preparations since 1988 and had extensive experience in international financial affairs more generally.[27]

At ministerial meetings, the presence of elected politicians (the finance ministers) means that discussions can be more political in nature, but finance ministers tend to be comfortable working within the parameters of a technocratic discourse and regular exposure to a round of international meetings and the complex financial issues they entail, socializes them into the norms of the prevailing technical discourse and mind-set fairly quickly.[28] Indeed, many finance ministers are chosen precisely because of their financial expertise and therefore their credibility (often translating as links to, or previous position) with financial markets. Notably, the attendance of the Central Bank governors at G7 meetings also tempers the political nature of G7 discussions and ensures the technocratic character of discussions is retained.

Surveillance, routines and shared social practices

G7 ministerial meetings involve a specific routine. They typically begin with a multilateral surveillance exercise. Multilateral surveillance consists of a series of frank and candid exchanges, whereby national authorities expose their policies to collective scrutiny and comments.[29] The world economic outlook is assessed and comment is passed on individual national G7 policies and economic conditions. Commonly agreed objectives, discussed in the last chapter, such as the importance of reducing inflation, a medium-term strategy for fiscal consolidation so as to increase national savings, reduce external imbalances and improve the outlook for exchange rate stability, have informed the discussions and exchanges over the last two decades.[30] Surveillance revolves around a one-page annotated agenda, together with a page on each country that is prepared by the IMF, and presented by the IMF director of research at officials' preparatory meetings and by the Managing Director of the IMF at ministerial meetings.[31] Economic indicators discussed have included growth, inflation, unemployment, budget deficits, trade balances, monetary conditions and exchange rates.[32] More recently, ways of quantifying the performance of national financial sectors and bank lending have been discussed, as surveillance has been extended from the public sector to the private sector.

Surveillance is essentially a form of peer review. According to officials, discussions proceed on the basis of conversations such as, 'if you do X, do you realize the effect this will have on us?'[33] Such exchanges of information are aimed at enhancing awareness of international interdependence and of the wider impact of national policies, so as to produce more informed and better national policy.[34] From 1997 onwards, the IMF's head of research started to provide a more regular assessment of the economic outlook to the senior officials charged with preparing for G7 ministerial meetings (the deputies), with this assessment paying more attention to medium-term structural reform of labour and financial markets, as well as to potential risks outside of the G7 that could result in international financial turmoil.[35]

Surveillance itself is a form of voluntary interaction which carries with it expectations concerning acceptable, or appropriate behaviour – an effective set of unwritten rules based on informal, non-binding exchanges of information and opinion.[36] Significantly, concerns over sovereignty and in particular central bank independence, tend to prevent authorities from making demands of other authorities' macroeconomic policies at G7 meetings during the course of the surveillance exercise. That states do not bargain over, or make specific demands of, their counterparts' macroeconomic policies has come to resemble what March and Olsen have termed a 'logic of appropriateness', whereby actors invoke a specific identity and match it to the particular social context they find themselves in, out of a sense of obligation and indeed 'appropriateness'.[37]

Causal beliefs concerning the limited gains from co-ordinating macroeconomic policies or targeting exchange rates, domestic institutional arrangements in the form of independent central banks and fiscal rules that place constraints on participants at G7 meetings, together with the extent, speed and scope of foreign exchange trading, have all combined to produce the accepted G7 norm that the finance ministries and central banks do not bargain with one another over their macroeconomic policies. In other words, it is the interaction of variables in the first three dimensions identified in Chapter 3 that produce the shared social practices and understandings that characterize routine surveillance, distinct from co-ordination, or bargaining. There is no single causal variable at work. To explain this further, through repeated interactions and discussions, G7 officials have developed a shared scepticism of the benefits of co-ordinating monetary and fiscal policies, or of joint exchange market interventions, which in turn is reinforced by a shared first-dimensional understanding or norm that finance ministries and more especially central banks do not make specific demands of one another's macroeconomic policies, although they might make recommendations concerning the overall orientation of policy in a particular country. Second, the rejection of co-ordination receives domestic institutional reinforcement in the form of independent central banks with national price stability mandates and fiscal rules. These domestic institutional arrangements restrict G7 participants' capacity to make pledges or give commitments to their counterparts, while the credibility of central bank independence would be threatened if these institutions were seen to respond to external pressure. Third, experiences of exchange rate turbulence and perceptions of the extent of international capital mobility have led to the downgrading of exchange market interventions as a policy instrument, a shared recognition of the need to send clear signals to the markets concerning domestic policy intentions and objectives, and a common acknowledgement of the futility of attempting to actively exercise some political management of financial markets, particularly the foreign exchange market.

To further illustrate the point that shared beliefs set the parameters for interactions between G7 finance ministries and central banks, consider the loose agreement amongst the G7 finance ministries and central banks that in the long term macroeconomic policy should prioritize low inflation. This belief was increasingly evident during the 1990s, in central banks with inflation or price stability targets and fiscal rules designed to deliver budgets that are either balanced or close to balance. The prioritization of low inflation, both in terms of beliefs and domestic institutional arrangements, puts the kind of international Keynesian style reflationary macroeconomic co-ordination practised at the Bonn summit of 1978, off the G7 agenda. Since the 1980s, the principal matter for debate and argument in the course of the multilateral surveillance exercise, has been how to most effectively achieve low inflation as a means to sustainable growth. More recently, in the aftermath of the Asian financial crisis and following slow US growth, there has been a growing interest in the contribution that macroeconomic policy can make to economic growth. However, beyond some isolated first-order policy changes including interest rate cuts and limited attempts at fiscal stimulus, this has not progressed into the kind of second-order institutional reforms that would surely be required if we were to talk about any far-reaching third-order (those overarching assumptions, priorities and objectives informing policy-making) paradigm shift.[38]

More generally, surveillance can be seen to have contributed to macroeconomic discipline in three principal ways. First, it has facilitated a system of peer review of national policies that can lead to peer pressure and criticism if a country is deemed to be following an inflationary policy course, although this has been less apparent in recent times due to slower levels of growth. In the 1990s at least, this system of peer review created powerful social disincentives for the pursuit of macroeconomic expansion, as G7 countries, with the exception of Japan, focused their policies on reducing inflation with some success. Not withstanding their technical or intellectual commitment to low inflation, finance ministers and central bankers are keen to avoid the embarrassment of unanimous condemnation from peers. Any G7 country departing from the course of macroeconomic discipline would have expected to experience peer pressure from their G7 counterparts.[39] The G7 have consequently had the character of an 'anti-inflationary' club over the last two decades.[40] Initial evidence suggests that this anti-inflationary character will be less pronounced in future years, although whether this is a temporary or more permanent development remains to be seen.

Second, surveillance and the associated data release enhances market scrutiny of national policies, disciplining national macroeconomic policy in accordance with market preferences of low inflation and balanced budgets, as countries face the risk of capital flight and exchange rate depreciation if markets take the view that macroeconomic policies are unsustainable.[41] Reports of criticism from G7 partners or from the IMF in the context of the surveillance exercise, are also likely to trigger market suspicions.

Third, the process of surveillance leads to deliberations and the sharing of experiences, on the best route to low inflation and best domestic institutional practice. These discussions as a corollary to the G7 surveillance exercise have undoubtedly contributed to the refinement and consolidation of the current consensus. The G7 have for example promoted the principle of central bank independence and today all G7 central banks, with the exception of the Bank of Canada, enjoy at least operational independence in the setting of interest rates. This was not the case in the 1980s. The widespread acceptance of central bank independence has been a distinctly 1990s phenomenon, not just in Europe, but also in Japan.[42] Obviously in the case of Europe, European Monetary Union and ECOFIN discussions played the prominent role in the conversion to central bank independence, but it is difficult to distinguish the role of the G7 process from that of other multilateral exchanges in this learning process and general shift among finance ministries and central banks, due to the overlapping nature of their networks and multiple memberships.[43] In other words, the process of multilateral consensus and agenda formation in financial and monetary affairs, consists of various strands and exchanges flowing into and contributing to a diffuse ongoing rolling process, with officials likening this to the various complex tributaries of the Amazon.[44] The G7 process may not have been the source of the current consensus, but as the principal mechanism through which the world's leading finance ministries and central banks exchange views and communicate, it has undoubtedly contributed to the formation and the subsequent refinement and adjustment of that consensus.

The domestic institutional products of the current consensus, such as independent central banks and fiscal rules, further institutionalize the anti-inflationary consensus. In particular they make it difficult for the G7 finance ministries and central banks to come together and talk about exchange rate targeting, target zone schemes, or co-ordinated growth initiatives. Aside from the intellectual scepticism such policies are regarded with, these policies conflict with current central bank mandates to meet a particular national inflation or price stability target. The shared priority of targeting inflation therefore not only sets the parameters for G7 discussions, but the nature of those discussions subsequently provide endorsement and reinforcement for the delivery of that objective.

The timing and annual rhythm of G7 meetings

The timing or annual rhythm of meetings is a key consideration for the routines and characteristics of any multilateral process. In the case of the G7 there are four scheduled ministerial meetings throughout the year. The first is early in the new year, the second is before the IMF interim and World Bank Development Committee meetings in the spring, the third is before the leaders' summit in the summer where a report is prepared for the leaders and the final meeting is before the annual IMF/World Bank meeting in the autumn. The first ministerial meeting acts as a benchmarking session in the surveillance exercise. At the spring and autumn meetings, actual performance is compared with what was projected at the benchmarking session. The last G7 ministerial meeting in the autumn is possibly the most significant G7 meeting. Not simply because it provides an overall assessment of the G7 countries' economic performance throughout the year in the context of the surveillance exercise, but also because decisions relating to the IMF and its future mandate and lending policies are officially reached by ministers at the IMF's annual meeting. Therefore, because the G7 process has a particular annual rhythm and because those meetings coincide with other multilateral meetings with wider memberships, the G7 can effectively act as a caucus group that formulates an internal consensus in an informal manner before promoting that consensus in more formal settings.

Informality and the deputies' network: statement drafting and questions of procedure

One of G7's most prominent and enduring characteristics has been its informality. As we have already seen, informality allows for meaningful, substantive and candid deliberations that can facilitate a process of mutual learning. Discussions at G7 meetings proceed on a face-to-face basis without the bureaucracy and proceduralism that hinders bigger more unwieldy settings such as ECOFIN or IMF ministerial meetings. In the case of the G7 process, the absence of a secretariat means that the process largely functions through 'the deputies' network'.

The deputies are the most senior officials from the international divisions of finance ministries, and the deputy governors of central banks.[45] These deputies meet between six and ten times a year to discuss and to prepare for tri-annual G7 ministerial meetings and have regular conference calls and email contact. As the quotation from Paul Martin on page 107 illustrates, the deputies carry out most of the work in the G7 process and their contributions are pivotal to the process of consensus formation.

During the 1990s, it was evident that a remarkable number of deputies involved in G7 preparations had previously occupied the position of national IMF Executive

Director at an earlier point in their career, or had held a senior staff position at either the Fund, the World Bank, the BIS, or the OECD and were therefore familiar with financial and monetary technocratic discourses (see Table 5.1). Those officials with no prior experience at an international institution dealing with financial issues, were usually either influential academic economists or private sector financial analysts. The table illustrates that five of the deputies were PhD economists in 1996, while several more had post-graduate economics qualifications, creating a group of technically capable individuals. Regardless, the crucial characteristics shared by all leading G7 deputies has been a preference for and a familiarity with the fundamental assumptions of neo-classical economics, irrespective of whether this was due to a process of career socialization through gradual exposure to the dominant currents of thought in institutions such as the IMF and the World Bank, and the neo-classical bias of finance ministries and central banks more generally, or through success in the economics profession with its growing neo-classical bias.[46] A basic consensus on the fundamental principles of sound money and open markets has followed.

In terms of domestic administrative hierarchies it is usual for the deputies to be more senior than those officials who are charged with the task of preparing leaders' briefings for the G8 summit, the so-called summit sherpas, who tend to be mid-ranking officials. Again this insulates and protects the G7 process from central direction. The deputies' more frequent contact with one another also ensures they tend to be a more tightly knit group than the sherpas. Figure 5.1 illustrates the relationship between the summit and the finance minister's and central bank governor's process. The problem with narrow close-knit policy networks with restricted agendas, debates and personnel such as the deputies' network, is that they run the risk of capture. Concerns over legitimacy have inevitably followed and allegations have been made that the IMF and the world's leading finance ministries and central banks have operated almost exclusively in the interests of

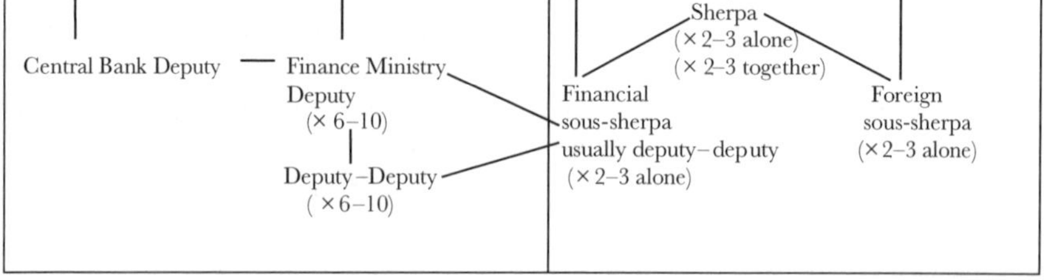

Figure 5.1 Linkages between the actors in the G7 Finance Minister's and Central Bank Governor's process and the Annual Summits

Table 5.1 Career details of Finance Ministry and Central Bank deputies in 1996

Country	*Finance ministry deputy*	*Central bank deputy*
Canada	Ian E. Bennett MA Economics University of Toronto, assistant secretary Treasury Board 1984–83, 1985–86 general director economic development policy, 1989–93 senior deputy minister tax policy, 1993–4 privy council deputy secretary to the cabinet, 1994–6 associate deputy minister revenue Canada, 1996–8 associate deputy minister finance special responsibility financial sector policy.	Paul Jenkins MSc Economics University of Western Ontario 1972, 1981–2 researcher in economics Princeton University, research department Bank of Canada 1983, deputy chief monetary and financial analysis 1983, chief of research department Bank of Canada 1984, advisor to Governor of Bank of Canada, Deputy Governor 1992.
France	Jean Lemierre 1976 Inspection générale de finance, 1987 head of tax policy, 1989 head of French inland revenue service, 1995 head of private office of minister of economy and finance, member of European monetary committee 1999–2000, Chairman of Paris club 1999–2000, Director EBRD 2000–present.	Hervé Hannoun Institute Etudes Politiques Paris, general inspector of finance 1975, technical adviser to prime minister's office 1981–4, technical adviser to the President of the Republic 1984, Deputy Director Ministry of Economy, Finance and Budget 1985, 1988 Charge d'mission President of the Republic, 1989 director of private office Minister for Economic Affairs, Finance and Development, 1992 Director of private office of Prime Minister, 1993 Second Deputy Governor Bank of France, 1994 member of monetary council Bank of France, member of board directors of BIS, chair of International Relations Committee of the European System of Central Banks, 1998.
Germany	Jürgen Stark PhD Economics University of Tübingen 1975, 1978 official economic policy department federal ministry of economics, 1988–92 head of foreign currency and financial markets unit Chancellor's office, 1992 Federal Ministry of Finance head of international monetary and financial relations section, State Secretary Ministry of Finance, became vice president of Deutsche Bundesbank 1998.	Helmut Schieber PhD Economics University of Freiburg, personal advisor to state central bank Baden-Württemberg 1984, vice president LZB in Baden-Württemberg 1985, Bundesbank board member 1992–2000 responsible for international relations, financial markets, credit and finance.

continued…

Table 5.1 continued

Country	*Finance ministry deputy*	*Central bank deputy*
Italy	Augusto Zodda PhD Economics, Director General Ministry of Treasury.	Padoa Schioppa 1968 joined Bank of Italy economics research department, 1973 head of money market development, economic adviser to the Italian Treasury 1978–9, 1979–83 Economic and Financial Affairs DG European Commission, 1983 Head of Research Bank of Italy, 1993 Deputy governor Bank of Italy and chair of BIS committee on Banking Supervision.
Japan	Takatoshi Kato BA University of Tokyo, MBA Princeton University, 1969–90 staff economist economic department OECD Paris, Executive Director for Japan at the Asian Development Bank Manila, 1990 Ministry of Finance International Affairs, vice minister International Finance Ministry of Finance.	Aikra Nagashima Director at the Bank of Japan 1989–90, Director of International Department 1990–3, Deputy Governor and executive director International Relations 1994–9.
UK	Nigel Wicks HM Treasury 1968–75, Private Secretary to Prime Minister 1975–8, HM Treasury financial markets 1978–83, UK Executive Director IMF and World Bank 1983–5, principal private secretary to the Prime Minister 1985–8, Second Permanent Secretary International Finance HM Treasury 1989–2000, Chair of EU monetary committee 1995–8.	Mervyn King 1972–7 Fellow St John's College Cambridge, 1977–84 Fairburn professor of investment University of Birmingham, 1984–95 professor of economics LSE, Co-director LSE financial markets group 1987–91, member City capital markets commission 1989–91, chief economist Bank of England 1991–8, Deputy Governor Bank of England, 1998. Currently Governor of Bank of England.
USA	Lawrence H. Summers PhD Economics Harvard, assistant economics professor MIT, 1983 economics professor Harvard, 1991 chief economist World Bank, 1993 Under Secretary International Affairs Treasury Department, 1995 Deputy Treasury Secretary (went on to become Secretary of Treasury 1999).	Edward Kelley MBA from Harvard, President and CEO of Kelley Industries Inc. in Houston 1959–81. Founding director of three Houston-area banks. Chairman of the Board of Investment Advisors Inc., Houston from 1981. Joined the Fed 1987. Member of the Board of Governors of the Federal Reserve System 1990–2004. Board's representative to the National Advisory Council, an inter-agency council providing advice on international financial matters to the Treasury.

the financial sector, due to a revolving-door policy between the private financial sector and these institutions, rather than in any wider public interest.[47] Consequently, a certain mind-set can come to reign relatively unopposed on grounds of technical supremacy, even if such a mind-set is far from uncontested, is inherently political and is even questionable in terms of its policy record. However, as the discussion above has illustrated such mind-sets are often self-perpetuating and routinized in the form of a series of micro social practices and shared understandings, which have the effect of curtailing and restricting debate and limiting the scope of potential policy outcomes.

The deputies are aided in G7 preparations by their deputy-deputies, officials usually one or two positions below the deputy in domestic administrative hierarchies. The deputy-deputies meet even more regularly than the deputies to compile detailed reports and recommendations. Many of the deputies also encounter one another in settings such as EU Economic and Financial Committee meetings, the G10 and the OECD's WP-3. As at ministerial meetings, there are no formally recorded minutes or transcripts of the deputies' meetings. Most work at G7 meetings is done not on paper, but in people's heads.[48] The deputies' regularity of contact also means that they tend to be on first name terms and know one another well, which enhances their capacity to arrive at consensus, or at the very least minimizes mistrust, tension and conflict.[49] The knowledge that they will enter into further interaction with their counterparts ensures that the deputies are reluctant to antagonize one another.

Deputies' meetings are often surrounded by secrecy, with only the deputies themselves attending.[50] Often even their closest colleagues only have a broad sense of what they discuss.[51] Confidentiality of this sort, together with the small numbers involved, encourages frank exchange and enables the deputies to test positions and policies, resulting in interactive debates, albeit within certain normative parameters. The result of these interactions is a sense of close collegiality amongst the deputies. The deputies and their deputies, the deputy-deputies, often dominate substantive G7 discussions. This means that preparations for G7 meetings tend to be conducted with only the occasional high-level steer from finance ministers (the only elected politicians who actually attend G7 meetings).[52] Finance ministers tend to have only one or two issues they will wish to push strongly.[53] In this respect, the G7 process is informal, collegial, secretive and exclusive and is predominantly characterized by exchanges of information and opinion.

Most of the preparatory work for G7 deputies' meetings flows through a G7 co-ordinator, who is usually a relatively junior finance ministry official and constructs G7 briefing packs, working for the deputy and the deputy's deputy. When assuming their post G7 co-ordinators frequently express surprise at the extent of the informality that characterizes the G7 process. Several co-ordinators referred to faxed agendas received from the host country ahead of a forthcoming G7 meeting that consisted of little more than a series of bullet-point headings.[54] The significance of each heading is something that is only learnt over time by junior officials, yet on the basis of previous discussions and experience, the deputies immediately understand the significance of each heading. Newcomers to the process are invariably struck by the intense networking that takes place in the margins of the main ministerial meetings.[55] In effect, the familiarity and close relations between officials brought about by the momentum of regular contact, enables them to discuss matters more informally and steer ministers in the direction of consensual outcomes. In other words, the G7 process has a specific culture and series of procedural and behavioural practices surrounding it that facilitates consensus formation and enables a small group of key senior officials to play a dominant agenda-setting role.

Chairing meetings and drafting statements

Responsibility for the chairing of meetings and drafting of statements is a procedure that is key in affecting the way in which consensus is formulated, interpreted and communicated. The country hosting the ministerial meeting undertakes both of these tasks. This means that the United States has a disproportionate ability to influence G7 agendas because it holds the highest number of ministerial meetings. Two of the three yearly G7 meetings precede the spring and annual meetings of the IMF/World Bank. Both institutions have their headquarters in Washington DC and hold most, although not all, of their meetings in the US capital.[56] Nearly two-thirds of all G7 meetings are therefore held either at, or within walking distance of, the Treasury Department or Federal Reserve buildings in Washington DC. This in part explains the use of the term 'Washington consensus' to describe the macroeconomic and financial orthodoxy that characterized the 1990s. The geographical location of both the IMF and G7 meetings also enables US financial firms to have most immediate access to policy-makers at G7 meetings, mainly on logistical grounds. On the fringes of the various meetings that take place in Washington, financial firms, most of them from the US, host lavish receptions in an effort to make their views and values known to finance ministers and central bankers. In other words, even G7 procedures give the US an enlarged capacity relative to other G7 states and that's even without considering factors such as the reserve role of the dollar and the US weighted vote at the IMF. The nature of the G7 as a process therefore enables the US to have an enormous influence over any prevailing economic discourse. Therefore, although Kirton's argument about the G7 representing a concert of international powers has some elements of truth, given the way the finance ministries and central banks conduct their business, it is also an argument that obscures many of the advantages and privileges the US enjoys and as such overstates the notion of equality amongst the G7 finance ministries and central banks.[57]

Crucial to the influence and impact that any multilateral process has, is the means by which outcomes and decisions are recorded and communicated. Statements or communiqués, which record what has been agreed, are released at the end of G7 meetings. The wording of these documents is precise, yet their meaning can appear ambiguous. They are in effect a form of code, and tend to emphasize areas of agreement and shared broad principles, illustrating that the G7 process is on the whole concerned with consensus formation, rather than the negotiation of precise agreements.[58] Statements and communiqués are often used as means of giving the G7 process continuity. They frequently refer to previous statements and replicate whole passages of text. In this respect, once something is in a G7 statement it becomes public property and can be referred to verbatim, because it is effectively a statement of common intent.[59] Moreover, this can be referred to in further discussions. Earlier statements can be referred to as a way of highlighting what was previously agreed and how this should provide the basis for future discussions.[60] Consequently, there is often an evolutionary and incremental dynamic evident in processes of multilateral consensus formation, while continuity and conservatism is an inherent characteristic of the G7 process.

The strategic direction for the drafting of G7 statements tends to come from the deputies. Communiqué drafters often scrutinize every word, full stop and comma in G7 statements. They frequently stay up to the early hours ahead of ministerial meetings to finalize drafts.[61] The content of the text of a statement is negotiated by telephone and at a meeting of the deputies held shortly before the ministerial meeting. Controversial issues are isolated for special attention from the finance ministers and central bank governors.

A crucial issue faced by the deputies is the extent to which communiqués should reflect the substance of actual G7 discussions. In theory, policy-makers face a difficult choice between producing open, public and transparent statements that are a genuine reflection of what has been discussed or highly cryptic statements that obscure differences. Where the intention is to arrive at detailed decisions, which G7 countries will be committed to, there is an obvious temptation to produce open transparent statements, because this reduces the potential for defection, or the so-called 'prisoner's dilemma'. However, consensus formation, system maintenance and crisis management have been a recurring focus for the G7 process. In this respect, G7 statements are used as an important tool of communication, with markets, with non-G7 governments, with multilateral institutions, transnational policy communities and with domestic publics, as well as with other sections of the state apparatus. We have to acknowledge therefore that alliances between bureaucracies and agencies from different states, in order for those agencies to maximize their influence through collective positions, what Keohane and Nye called transgovernmental coalitions, can form so as to influence developments in locations other than just the domestic setting.[62] The effectiveness of collective communications and statements is highly dependent on how the press report and interpret the statement released. Statements are therefore intended to be a form of press guidance and this is particularly the case when policy-makers are trying to influence markets.[63]

Some research on the G7 process has argued that it is possible to examine G7 statements in terms of domestic compliance with the commitments contained in those statements.[64] The problem with this approach is that G7 statements contain few clearly identifiable commitments. There is rarely evidence of a recorded agreement that participating parties are supposed to comply with. In this regard, the G7 process has proved effective at raising consciousness, setting agendas creating networks and 'lighting fires under civil servants and bureaucrats'.[65] On the basis of this limited decision-making role, research into the G7 process should place rather less emphasis on issues of 'compliance'. Rather more attention should be paid to the linkages and relationships between different networks of officials from the G7 countries, from multilateral institutions, specialist regulatory bodies, the private sector and with authorities from various emerging market economies. Ultimately, it is these networks that facilitate the formulation and institutionalization of the consensual 'mind-sets' or 'belief systems' that are increasingly shaping and setting the parameters for multilateral diplomacy on monetary and financial issues.

Applying second-dimensional analysis to the G7: domestic institutions and interests

Domestic institutional mandates and decision-making procedures

Finance ministries with fiscal rules and independent central banks with national price stability targets are currently the most prominent domestic institutional features of the G7 process. Fiscal rules such as the fiscal stability pact, the golden fiscal rule in the UK, make internationally negotiated fiscal policy difficult to execute. All G7 countries have made moves in the direction of institutionalizing annual deficit reduction targets of various sorts and have introduced various limits on spending and deficits as Table 5.2 indicates, although these have been revised, or at least suspended recently in the case of the US and Japan in response to slow growth. The key point is that this has to some extent limited the discretion enjoyed in fiscal policy by all G7 countries. Certainly these institutional arrangements mean that we are a long way away from a return to some sort of international locomotive strategy as some authors have claimed,[66] and we can see how these institutional arrangements have been informed by one of the fundamental defining consensual principles referred to in the last chapter. Policy co-ordination is of course largely rejected in ideational terms anyway, but current institutional arrangements appear to be reinforcing this rejection.

Where the central banks are concerned, all of the G7 central banks, with the exception of the Bank of Canada, enjoy operational independence.[67] The ECB,[68] the Bank of England and the Bank of Canada have specific price stability or inflation targets, while the Bank of Japan and the Fed have more general mandates to deliver national price stability.[69] These national inflation targets provide little incentive for central banks to worry about how their domestic interest rate policies might affect the rest of the world, unless events force their hand. Furthermore, committees of officials, such as the Federal Open Market Committee, the Bank of England's Monetary Policy Committee, the ECB's Governing Council and the Bank of Japan's Policy Board, reach collective decisions on interest rates. In other words, the governors and their deputies do not have the authority to negotiate on domestic policy decisions with their foreign counterparts at G7 meetings, because they have difficulty in speaking on behalf of expert colleagues that supposedly have some degree of independence when decisions are made on interest rates. Domestic institutional mandates in both fiscal and monetary policy therefore restrict

Table 5.2 Fiscal frameworks in G7 countries

Country	*Current fiscal situation and targets for fiscal consolidation*	*Initiatives aimed at fiscal consolidation*
USA	• To balance the fiscal budget of the federal government by FY2002 (Balanced Budget Act enacted in FY1997 following agreement between the President Clinton and Congress). * Fiscal surpluses were recorded in FY1998–2001. • According to the FY2003 President's Budget (announced in February 2002), the fiscal balance in FY2002 will be $106.2 billion in deficit.	Under the 1985 Gramm–Rudman–Hollings Act, fiscal deficit reduction targets were set for each year, with the target of balancing the federal budget by FY1991. In 1987 the Act was amended and the target of balancing the federal budget deferred to FY1993. Subsequently, under the 1990 and 1993 Omnibus Budget Reconciliation Act (OBRA), measures to reduce specific individual expenditure categories (e.g. Medicare) and increase tax were implemented. Spending caps and pay-as-you-go (no increased spending without revenue sources) were introduced in an attempt to further improve the fiscal balance. In 1997, the Balanced Budget Act was enacted with the target of balancing the fiscal budget by FY2002. Among others, it incorporated measures for further spending cuts.
UK	• Medium-term target: to conduct prudent fiscal administration. To ensure that the effects of spending and taxation are fairly balanced within and between different age groups. • Short-term target: to support financial policies. Not to obstruct automatic stabilizer functions. • Budget 2002 projections show that the current budget remains in surplus over the economic cycle, indicating that the Government remains on track to meet the golden rule and that public sector net debt is expected to remain around 31% of GDP, comfortably meeting the sustainable investment rule.	In 1993, 'Control Total' was introduced in public spending plans (formulated in advance of the budget) for the subsequent three years. The aim of this was to curb growth in spending by setting limits on real growth rates. The Blair administration that came to power in May 1997 has remained true to the line of austerity in public finances, and has attempted to reform the budget system. To replace the 'Control Total' it has (1) drawn up fiscal stabilization rules, including targets for fiscal policies, fiscal discipline, preparation and publication of various reports, etc., and (2) introduced a system of (comprehensive) spending reviews and a system of multiple-year budget formation based on these.

continued…

Table 5.2 continued

Country	*Current fiscal situation and targets for fiscal consolidation*	*Initiatives aimed at fiscal consolidation*
Germany	• To balance the general governmental budget by 2004, and to bring the GDP ratio of outstanding debt to 57% in 2004 and 55.5% in 2005. To balance the federal budget by 2006. ('Stability Programme' based on EU Stable Growth Agreement, Dec. 2001). • The GDP ratio of the general governmental deficit is forecast at 2.6% and the GDP ratio of outstanding debt at 60% in 2001. • The FY2002 federal budget shows a fiscal deficit of 23.7 billion euros (9.6% of spending).	Efforts aimed at fiscal consolidation include a 'Construction Bond Principle' (a principle under the Federal Constitution, whereby revenue from bond issues must be no greater than investment spending), a 'Medium-term Fiscal Plan' (5-year fiscal plans, starting with the year of formulation, drawn up since 1967 to secure the medium-term perspective of the fiscal administration), a 'Budget Circular' (issued by the Federal Ministry of Finance to the other ministries in advance of budget requests, indicating budgetary limits for the government as a whole), and a 'Moratorium Principle' (permitting new budgetary measures only if equivalent existing measures are scrapped; introduced in the FY1994 Budget). The fiscal situation worsened at the beginning of the 1990s due, among others, to support measures for the former German Democratic Republic. However, a series of fiscal austerity measures stipulating medium-term fiscal targets have also been implemented.
Japan	The Fiscal Structural Reform Act enacted in 1997 was suspended in 1998. The aim was to deliver a deficit below 3% of GDP, first by 2003 then by 2005. The act will be re-enacted when Japan's economy returns to growth. According to the 'OECD Economic Outlook' issued in June 2002, the fiscal deficit in Japan in CY2002 will be 8.0% of GDP on a general government basis, and 8.4% excluding social security funds, which is the worst deficit among G7 countries.	The Fiscal Structural Reform Act was enacted in 1997. By FY2003 Japan was to bring its fiscal deficit below 3% of GDP. An intensive reform period 1998–2000 to tackle the deficit and numerical targets for the reduction of major expenditures in social security and public investment was announced. In May 1998 the act was amended with the year for attainment of the fiscal consolidation target put back to 2005. The wording for reductions in social security expenditures was changed from 2% to as much as possible. In December 1998 all effects of the Fiscal Structural Reform Act were temporarily suspended. Provisions were announced to re-enact the act when its suspension was lifted, which in turn was dependent on Japanese recovery.
France	• To balance the general governmental budget by 2004, to achieve a surplus GDP ratio of 0.3% in 2005, and	Since the Maastricht Treaty came into effect in 1993, an all-out reduction of the fiscal deficit has been launched. Attempts have been

	to bring the ratio of outstanding debt to GDP to 51.8% in 2005. ('Stability Programme' based on the EU Stable Growth Agreement, Dec. 2001). • According to the FY2002 Budget (established in Dec. 2001), the GDP ratio of the fiscal deficit is forecast at 1.4% and the GDP ratio of outstanding debt at 56.3% in 2001.	made to curb spending under a 'Fiscal 5-Year Program Law' enacted in 1994. Since President Chirac's election in 1995, aggressive efforts have been made to reduce the fiscal deficit, with sights on the single European currency. As well as a continuing drive to reduce defence expenditure, civil servants' salaries, etc., tax revenue has also been increased by raising Value Added Tax and introducing a Corporation Special Tax (1995). Based on the EU Stable Growth Agreement, multiple-year fiscal plans for the subsequent three years have been submitted every year since 1998, and continuing efforts are being made to reduce the fiscal deficit, mainly by curbing spending.
Italy	• To bring the GDP ratio of the general governmental fiscal deficit to 0.5% in FY2004, and to achieve a surplus GDP ratio of 0.1% in FY2005. (Economic Fiscal Plan, July 2002). • The GDP ratio of the general governmental deficit is forecast at 1.1%, and the GDP ratio of outstanding debt at 108.5% in FY2002.	In 1988, a system of formulating Economic Fiscal Plans (DPEF) in advance of budget drafts and obtaining the approval of the legislature was introduced. Budget drafts are formulated on the basis of these plans, with respect to upper limits on spending, etc. In 1993, moreover, parliamentary procedures were amended and 'Obbligo Copertura' (whereby fiscal resources must be demonstrated for new or increased spending) rigorously implemented. Also, as well as reducing expenditure through reforms of the pension and medical care systems, efforts on the revenue side include the introduction of a 'Euro Tax' in 1997 (for one year only) and pursuit of tax evasion by the 'Finance Police' (Fiamma Gialle).
Canada	• To continuously reduce the GDP ratio of the federal government's outstanding debt (to be brought down to below 50% in FY2002 under the FY2001 Budget Plan). * Fiscal surpluses were achieved in FY1997–2000. Outstanding debt has also decreased in net terms since FY1997.	In 1994 a Program Review was introduced to judge spending program priorities based on 6-stage judgment criteria, and spending reduction rates were set for different policy sectors. Since then, an Expenditure Management System (EMS) has been introduced as a framework for spending management in order to normalize these Program Reviews. Apart from this, other efforts have included a revision of the system of federal grants to the states (1995; the existing subsidy system was amended to a comprehensive grant system aimed at social welfare, higher education, and health care sectors), and revision of the budget process by Congress (introduction of a preliminary budget consultation process, and greater transparency of the budget formation process).

the capacity of the G7 to reach decisive binding agreements at their meetings and to co-ordinate their monetary and fiscal policies. This means that G7 meetings tend to be restricted to a directional or advisory role concerning the overall monetary and fiscal stance in particular countries. These domestic institutional arrangements also effectively institutionalize the shared dimension I G7 understanding that the finance ministries and central banks do not engage in hard bargaining over their monetary and fiscal policies at G7 meetings. In other words, this shared understanding and the belief in sound money and national price stability more generally (fiscal consolidation and low inflation) is embedded in domestic institutional arrangements.

Traditionally, the policy instrument most favoured at G7 finance ministry and central bank meetings has been foreign exchange market intervention. This is explained by the fact that it is in this area where the direct participants at G7 meetings have enjoyed most discretion (see Table 5.3).[70] Whereas boards of experts reach decisions on interest rates and fiscal policy is subject to legislative ratification and approval through the presentation of annual budgetary statements, foreign exchange interventions are usually made by key individuals advised by a coterie of senior officials and this suits the G7's informal, personal and sometimes secretive working methods. However, such joint interventions usually require the participation of the United States if they are to convince the markets and Congress was able to freeze the Exchange Stabilization Fund after the Mexican peso bail out in 1994–5, placing rather obvious limitations on the capacity of the G7 to engage in joint foreign exchange market interventions. Moreover, as we saw in the last chapter, large-scale interventions are currently out of fashion amongst the finance ministries and central banks.

However, in an era of international capital mobility and market-determined exchange rates, formal institutional mandates are only part of the picture where exchange rate outcomes are concerned. The relations finance ministries have with other agencies, particularly trade and commerce departments, is crucial. Market actors increasingly scrutinize government statements on the economy of all descriptions and attempt to interpret them. In this respect market actors are interested in profits and therefore engage in speculative activities on the basis of very little in order to move prices. If trade departments are prone to issuing independent statements concerning trade deficits and the causes of those deficits, this can lead to market sentiment shifting quite suddenly, causing an exchange rate valuation to change, thwarting finance ministry objectives through what might appear to be a happy coincidence. The skilful trade representative is often able to exploit this and release statements designed to shift market sentiment in the desired direction. If however, statements on trade balances have to be approved by finance ministries, the trade department will have less potential to act independently and influence exchange rates. A similar situation applies where foreign ministries are concerned. Here the relationship the foreign ministry has with the head of state or government is crucial. If the foreign ministry is able to persuade the leader of the desirability of a particular exchange rate action then the finance ministry can be overridden or forced to follow a particular course of action.

Table 5.3 Procedures for foreign exchange interventions in G7 countries

	United States	*Euro area*	*United Kingdom*	*Japan*
Authority for intervention	Government (Treasury Department) and Federal Reserve Board (FRB). Government has priority with regard to the decision.	European Central Bank (ECB). Intervention should be consistent with the general orientations formulated by ECOFIN. The general orientations are formulated after consulting the ECB, or on a recommendation from the ECB and 'shall be without prejudice to the primary objective of the ESCB to maintain price stability'.	Government (the Treasury) and Bank of England. Intervention by BOE is restricted to occasions when it is necessary to attain the monetary policy objective.	The Minister of Finance authorizes intervention.
Operation of intervention	Federal Reserve Bank of New York	ECB	BOE	BOJ acting as the agent of MOF
Funds for intervention	Government (Foreign Exchange Stabilization Fund) and FRB (usually, each finances half of the amount used for intervention). Intervention results are reported to the Congress every quarter (also published in Federal Reserve Bulletin).	ECB	Government (Foreign Exchange Operation Account) and BOE. The Treasury is planning to disclose intervention on a monthly and quarterly basis on its website.	Minister of Finance entrusts operations involving the Foreign Exchange Fund Special Account to the Bank of Japan. Operations are entirely at the Minister's discretion.

Institutional relationships are also crucial in the sphere of financial supervision and regulation. In particular, the degree of autonomy that regulatory agencies enjoy *vis-à-vis* finance ministries and central banks is crucial in determining the capacity of G7 authorities to catalyse global regulatory initiatives. With the emergence of independent regulatory authorities consisting of personnel from the private sector, the capacity of G7 finance ministries and central banks to take decisive action is being further constrained and simple persuasion, encouragement and endorsement are becoming more common activities. If a national regulatory structure is relatively fragmented, as in the case of the US, reform in the direction of a more integrated regulatory structure is problematic, as are international initiatives to produce greater information exchange between different but related sectors.[71] If there is a single super-regulator, as in the case of the UK's Financial Services Authority, such initiatives are obviously easier to implement.

The picture being painted by this review of domestic institutional arrangements is that it is very difficult for G7 meetings to reach concrete implementable decisions, or specific agreements. Some would see this as evidence of the decline in significance of the G7.[72] However, this is a simplistic assessment that fits rather too conveniently with the liberal institutionalist perspective's current obsession with legalism in American IR, which views the effectiveness of institutions in terms of compliance and legal obligation.[73] This review of domestic institutional arrangements again points us in the direction of the G7 processes role in facilitating consensus formation amongst the leading industrialized powers on global financial governance issues that in turn sets parameters and guiding principles for economic policy-making more generally, and as Robert Cox has pointed out, circumscribes what can be thought and done.[74] The G7 finance ministries and central banks seek to set agendas in global financial governance by formulating their own consensus and seeking to influence debates, agendas and activities in other spatial dimensions, such as their domestic arenas, globally networked markets, and wider multilateral and transnational bodies including the governments of non-G7 states. Given their financial resources and their intellectual expertise, the G7 finance ministries and central banks reaching a common view is not something that is insubstantial, nor is it something that can be easily resisted. Simply writing the G7 off on the basis of the absence any formal decision-making capacity is to miss a significant concentration of influence in the global political economy. Ignoring the informal directional and agenda-setting influence of the G7 because it does not fit with the methodological and theoretical imperatives of certain schools of thought in International Relations is a serious oversight.

Finance ministries, central banks and differing domestic political economies

One of the principal differences between the G7 countries in financial and monetary affairs is rooted in the different domestic political economies of G7 states. As we saw in the previous chapter the fundamental divide is between the US and UK with open financial sectors with arms-length relations between financial institutions and industry, and Germany and Japan with controlled financial sectors with close relations between banks and industry. Indeed in Germany and Japan the financial sectors have been designed to facilitate industrial expansion and productivity growth, rather than existing as a means of capital accumulation in their own right.

Numerous authors have referred to a Dollar–Wall Street regime, or a Wall Street–Treasury–IMF complex.[75] The US financial sector and the agencies most closely connected to it – the Treasury Department and the Federal Reserve – have been keen to push and promote the agenda of financial liberalization, in their efforts to expand market share into new countries and new sectors, and to increase capital inflows into the US financial system. Since the 1970s, Wall Street and the US Treasury have pushed to weaken the barriers to US financial firms' penetration into foreign financial systems. This pressure has been designed to free up the movement of funds from and into Wall Street and other financial centres, to redesign foreign financial systems and to allow Wall Street operators full rights to do business in the financial systems of other states.[76] In this respect, exchange rate turbulence means that other states have to accumulate large foreign currency reserves, predominantly dollars. Such reserves have been placed in US financial markets such as US Treasury bonds because their liquidity means they can easily be withdrawn for exchange rate stabilization purposes. Wall Street has consequently benefited through the inflow of foreign funds pushing up market values, while it has also pioneered the development of a variety of derivatives markets that are intended to hedge against exchange rate risk (although they often create new forms of risk in their own right). Currency volatility can also increase governments' trade deficits, increasing their need to borrow on Wall Street or from the IMF. Wall Street and the IMF can then demand macroeconomic adjustment in the form of spending cuts and further liberalization of markets and financial systems in return for their loans.[77]

Financial crises and volatility in emerging markets also result in funds flowing from affected markets into Wall Street. The boost in liquidity that the New York–London Anglo-Saxon financial nexus experiences from financial crises in various parts of the world has also resulted in lower interest rates. Low interest rates are of enormous significance for US prosperity due to its burgeoning equity culture and the expansion in share ownership that saw 53 per cent of Americans holding some stocks or shares by 1998. Lower interest rates increase the funds flowing into equities markets and in turn boost share performance. Changes since the 1970s have meant that speculative market-based financial activities have come to dominate Anglo-Saxon financial markets, changing domestic interest-based politics in the US and UK and changing policy-makers' perception of national interest in the sphere of international financial and monetary governance. Anglo-Saxon financial conglomerates are the most clear beneficiaries of financial liberalization. Increasingly, credit to companies in the US is not offered in the form of bank loans, but in the form of bonds offered by mutual funds, which in turn also offer higher returns to savers. The supply of capital to American employers and the savings of vast swathes of America have subsequently become tied to price movements in securities markets. This has been accompanied by the emergence of a new tier of securities called derivatives whose prices are derived from the movement in other securities or currencies and hedge funds, which are offshoots of major investment banks that buy and sell securities on their own account to exploit price differences over time and price differences between markets. The biggest banks lend huge sums of money so that the hedge funds can play the markets with enormous resources. The scale of resources is vital because it enables the speculator to move prices in a particular market in the direction they want them to move in.

Consequently, not only has the American economy as a whole become dependent on the performance of Wall Street, but the support of Wall Street, both financial and verbal, has become essential for those hoping to obtain power in Washington.[78] The income and wealth of the large US corporations have become tied to future prices on stock and bond markets, as they have invested in various mutual and hedge funds. They have also made the delivery of shareholder value their overwhelming priority, which in turn determines structures and policies in operation within corporations. US workers too have become dependent upon the securities markets for their pensions, health care and even their wages in the form of share option schemes. In other words, most aspects of US society have an interest in rentier finance and financial speculation. However, while the US economy depends on Wall Street, which in turn depends upon on monetary and financial turmoil elsewhere, its manufacturing sector depends upon steadily growing emerging markets capable of absorbing US products to generate profits for US companies and needs a competitively valued currency to facilitate exports.[79] The financial bias of US and UK capitalism has resulted in both countries having sustained long-term current account deficits that have been funded by capital account surpluses. In interviews for this study one British Treasury official even claimed that trade deficits had ceased to matter in an era of capital account liberalization.[80] This kind of attitude has resulted in a degree of de-industrialization in each country.

In contrast to the US and the UK, the continental European and Japanese economies are not as financialized as the Anglo-Saxon economies and therefore have a different set of interests and a different distribution of power in their domestic political economies.[81] Europe and Japan have not deliberately pursued financialization and have not displayed the contempt for domestic productive activities that have often been evident in the policies of the US and the UK. Unlike the UK and the US, Germany has not made building a large internationally dominant set of financial markets a central priority. Attempts have been made to maintain a financial structure centred on large regulated banks, relatively small securities markets and large parts of the financial system in state hands. Commercial credit banks have been closely connected to manufacturing, providing long-term loans facilitating a continuous, incremental investment ethic and a solid manufacturing base that in turn has been dependent on some degree of exchange rate stability. Limited securities markets has meant that shareholder value has not been prioritized over productivity in Japan or Germany the way it has in the US and UK, and in Germany this has enabled the trade unions to have a key participatory role in the way leading German firms are run and in labour market governance more generally. This more controlled and less speculative form of financial system is therefore based on and has facilitated an entirely different vision of society and economy than the speculative, profit-driven Anglo-Saxon one.

Unfortunately for labour groupings and some sections of manufacturing, rentier interests, although not enjoying the same prominent position as in the UK and the US, have enjoyed increasing political success in Europe. The principal reason for this has been a perceived loss of European competitiveness, relative to dynamic growth regions in North America and Asia, which has convinced some European policy-makers of the need to promote the restructuring of European labour markets and to introduce more innovation and dynamism into the European economy so as to expand market share.[82] Financial interests have pushed the structural reform agenda and emphasized the need for labour-shedding measures in continental Europe, while advocating the need to develop an equity culture and to embrace more fully the concept of shareholder value. This is a political struggle that has a long way to run, and labour market reform in Europe is likely to take the form of slow incremental adjustment rather than wholesale change, due to the politically prominent position of organized labour. Despite this, almost everywhere in continental Europe labour spent most of the last decade on the retreat, rather than on the offensive.[83] Furthermore, the single market programme and some EU directives favour greater liberalization in the areas of investment services and capital adequacy standards, and offer potential for Anglo-Saxon concerns to increase their business in European markets. At the same time, state aid provisions are being used to challenge the role of the state-owned Lander bank in Germany.[84] European states have accepted some of the activities of the US, precisely because these activities have opened economies elsewhere and made it easier for European capital to turn outwards and enter new markets. This was starkly evident in the G7's response to the Asian financial crisis. For some this represented a new transatlantic alliance between the US and the EU as they sought to co-operate to gain new positions in the economies of South East Asia by opening these economies and increasing their holdings of assets in this part of the world.[85]

Rentier interests in the European Union are the social groupings with the closest links to the finance ministries and central banks. This provides us with a stark reminder that the consensual ideas, or the mind-set referred to in the last chapter, do not exist in a political vacuum. The rise to prominence of neo-classical approaches to finance and markets has been intimately intertwined with changes in social relations in national locations brought about by the transnationalization of finance and production more generally. The construction of open market-based financial systems has enabled rentier financial interests to emphasize the importance of shareholder value, low inflation, wage restraint, labour shedding and capital account liberalization if economies are to be competitive in the changed material conditions of increasing international capital mobility. G7 finance ministries and central banks have in turn been quite successful in promoting the beliefs referred to in the last chapter as received wisdom and have in the process managed to increasingly insulate their own policy-making activities (macroeconomic policy and overall responsibility for the financial system) from democratic accountability and scrutiny. Furthermore, strong societal preferences in favour of stable and competitively valued exchange rates in both Japan and Germany, because of close banking industry relations, appear to be being progressively overridden. For example, by the mid-1990s scepticism about the utility of exchange market interventions was widespread across the G7, following the failure of efforts to support the dollar in 1994, the ERM crisis of 1992–9 and the Mexican peso crisis of 1995, all of which resulted in considerable losses for central banks. G7 policy-makers have since displayed a marked reluctance to intervene in markets and attempt to manage exchange rates. The difficulty in following proactive exchange rate policies has also been compounded by the movement towards independent central banks with national inflation targets across the G7. Therefore, while we might expect international economic integration to increase the political prominence of exchange rate issues because of the increasing number of socio-economic actors affected by currency movements,[86] policy-makers' capacity to respond to increasing societal demands on exchange rate matters appears to be receding. At the same time, an increase in relative insulation of national treasury and central bank officials from direct societal pressures has made it more difficult for societal groupings to mount significant lobbying on exchange rate or monetary issues.[87] The market has assumed a new level of primacy in exchange rate determination over the last decade, bringing with it large gyrations and fluctuations. This has been convenient for the finance ministries and central banks in excusing them of an important responsibility. It has suited rentier interests concerned with opening economies and financial systems in South East Asia, and it has ensured that assets have flowed into safe-haven markets in Europe and North America.

While it would be premature to suggest that Japan and continental Europe have abandoned their credit banking traditions, as the last chapter demonstrated, evidence is emerging to suggest that the finance–industry coalitions and alliances in Japan and Germany are being challenged, while speculative rentier interests have been more successful in forming alliances not only with Wall Street and the US Treasury, but also with their own finance ministries and central banks.

The financial sector–finance ministry–central bank axis

As the discussion above demonstrated there has been no convergence between the G7 states on any single model of capitalism. However, some authors have pointed to a process of 'hybridization'.[88] This involves the emergence of Anglo-Saxon practices oriented to the speculative management of share prices, share splits, mergers, stock buy-backs, incentive compensation and their uneasy existence alongside the traditional Japanese–German orientation towards maintaining stable long-term employment and social solidarity. At the very least there are social forces in both Japan and Germany who promote reform in the direction of the Anglo-Saxon model, including academic US-educated neo-classical economists, economic analysts in the private sector, certain corporations and financial institutions seeking to increase their competitiveness and global market share, and sections of the business and financial press in both countries who are again often educated in the US.[89] It is not surprising that these groups and individuals find that their most sympathetic audience within the state apparatus are the finance ministries and central banks. These institutions employ a large number of neo-classically trained economists who tend to see the economy in more conservative and market-oriented terms than the communitarian socially-oriented vision that has traditional characterized both Japanese and German society. A state–society axis has formed in both countries between these groups and the finance ministries and central banks, and in particular with those officials with extensive experience of the international side and with most direct exposure to Anglo-Saxon norms.[90] This state–society axis has at least in part promoted an agenda of 'financialization' – the increasing dominance of the finance industry in the sum total of economic activity, of financial controllers in the management of corporations, of financial assets among total assets, of marketized securities and particularly equities among financial assets, of the stock market as a market for corporate control in determining corporate strategies, and of fluctuations in the stock market as a determinant of business cycles.[91]

Finance ministries and central banks have come to act as the representatives of financial interests in both international and national policy processes, often single-mindedly pursuing the objectives of sound money and open markets at the expense of other social and economic objectives such as growth, unemployment and widening inequality between high and low earners. Financialization is therefore a self-perpetuating cycle, initially stimulated by states' desire for competitiveness, market share and foreign investment, but increasingly driven by the growing leverage and influence of finance ministries and central banks from the wealthiest nations, which in turn is the result of both the growing importance of financial markets, and the finance ministries and central banks' close relationships with globally active financial concerns. The axis between G7 finance ministries and central banks and their rentier financial sectors is one of the most powerful state–society axes in today's global political economy.

Of course, sound money and capital liberalization have not always been prioritized and promoted by finance ministries. It is well known that John Maynard Keynes spent some of his career at the British Treasury, and as a consequence HM Treasury became a bastion of Keynesian economics.[92] However, the failure of Keynesian policies in the 1970s following the collapse of Bretton Woods and the US decision to abolish capital controls, saw finance ministry officials both in Britain and elsewhere in the G7 move away from Keynesianism and adopt neo-classical and neo-monetarist approaches to economic policy.[93] A new generation of officials shaped by the experiences of the breakdown of Bretton Woods and the stagflation of the 1970s emerged. Despite the post-war Keynesian orientation of the British Treasury it is worth noting that its overseas finance section, that participated in the kind of international networks of which the G7 is a latter-day version, always sought to promote a sound currency over growth objectives and full employment. The overseas section of the Treasury was one part of a *de-facto* 'sterling lobby' at the heart of the British establishment, which also comprised the Bank of England and sought to promote the interests of the City of London in Whitehall.[94] Generally, it has been true that the international sections of finance ministries (those most directly involved in G7 preparations) have been most sympathetic towards those financial interests involved in rentier and speculative international financial business.

In accordance with this last point and in relation to this finance ministry–central bank– financial sector axis, the G7 process itself is a very one-sided process. While the IMF has attempted to expand its underdeveloped dialogue with civil society actors, the institution remains susceptible to the criticism that it only listens and does real business with finance ministries and central banks in affected countries who are themselves much more open to the sound money open markets agenda.[95] If anything, the record of the G7 finance ministries and central banks concerning societal consultation on important international financial questions is even worse than that of the IMF. The G7 finance ministries and central bankers' process is a closed, not an open one. The range of interests represented at G7 meetings is narrow, not broad and the process of G7 agenda setting is greatly circumscribed. There is simply very little in the way of societal-wide agenda-setting discussions prior to G7 meetings. Most of the officials involved in G7 preparations that were interviewed for this study considered their constituency to be financial interests on Wall Street in the case of the US, or the City of London in the case of the UK. The interests of Wall Street or the City accordingly translated into officials' conception of 'national interest'.[96] Moreover, societal consultations prior to G7 meetings are invariably restricted to the occasional seminar with representatives of some of these financial interests on specific issues or initiatives.[97] The consequence of this is that certain issues such as a return to a system of capital controls, managed exchange rates, increased public sector investment, or redistributive macroeconomic policies based on criteria other than financial and monetary ones, are unlikely to feature in any significant way on the G7 agenda. In other words, the consensual economic ideas that are shared across the G7 reflect the societal interactions finance ministries and central banks engage in and the patterns of interest representation in the international sections of theses institutions. Of course, occasionally a finance minister who is interested in pursuing ideas that fundamentally challenge the status quo emerges, and these individuals may engage in a greater degree of societal consultation, but their ideas are rarely taken seriously or discussed in any great detail by finance ministry and central bank colleagues who on the whole remain wedded to the prevailing mind-set.[98] In one sense, this would appear to confirm the liberal intergovernmentalist view that societal preferences are independent causal variables. However, as the discussion in the next section will confirm, priorities in monetary and financial policy are not arrived at via simple societal consultation, but via a more complex diffuse series of interactions.

G7 transgovernmentalism and the domestic arena

In the original account of transgovernmentalism, Keohane and Nye argued that the critical variables affecting both the capacity of bureaucracies and the incentives they face to engage in transgovernmental activities are domestic. Some degree of independence from central co-ordination was required for transgovernmental coalition building. As we have seen this clearly applies to the finance ministries and central banks. Transgovernmental coalitions were also thought to be more likely when there was a high degree of conflict among different governmental sub-units, creating an incentive for agencies to act collectively with like agencies from other countries to influence domestic decisions. Yet I would argue that while some degree of national autonomy is clearly a necessity for transgovernmental activity, the degree of conflict between national sub-units is not necessarily a good indicator or reliable predictor of the incentives agencies face to collaborate in a transgovernmental fashion for a number of reasons. Crucially, as finance ministries and central banks have become more insulated from societal and political pressures, and have become convinced that their principal function is to deliver financial and price stability, which in turn is conceived of as a primarily technical task, finance ministry and central bank elites appear to be becoming more concerned with using their dimension I discussions to affect, rather than respond to, public opinion.[99] With the exception of the immediate period following the Asian financial crisis, the leaders at the annual G8 summits have disengaged from substantive discussion of international financial and economic questions, so the G7 finance ministries and central banks have become less inclined to mediate between competing domestic political pressures in the field of international monetary and financial affairs.[100] The G7 finance ministries and central banks' primary transgovernmental activity in relation to the domestic setting has been discourse construction. To prevent counter-arguments emerging against independent central banks and to make the overturning of existing arrangements more difficult, finance ministries and central banks have found it useful not only to refer to their technical expertise but also to cite practice elsewhere in the industrialized world and the existence of a loose consensus on macroeconomic governance, so as to defend their ascendancy in macroeconomic policy as the 'norm' throughout the industrialized world.[101] The targets of this macroeconomic discourse are other government agencies and domestic electorates and the principal aim is to minimize expectations and create the impression that there is 'no alternative' to central bank independence and policies oriented towards price stability and deficit reduction. In other words, despite the possibility that there are low levels of conflict between finance ministries, central banks and other domestic agencies across the G7, or that finance ministries and central banks enjoy supremacy over other domestic agencies in determining the domestic economic agenda, finance ministries and central banks still have an incentive to build a transgovernmental coalition so as to ring-fence and protect what are relatively recently won institutional gains (over the last ten years in the case of central bank independence in most cases). Moreover, in an era of 'decentralized globalization', as described in Chapter 3, we would expect the domestic setting to become less important for G7 transgovernmental activities, with the G7 becoming more inclined to collaborate to influence and communicate with wider international institutions and bodies, with authorities in systemically important emerging markets and with financial markets themselves.

Applying third-dimensional analysis to the G7

Decentralized globalization and the third dimension

Dimension III consists of the space occupied by networked financial markets. Since the 1970s and the switch to floating exchange rates, the growth in the need for foreign currency associated with the growth in international trade, the abolition of exchange controls, the mushrooming of international investment flows of portfolio investors, life insurance companies and pension funds, have all combined to generate a rapid expansion in the market for foreign exchange. The sheer number and short-term nature of trades makes the calculation of precise volumes difficult. However, the Bank for International Settlements estimated that around $1,210 billion a day were traded in foreign exchange by 2001, far out-stripping trade in manufactured goods.[102] Trade in money proliferated initially through new derivative instruments such as futures, swaps and options, designed to offset foreign exchange risk, but these sophisticated instruments have become an important source of profit for financial institutions, leading to new forms of risk and creating the potential for further currency instability.[103] One development in financial markets has been the emergence of secondary markets enabling people to buy and sell pieces of paper entitling the holder to future royalties. Today it is possible to buy and sell paper giving the holder the right to buy or sell a currency, a commodity, or certain shares at a certain price at a certain time in the future. The generic name for these tradable pieces of paper is securities. Securities do not contribute to productive investment and have nothing to do with supplying funds for capital investment. Instead investors in securities markets are buying and selling claims on future value created in future productive activity. Rentier activity such as this is based on efforts to derive income by extracting royalties from future production through trading in securities or currencies, by selling at prices higher than initially paid. Increasingly, rentiers and speculators conduct their activities through hedge funds. As we have already seen in this chapter, in the discussion of the US financial sector, hedge funds are often the creation of large US banks allowing them to engage in speculative activities by creating a partnership, often registered offshore. Big banks then lend huge sums of money to these hedge funds, with the scale of resources critical, because it enables hedge funds to shift prices in a market, through the sheer scale of the resources deployed. The most dynamic growth sector in which hedge funds have been involved is the international foreign exchange market and foreign exchange derivatives markets. Foreign exchange is a very psychological market and when others in the market see a powerful hedge fund moving in a certain direction, they are liable to follow suit and start buying, enabling the hedge fund to sell to them and take profits. Financial markets therefore often function on the basis of traders' analyses of the behaviour of other traders, rather than any analysis of underlying economic fundamentals as the finance ministries and central banks' current focus on transparency would have us believe.

Derivatives markets have come to dwarf other financial sectors and the biggest single market is that for foreign exchange derivatives. Seven financial centres, London, New York, Toronto, Tokyo, Frankfurt, Bahrain and Singapore, dominate foreign exchange trading. Five of these centres are located in G7 countries. In this sense it is clear that the G7 countries have a clear interest in maintaining an open financial system that generates large profits for its financial sector. We can also see that the interconnectedness of the current globalized financial system is also accompanied by a certain degree of geographical dispersion – what Randall Germain calls 'decentralized globalization'.[104] This in turn creates a mutual vulnerability to disruption in any of these centres, creating a need for collaboration and consensus formation in relation to regulatory initiatives and information exchange, which is why financial governance is more heavily reliant on consensus than an area like trade. At the same time, as Tony Porter has recently argued, global finance is developing more of the features of a technical system, reliant on machines, computer networks and technology and the technical expertise of operators in this field.[105] This in turn has meant that governance of this field is increasingly conducted by specialists and technocrats. The key point is that governance initiatives are part of the constant response to the evolution and development of the third-dimensional space of global finance. Policy-makers are continuously responding to the challenges emerging from the latest developments in global financial markets as an interconnected but decentralized technical system.

Today, a number of global or stateless banks and financial institutions that have offices around the world, dominate trading in foreign exchange and securities. The IMF estimated that 75 per cent of business in the centres listed above is handled by just ten hedge funds and that collectively these funds can mobilize between $600 billion and $1 trillion to bet against currencies in speculative attacks.[106] At the same time, names such as Citicorp, Chase Manhattan, Merrill Lynch, Barclays, National Westminster, Warburg, UBS, Bank of Tokyo and Nomura, continuously recur across several product markets. Such institutions are able to develop global networks and achieve economies of scale and scope, enabling them to move money and financial instruments around the globe almost instantaneously.[107]

In this respect, financial markets are themselves structured networks of social relations, interactions and dependencies, comprising communities of actors and agents with interests, values, rules of behaviour, trust, co-operation and competition.[108] Financial flows take off and land at the major world urban financial centres, which comprise the hubs of a global network.[109] Such flows respond to rapidly changing market signals about risk and return. Today's financial markets are characterized by electronic fund transfer systems that allow banks to move capital around at a moment's notice, arbitraging interest rate differentials, taking advantage of favourable exchange rates and avoiding political unrest. Reuters, with 200,000 interconnected terminals world wide, accounts for 40 per cent of the world's financial trades each day, through systems such as Instinet and Globex.[110] Such networks mean that the average trade takes less than 25 seconds. This in turn means that fortunes can be won and lost by staying micro-seconds ahead of the rest of the market.

Electronic money has created a culture of transacting rather than investing, institutionalizing volatility and wild swings in prices in the process.[111] In this context, information and communication become all important because access to important information can bring huge rewards if it is interpreted in a fashion that allows a dealer to predict market movements. Authority can therefore be said to rest with those market watchers who have over time offered the most convincing interpretations.[112] Their words, analyses and discourses can trigger market movements, giving them a form of communicative power based on the flow of communication and a real degree of discursive authority.[113] Feel for the mood of the market and prevailing market is therefore essential for the successful trader.[114] In this respect, third-dimensional diplomacy is the series of communications that are played out within the market itself, both between traders, and with states acting either unilaterally or multilaterally.

Third-dimensional diplomacy at G7 meetings

Third-dimensional diplomacy involves policy-makers' collective attempts to communicate with prevailing sentiment in financial markets as transnational networks, or global cross-border spaces, as well as the process through which market actors scrutinize national government economic policies and policy-makers' statements, and the collective statements of group of states such as the G7. In the week leading up to a G7 meeting, the public statements of policy-makers and prominent market spokespeople intensify. Each expresses an opinion based on their own calculations and data, tempered in the case of the official community by some political considerations, and in the case of market actors by a desire to enhance their own institution's capacity for short-term profit. The significance of this third-dimensional diplomacy between markets and national authorities for macro-economic policy is that it determines access to foreign credit. Access to private sources of credit enables national authorities to postpone macroeconomic adjustment and to run deficits – what Benjamin Cohen has called the 'power to delay'.[115] If markets reach a negative judgement on an economy, the cessation of lending can precipitate adjustment to address those deficits through fiscal retrenchment, currency depreciation, and/or interest rate adjustments. Ultimately therefore, market judgements determine a state's 'power to delay' and to exercise macro-economic freedom.

For some observers the process of perpetual market scrutiny that characterizes third-dimensional diplomacy and policy-makers' subsequent attempts to demonstrate their 'credibility' has resulted in a structural dynamic of 'market followership', as central bankers respond to market movements by delivering an interest rate path that financial markets themselves have embedded in asset or currency price movements.[116] Market analysts continuously comment and offer opinion on what different financial markets need in terms of interest rate policy. When central banks respond to market consensus, this rather sheds doubt over the realities and true extent of their independence, as formal independence from partisan politics and general public opinion does not appear to be accompanied by informal independence from those operating in financial markets.[117]

Two particular forms of third-dimensional diplomacy are evident at G7 meetings. The first of these is connected to the surveillance exercise in which public authorities release data on their macroeconomies and their financial sectors, as part of a process of peer review for the benefit of a world-wide audience of investors. A continuous flow of data is expected to be made available to investors on the performance of countries' macroeconomies and financial sectors under new international codes of practice promoted and initiated by the G7. All of this was captured under the banner of 'transparency', particularly the notion that macroeconomic credibility could be enhanced through 'transparency'. To minimize time inconsistency and with it investors' suspicions about macroeconomic intentions, authorities are expected to engage in timely data release, so as to prevent unsustainable policies from being hidden from view.[118] In this respect, 'credibility through transparency' involves authorities playing to a third-dimensional audience of investors – predominantly the foreign exchange market, as policy-makers release timely data on their macroeconomies often in accordance with multilateral (dimension I) procedures and norms.[119] Efforts to increase transparency and improve the disclosure and flow of information between market participants and market authorities have however been asymmetrical. For national authorities, particularly those in emerging markets, the emphasis is on building a sustained dialogue with both markets and the wider international community including the G7 and the IMF, or risk being shut out of international financial markets. Transparency is therefore designed to operate through a three-sided process involving multilateral standards and scrutiny, market scrutiny and national policy and practice. Most worryingly, governments now seem to be more accountable to non-citizens – other finance ministries and central banks, various international organizations and international investors and foreign currency traders – for their national macroeconomic and financial policies.

The second form of third-dimensional diplomacy is a direct product of the G7's approach to exchange rate policy. The shared G7 view is that exchange rate misalignments result in resource misallocations within and between economies, but that correct exchange rate valuations change on a daily and even on an hourly basis.[120] On the basis of this view, the G7 finance ministries and central banks' multilateral surveillance exercise concentrates on the identification of sustained and pronounced exchange rate misalignments that fail to reflect underlying domestic fundamentals. When finance ministries and central banks agree that a particular currency's value represents a clear misalignment, they release a joint statement in an effort to persuade the foreign exchange market to initiate a correction. The release of collective public statements by the G7 on exchange rates is a form of declaratory policy. Declaratory policy constitutes the expression of a collective G7 view and represents a form of code the market is expected to interpret.[121] However, statements are little more than a form of persuasion or an opinion that the market is effectively free to reject if they feel a different interpretation, offered by market analysts at private financial institutions, is more convincing. Again the implication of this form of third-dimensional diplomacy is that ultimate sanction lies with the dynamic of the market, with public authorities' role reduced to that of presenting arguments and data to the markets. The consequence of these activities is that domestic policies implemented in the dimension II setting tend to be disciplined by market scrutiny and focus on the criteria most monitored by global financial markets – current and projected rates of inflation and fiscal deficits, to provide some degree of market reassurance.[122]

Applying fourth-dimensional analysis to the G7

If the timing of G7 meetings is a significant first-dimensional variable, it also heavily influences fourth-dimensional diplomacy. G7 meetings are timed so that they take place the day before the spring and autumn meetings of the IMF and World Bank. Effectively this means that the G7 can act as a caucus group, in which a consensus is reached before that consensus is promoted elsewhere. For example, one deputy's deputy interviewed for this study revealed that he spent the majority of his time in the margins of G7 meetings trying to persuade non-G7 countries to accept certain G7 proposals, so as to create workable positions at IMF/ World Bank meetings.[123] In other words, fourth-dimensional diplomacy is an ongoing and integral part of the G7 activities that is aided by the timing of G7 meetings and is pivotal to the G7's defining characteristics as a transgovernmental coalition.

Notably, the Managing Director of the IMF also attends G7 meetings and is part of the collective exchanges and lesson drawing that characterizes the G7 process, and is therefore also a part of the G7 network, despite supposedly acting as an impartial observer representing the rest of the world. Intellectually, it is rare for the Managing Director's views to diverge fundamentally from that of the deputies, ministers or governors.[124] Differences that do arise tend to stem from the Managing Director's slightly enlarged view of the role of the IMF.[125] While the Managing Director is supposed to communicate the rest of the world's interests to the G7, it is more common for the G7 to attempt to use the IMF and the Managing Director to express their views to the rest of the world. Forty-five per cent of voting rights, a strategic capacity to provide liquidity and financing through the IMF, to secure associated concessions through the principle of conditionality and a shared broad outlook, ensure that the G7 can usually make things happen in relation to the IMF.[126]

There are four key fourth-dimensional variables where the G7 process is concerned. These are the functional responsibilities of various bodies, the institutional culture and resources of these bodies, the degree of independence and autonomy these bodies enjoy *vis-à-vis* national authorities (finance ministries and central banks), and finally their involvement in and relations with non-G7 countries. Where global financial governance and the G7 process is concerned, three bodies are to the fore, the IMF, the Basle Committee and ISOCO.

The IMF

The IMF remains the crucial institution in the international financial architecture. It provides emergency lending to countries affected by financial crises in return for strict conditionality and it now oversees new codes of practice on monetary and fiscal policy. It is essentially an inter-governmental organization (although it has a secretariat) that places a high priority on carrying the voting support of broad array of individual governments for its programmes. With over 180 members, the IMF is a large sometimes unwieldy organization with limited budgetary and resource autonomy or flexibility that cannot change course easily. Moreover, its specialist analysts as professional trained economists set a considerable stall by technical knowledge, yet the organization is often criticized for its formulaic orthodox prescriptions.[127] The principal foci of the IMF include monitoring and advising governments on their public finances, balance of payments and the overall efficiency of markets. At times of financial crisis the IMF acts as lender of last resort, but often makes the provision of liquidity dependent on the countries receiving financial assistance following its prescriptions on financial liberalization, macroeconomic and exchange rate policy and even structural reform.

The IMF's wide membership, together with the frequency with which it is called upon to provide financial assistance to middle- and low-income countries, has meant that it has provided the G7 finance ministries and central banks, as the institution's principal creditors, with an effective means of extending their influence. In other words, nothing of substance in the Fund can take place without G7 approval, or for that matter US approval. With 17.11 per cent of votes (see Table 5.4), the US has enough votes to block a quota increase. No other G7 power has that capability, again demonstrating the limitations of Kirton's concert equality model, and that is before we consider US advantages such as chairing and drafting more G7 meetings and statements than any other country, the Treasury Department's close geographical proximity to the Fund and the fact that the US trains more Fund economists than any other country.

The G7 countries are represented at the Fund by national executive directors, most of whom are usually national civil servants on secondment. In almost all cases, while the executive directors might handle day-to-day business, crucial strategic decisions are made by national finance ministers and the deputies. It is commonly understood that the executive directors act on behalf of, and are answerable to, the national finance minister and national (G7) deputies.[128]

Table 5.4 G7 countries percentage share of IMF votes

Country	*Percentage of IMF votes*
United States	17.11
Japan	6.14
Germany	6.00
France	4.95
United Kingdom	4.95
Italy	3.26
Canada	2.94
Total G7 IMF votes	45.35

Consequently, real debates over future IMF policy and controversial cases are discussed outside of the IMF's executive board at meetings of smaller groups of states such as the G7, and more lately and infrequently the G20. As Ngaire Woods has pointed out, for example, a loan that did not meet with US approval would seldom be pointed to the Board for discussion.[129]

Notably, the Fund itself has traditionally been restricted in terms of with whom it could consult. Negotiations were restricted to being held with a nation's finance ministry, and although the IMF has attempted to increase its consultations with civil society groupings, historical legacies and institutionalized patterns of behaviour are not easily changed. Consequently, it has often appeared that the IMF would be willing to talk to the members of an elite in a developing country, senior figures in the finance ministry, or central bank, but beyond that there was little point in talking as the Fund was the purveyor of a technical financial orthodoxy too subtle to be grasped by wider societal groupings.[130] Of course, as we have already seen, elites in finance ministries and central banks tend to be more amenable to the kind of monetary and financial orthodoxy the IMF and the G7 have promoted. In other words, the very nature of the IMF, its historical legacy as an institution and its decision-making procedures that would consult with only finance ministries has enhanced the capacity of G7 finance ministries and central banks to realize their objectives and ensure that IMF agendas reflect their own preferences. In many respects this is the very essence of the transgovernmental nature of contemporary global financial governance.

The Basle Committee

The Basle Committee on Banking Supervision (BCBS) is based at the Bank of International Settlements (BIS) in Basle and consists of representatives from specialist national regulatory bodies from the G10 countries, many of whom enjoy considerable autonomy from national authorities, and regulatory specialists from national central banks. Many regulators have had careers in the private sector, from where they have gleaned their specialist knowledge. The result is a circumscribed transnational policy community that privileges technical knowledge over public debate in what is a relatively inaccessible policy area.[131] Certainly, the Basle Committee is not easily susceptible to influence from elected governments or wider societal interests, other than the banking industry which it is charged with regulating. The G7 finance ministries and central banks can therefore play a role in highlighting priorities and challenges for an organization like the Basle Committee, but the technical nature of the issues, together with the independence of many regulators, mean that their influence is nowhere near as great as is the case with the IMF. Over the years the Basle Committee has developed an agreed division of responsibilities between home and host country regulators, codified in 1983 and updated in 1992, and a risk-based capital accord in 1988, which agrees minimal levels of bank capital for internationally active banks. From the mid-1990s onwards the Basle Committee, at the instigation of the G7, began working more directly with non-G10 countries. Following consultation with sixteen emerging markets and developing countries the committee published the *Basle Core Principles for Effective Banking Supervision* in 1997. The Basle Committee also established the Core Principles Liaison Group to institutionalize links with non-G10 countries.[132] In effect, the G7 have used the Basle Committee as an intermediary to extend the principles governing their own banking sectors into other countries, in a form of fourth-dimensional diplomacy. However, the Basle Committee's focus on prudential regulation and the stability of the financial system means that it is inclined to take a slightly more circumspect approach to financial liberalization, acting as a much needed antidote to the IMF's sometimes over-zealous and hasty enthusiasm for further liberalization.[133]

IOSCO

The International Organization of Securities Commissions (IOSCO) is a group of securities regulators that came into existence following the extension of the American securities regulator in 1984. Securities regulators are usually autonomous agencies mandated by legislation to take on the responsibility of supervision, although some finance ministry and central bank officials attend IOSCO meetings. Many trade associations are affiliate members of IOSCO and engage in self-regulation. Significantly, IOSCO considers itself as a non-governmental organization and given the rate of product innovation, is heavily dependent on the expertise of industry analysts. It is another example of a closed insider policy community and is even less susceptible to outside influence than the Basle Committee. To some extent it has been characterized by a desire to keep governments at arms length, legitimating this through claims to technical expertise. Obviously, this limits the capacity of the G7 to influence IOSCO's activities.[134] By 1998, IOSCO's membership had reached 159 countries, as it too has progressively extended its reach, although its most powerful committees remain dominated by the G10 and G7 countries. As Chapter 7 will demonstrate, one of the trends evident in the last five years has been an effort to involve developing countries more actively in the activities of regulatory committees such as Basle and IOSCO. The other major trend has been the effort to mirror the increasing integration of banking and securities markets at an industry level, by improving consultation and communication between IOSCO, the Basle Committee, insurance regulators and even the IMF. This has been evident in initiatives such as the Tripartite Group, the Joint Forum and most recently the Financial Stability Forum. While these new forums have cluttered the stage as far as global financial governance is concerned, they are also leading to the emergence of new forms of fourth-dimensional diplomacy, extending the influence and reach of the G7 by improving their channels of communication with authorities in emerging markets and by persuading them to adhere to a growing range of multilateral standards and codes monitored by the IMF, the Basle Committee and IOSCO, and thereby enhancing and institutionalizing dialogue with international investors (third-dimensional diplomacy), supposedly resulting in sounder more stable financial systems.

Fourth-dimensional diplomacy and complex stratified transgovernmentalism

There is no better illustration of the G7's transgovernmental activities in relation to this fourth spatial dimension than their drafting of reports on the so-called global financial architecture, from those published at the Halifax summit of 1995 right through to the Cologne summit reports of 1999 and more recent updates (see Chapter 7). The finance ministries and central banks largely settled for setting strategic priorities and deadlines for more specialist bodies and for catalysing increased communications between technocrats engaged in banking and securities regulation. Regulators' reports fed back into and informed G7 agendas and proposals. Inevitably, these networks of regulators built upon their previous work and existing technical knowledge, giving proposals a kind of evolutionary technocratic dynamic.[135] While the upper echelons of the hierarchies of finance ministries and central banks participated in G7 meetings and preparations, those at lower ranks tended to get more involved with the specialist detailed work of the Basle Committee, the Paris Club, specialist G10 and IMF committees, and various specialist working parties.[136] Consequently, the G7 process has acted as the most senior of a number of overlapping technocratic transgovernmental networks that are in turn often embedded in their hierarchies of national administrative structures. Many of the more junior officials involved in specialist Basle committee or G10 work, were directly answerable to the finance ministry and central bank deputies who prepared G7 agendas. The deputies themselves rarely involved themselves in the technical specifics of the work of more specialist regulators and have largely restricted themselves to setting strategic priorities and deadlines. In effect, the G7 have increasingly delegated technical detail to more specialist transgovernmental problem-solving networks, resembling those described by Anne-Marie Slaughter,[137] with the G7 itself assuming the role of a senior or co-ordinating transgovernmental coalition exercising a loose oversight function, setting agendas, priorities and deadlines for the technical work of these networks. Transgovernmentalism has consequently become considerably more complex and stratified in the time since Keohane and Nye laid out the definitive account of this kind of activity. A key challenge for analysts therefore is to reflect and explain the increasingly complex overlapping nature of transgovernmentalism and transgovernmental networks by creating typologies and identifying the different levels at which they operate and how they interact. Senior or master transgovernmental coalitions such as the G7, predominate in a particular issue area and operate as first among equals, offering strategic direction to a series of more specialist and partially autonomous junior transgovernmental networks that engage in technical problem solving. The defining characteristic of 'master transgovernmental coalitions' such as the Group of Seven, is that they retain the overriding transgovernmental characteristic of like-minded senior officials from comparable domestic agencies collaborating so as to maximize their influence collectively over a particular transnational issue area – in this case finance. Complex, overlapping, but stratified, transgovernmentalism involves a functional and specialist division of labour between technical problem solvers and technically minded but more senior strategic priority setters and is a direct response to the process of 'decentralized globalization' and the emergence of global finance as an increasingly complex technical system. In the process, the G7 have been quite successful in depoliticizing inherently political issues and institutionalizing them as technocratic matters, creating an issue area that is difficult for outsiders to penetrate or influence. This will be discussed in more detail in Chapter 7.

Conclusions

Analysis of G7 transgovernmentalism in terms of the four spatial dimensions discussed here, helps us to understand how the Group of Seven operate as a transgovernmental coalition. In the context of decentralized globalization, the audiences finance ministries and central banks may wish to influence are not just other domestic state bureaucracies, as suggested in Keohane and Nye's original discussion of transgovernmentalism, but also domestic electorates and societal interests, whose expectations and perceptions they will seek to shape. Likewise, in a quite different dynamic and given transgovernmentalism's overriding characteristic of small group collegiality, finance ministries and central banks have also sought to create internal consensual positions, prior to collectively promoting those positions in wider multilateral institutional settings, or to influence the priorities, mandates and agendas of a whole host of other bodies involved in global and international financial governance – fourth-dimensional diplomacy. Finally, the emergence of transnationalized financial markets and the risk of contagious financial crises that spread quickly, often sees finance ministries and central banks seeking to communicate collectively with financial markets as transborder spaces, to provide them with reassurance and collective messages concerning future policy intentions – third-dimensional diplomacy. In the context of 'decentralized globalization', finance ministries and central banks have multiple incentives to engage in transgovernmentalism so as to collectively maximize their influence with the multiple authorities and spaces that comprise the global financial system.

Contemporary global financial governance depends on consensus. Consensus is crucial because of the need for a variety of states and bodies to implement shared initiatives if the omnipresent threat of systemic contagion and financial crisis is to be minimized, and because the diffused nature of decision making across a number of specialist bodies means that no one actor can control the entire complex of global financial governance. Crucially, the technically specialist nature of finance as an emerging technical system has also seen technocrats use argument and reason as guiding precepts of debate and deliberation out of respect for one another's professional expertise and the collegiality this engenders.[138] This has been particularly evident in the operation of the network of G7 deputies who have engaged in a technical process of argumentation and deliberation, contributing to the G7's transgovernmental characteristics. These processes of deliberation and respect for technical authority enable smaller states to display leadership at G7 meetings if they have capable personnel who are able to advance convincing arguments and ideas. However, this does not mean the G7 operate as a concert of equal international powers as John Kirton has suggested. International financial affairs continue to be characterized by some fundamental asymmetries between the United States and other states. Even if technical deliberations appear to involve a degree of equality between the finance ministries and central banks, these deliberations do not take place on a level playing field and the US continues to enjoy a number of privileges, including a substantial power of veto.

In this chapter, I have suggested that the Group of Seven resemble a 'senior transgovernmental coalition' that operates in the context of a stratified technical transgovernmental governance system characterized by hierarchy and a complex division of labour. Increasingly, the G7 finance ministries and central banks oversee a range of more junior but highly specialized technical transgovernmental networks. Complex stratified transgovernmentalism of this sort has proved to be a very effective way of channelling policy debates on crucial global governance questions and determining which social and political interests participate and are included in a given policy area, and just as crucially which are excluded. Acting as a senior transgovernmental coalition the G7 finance ministries and central banks have ring-fenced global financial governance, vesting control in the hand of technocratic elites, while making financial governance practically impenetrable for a broader range of social and political constituencies. The discussion will now turn to the implications of this for the issues of macroeconomic governance and the global financial architecture.

6 The Group of Seven and macroeconomic governance

Discourse, declaratory policy and market supremacy

Since the 1970s and the collapse of the Bretton Woods exchange rate regime, the world's leading finance ministries and central banks have concerned themselves with two principal areas of activity at their meetings. First, they have continuously discussed and reviewed macroeconomic performance and policy in their own economies, examining how this has contributed to the performance of the world economy. Second, they have monitored the stability of the international monetary and financial system, seeking to identify and minimize threats to systemic stability, as well as periodically reviewing the design and functioning of the system as a whole, albeit in a gradualist incremental fashion. This chapter looks at the G7's treatment of the first of these areas over the last decade. The second area of activity is also touched upon in this chapter because liquidity levels, capital flows and currency valuations are crucial component parts of the macroeconomic picture of any state, but the issue of systemic design and financial (in)stability is primarily dealt with in the next chapter.

As the last chapter established, G7 meetings involve a specific routine. They begin with a process of multilateral surveillance, whereby countries expose their macroeconomic and exchange rate policies to collective scrutiny and comments. Surveillance, or peer review, helps to maintain macroeconomic discipline, assists in the identification of exchange rate misalignments and generally frames deliberations on macroeconomic and exchange rate issues at G7 meetings. In this chapter, macroeconomic discussions and outcomes at G7 meetings throughout the last decade are tracked in a chronological fashion and three specific questions are explored. First, what contribution do G7 deliberations make to macroeconomic governance in the G7? Second, what is the biggest single influence on G7 deliberations on macroeconomic matters and subsequent outcomes – key state–society coalitions, the shared social practices and causal beliefs of finance ministry and central bank elites, or the strategic interests of the United States? Third, what does this tell us about prevailing patterns of power and authority in macroeconomic governance?

The chapter is divided into four sections. The first three sections reflect the G7's three principal macroeconomic activities over the last decade. Section one examines G7 collective discourse on macroeconomic conditions, priorities and challenges as expressed through G7 statements. The next section looks at the continuous monitoring of major currency exchange rates and collective G7 policy that has periodically emerged from this monitoring process. The third section considers several recent episodes of concerted interest rate easing and looks at the factors that influenced and shaped G7 deliberations and action on interest rates. The final section briefly comments on the G7 process's relationship with the act of monetary union in Europe, which has irrevocably changed monetary and fiscal politics in three of the Group of Seven's members.

Discourse construction and the reinforcement of macroeconomic discipline

At the end of the 1980s, European countries were managing exchange rates within the narrow bands of the exchange rate mechanism of the European Monetary System, while the US, Japan and Germany briefly flirted with an informal system of currency reference ranges, following the Louvre accord of 1987.[1] However, efforts to manage exchange rates were soon replaced by a more explicit focus on the delivery of domestic price stability. Macroeconomic discipline was progressively institutionalized over the course of the 1990s, as evidenced by the rise of central bank independence and fiscal rules. Private international capital flows grew exponentially following capital account liberalization in Japan and Europe in the second half of the 1980s, and the brave new world of international finance convinced G7 policy-makers of their limited capacity to manage exchange rates, especially after the ERM crisis of 1992 (see Chapter 4).

At the same time, policy-makers became convinced of the importance of achieving macroeconomic credibility by signalling their intention to deliver macroeconomic discipline to private international investors. In this respect, the institutional fixes favoured by G7 policy-makers of central bank independence and fiscal rules that targeted and institutionalized low inflation and low budget deficits were a message to institutional investors designed to symbolize policy-makers' 'good' intentions.[2] Inflation and current and projected budget deficits are the macroeconomic outcomes most damaging to the long-term returns private investors can expect on investments and are therefore the indicators monitored most by institutional investors.[3] In short, the drive towards macroeconomic 'credibility' and the series of social relationships this has entailed, has involved macroeconomic policy coming to reflect the concerns and priorities of transnational institutional investors rather more than those of national citizens who do not have significant capital investments. Moreover, transnational investors are effectively engaged in a continuous ongoing referendum on national policies and policy-making, through their buying and selling activities and through the public statements of prominent market spokespeople who provide continuous analyses of prevailing market sentiment in relation to particular national economies (see Chapter 5).

For most of the 1990s, G7 finance ministers and central bank governors promoted and facilitated this narrow anti-inflationary focus for macroeconomic policy.[4] The prioritization of low inflation has had the effect of strengthening the finance ministries and central banks' hand in relation to other sections of the state apparatus and created a buffer zone or institutional distance between societal interests and politicians and technocratic policy-makers. Freed from the constraint of having to balance the interests of a range of constituencies in their decision making, macroeconomic policy-makers have had more scope to base their decisions on their own causal beliefs, social practices and professional norms and less on political pressures and considerations.[5]

A collective G7 discourse emphasizing there was no alternative to macroeconomic discipline was repeatedly evident in G7 statements in the 1990s. This was an explicit effort to set limits to what was thinkable and achievable in macroeconomic policy, and to protect what were in most cases the relatively recently won institutional gains of central bank independence and fiscal rules.[6] Finance ministries and central banks sought to externalize their shared beliefs, spreading the message of macroeconomic discipline to other domestic actors who did not necessarily share their commitment to low inflation and fiscal austerity. With the collective expertise of the G7 finance ministries and central banks promoting this message, and with this being backed by private financial investors and analysts, it became difficult for other state actors to dispute such a message. G7 statements on macroeconomic policy were primarily designed to influence the expectations of other domestic and wider societal actors by emphasizing that macroeconomic austerity was the norm throughout the G7. In this respect, those state agencies charged with the delivery of price stability, clearly had a shared interest in publicly emphasizing to electorates and other domestic actors that all G7 states were committed to the pursuit of macroeconomic austerity. It was for this purpose that G7 meetings were principally used in the 1990s and the construction of a specific sound money discourse was the G7's principal contribution to macroeconomic governance throughout the 1990s.

G7 macroeconomic discourse 1990–8

The most commonly cited G7 policy objective in the 1990s was non-inflationary global growth and the decade began with the G7 publicly warning of price pressures and the need for vigilance against inflation.[7] By September 1990, the fear of inflation intensified due to oil price rises associated with the situation in the Gulf following the Iraqi invasion of Kuwait. In these circumstances the message of the finance ministers and central bank governors was that stability-oriented monetary policies and sound fiscal policies constituted the correct response, because this would guard against inflation, reducing the risk of lower growth.[8] In other words, in 1990, low inflation was seen as a route to higher growth and therefore as the principal macroeconomic priority across the G7.

Following the Gulf War, the finance ministers and central bank governors noted the persistence of high real interest rates. The route to lower real interest rates was identified as involving a medium-term fiscal strategy of consolidation and deficit reduction that provided the global basis for higher savings and lower interest rates.[9] By the start of 1992 the ministers and governors were expressing concern at slow rates of growth, but emphasized that the outlook remained positive because inflation expectations had eased and wage and price pressures had declined in most countries. The general tone of the G7 message throughout 1992 was that fiscal deficit reduction through medium-term consolidation strategies was central to economic performance and growth, because it reduced governments' call on private savings. It was however conceded that those countries that had been more successful in bringing deficits down might look at how expenditure might be targeted at strengthening demand, enhancing growth and productivity, but that crucially expenditures needed to be kept under control and should operate within the context of medium-term consolidation strategies. These sentiments can be viewed as an attempt to keep other bureaucracies and interest groups' public expenditure expectations low. In monetary policy, the priority highlighted was the achievement of low inflation as a pre-requisite for lower interest rates, which in turn were seen as the engine of growth. In short, containing inflation and deficit reduction were repeatedly emphasized as macroeconomic priorities in the first half of the 1990s, and as crucial pre-requisites for sustainable growth.[10]

In the second half of the 1990s, the Clinton administration's deficit reduction efforts were repeatedly congratulated and endorsed by the finance ministries and central bank governors' statements. The United States pointed to successful deficit reduction as evidence they were beginning to 'put their own house in order'. A G7 statement from February 1995 made the point that there was 'a fundamental need for continued fiscal consolidation beyond fiscal windfalls from cyclical rebounds'.[11] In other words, the principled commitment to deficit reduction as a principle of good macroeconomic management went beyond the vagaries of increased tax revenues brought about by economic growth. After 1997, the G7 continued to endorse fiscal consolidation and low inflation, but G7 statements on macroeconomic policy also became increasingly self-congratulatory. They highlighted the progress made towards improved fiscal positions and low inflation throughout the G7, but pointed to the need for structural reform of labour and financial markets.[12]

Domestic politics, peer pressure and the use of macroeconomic discourse during 1998

By the start of 1998 the economic situation in G7 countries was quite divergent. With the exception of Japan, which was suffering from a chronic shortage of domestic demand, all the G7 countries had pursued low inflation and fiscal consolidation throughout the 1990s, albeit with quite differing outcomes. The US, the UK and Canada had experienced rapid and sustained growth, while inflationary pressures were less then previous experiences would have suggested. In contrast, France, Germany and Italy had experienced low levels of growth, as the pursuit of both low inflation and fiscal consolidation in the lead up to EMU appeared to have contributed to lower than expected growth and persistent unemployment. However, the G7 statement issued in February 1998 advocated no macroeconomic response to continuing European unemployment. Rather the emphasis was placed on further structural reforms, especially of the labour market as a means of creating jobs.[13] Certainly, there was no denouncement of the focus on low inflation and fiscal consolidation, or the extent to which these objectives were pursued. Instead, the European finance ministries and central banks preferred to highlight labour market governance – a policy process over which they had limited control. In traditionally corporatist Europe, powerful trade unions and other social partners have ensured that labour market reform has been a protracted and negotiated process. However, European finance ministries and central banks have occasionally been happy to endorse the message of structural reform coming from the Anglo-Saxon countries, especially when it has deflected attention away from the role macroeconomic policy can play in restoring growth and generating jobs. Vague endorsements of the need for future structural reform of continental European economies have therefore protected hard-won gains the finance ministries and central banks have made in the context of the EMU process, in the form of central bank independence and fiscal rules. Furthermore, in the lead up to European Monetary Union, the finance ministries and central banks had an interest in ring-fencing macroeconomic policy, so they could meet the Maastricht convergence criteria on budget deficits and inflation rates. Emphasizing the importance of structural reform in restoring growth had the effect of putting more critical voices on macroeconomic austerity, such as trade unions, on the back foot.[14] In effect, the G7 process was used as part of a collective transgovernmental strategy by European finance ministries and central banks to protect and reinforce macroeconomic discipline during 1998.

The notion of a macroeconomic sound money consensus is most difficult to apply to Japan. Japan found itself in exceptional economic circumstances in the second half of the 1990s. Growth was non-existent and consumer demand had all but collapsed. Faced with this situation, the rest of the G7 urged Japan to administer expansionary fiscal measures and structural reform of its financial system including a series of big bang financial reforms in the first half of 1998. Peer pressure was applied by the G7, but precise demands concerning the size of any fiscal stimulus were avoided. In accordance with the G7's powerful sense of appropriate behaviour, the finance ministries and central banks tended to concentrate their recommendations and comments on the overall orientation of monetary and fiscal policy rather than becoming too involved in the specifics and the politics of national policies. In this respect, G7 activity on macroeconomic policy most commonly takes the form of suasion and exchange of opinion rather than policy co-ordination, bargaining or horse trading over national policies.

Unfortunately, in the Japanese case forthcoming elections limited the extent to which the ruling LDP were able to pursue fiscal activism, although following a G7 meeting in London in February 1998, Koichi Kato, Secretary General of the LDP, conceded that extra spending and further tax cuts might be considered in April and May of that year. The application of collective G7 pressure on any one of its members can therefore have very real effects, although this is difficult to measure in any precise fashion, because the most common effect of such pressure is to trigger, or change the terms of, domestic policy debates, which can themselves turn out to be quite protracted. When such international peer pressure is more or less unanimous, it is hard to resist. A Japanese stimulus package of ¥10,000 billion, including ¥7,000 billion of tax cuts, followed in the autumn of 1998 under a new prime minister and collective G7 pressure and sentiment helped to convince the new administration of the importance of fiscal activism.

The sound money consensus under strain

By the late 1990s, G7 discourse had emphasized the fight against inflation as the principal macroeconomic policy objective for nearly twenty years. By 1998 however, inflation was low across the G7 countries. Two exogenous shocks then shook the international economic system, leading to a change in emphasis and tone in macroeconomic discourse. However, it remains difficult to make precise assertions on the full extent and nature of this change. In particular, it is difficult to find evidence to support the claim that the G7 finance ministries and central banks have abandoned the basic causal beliefs they have held about macroeconomic policy for the last twenty years, or that they have adopted qualitatively different ideas that constitute a new consensus.[15] Based on the lack of any attempt at far-reaching institutional reform to reverse the institutionalization of macroeconomic discipline that characterized the 1990s, the evidence would seem to suggest that there was a mere temporary abandonment of the focus on low inflation as a short-term pragmatic response to the particular economic circumstances at the end of the twentieth and beginning of the twenty-first centuries. Certainly, the finance ministries and central banks have been increasingly prepared to accept that macroeconomic policy can play a role in restoring economic growth, but this is not the same as suggesting that we are witnessing a return to some form of macroeconomic Keynesianism or global locomotive strategy.[16]

The change in tone in the G7's macroeconomic discourse first came in September 1998, when financial contagion spread from South East Asia to Latin America and Russia. A predominantly regional financial crisis had become a global one, and the G7 became concerned that financial turmoil was having a detrimental impact on their own economies.[17] On 14 September 1998, the G7 released a statement pointing out that the balance of risk in the world economy had changed.[18] This appeared to be a reference to the fact that having spent the previous twenty years primarily fighting inflation, the finance ministers and central bank governors recognized that the biggest threat to their economies was falling growth, brought about by a fall in world-wide economic activity.

A follow-up statement in October 1998 pointed out that the UK, US and Canada all had obligations to take appropriate action to maintain conditions for sustainable growth, while the European economies had to maintain robust domestic demand and Japan had to take measures to boost domestic demand-led growth.[19] Indeed, all the G7 central banks moved to ease interest rates before the end of the year. However, Peter Hall's distinction between first-, second- and third-order policy changes is useful here.[20] Simple interest rate adjustments are more indicative of first-order policy change, rather than more far-reaching third-order paradigm shifts, or even second-order changes to the policy frameworks, instruments and institutional mandates that frame a given policy area. These types of institutional second-order changes have been conspicuous by their absence despite increasing G7 references to growth in their macroeconomic discourse.

The shift in the G7's macroeconomic discourse was consolidated further in April 1999. The G7 statement of 26 April 1999 referred to a growth strategy based on a strengthening of domestic demand in the context of a favourable outlook for continued price stability.[21] Moreover, there was for the first time in the April 1999 statement, evidence of a gradual sea change in the G7's attitude to macroeconomic austerity in the developing world, which had traditionally been the option favoured in terms of macroeconomic responses to financial crises. At the end of a statement under the heading *social principles*, the G7 emphasized the need to ensure the protection of the most vulnerable and called for greater IMF and World Bank collaboration on public expenditures and the social impact of fiscal choices.[22] This was undoubtedly a minor concession, but nevertheless it was the first acknowledgement that fiscal policy was more than simply a technical matter, to be used to restore financial stability in crisis-affected countries, but should also be considered in terms of its social impact.

Clearly, changing the course of a bureaucracy like the IMF is not something that can be achieved overnight, and the process of changing established mind-sets, as Joseph Stiglitz has pointed out, will be a long and arduous one,[23] but if the G7 as the leading IMF shareholders are prepared to support work that looks at how public expenditure can be targeted towards alleviating social distress, then that is indicative of a desirable change in priority in macroeconomic policy. At the very least, it should ensure that the macroeconomic policy prescriptions recommended in future IMF structural adjustment programmes will not simply be universal standard prescriptions generated on autopilot by a prevailing mind-set. Indeed, the concessions made in the April statement were further built upon the following September, when the G7 welcomed the IMF's decision to replace the Enhanced Structural Adjustment Facility with a new Poverty Reduction and Growth Facility, which was to include more effective targeting of fiscal expenditures towards poverty reduction, especially in basic health and education provision, the treatment of AIDS and measures to improve child survival.[24] However, this was accompanied by references to the need to improve monitoring and control over fiscal expenditures, suggesting that sound money and fiscal consolidation were still on the G7 and IMF agenda. The key for future world macroeconomic governance will be how the inevitable conflicts and tensions that arise between the tighter control of public expenditure and the targeting of poverty will be managed.

A marginal improvement in the economic outlook across the G7 by the start of 2000 suggested that the G7 finance ministries and central banks had certainly not abandoned their commitment to tackling inflation. The G7 statement of January 2000 pointed to the need for the US and Canada to follow prudent monetary policy and maintain fiscal consolidation, while in the light of improved UK growth the importance of the Bank of England meeting its inflation target was also emphasized.[25] The sound money discourse was revisited the following April when it was highlighted that in the case of the United States, Canada and the UK, fiscal surplus policies should not be relaxed and monetary policy should continue to be prudent. Moreover, in the case of Europe there was less emphasis on using macroeconomic policy to stimulate demand.[26] In other words, with the notable exception of Japan, which had to all intents and purposes entered a period of deflation and now had a zero interest rate policy, the G7 were beginning to re-emphasize the importance of low inflation following recovery, and the management of the fall-out from the Asian financial crisis. Indeed, the emphasis on the need for sound macroeconomic policies and the need to keep inflation low was evident in G7 statements in 2000 and 2001, despite slowing US growth (and references to the need for monetary policy in the US to target both growth and price stability).

A cautious approach to inflation continued to be evident in G7 discourse right up to September 2001 and the second shock to rock the international economic system in the space of three years. In other words, far from abandoning their focus on low inflation, the G7 finance ministries and central banks, with the exception of Japanese authorities, gradually returned to their emphasis on price stability in their collective discourse, once the initial negative affects of the Asian financial crisis on the world economic outlook had been mitigated through some short-term expansionary macroeconomic policies.

Following the attacks on the United States by al-Qaeda, the G7 finance ministries and central banks responded swiftly, releasing a statement in an effort to protect economic confidence in which they stated that central banks would provide liquidity so as to ensure financial markets operated in an orderly fashion.[27] Subsequent statements made reference to the need to take action to preserve growth, but G7 statements after 9/11 began to contain less and less information on G7 macro-economic policies.[28] By the start of 2003 in the context of a low interest rate, low inflation environment there were few references to macroeconomic stimulus in G7 statements. Increasing emphasis was placed on structural reform of labour, product and capital markets as a means of generating growth as it was recognized that the potential for macroeconomic expansion had been exhausted. Indeed, the G7 even took the opportunity to re-emphasize their 'commitment to sustainable public finances and price stability'.[29] Moreover, the release of a growth strategy document following a G7 meeting in Dubai in 2003 suggested that demand side problems had been addressed and longer term supply side impediments were where future challenges and impediments to growth lay.[30] Despite recent growth-oriented policies therefore, finance ministries and central banks remain reluctant to travel too far down the route of macroeconomic stimulus.

A variety of measures in individual countries were outlined in the Dubai document, which the finance ministries and central banks will champion in their own domestic context. These included tort reform in the US, labour market and pensions reform in Germany, public sector and health care reform in France, pension reform in Italy, structural reform in Japan, and skill and productivity improvement in the UK. Moreover, there were proposals from the G7 to introduce a form of supply side surveillance to accompany macroeconomic surveillance revolving around certain shared benchmarks.[31] This is designed to create international norms of structural reform, which the finance ministries and central banks can promote, despite having only limited influence over domestic reform processes. Clearly, there is variation in the types of structural reform being advocated by the finance ministries and central banks, but all are designed to encourage the emergence of more flexible market-orientated societies.

In Europe, debate has raged about the viability of the growth and stability pact, while poor growth performance in both France and Germany has ensured that both countries have breached the terms of the pact.[32] However, reform of the growth and stability pact has entailed some relatively modest adjustments to existing rules. As the designers of the pact, the European finance ministries and central banks appear to see little need for fundamental reform and seemingly remain committed to the principles of fiscal discipline and consolidation, albeit not necessarily the narrow 3 per cent of GDP criteria, but rather individual calculations for annual deficits based on levels of total public debt.[33] The principal criticisms of European monetary and macroeconomic frameworks have come from the US and the UK, but within the G7 setting the extent of that criticism has been surprisingly muted owing to the collegiate nature of the process.[34]

There is also little evidence to suggest that the consensus of the 1990s referred to in Chapter 4 has been replaced by a qualitatively new Keynesian-style consensus.[35] Certainly, macroeconomic policy became more growth focused throughout the G7 between 1998 and 2002, but this was a specific response to two international economic shocks, rather than any principled commitment to Keynesian-style macroeconomics, or the rejection of the anti-inflationary sound money bias of neo-classical economics. There has been no public denouncement of the excessive anti-inflationary focus of the 1990s. Admittedly, the United States has gone from fiscal surplus back to a position of deficit and this would appear to be at odds with the policies and discourse of the 1990s, but this is more to do with the political pragmatism of an administration that has on the whole appeared to have little interest in economic policy and has adopted the traditional Republican stance of lower taxes and higher military expenditures, with little thought for how this fits into a wider economic strategy. Certainly, the practice of persisting with tax cuts when recovery was well under way was contrary to the counter-cyclical role of fiscal policy envisaged by Keynes.

Currently, the biggest threat to 'sound money' as a principle for international monetary governance has come not from the finance ministries and central banks' own learning processes and exchanges, or through increased resistance from a coalition of wider societal actors, but from the Bush administration's 'securitization agenda', which sees globalization not just in terms of neo-liberal economic benefits, but also as a series of security threats and challenges, which override economic imperatives and necessitate military activism that requires funding.[36] The US remains extraordinary and is the country least constrained by prevailing international economic discourse, particularly when there is a Republican president in the White House. In particular, US governments continue to have what Benjamin Cohen calls the 'power to delay' macroeconomic adjustment by funding deficits with inflows of foreign capital (see Chapter 3).[37] One manifestation of the securitization agenda was the downgrading of the Treasury department, particularly under Paul O'Neill, as military and security imperatives rather than economic ones determined the foreign policies of the Bush administration, contrasting starkly with Treasury (Rubin–Summers) inspired economic policies under Clinton.[38] Stimulus-oriented US macroeconomic policies have largely been engineered by White House advisors, but there has been no ringing endorsement of these policies in G7 statements. Rather, Japanese and European officials continue to express reservations about the size of US budget and current account deficits, as well as the falling dollar.[39] Indeed, many at the Treasury appear to have had reservations about recent policies and O'Neill's resignation in December 2002 was a direct result of continuing differences with the White House, particularly over further tax cuts. The finance ministries and central banks themselves have not turned their back on 'sound money' principles, but are operating in the context of reckless White House-engineered deficit budgeting to support equally reckless military campaigns.

That the White House has been able to downgrade the Treasury so easily, is due to the unique circumstances of US domestic politics. Neo-conservatives were able to pursue the securitization agenda, partly because the sound money focus is not as heavily institutionalized in US policy frameworks as in other G7 countries, and partly because of the continuing power of the US to delay macroeconomic adjustment by attracting capital inflows from abroad. Yet these developments should not be used to make the argument that the finance ministries and central banks have abandoned their sound money focus, or their capacity to pursue this agenda. The experiences of the Bush administration merely reinforces arguments about the continuing exceptionalness of the United States and the continuing capacity of powerful political coalitions in the US to step outside the financial orthodoxy that continues to bind the rest of the world.

Currently, the US and the UK have been keen that both Japan and continental European economies assume more active roles as locomotives for the world economy, and while they have been keen to promote structural reform, they have been aware that hectoring the European Central Bank to ease interest rates at G7 meetings would prove counter-productive and might produce intransigence as the ECB strives to consolidate its independence and anti-inflationary credibility. More generally, there is a shared understanding that states should refrain from making specific demands of one another's interest rate policies, although the expression of general opinions concerning the overall orientation of policy is acceptable. In this respect, the US and the UK have both been critical of the restrictive nature of the fiscal stability pact, but have avoided being too strident in those criticisms. In other words, shared understandings and a general sense of collegiality amongst the finance ministries and central banks have meant that they continue to avoid making explicit specific demands of one another's macroeconomic policies, reflecting the consensus-oriented nature of the G7 process. Shared social practices and notions of appropriate codes of behaviour continue to display a strong determining influence on the collective behaviour of the G7 and consequently on G7 outcomes.

Discourse and the macroeconomic contribution of the G7 process

To summarize therefore, as Bergsten and Henning noted in their 1996 study, macroeconomic policy has largely been immobilized by the rise of central bank independence and fiscal rules.[40] Little or no negotiation over the formal detail of macroeconomic policies takes place at G7 meetings and the kind of co-ordination that characterized the first decade of the G7's existence is largely off the agenda. Instead, the principal function of G7 meetings in relation to macroeconomic policy has been to signal and publicize strategic priorities. This has had the effect of buttressing or reinforcing the courses of action that finance ministries and central banks were already intent on pursuing, and has proved a useful strategic device for providing mutual endorsement of policy positions from peers at other finance ministries and central banks. Exchanges of information and opinion have also had the benefit of increasing the pool of information on which macroeconomic authorities base their decisions. Occasionally, when a collective G7 verdict has been unanimously critical of domestic economic performance, as in the case of Japan in 1998, G7 statements have triggered, or given a sense of urgency to, domestic policy debates, both stimulating and consolidating domestic policy change.

In other words, given the relative immobilization of macroeconomic policy, the principal contribution of the round of G7 meetings to macroeconomic governance has been in producing a discourse that sets the parameters for and defines the terms on which macroeconomic policy debates are conducted, while providing signals and reassurance for markets concerning policy-makers' future intentions. The Group of Seven's interactions and exchanges reflect the growing autonomy of finance ministries and central banks in national macroeconomic policy. Their interactions are increasingly sectoral and transgovernmental in nature, reflecting their increasing isolation and insulation from the rest of the policy process, with the notable exception of the US. This has made the possibility of cross-sectoral co-ordination that can facilitate interventionist, fine-tuned and negotiated Keynesian-style re-distributive solutions to particular policy problems less likely.[41] This has been particularly apparent, as we shall see, in the field of exchange rate policy, resulting in market-determined outcomes and enhanced market discipline, contributing to the institutionalization and reinforcement of a decidedly neo-liberal regime in global financial governance.

For most of the last decade and beyond, the G7 have restricted themselves to promoting low inflation and fiscal consolidation in their discourse. Subsequent success in achieving low inflation, combined with two shocks to the international economic system, saw the collective focus of the G7 finance ministries and central banks shift to more growth-oriented macroeconomic policies. Certainly, the finance ministries and central banks appear to have adopted a more pragmatic approach. They are less dogmatic in their commitment to macroeconomic discipline than they were for most of the 1990s and recently have been more willing to explore the potential of go-for-growth policies. However, the current situation seems to involve an acceptance that the potential for macroeconomic stimulus has been exhausted. The finance ministries and central banks have consequently again shifted their attention, this time to the more difficult task of structural reform. Moreover, evidence to suggest that the finance ministries and central banks have completely abandoned their attachment to low inflation and sound money as the principal objectives of macroeconomic policy, is at best anecdotal. Recently, inflation has not been a major problem for the finance ministries and central banks, but there are precious few signs that they are considering reforming their macroeconomic frameworks in the direction of more permanently growth-friendly arrangements.

The austerity consensus of the 1990s has created economic and social problems – lower than expected growth, persistent unemployment and widening inequality – and it may be under strain, but it does not as yet appear to have been replaced by anything economically coherent, while the institutional fixes it has advocated – independent central banks, fiscal consolidation frameworks and intensified multilateral surveillance mechanisms and codes of practice oriented towards sound money and open markets, remain in place. Ultimately, we are faced with the reality that G7 finance ministries and central banks continue to cling to a mind-set emphasizing the principles of sound money and open markets – a mind-set whose time may have come and gone. However, they appear incapable of thinking more radically or of admitting past mistakes, nor do they appear to have the political inclination to do so, while other actors, with the exception of a White House intent on pursuing a securitization agenda on behalf of a US military–industrial complex, lack the political initiative and resources to challenge the finance ministries and central banks' current intellectual and political monopoly of macroeconomic and financial policies. Finally, a real concern has to be that the kind of incremental adjustments and slow learning processes finance ministries and central banks are predisposed towards, or at least their unwillingness to relinquish closely held beliefs that may no longer apply, may ultimately be insufficient to restore the world economy towards a path of steady sustainable growth and equitable wealth generation. In other words, the G7 finance ministries and central banks are inherently conservative, have an unwillingness to discard what is regarded as legitimate technical knowledge and have a disposition towards refining and building upon that knowledge, which inevitably informs and leaves a lasting imprint on future decisions and development trajectories.[42]

Exchange rate management

The G7 have always been traditionally most active on the issue of exchange rates, primarily because exchange market intervention has been always a relatively secretive policy area where finance ministries and central banks have enjoyed most discretion.[43] Since the initial G7 agreement on the future of the international monetary system at Rambouillet, an informal continuous monitoring process has been assigned to the finance ministries and central banks, so as to ensure that excessive exchange rate movements are avoided, or at least minimized (see Chapter 2). One of the principal functions of the G7 process therefore has been to perform a minimal stabilizing oversight function for an international monetary system consisting of floating exchange rates and large and sometimes volatile private international capital flows. While in the 1980s we saw periodic attempts by the G7 to directly intervene and manage exchange rates, in the 1990s we saw a looser mode of G7 operation, which involved a changing relationship with private international investors.

One of the fundamental purposes of the finance ministries and central banks' surveillance exercise has been to identify sustained and pronounced exchange rate misalignments on the basis of a thorough ongoing review of domestic economic indices. During the 1990s, the G7 increasingly came to rely on declaratory policy. Declaratory policy involves the release of collective public statements that present a particular interpretation of exchange rate patterns to the market. There are several reasons for declaratory policy's rise to prominence. First, the policy instrument traditionally favoured at G7 meetings, foreign exchange market intervention, was partially discredited by events in 1992–3, when US authorities failed to prevent a sharp decline in the value of the dollar, while repeated interventions by European Central Banks failed to prevent turbulence in the ERM, resulting in considerable losses for the central banks. In contrast, all seventeen episodes of concerted intervention between 1985 and 1991 had been successful in moving exchange rates in the desired direction. The view that intervention could only have short-term impact and only in special circumstances, became the accepted wisdom. Second, the rise of central bank independence involving committees of technocrats reaching collective decisions to deliver a domestic price stability mandate, has meant that using interest rates to target particular exchange rates is off the agenda, while the co-ordination of interest rate decisions is, as we shall see, institutionally problematic. Third, as we saw in Chapter 4, there is a basic belief, or faith that markets will deliver efficient rational outcomes, which means that intervention to manage exchange rates is viewed as undesirable and is generally rejected. All of these factors leave declaratory policy, as an effective appeal to market operators' better nature so as to curb excessive price movements, as the policy option that sits most comfortably with policy-makers' current beliefs and the domestic institutional arrangements that reflect those beliefs.

Various G7 statements explicitly laid out the approach to exchange rates throughout the 1990s. For example, the finance ministers' report to the leaders at Lyon in 1996 pointed out that flexibility was a feature of the system because unanticipated events occur, economic fundamentals change, and national financial and economic developments are sufficiently different that they require policies to be able to respond.[44] Co-ordinated government intervention to influence exchange rates was rejected unless there was a clear agreement that a currency's value was not reflective of underlying domestic fundamentals and was therefore misaligned. When a consensus is reached, G7 authorities issue a statement in an effort to persuade market actors to correct the perceived misalignment, as well as engaging in some minor exchange market interventions.[45]

Based on his prior experience at Goldman Sachs, former Treasury secretary Robert Rubin believed that the trading flows in foreign exchange markets were:

> too vast for interventions to have more than a momentary effect, except in very unusual circumstances. Currency levels reflect the markets expectations – and the realities – of a country's fundamental economic situation relative to the economic fundamentals of other countries' fiscal conditions, interest rates, inflation, and growth.[46]

It is beliefs such as these and a subsequent unwillingness to proactively manage exchange rates that has meant that today exchange rates essentially constitute market players' judgement on the suitability of national policies.

Exchange rate abstention 1993–4

During 1993–4, exchange rates were largely ignored in G7 statements due to a difference of opinion between US and Japanese authorities.[47] Upon becoming US Treasury Secretary in February 1993, Lloyd Bentsen indicated that he thought there was a case for a higher yen at a press conference at the National Press Club in Washington.[48] The yen subsequently rose, leading to a Japanese perception that Bentsen had intentionally encouraged a yen appreciation so as to improve US export performance. While US policy-makers maintained that major currencies were roughly in line with fundamentals, the Japanese asserted that the rise in the yen had been excessive.[49] Consequently, differing interpretations of the scope and extent of the subsequent rise in the value of the yen were the principal cause of the US–Japanese tensions. In other words, it was not the fundamental approach to exchange rates that was the cause of disagreement, but differing interpretations of economic data, illustrating how disputes and differences exist within the parameters of a broad G7 consensus on the approach to exchange rates.

In this respect, a great deal of deliberation at G7 meetings involves differing interpretations of economic data and differing diagnoses of exchange rate movements. This kind of arguing and deliberation is distinct from straightforward intergovernmental bargaining in the sense that the positions expressed are technical ones, rather than simply political ones, although clearly technical evidence can be manipulated to suit a politically convenient case. However, there are limits to which individuals can adopt politically convenient interpretations of data where exchange rates are concerned. G7 meetings, as we established in the last chapter, are characterized by a technical discourse, while the participants tend to have similar, or at least comparable levels of expertise, and so consequently tend to speak to one another as equals. Their authority is a function of their personal performance and their ability to advance technically credible and convincing analyses over time. Continuous attempts to make politically convenient arguments where exchange rates are concerned, with insufficient attention being paid to the underlying data, will undermine the credibility and track record of the individual concerned, not only with their peers, but also with key players in foreign exchange markets, who monitor policy-makers' every word on exchange rate matters. Consequently the technical authority of these individuals, or the extent to which others trust in and believe their interpretations, will also decline. Robert Rubin has provided insights into this issue of technical competence and also the ongoing coded third-dimensional diplomacy that means finance ministers have to be extremely vigilant in terms of their comments on exchange rates:

> Because of the Treasury's ability to buy and sell currencies for the purpose of affecting exchange rates, the markets would respond to almost anything I said that seemed to make intervention more or less likely. Affecting exchange rates unintentionally would make me look undisciplined and unsophisticated. My credibility with respect to our currency, could be especially critical if at some subsequent time we had a weak dollar and faced the possibility of a dollar crisis ... My substantive view was that economic fundamentals determine exchange rate levels over time, and that we should focus our attention on strengthening US economic policy and performance, not on influencing the level of the currency.[50]

These comments are also an insight into the unique power of the US Treasury secretary to influence exchange rate movements simply by opening his or her mouth. Unfortunately, the situation is not as straightforward as this might imply. As we shall see, Treasury secretaries are in fact constrained in their capacity to influence the dollar through spoken words and their record over the last decade has been mixed. Indeed we might suggest on the basis of Rubin's comments that the capacity to influence currency valuations through verbal signalling is finite and something to be used sparingly.

The shift to a policy of dollar appreciation

In May 1994, G7 abdication on the yen–dollar issue ended with concerted interventions by the G7 central banks to support the dollar. The US Treasury's position shifted as it began to argue that the dollar's depreciation had gone beyond a level justified by underlying fundamentals. The intervention was accompanied by a two-paragraph statement pointing out that the US administration saw no value in an under-valued currency.[51] After an initial rise, the dollar resumed its downward slide, causing the Treasury Department great frustration at the failure of exchange rates to reflect their analysis of underlying fundamentals. Treasury Secretary Lloyd Bentsen even admitted that he had 'given up trying to anticipate what would happen with regard to the markets'.[52]

Declaratory policy of the sort practised in 1994 (presenting analyses or arguments to the market through public statements – third-dimensional diplomacy) is thought to have added credence if a statement is agreed upon collectively by national authorities with technical expertise on exchange rate matters – the G7 finance ministries and central banks. The problem with declaratory policy, as the experience of the 1990s has demonstrated, is that market participants have on occasion failed to interpret policy-makers' statements correctly or alternatively have simply chosen to ignore or reject policy-makers' arguments, and in the absence of sufficient public financial resources to have a long-term impact in the market (or at least the reluctance to try) policy-makers have simply had to suspend their judgement and accept the market's collective verdict. In such circumstances, market analysts have been quick to rationalize the market response and point to the inadequacy of policy-makers' analysis. This points to an increase in market authority at the expense of public authority as private market analysts have become more prepared to challenge and dispute the judgement of policy-makers. However, the pattern is not absolute. More research is needed not only on the record of market analysts and policy-makers in moving exchange rates, but also the circumstances in which policy-makers have been successful and unsuccessful in moving exchange rates.

It is important to note that the Treasury's capacity to initiate changes in dollar policy is not a constant but varies in accordance with a range of factors, and we must be cautious when generalizing about US power in the field of exchange rate policy. In particular, we need to look at the circumstances in which the Treasury has been both successful and unsuccessful in influencing dollar movements. If, as Peter Gowan has claimed, the US Treasury secretary can talk the dollar up or down simply by opening his or her mouth, then the United States government has an enormous capacity to arbitrarily influence economic conditions throughout the world and can therefore use exchange rate policy to engage in politically advantageous aggressive economic statecraft.[53] However, Gowan's assertions are bold and the extent of US power in dollar policy needs to be debated and explored further.

The reasons for the failure to secure dollar appreciation in 1994 were complex. Most significantly, the United States is not a unitary rational actor in international affairs. Different bureaucracies have different agendas and achieve their objectives to varying degrees in accordance with their resources and the expertise and reputation of key personnel at any one time. In 1994, two notable constraints on the US Treasury were evident. First, following G7 intervention to lower the dollar, US trade officials publicly complained about the closed nature of Japanese markets and their contribution to the US balance of payments deficit.[54] Key players in financial markets subsequently interpreted these complaints as a signal that the US really wanted a lower dollar so as to reduce the trade deficit with Japan. In reality, this situation simply reflected the differing constituencies and priorities of the USTR and the Treasury and poor intra-agency co-ordination in Washington. The Treasury and the Fed's priorities focused on maintaining the value of the dollar, while trade officials were more concerned with the size of the US trade deficit and responding to voices in Congress concerned about the size of that deficit. Notably, neither the Commerce Department nor the USTR were directly represented at G7 meetings in 1994. Ultimately therefore, G7 efforts to initiate dollar appreciation failed because of the actions of US domestic actors that were not even present at the G7 meeting in 1994.

Second, the growth in the foreign exchange market to the point where it has come to resemble an extra-territorial space[55] and the tendency of market actors to scrutinize policy-makers' statements has exacerbated the problems associated with poor intra-agency co-ordination in Washington, especially when contrasting messages from different US agencies have created confusion in the markets. As a consequence of trade officials' actions the dollar resumed its downward slide in 1994, falling to a post-war low of ¥93.365 and DM1.528. Market analysts justified the downward movement of the dollar by referring to concerns that the Fed had not moved sufficiently aggressively to contain inflationary pressures, given the rates of growth in the US economy. Crucially, declaratory exchange rate policy means casts market actors in a dominant role, because it is their collective interpretation that is crucial in determining exchange rate valuations. The point here is that an approach to exchange rates based on a series of subtle nods and winks, together with the presentation of contestable arguments or opinions to the market, is unpredictable, open to interpretation or misinterpretation by markets with regard to authorities' intentions, or markets can simply reject policy-makers' analysis. It is consequently more difficult for US policy-makers to move the dollar exchange rate than is frequently assumed. In particular, the 1994 attempt to instigate an appreciation in the value of the dollar illustrated that exchange rate shifts will not simply occur because the US Treasury wants them to. The US Treasury cannot simply wish exchange rate movements into existence, but has to present a convincing technical case for any exchange rate movement that convinces technical experts at other G7 finance ministries and central banks of the case and more crucially convinces market analysts and sentiment more generally that there are the grounds for such a shift on the basis of review of economic fundamentals and future policy projections. This is a real constraint on the United States and means that exchange rate policy cannot simply be formulated on the basis of US political preferences or strategic objectives. Furthermore, if the markets are sometimes unconvinced even when there is a consensus amongst G7 finance ministries and central banks, then clearly in the absence of G7 consensus it will be even more difficult to persuade the market of a particular case.

The events of 1994 demonstrated that where dimension I exchange rate policy is concerned, successful outcomes are dependent upon other national government agencies in the domestic (dimension II) setting behaving in a fashion that is consistent with an agreed multilateral (dimension I) line, and moreover how this in turn is interpreted in the third-dimensional space of extra-territorial markets. The result is a delicate form of three-way or three-dimensional diplomacy on macroeconomic and exchange rate matters. In the case of the 1994 episode, the interconnections between the various spatial dimensions were clear. US trade officials' statements caused the market to move in the opposite direction to that desired by Treasury officials. The Treasury consequently lost the trust of their G7 finance ministry and central bank colleagues, particularly the Germans, who had only agreed to contribute to the intervention after much US persuasion.[56] The Germans felt that the US had reneged on the G7 consensus. This increased the tension in the dimension I setting and created difficulties for the US Treasury in securing support for future exchange rate ventures. Indeed, the US Treasury attempted to revisit the issue of dollar appreciation at the autumn meeting of the G7 in 1994, but German hostility over the earlier failed attempt prevented the issue being pursued any further. It was a further eight months before the US were able to return to dollar appreciation at a G7 meeting the following April. Significantly, the US had to conduct interventions to support the dollar unilaterally without the support of European central banks in November 1994.[57] This alone was insufficient to move the dollar upwards, suggesting the US needs domestic unanimity, or at least acquiescence, support from other G7 powers and a convincing technical argument to move the dollar.

On 25 April 1995, following a meeting in Washington ahead of the IMF/World Bank spring meeting, a statement was issued by the G7 finance ministers and central bank governors that called for an orderly appreciation of the dollar. The important part of the statement was contained in point 5 and was phrased in the coded language beloved of finance ministers and central bankers. Its target was the foreign exchange market. It read:

> The ministers and governors expressed concerns about recent developments in exchange markets. They agreed that recent developments have gone beyond levels justified by underlying economic conditions in the major countries. They also agreed that orderly reversal of these movements is desirable, would provide a better basis for continued expansion of international trade and investment, and would contribute to our common objectives of sustained non-inflationary growth. They further agreed to strengthen their efforts in reducing internal and external imbalances and to continue to co-operate closely in exchange markets.[58]

The G7 finance ministers and central bank governors were effectively expressing the collective opinion that the continuing slide of the dollar was a misalignment not reflective of underlying economic conditions, and that it needed to be corrected.

The statement and some 'skilled' intervention had the desired effect and a relatively orderly appreciation of the dollar ensued. At the same time an excessive depreciation of the yen was avoided.[59] According to US G7 deputy, Larry Summers, the 1995 realignment of the dollar was achieved through a more selective use of the tool of exchange market intervention. The US authorities intervened on only four occasions in 1995, less than during any other year over the previous decade. This was assisted by 'a co-ordinated signal that meant something' (third-dimensional diplomacy), leading Summers to conclude that 'sometimes less is more'.[60] However, the US and the G7 had been trying to secure a dollar appreciation for over a year, suggesting that it was not achieved with quite the degree of ease Peter Gowan has suggested in his account.[61]

By April 1995, three things had changed in the intervening twelve months. First, the US economy had continued to grow and the inflation the markets feared had not materialized. In other words, there was an even stronger economic argument for dollar appreciation than there had been in 1994 and this was added to by the dollar becoming a much more attractive proposition for Latin American investors following the Mexican peso crisis. Second, the US had spent the eight months since the 1994 autumn G7 meeting reconstructing multilateral consensus. In particular, they were able to convince the Germans of the strong economic case for dollar appreciation in the absence of inflation in the US economy. Third, there was a change in Treasury personnel. Robert Rubin, an urbane career investment banker (ex-Goldman Sachs) had become Treasury secretary. His market experience meant that his words carried more weight with financial markets. Rubin also appeared to have a better relationship with the White House, having briefly worked on the National Economic Council. This meant he was better positioned in Washington policy networks, and both the markets and other US domestic agencies were more likely to accept his views on the need for dollar appreciation. The 1995 dollar appreciation also reaffirmed the point that in a technical area like exchange rate policy, authority is not static but fluctuates over time and is often a function of personal reputation and individual credibility and expertise.

However, the increased authority of Rubin, both domestically and in international markets, together with a better technical argument in favour of dollar appreciation, offer only a partial explanation of the episode. By 1995, the Clinton administration had strong incentives for dollar appreciation that went beyond the Treasury team's own views. A sliding dollar added a risk premium to foreign investments in the US. More notably, it was producing an export boom, rising import prices that brought with them the threat of inflation and a danger that the Federal Reserve would raise short-term interest rates. Nineteen ninety-six was a scheduled election year in the United States. By the second half of the 1990s, 53 per cent of the US electorate owned stocks and shares. Potential interest rate rises threatened stock market performance and therefore the wealth and earnings, through various insurance and pension holdings, of a large swathe of the US electorate.[62] President Clinton's re-election prospects the following year would have been severely damaged by such an outcome. A dollar appreciation on the other hand, would lessen the necessity for interest rate rises by reducing inflationary pressures in the US economy. US domestic politics therefore gave a sense of urgency to the Treasury department's efforts to secure an appreciation of the dollar through the G7 process in 1995. Most importantly, it ensured that Treasury support for a higher dollar would not be undermined by the actions and words of officials from other government departments. Political motivation and a favourable domestic political context came together with a strong technical case to produce the dollar appreciation of 1995.

In other words, a variety of favourable factors in three of the spatial dimensions identified in earlier chapters came together to create the conditions for dollar appreciation in 1995. Certainly the US had both domestic and international political reasons for switching to a strong dollar policy in 1995. But if 1994 demonstrated anything it was that the US Treasury can't simply impose its wishes on the foreign exchange market. Declaratory policy is only successful if there is a credible technical argument for an exchange rate movement. Of course, it is not possible to say whether, in the absence of a strong credible economic argument, we would have seen a dollar appreciation anyway, given the stronger domestic political support in the US for that outcome in 1995. However, given the G7's working method, and the preference for technical argumentation, together with financial markets that seem to respond to individuals with 'market credibility' and 'technical authority' that is established over time, it is doubtful that the US would have been able to initiate an exchange rate change without forwarding a solid convincing technical case for such a movement. Certainly there is little evidence to suggest that the US can arbitrarily influence exchange rates without paying due attention to technical considerations. Indeed what 1994 and 1995 demonstrate is how difficult it is for the US Treasury to move exchange rates. Declaratory policy has been the principal weapon employed by the G7 over the last decade and it relies upon technical authority. To be credible and effective, public G7 statements on exchange rates must pay due attention to the technical case for a particular exchange rate valuation. Without this markets will remain unconvinced, as will other public policy-makers, and the reputation and authority of officials who rely solely on power and exhortation rather than convincing technical arguments, will suffer and diminish accordingly.

Efforts to stabilize the dollar and appreciate the yen 1997–8

The trend of G7-supported dollar appreciation continued until early 1997. At a G7 meeting in Berlin in February 1997, the G7 issued a statement in an effort to stabilize the rise of the dollar initiated in 1995. The statement read:

> We believe the major misalignments noted in our April 1995 communiqué have been corrected. We reaffirmed our views that exchange rates should reflect economic fundamentals and that excess volatility is undesirable. We agreed to monitor developments in the currency markets and to co-operate as appropriate.[63]

The statement expressed the authorities' collective opinion that the predominantly market-led appreciation of the dollar initiated at Washington in 1995, had gone far enough based on the available data on fundamentals. Little in the way of concerted exchange market intervention accompanied the 1997 statement[64] and crucially, the markets were left to either accept or reject the collective view of the G7 authorities. In this case, in contrast to the April 1995 statement, investors rejected authorities' views and the dollar continued to appreciate.

Initially, the market failed to interpret the significance of the coded language in the statement, illustrating how haphazard and precarious this sort of exchange rate diplomacy is. Only in the days after the meeting, when German and Japanese officials emphasized that they wanted a stronger yen, did the market fully appreciate the sentiment of the statement. The yen subsequently rose ¥15 against the dollar, but then slid back and continued its steady long-term depreciation.

Third-dimensional diplomacy or the practice of presenting arguments to market players (declaratory policy) is designed to minimize excessive market movements. The principal means of tackling these excessive movements has been the release of joint statements together with improved data release or increased transparency, thus giving markets more information on the state of economies in an effort to allow them to reach more informed judgements. Ultimately, declaratory policy of this sort is dependent upon investors interpreting policy-makers' statements and agreeing with their diagnosis of underlying fundamentals. It also requires that policy-makers' develop convincing explanations. At the Berlin G7 meeting in 1997, there was effectively a difference of opinion between policy-makers and the markets, with the consequence that yen depreciation continued, eventually creating problems for G7 policy-makers during the Asian financial crisis of 1998. In this instance policy-makers were forced to suspend their judgement and accept the collective market verdict.

The non-response of market actors to the 1997 statement should not be surprising. The G7 were simply calling for the market to stabilize, rather than move decisively in any one particular direction. In the view of policy-makers, the dollar had reached its peak. Unfortunately, market actors depend on exchange rate movements for profits. The last twenty years has witnessed repeated gyrations and overshooting in the valuation of currencies brought about by market speculation and volatility. Yet the major powers' reliance on declaratory policy reflects a faith in floating exchange rates and the rationality of financial markets. Declaratory policy rests on the notion that markets will overshoot occasionally but will respond to sound technical analysis. The evidence of the last decade is not reassuring on this count. Moreover, the reliance on declaratory policy also hands ultimate sanction to the dynamics of the market and gives authority to market analysts who will endlessly justify and rationalize the market's response, knowing that public officials will in all likelihood suspend their judgement and accept the market's verdict. It is an approach to exchange rate policy based on a fundamental misreading of the nature of currency markets as rational entities that respond in a predictable fashion to the latest data. Of course, the United States can continue to exploit currency movements and fluctuations for political and economic gain, but as we have seen these movements can also prove to be a source of frustration when markets do not respond to the views forwarded by officials.

It is important to emphasize at this point that interest-based politics have not disappeared from exchange rate policy, but as the G7 have increasingly relied on declaratory policy, exchange rate policy has become dependent on technical arguments, societal interests have become increasingly restricted in their capacity to influence exchange rate policy, and finance ministries and central banks have become less responsive. If exchange rate policy is becoming more market driven, more technical, less democratic and less susceptible to influence by concerned citizens, then this is offset by the fact that exchange rate policy cannot solely be determined by the political whims of the United States and exploited arbitrarily for US financial gain.

In September 1997, the Japanese trade surplus with the US, exacerbated by yen–dollar rates, rose to ¥742 billion. Powerful pressures connected to US exporters became vocal in Congress and began to call for a lower dollar in response to this record US trade deficit with Japan. Yet still the Treasury refused to take action on the yen. The Treasury response was that it was unwilling to take action to initiate a lower dollar because this would not reflect underlying fundamentals. The Treasury argued that the strength of the US economy mitigated against a sustained fall in the value of the dollar. They also feared that any exchange rate action at that time would damage the credibility of future actions. In other words, the response of the Treasury was that on the basis of a review of fundamentals there wasn't much of a case for a lower dollar, although they repeatedly emphasized they didn't want to see the dollar climb much higher, or the yen fall much lower, because by this stage the Treasury had an interest in the export-driven recovery of South East Asian economies. Of course, the Treasury was also happy to continue to accept the anti-inflationary benefits of a higher dollar and healthy stock market performance that was partly derived from low interest rates.

During this period, the markets interpreted Treasury Secretary Robert Rubin's position as 'strong dollar good, weak yen bad'.[65] One market analyst pointed to the zero sum nature of foreign exchange markets and the incompatibility of having both a strengthening dollar and a strengthening yen.[66] Another market participant summed up the G7 dilemma by suggesting there was not a lot the G7 could do: 'no one in the world wants the Japanese currency to get much weaker, but there's not much of an economic argument for a stronger yen'.[67] The markets' message to the G7 deputies was that without a strong collective support for the yen, it would come under further pressure.[68] Moreover, in their own form of third-dimensional diplomacy, the markets were beginning to accuse the Bank of Japan of pursuing a policy of 'benign neglect', because it was continuing to cut interest rates in an effort to stimulate demand despite the slide in the value of the yen.[69] Such sentiment made it difficult for the G7 to take action to reverse the fortunes of the yen. What was particularly alarming for the G7 deputies was that the low level of the yen was leading to a series of falls in the value of other Asian currencies. Amid fears of a round of further devaluations, market spokespeople continued to argue publicly in favour of the G7 taking joint action to support the yen, but at the same time pointed out that it was unlikely to have a serious impact without supportive domestic policy action.[70]

The situation eventually came to a head in June 1998, when the US finally decided to act. The alarm of US exporters at the continuing fall of the yen against the dollar was certainly part of the equation in moving the US to a more proactive exchange rate stance in the summer of 1998, but it was not the only factor, nor does it appear to have been the decisive one. Three other factors were key in explaining the shift in US policy. First, by June 1998 the yen–dollar exchange rate appeared extreme at ¥147 to the dollar and was contributing to the slow pace of recovery in Asia as a whole as the export economies of the region struggled due to the chronically low yen. Second, Japanese officials were prepared to make statements supporting economic reforms that the US were encouraging such as the closing of insolvent banks. The US had been reluctant to take action on the yen precisely because they feared this might detract from pressure for structural reform. That Japanese officials were willing to go on the record supporting reform efforts was viewed as progress.[71] Third, Robert Rubin's well-known bias against currency intervention provided the Treasury with the element of surprise which could be crucial in affecting the psychology of the market.[72] The decision to intervene was successful as the yen rose back to ¥136 to the dollar and never again dropped to the levels of the summer of 1998.

The weakening dollar and the rise of exchange rate tensions

By 2000, attention had shifted from the yen to a weak euro. At the instigation of the ECB, the G7 moved to support the euro with a series of interventions on 22 September 2000. The interventions were publicly announced in a G7 statement released the next day, following a meeting in Prague.[73] The move indicated that the G7 as a group are not solely concerned with the dollar and that it is not just the US who can catalyse G7 action, although it is clearly most well placed to do so. By the end of 2000, the euro had lost 28 per cent of its value against the dollar since its creation. Its weakness was also exacerbating the inflationary impact of rising oil prices in the Eurozone and was worsening the US trade deficit. The interventions only had a temporary effect in stemming the fall of the euro, but a G7 meeting in February 2001 was more successful in supporting the euro. First, the IMF forecast made public at the meeting saw Eurozone growth increasing to 3 per cent, with US growth falling to 1.7 per cent. Second, the lack of any reference to European interest rates in the G7 statement indicated that further rate cuts by the ECB were unlikely. The euro slowly began to rise against the yen, and more especially against the dollar on the basis of forecasts, with the incoming Bush administration seemingly happy to accept the export-related benefits of a weakening dollar. The implication of this is that the G7 finance ministries have been most effective in moving exchange rates in the desired direction when their preference is supported by economic data and a solid technical case.

The next major G7 collective exchange rate statement came following a meeting in Dubai, in September 2003. The G7 statement called for more flexibility in exchange rates for major countries or economic areas.[74] The dollar subsequently fell against a range of currencies and this was exacerbated by lower US growth forecasts and a general market sense that the dollar had further to fall as part of the process of correcting the US current account deficit. The dollar has continued to decline right up to the time of writing. What is currently at stake is the extent of this decline. By the autumn of 2003, and in the context of a sharp acceleration in the decline of the dollar, commentary in the international financial press was increasingly warning of the dangers of a dollar rout.[75] Recent G7 statements have tried to guard against such an eventuality by warning against excessive volatility, but the dollar has continued its long-term depreciation. Indeed, but for central banks in Japan, China and a number of South East Asian economies, who intervened in the foreign exchange market by buying dollars in an effort to prevent an excessive appreciation of their own currencies and preserve some degree of export competitiveness, the decline of the dollar would have been even more severe. What happens to the dollar in the context of large current account and budget deficits will be important for US exceptionalism. Should something approaching a dollar rout materialize, this will prove to be the real test of capability for the so-called Dollar Wall Street Regime, in terms of its ability to manipulate exchange rate outcomes.

The G7 have a mutual interest in avoiding a dollar rout. This would undermine competitiveness in export-based economies in Europe and Asia and undermine foreign willingness to hold US bonds, with the resulting jump in long-term US interest rates choking off US growth, and having a detrimental affect on global growth prospects more generally. What the G7 would prefer is an orderly adjustment in which excessive movements are avoided, yet it is precisely the former scenario that became a distinct possibility following the G7 Dubai statement, which called for more flexibility between currencies and was interpreted as a condemnation of the intervention activities of Asian authorities, which were effectively propping up the dollar. Subsequently, the euro rose sharply against the dollar.

In the past, the US has largely been immune from investor fears over current account deficits because foreign investors have always been keen to accumulate foreign exchange reserves. The most secure way of doing this has been to invest surplus funds in the country with the world's biggest economy and most liquid capital markets. If and when foreigners can no longer be persuaded to finance the US, the dollar will decline. Between the spring of 2001, when the dollar began its decline, and October 2003, global foreign currency reserves rose by $831 billion. Of these $611 billion were accumulated by Asian countries. Japan led the way with $219 billion, with China and Taiwan accounting for $184 billion and $73 billion respectively. These foreign currency reserves were predominantly invested in US official obligations and accounted for 4.5 per cent of US GDP. In other words, Asian countries have followed a strategy of exchange rate protectionism, managing an undervalued exchange rate through sizeable exchange market interventions, accumulating reserves and encouraging export-led growth. The willingness of Asian countries to invest in these ways has helped keep both US bond prices and the dollar afloat, thus financing the borrowings of the US government and households.

What has emerged is a *de facto* alliance or bargain between the US and Asian economies, in which the US has been quite happy to accept Asian currency policies because these policies have effectively financed US payment imbalances by bringing inflows of foreign funds into the US financial system through the purchase of dollar-denominated US Treasury debt securities. However, these interventions have limited the extent of market-induced dollar adjustment, meaning that the dollar adjustment has fallen with full force on those currencies left to float, most notably the euro and sterling. This has caused great frustration within the Eurozone because the deterioration in net trade brought about by the appreciation of the euro has, according to OECD forecasts, reduced Eurozone growth from 1.2 per cent to 0.5 per cent. In these circumstances, Eurozone states have struggled to emerge from a prolonged period of stagnation. The result has been rising tensions between the G7 powers concerning future exchange rate policy. The Europeans desire a more competitive currency, but the Asian–US bargain, which involves a tacit acceptance of Asian mercantilism in return for a source of financing for twin US deficits, have resulted in G7 statements having little or no impact in currency markets, other than to hasten the fall of the dollar against the euro.

These tensions reached a peak as the G7 prepared for their first meeting of 2004. In the lead up to the meeting German Chancellor Gerhard Schroeder, French Finance Minister Francis Mer and ECB president Jean Claude Trichet all complained about the brutal and abrupt rise in the euro against the dollar, while

Alan Greenspan appeared unconcerned, claiming that the falling dollar created no 'measurable disruption' and was vital to thwart creeping protectionism.[76] Indeed, in an election year the Bush administration appeared to favour a lower dollar as means of helping US manufacturers. Yet the impact of a lower dollar on US exports is far from clear. Despite a strong dollar from 1995 to 2000, US exports rose by 35 per cent, suggesting global demand is a more important factor determining US export performance than a competitive currency. Moreover, since 1976 the yen has roughly trebled against the dollar, yet there has been no significant improvement in the trade deficit with Japan, which has long been the cause of most consternation with US manufacturers.

The G7 statement released following a meeting in Boca Raton, Florida in February 2004 did refer to the need for currency flexibility and warned about the dangers of excess volatility, but it carried little weight in the markets, despite European and Japanese officials expressing satisfaction at the content of the statement.[77] The market response was that the statement appeared designed to please all G7 members and was too limited to place an effective break on the dollar. Of particular concern was that the statement appeared to reflect an agreement on words rather than policies. Ultimately, the references to disorderly and excessive currency movements appear to have been included in the statement at European and Japanese insistence. Unfortunately, problems have arisen because of an apparent disagreement over whether the decline in the dollar has constituted an excessive and disorderly movement. Currently, there is little evidence to suggest that US policy-makers see it as such. Furthermore, there was also little evidence that the G7 were committed to joint interventions, or that the ECB stood ready to cut interest rates in response to the rising euro. Again the G7 relied on declaratory policy as their principal exchange rate policy instrument and the markets were again left to act as arbiter or judge and jury. In this respect, the G7 have always had a common interest in avoiding disorderly market movements and seeking to restrain and minimize sudden market movements. It is the interpretations of what constitutes sudden and excessive movements that sometimes differs. The problem the G7 often face is in trying to present a common position in accordance with the consensual orientation of the G7 process, while papering over any differences. Frequently, the markets often remain unconvinced of the significance of collective G7 statements, which means that the G7 frequently appear to be fighting a losing battle against growing market volatility and currency gyrations, although the root cause of this is the finance ministries and central banks' preference for declaratory policy, the importance they attach to technical authority and credibility and differing political and economic priorities at any one time that prevent them from taking more substantial joint policy action.[78]

Implications for US power, market authority and G7 governance

G7 exchange rate activities tell us a great deal about some of the key debates in IPE, including the extent of US power, the restrictions on it, relations between the major industrialized powers, the rise of market authority, how monetary authority is exercised and its consequences for social and political order. Debates on US power tend to have been polarized between those who have followed Robert Keohane's lead believing US hegemony to have been replaced by a system of collective management involving international institutions and major powers, and those who contend that US hegemony remains undiminished and has even been accentuated as a consequence of globalization.[79] More recent applications of both extreme perspectives have been evident in the work of John Kirton on the role of the G7/G8 as an organ of global governance and Peter Gowan's work on US dollar policy.[80]

Kirton has suggested that the G7 operate as a modern concert of international powers with each state having roughly equal capability and even the weakest state having the capability to exercise leadership in the G7.[81] Yet it is difficult to see how such a model can be applied to G7 exchange rate policy. While there is clearly an open exchange of views and each country has the opportunity to make their case and shape the G7 consensus by forwarding a convincing and authoritative interpretation of exchange rates at G7 meetings, this does not necessarily equate with each G7 country having an equal capacity to influence exchange rate outcomes. There are notable asymmetries in contemporary international monetary relations, which continue to give the US strategic advantages relative to other states at G7 meetings.

First, as we have seen the dollar's role as the major reserve currency in the international monetary system means that it is often the focus of attention at G7 meetings. Consequently, the US has more opportunity to pursue its exchange rate interests in relation to its own currency than other G7 states. Second, as the G7 have come to rely on declaratory policy to influence exchange rates, markets have come to occupy the role of arbiter. Market analysts and operators pay most attention to US policy-makers' statements and to US interpretations of collective G7 statements, because they know that the US economy is the largest economy in the world and that it will be US policy-makers' future decisions that will have most effect on future exchange rates. Third, no other state enjoys the kind of veto power the US holds within the G7. No major monetary or exchange rate initiative can be pursued successfully if the US is not on board, simply because the United States has the world's most liquid capital markets and is the home country regulator to most of the major players in global financial markets.

Of course, Kirton is right in so far as other G7 states can exercise leadership at certain times. In this respect, the G7 process does not simply exist as a mechanism for executing US political objectives. As the discussion above illustrated, both the Europeans and the Japanese have catalysed collective G7 exchange rate action or G7 statements on exchange rates, but this is a much less common occurrence than the US doing likewise and this does not amount to an equality of capability amongst the G7. In other words, despite an appearance of deliberative equality and a privileging of technical concerns by the finance ministries and central banks that allows individual policy-makers to display authority, international monetary relations are still characterized by a structural asymmetry which gives the US a greater capacity to influence exchange rate patterns than other G7 states. The concert equality model is a hugely overstated expression of the fact that Japan and Europe can influence G7 exchange rate policy, or that a certain exchange rate policy is much more likely to exceed if it is collectively backed by the G7 as a group. It is still much easier for the US to take action and lead exchange rate policy, indeed the 1990s illustrated how the US was able to use the G7 to lend crucial support to a change of dollar policy. Moreover, the US doesn't appear to have to wait until there is a clear undisputable misalignment in the value of its currency, which appears to be the case for Japan and Europe. Certainly there is little evidence of either Europe or Japan initiating policy changes outside of extreme circumstances, as the US did, most notably in 1994–5.

Despite the fact that the G7 is characterized by an inequality of capability, rather than an equality of capability, this is not the same thing as arguing that US policy-makers can arbitrarily talk the dollar up or down in accordance with political objectives, as Peter Gowan has suggested. One of the key arguments in Gowan's Dollar Wall Street Regime thesis was that the Treasury Department were able to engineer dollar appreciation in 1995 by talking up the dollar and mobilizing Wall Street trading activities as part of a strategy of aggressive economic statecraft, designed to lever Asian economies open and increase US ownership of assets in the region, while stimulating an inflow of foreign funds into the US stock market. It is certainly true that Wall Street is a liquidity-driven market whose constant re-supply of funds from abroad is essential to offset low levels of domestic savings, to keep the domestic economy booming and to fund sustained current account deficits. American governments have had a strong interest in maintaining a liberalized financial order for precisely these reasons, as discussed in Chapter 4.[82] However, suggesting that US authorities have such a degree of control that they can direct movements in the value of the dollar at will is quite another thing.

Certainly, dollar appreciation in 1995 helped the US secure domestic and international political and economic objectives, but the question of how important US strategic considerations are in determining exchange rate outcomes is far from clear cut. The experience of the 1990s, discussed in the previous section, demonstrated that exchange rate movements cannot be simply wished into existence by the United States. The record of US Treasury Secretaries, and of the G7 collectively, has been decidedly mixed throughout the last decade. The discussion above suggested that policy-makers' exchange rate statements need to be based on technically credible arguments, rather than simply being motivated by political considerations, if they are to convince market operators. In this respect, exchange rate policy is characterized by a dynamic interaction between power and political motivation and technical authority. Moreover, there are obvious tensions between state authority and market authority in exchange rate policy as a consequence of policy-makers' increasing reliance on declaratory policy. Authority on exchange rate matters is something that varies over time in accordance with the individuals in key strategic positions, their expertise, their reputation, their resources and the priorities of an administration. US domestic politics are crucially important for dollar policy, but they do not determine exchange rate outcomes. The evidence highlighted in the last section indicated that exchange rate policy is a complex area, characterized by a multi-spatial (three-dimensional) governance process that no one single actor is able to control, with a complex combination of factors being required to move an exchange rate in a particular direction.

Notably, domestic politics and pressures are mediated by finance ministry and central banking elites with their own sets of beliefs and social practices. These elites appear unable to impose their preferences on the global foreign exchange market without paying due consideration to technical matters. The G7 appear to have been most successful in influencing exchange rates when three conditions have been in place (see Table 6.1). A strong technical argument for an exchange rate movement has existed, there has been strong domestic support for such a movement, most especially in the United States, so as to avoid the risk of market confusion brought about by conflicting domestic signals, and finally a successful exchange rate outcome has been most likely when a broad consensus has existed amongst G7 authorities.

Markets and market watchers continue to play close attention to G7 statements on currencies and go to considerable lengths to decipher the language contained therein. Markets often react to G7 statements, although not always in the way policy-makers hope. Indeed G7 meetings and discussion of exchange rate matters can even exacerbate volatility. G7 statements clearly continue to matter and this alone would suggest that states retain a capacity to steer market movements. Moreover, markets clearly continue to look to states for leadership and guidance at times of market turbulence. Increasingly however, the argument coming from markets appears to be that collective G7 statements need to be accompanied by supportive domestic policy action. Declaratory policy alone has enjoyed a mixed record. This is partly due to the nature of declaratory policy. The wording of G7 statements is often ambiguous or difficult to decipher, which can lead to the markets misinterpreting the true sentiments behind a statement, or alternatively doubting the conviction behind it and the commitment to a particular policy stance. Ultimately, the G7 have turned their backs on a proactive approach to exchange rates and have adopted a reactive stance to market developments. Declaratory policy is the principal defining characteristic of this reactive approach. The G7 have downgraded collective exchange market interventions and exchange rate attentive interest rate policy has been rejected, due to authorities' perceptions of the speed and scope of private financial transactions and the domestic macroeconomic institutional reforms that have resulted from this.

Declaratory policy is effectively a form of persuasion – an appeal to market operators' better nature or rational decision-making capacities – and it suffers from two major flaws. First, market operators are often swept along by the exuberance of the market. Declaratory policy relies on some degree of self-awareness on behalf of markets to acknowledge and correct excessive movements. In other words, it rests on a faith in markets' willingness to respond to data on fundamentals and to the reasoned analysis of the policy-makers. The experience of the last decade suggests that such faith cannot always be justified. Markets do not always behave rationally, which obviously limits the effectiveness of declaratory

Table 6.1 G7 declaratory policy in the 1990s

Year	*US Treasury position*	*Multilateral consensus among technocrats?*	*Consensus among US domestic actors?*	*Desired market outcome?*
1994	Strong case for dollar appreciation	Yes, but some doubts (Germany)	No	No
1995	Strong case for dollar appreciation	Yes, strong consensus	Yes	Yes
1997	Qualified support for dollar stabilization	Yes, but only on the need for dollar stabilization	Yes, strong pressure from exporters	No

policy. In particular, markets are less likely to respond to public statements that call for a stabilization of exchange rates around existing levels, rather than those that call for a decisive movement in one direction or another. Price shifts make financial markets lucrative and attractive for those who operate in them and it is this that makes them prone to volatility and unsuited to becoming authorities in their own right.[83]

Second, markets can simply reject policy-makers' analyses or arguments on the grounds that prevailing market thinking is superior to that of public officials. Declaratory policy gives policy-makers no real come-back in such circumstances. When the markets refuse to respond to policy-makers statements, the impotency of declaratory policy becomes all too apparent, and the belief that financial markets are all-powerful is further consolidated and augmented. In short, markets have become authorities in their own right because states have treated them as such and have been reluctant to intervene, or to attempt to direct them in a proactive fashion. In the absence of any sanction, market operators can offer alternative views to those of policy-makers, while claiming they have a better feel for market dynamics. Even in their modest assumed role of containing extreme movements and minimizing exchange rate misalignments therefore, finance ministries and central banks have not always been successful because of their preference for presenting arguments to markets and their questionable assumption that financial markets behave rationally.

Technical authority has therefore become just as important in determining the course of exchange rate policy as political motivation, if not more so. Exchange rate policy is becoming more technical, more market determined, but less democratic. Finance ministries and central banks have greater institutional distance between themselves and wider societal interests and are becoming increasingly concerned with cultivating their technical authority and credibility, rather than responding to the demands of key societal interests. However, the increasing reliance on declaratory policy and the associated rise in technical authority has also restrained the power of the United States. The US cannot simply follow its exchange rate preferences on political grounds, but has to come up with technically convincing arguments for any proposed course of action. Failure to do this will diminish the credibility and authority of US officials, with both their peers in other finance ministries and central banks and most crucially with the markets. Technical authority places a vital constraint on the United States and prevents arbitrary US action on exchange rates. Moreover, it creates incentives for the US to conform with the accepted social practices of finance ministries and central banks and engage in technically grounded multilateralism. International monetary relations clearly continue to be asymmetric, but the United States has to pay attention to technical credibility and authority as well as acting on the basis of political motivation. The capacity of US monetary authorities to engineer monetary and economic outcomes through the act of currency manipulation should therefore not be overestimated. The dollar appreciation of 1995 for example, delivered political and economic benefits for the US, but it was the result of a complex and somewhat fortuitous combination of factors. In an age of growing market and technical authority, such outcomes will not always be within the gift of the United States.

This last point should be a salutary lesson for the Bush administration as they enter their second term of office. If and when foreigners can no longer be persuaded to finance the US, the dollar will decline. With voices on Wall Street increasingly warning that the Bush tax cuts are a fiscal time bomb waiting to happen when baby-boom retirees lead to spiralling health and pension costs, the US fiscal deficit is expected to continue to grow, particularly with further tax cuts having been pledged in the Bush election campaign and the distinct possibility of further expensive military campaigns. In this context, the capacity of the US government to persuade foreigners to invest in US Treasury securities and in equities might well be squeezed. Indeed, the reckless fiscal policies of the Bush administration may well be hastening the decline of US monetary exceptionalism, and by association military exceptionalism. There is a potential limit to the willingness of foreigners to go on lending to the US. Ultimately, the capacity of the United States to postpone macroeconomic adjustment has been dependent on a perpetual opinion poll, involving the judgement of private financial market actors. Crucially, should market sentiment change, the portents from the experience of the Clinton administration, during a period of economic strength and sound fundamentals, in terms of their capacity to manipulate and control exchange rate outcomes, do not bode well for the Bush administration's ability to prevent an extreme market-led decline in the value of the dollar (a dollar rout). The record of an administration with a sound economic record that paid close attention to macroeconomic credibility and on the whole respected technical authority, was decidedly mixed in terms of its ability to achieve desired exchange rate outcomes. An administration that has displayed little interest in economic policy beyond populist tax cuts could be about to suffer the consequences of its earlier disinterest and find painful macroeconomic adjustment unavoidable.

Exogenous shocks and episodes of concerted monetary easing

As well as identifying exchange rate misalignments, surveillance can also help to identify when national policy is out of step with global conditions. In this respect, the surveillance exercise structures and informs debate and discussion of how to respond to what economists refer to as 'exogenous shocks'. The globalization of finance, new and innovative means of financing commercial enterprises, combined with growing trade interdependence, have meant that events in one part of the world can have a major global impact and affect growth prospects in other parts of the world. Such events can be referred to as exogenous shocks. Two major exogenous shocks have rocked the global financial system and adversely affected global demand in recent times. Both shocks have required action from policy-makers to counter their impact on demand and consumer confidence. The first shock was contagion in Asian financial systems and exchange rate depreciation, which spread to Latin American countries and Russia in 1998. The second exogenous shock was caused by the events of 11 September 2001, when terrorist attacks on the two World Trade Centre buildings in New York rocked global economic confidence. Both incidents led to a concerted monetary easing across the G7.

Concerted monetary policy should be distinguished from co-ordinated monetary policy. Co-ordinated monetary policy involves precise agreements on domestic policy adjustments, often in different directions, usually with the aim of addressing payments or exchange rate imbalances, or as part of a co-ordinated growth strategy. Concerted monetary policy on the other hand is a joint response to an exogenous shock that pushes policy in a similar direction in different countries. Concerted policy, in this case the simultaneous easing or raising of interest rates, tends to happen once a broad reasoned consensus is reached in a dimension I setting on the diagnosis of a particular event, its impact and the role national policy can address in alleviating the situation. A common recognition of the threat of global recession or world-wide inflation can then be internalized into national policy processes and the impact of the particular event can be assessed in distinctly national terms within the terms of the reasoned consensus arrived at in the dimension I setting. Such a process can lead to national policy moving in a similar direction in different countries in a short space of time, albeit to varying extents. Concerted policy emerges from a process of deliberation and arguing in dimension I settings. Concerted policy is therefore a policy output that is compatible with, and indeed a product of, the G7's sense of appropriate social practice.

In the case of the response to the Asian financial crisis, the G7 held a meeting in September 1998 in London and then released a statement that acknowledged that 'the balance of risks in the world economy had shifted' away from inflation. The G7 identified the need to preserve or create the conditions for economic growth. However, reports that the G7 statement was a prelude to a co-ordinated interest rate cut by G7 policy-makers were inaccurate.[84] Two days later Alan Greenspan, Chairman of the Federal Reserve, reiterated the G7 consensus. According to Greenspan, policy would remain focused on national economies. There was 'no endeavour to co-ordinate interest rate cuts'.[85] A day earlier a similar rebuttal had come from Hans Tietmeyer, President of the Bundesbank. Certainly the meeting produced no specific negotiated agreement. However, the G7 meeting did reach a broad consensus that central banks in the industrialized world should move in the direction of monetary easing, with the size and timing of interest rate cuts to be determined by national considerations. In this respect, the G7 meeting was used to form a collective view, before conveying this view to national monetary policy committees. In other words, the monetary easing of 1998 was not the result of a co-ordinated agreement stemming from intergovernmental bargaining. Rather it was based on a more subtle process of consensus formation amongst elites in the dimension I setting, and subsequent efforts to communicate that consensus to the domestic dimension II setting, while sending a signal of intent to market participants that the seriousness of the situation was grasped, in an effort to improve market confidence.

Attempts to arrive at a consensual view, together with efforts to communicate that view to other settings, are likely to become an ever more common form of activity at G7 meetings. Central banks have become increasingly independent. The G7 provides one of the few settings where finance ministers can collectively pressurize 'independent' central bankers in informal and intimate surroundings, with the objective of persuading them to pay more attention to 'global developments' in the setting of national policy. Yet hard bargaining over national monetary policy would only infringe the independence of central banks.

In October 1998, following the Federal Reserve Open Market Committee's decision to cut short-term interest rates by a quarter of a percentage point, there was an orgy of selling of stocks and shares around the world. Investors had been hoping for a half point cut and saw the quarter point cut as an indication that the Federal Reserve did not fully grasp the seriousness of the situation. In this sense, third-dimensional pressure for further cuts mounted from private sector investors around the world. A subsequent G7 meeting in London produced a further recognition of concerns about low growth. German and British finance ministers suggested that given the consensus on this in the G7, their central banks should be looking to move in the direction of monetary authorities in the US and Canada. The resulting G7 statement called for individual G7 countries to 'take action to bolster growth in their own economies, for each country in the global economy to play their part in the promotion of recovery, but that different countries faced different challenges'.[86]

The wording of the statement clearly indicated that there was no intention to co-ordinate interest rate cuts across the G7, but that monetary easing was on the agenda. Central bank governors acknowledged in interviews that there was a consensus that the balance of risks in the world economy had shifted, but pointed out that international factors were only one consideration and that they would not be swayed by international pressure.[87] In this sense, the avoidance of a pre-negotiated agreement meant that the independent status of central banks and accepted G7 practice was not compromised. Furthermore, central bank governors can offer no guarantees on how domestic colleagues on monetary policy committees such as the Bank of England's Monetary Policy Committee or the Federal Open Markets Committee, will vote, especially when these committees have independent technocrats amongst their membership. There is also a recognition that making demands of other central banks and the appearance of sensitivity to international pressure would undermine the credibility of central bank independence more generally. What the governors can do at G7 meetings is agree to present arguments, based on a consensual G7 view, to their national colleagues.

In this respect, statements from London and Washington meetings in the autumn of 1998 represented little more than a signal to national monetary policy committees, whether it be the Board of the Bundesbank, the FOMC, or the MPC. The message was for these committees to shift the focus of their debate, but actual decisions on interest rates were made nationally, not in the multilateral setting of the G7. The G7 statement constituted a form of suasion. Both the Bank of England and the Federal Reserve subsequently cut interest rates. This was followed by delayed interest rate cuts amongst European central banks before Christmas, ahead of the launch of the euro. Therefore, while G7 meetings did not produce an international agreement involving specific national commitments, the process of arguing and deliberation that took place at G7 meetings did act to shape national policy discussions, and subsequently the course of monetary policy throughout the industrialized world. G7 meetings were effectively used as a platform for persuading national institutions to pursue more globally sensitive policies, although this method of arguing and persuasion does not guarantee the necessary national policy shifts.

Concerted monetary easing also followed the terrorist attacks of September 11 in the United States. With the US already entering recession and the Federal Reserve having already cut US interest rates seven times in 2001, the Federal Open Markets Committee (FOMC) moved to cut rates by half a percentage point on the morning of Monday 17 September, the day traders and analysts were due to return to work in New York following the attacks. Later that day the ECB cut its rates by a similar margin, following a telephone conference call of its governing council, instigated from the Finnish central bank's headquarters by president Wim Duisenberg. This was the first time the ECB had initiated a change in interest rates in between scheduled meetings of its Governing Council. Likewise, the Japanese central bank also cut its interest rates. The Federal Reserve appeared to have only communicated its decision to the ECB after the FOMC had met early on the Monday morning of the 17 September, shortly before publicly announcing its decision.[88] Interest rate cuts dribbled out of central banks in an ad-hoc fashion over the next 24 hours. The notable exception was the Bank of England, which preferred to wait for the next formal meeting of its MPC before cutting its rates. Matti Vanhala of Finland's central bank explained that the decisions were made separately, albeit on the basis of a flow of information, with other central banks following the Fed's lead. Reports also suggested that there was no request from US officials concerning the policies of other central banks.[89] Central banks exchanged information and possibly opinions, but they came to their own decisions.

In other words, there was no hard bargaining over monetary policy following the September 11 attacks, and there was no co-ordinated monetary policy. G7 beliefs and understandings that monetary policy is a national enterprise, central banks should reach decisions independently, and countries shouldn't engage in hard bargaining over macroeconomic policy, were not breached. Indeed, the shared understanding that it is inappropriate for states to bargain over their macroeconomic policies at G7 meetings appears to have been a fundamental consideration affecting the interactions and outcomes of the central banks.

These episodes of monetary easing amongst the G7 demonstrate that G7 interactions serve as a useful safety valve mechanism that can on occasion offset the damaging deflationary effects of an excessive focus on domestic price stability. G7 interactions and discussions can do this by steering domestic policy debates in the direction of interest rate cuts, but they do so within the parameters of the constituent normative and causal beliefs of the G7 finance ministries and central banks and the prevailing social practices that inform their interactions. In this respect, in recent times concerted monetary policy easing has not resulted from simple intergovernmental bargaining that has modified national positions, but has resulted from a more complex interplay of shared ideas, multilateral norms, domestic institutional practice, and market expectations. The major point here however, is that the G7's preferred method of securing a concerted international monetary easing is not guaranteed. Like third-dimensional diplomacy (communicating with the market), the method of attempting to steer or initiate domestic debates – second-dimensional diplomacy – remains haphazard, reflecting the constraints of national institutional arrangements, such as interest rate decisions by committees of independent experts and territorially defined price stability targets. Theoretically at least, national committees that make decisions on interest rates remain in a position to reject the arguments presented to them by governors and deputies who have participated in G7 discussions. Ultimately, the ability of the G7 process to steer the world economy away from deflationary crises remains uncertain, largely due to the faith the G7 continue to place in the current sound money orthodoxy and the series of social practices surrounding that orthodoxy.

EMU and the Group of Seven

One of the most momentous developments of the last decade has been the movement towards a single European currency. Throughout the 1990s, the focus of France, Germany and Italy was on the process of European Monetary Union. This has been cited as being one of the major reasons behind the demise of G7 policy co-ordination.[90] It certainly affected domestic politics in these countries and has had a restrictive effect on G7 co-operation. EMU has not been conducive to more proactive and extensive forms of international exchange rate management, or G7 macroeconomic policy co-ordination. To US participants it has at times appeared that European countries have been willing to abandon national exchange rates and monetary policy but have been totally opposed to co-operation with the rest of the G7.[91] For the Germans and the other Europeans, the EMS assumed primacy over global co-operation.[92] European countries have also directly opposed any wider consideration of European exchange rates by the G7, even if these issues clearly had wider global ramifications.[93] This disengagement from exchange rate issues and a focus on regional or European arrangements has, however, paradoxically reinforced the wider G7 view that exchange rates should be determined by markets. At the same time, the Maastricht convergence criteria on budget deficits and treaty provisions on independent central banks have constrained European economic policy-making and made it less susceptible to international pressures from other G7 governments.

As the deadlines for the EMU convergence process approached, European countries focused on ways of meeting the convergence criteria and concentrated on maintaining and establishing the 'credibility' of their parities within the EMS, through a focus on domestic economic fundamentals in accordance with the general consensus in the G7. The mandate of the new European Central Bank is to deliver domestic price stability. Despite the fact that the Euro 12 group can set general external orientations for the euro, without operational control of interest rates, finance ministries and governments will have difficulty in compelling the ECB to follow an exchange rate policy, or to co-operate with US and Japanese authorities to manage exchange rates, without negotiating a treaty amendment concerning the ECB's mandate, which in turn will require unanimity amongst Eurozone governments. Furthermore, the 'fiscal stability pact' continues to constrain fiscal policy.

Notably, the monetary easing that took place across the industrialized world in 1998 in recognition of a global slow-down, was introduced last in continental Europe as the focus of central banks remained on the launch of the euro. In other words, the general pattern in Europe is that the EMU process has effectively demobilized European macroeconomic policy. With the exception of the loose form of co-operation based on a common identification with the principles of sound money and open markets at the core of shared G7 beliefs, more ambitious forms of monetary co-ordination have been impeded.

The Europeans' apparent disengagement from the G7 process was also partly due to the time consuming nature of monthly ECOFINs, European Monetary Committee meetings and European Central Bankers' meetings and more recently Euro Group meetings. This meeting cycle intensified as the process of European monetary union gathered momentum. Senior officials working on European monetary affairs were invariably also G7 deputies. They had to liaise with Commission officials, and officials from COREPER in a more extensive and elaborate series of networks than the relative informal intimacy of the G7.[94] It has not been uncommon for these officials to spend half their working week in Brussels.[95] This has detracted from the energy and attention European officials have been able to devote to the G7 process. EMU countries do now have a more streamlined representation at G7 meetings with the President of the ECB representing all Eurozone countries, with the national central bank governors of these countries no longer attending, although individual finance ministry representation continues.

European abdication from G7 matters was also more or less endorsed by the US, through its position on the euro. The Clinton administration adopted the position that EMU was a positive development and that a strong euro would be good for Europe, good for the world economy and therefore good for the US. They repeatedly applauded the increased fiscal discipline and the movement towards more central bank independence that the implementation of the Maastricht Treaty brought throughout Europe.[96] However, there was very little serious discussion on the process of EMU, or its likely impact on the future international monetary system, other than to indicate that this would be a topic for future discussion. At the same time, there was a general unwillingness amongst US officials to make public comments on the euro for fear of upsetting the Europeans and risking charges of interference.[97] Amicable diplomatic relationships with Europe have been the most important consideration for the US, leading to something of a non-policy on EMU, other than to emphasize shared objectives of low inflation and fiscal consolidation, thus reiterating and reinforcing existing G7 beliefs concerning sound money.[98]

Conclusion

Based on a reading of this chapter it would be easy to reach the lazy conclusion that the G7 process has become an anachronism and is only of marginal relevance where macroeconomic governance is concerned. Certainly, the Group of Seven does not act as some form of international macroeconomic government. In this respect, as Fred Bergsten and Randall Henning have argued, macroeconomic policy co-ordination, with which the G7 has long been associated, has been immobilized.[99] The reasons for this immobilization help to shed light on the role the G7 process has played and continues to play in constructing and reinforcing the current macroeconomic regime. A combination of central bank independence, fiscal rules, perceptions of the foreign exchange market and G7 beliefs and social practices have all contributed to the immobilization of macroeconomic policy. But all of these developments are the product of deliberate choices made by finance ministries and central banks. These choices, and the beliefs on which they are based, have been informed by the finance ministries and central banks' continuous exchanges in the context of the G7 process, resulting in a loose consensus on macroeconomic policy. Moreover, this consensus has resulted in a particular form of interaction at G7 meetings and a particular way of reasoning, that has in turn facilitated and encouraged the pattern of market supremacy and the relatively narrow focus on sound money referred to in this chapter.

Ultimately, Group of Seven meetings have no formal macroeconomic decision-making or co-ordination role, but rely on collective communication and signalling to a range of actors that make up the global political economy of finance and money. This has been evident in all three principal G7 contributions to macro-economic governance discussed in this chapter – collective discourse, declaratory exchange rate policy and strategic signalling in the direction of monetary easing. The Group of Seven is a consensus-based process, which is aided by its small group nature and the technical character of exchanges that foster professional collegiality and improve the prospects for arriving at consensus. Discourse, declaratory policy and strategic signalling all involve the construction of consensus, followed by the promotion and communication of that consensus to other actors, whether it be other government departments and officials, legislatures, electorates, transnationally networked markets, an increasingly global financial press, wider multilateral international institutions, social movements and states outside of the G7. Consequently, the G7 finance ministries and central banks principally use their meetings to maximize their influence, by arriving at collective consensual views on macroeconomic matters, and publicizing and rationalizing those collective views in terms of economic data and future policy priorities. In the course of this transgovernmental coalition-building process, the finance ministries and central banks primarily derive their authority from their technical expertise in monetary and financial matters and their track record in delivering accurate economic analyses. Finance ministries and central banks are in affect engaged in a continuous process of argumentation and persuasion, both with one another and with a wider range of actors.

Because the G7 is based on discourse and strategic signalling, it is difficult to measure in any precise way the impact that G7 meetings have on macroeconomic governance. However, several points can be made to demonstrate that the G7 process is far from irrelevant in a macroeconomic sense. First, repeatedly emphasizing that fiscal discipline and independent central banks focused on price stability are the 'norm' throughout the G7, reinforces these developments and acts as a considerable barrier to the possibility of reforming the status quo. Consequently, the G7 process is a collective resource the finance ministries and central banks can exploit to cultivate peer approval that secures their domestic institutional position and reinforces their increasing autonomy in the field of macroeconomic policy. Second, financial markets continue to look to G7 meetings for guidance and signs of collective action at times of turbulence. On several occasions over the last decade or so, the G7 have successfully steered the foreign exchange market. However, G7 declaratory policy has a mixed record and more importantly casts the market as judge and jury in the determination of exchange rates and macroeconomic priorities, effectively inviting the market to engage in an ongoing referendum or opinion poll on national macroeconomic policies. Current G7 beliefs and social practices have encouraged and facilitated this continuous form of communicative diplomacy and signalling between private markets and public authorities, which is a key defining feature of the contemporary international monetary order. Third, G7 interactions and discussions have made a contribution to concerted monetary easing, successfully steering domestic policy debates in the direction of interest rate cuts to boost global liquidity. G7 meetings can act as the catalyst for vital national policy shifts, although in recent times they have not delivered them in their entirety. Senior figures have used G7 meetings to set agendas and signal priorities, but interest rate decisions have still been the product of national decision-making processes and have not been pre-negotiated at G7 meetings, even if G7 meetings have been influential in defining the terms on which national policy debates have subsequently been conducted.

In terms of the crucial determinants that have exerted most influence on G7 interactions, G7 macroeconomic deliberations take place in the context of some fundamental asymmetries. The US remains in the strongest position to influence G7 macroeconomic debates and outcomes because of the status of the dollar, the fact that the US chairs more meetings than any other G7 state, its power of veto in international monetary affairs, as well as a continuing capacity to delay macro-economic adjustment. However, we should be careful about endorsing strong versions of the American hegemony thesis on the basis of this. This chapter has revealed that there are notable constraints on the US at G7 meetings. If the US wishes to arrive at a collective G7 position, it has to respect the shared social practices and norms of the finance ministries and central banks. In particular, on exchange rate matters, the US have to advance arguments that have technical credibility, both with their peers and with the markets, if they are to successfully steer outcomes. The experiences of the 1990s revealed that the US cannot just arbitrarily wish exchange rate outcomes into existence, or impose their preferences on other G7 members and the markets. Neither can the US successfully make specific demands of other countries' macroeconomic policies. US policy-makers have to respect accepted finance ministry and central bank practice and restrict themselves to the expression of opinion, or in the case of central banks and interest rate decisions, risk delaying their desired course of action. The more persuasive and technically sound their argument, the more likely it is that other actors will respond to the US position, and the more monetary authority the United States will enjoy at any one time.

There is a powerful sense of accepted social practice at G7 meetings that continues to exert a strong hold on G7 interactions. In particular, respect for technical expertise amongst finance ministry and central bank elites means that there is a sense of equality at G7 meetings, and technically capable individuals have some capacity to critically influence and lead debates, regardless of the country they represent. Japan and European states have managed to get the yen and the euro to feature on G7 agendas and to critically influence G7 debates over the last decade. Yet this should not be read as an endorsement of John Kirton's concert equality model, which remains an extreme characterization of G7 diplomacy. A respect for technical expertise and the fact that there are opportunities for technically capable individuals to lead G7 debates, does not mean there is an equality of capability among G7 states. Clearly, opportunities to exercise influence and leadership are greatest in the case of the United States and the resources noted above continue to tilt the playing field on which G7 discussions take place. Nevertheless, causal beliefs and accepted social practice continue to frame G7 discussions. As former German Finance Minister Oskar Lafontaine discovered in 1998–9, newcomers to the process make little progress if they adopt an adversarial tone and step outside accepted social practice, or if they radically challenge existing causal beliefs. Finance ministries and central banks have an unwillingness to discard what is regarded as legitimate technical knowledge and have a disposition towards refining and building upon existing knowledge, which inevitably informs and leaves a lasting imprint on future decisions and development trajectories. The G7 process is inherently conservative. It is heavily reliant on communiqués, which often simply repeat previous passages of text, giving the process continuity and creating strong resistance to sudden shifts in prevailing economic beliefs and approaches.

While ideas and social practices continue to exert a considerable hold on the G7 process, the pattern is not absolute. It is certainly true that finance ministries and central banks have become increasingly insulated from the wider political process, as a consequence of developments such as central bank independence and fiscal rules. Yet key societal coalitions continue to exert a pull, even if their influence on finance ministry and central bank technocrats is diminishing. For example, the commitment to capital account liberalization and speculative, rentier financial activities remains less pronounced in Japan and Germany than in the US and the UK, and both of these countries continue to have a basic preference for export-led growth and competitively valued exchange rates, which is largely a function of historical experience, even if the capacity of monetary authorities to deliver exchange rate outcomes is diminishing due to financial globalization, the prevailing G7 consensus, existing domestic institutional arrangements and even, in Germany's case, European Monetary Union. Most significantly, the Bush administration has been able to follow a securitization agenda, downgrade and impose their fiscal preferences on an at times reluctant Treasury, in a fashion no other state would have been able to contemplate.[100] Yet the decline of US financial exceptionalism may be being hastened by Bush's fiscal recklessness, in the context of a declining dollar, which in turn may reduce foreign investors' willingness to continue financing US deficits and to compensate for low levels of domestic savings.

Finally, surveillance, discourse, strategic signalling and declaratory policy have produced an empirically observable pattern of three-dimensional governance in contemporary macroeconomic policy involving peer and market scrutiny of national economic policy and conditions.[101] The very essence of the G7's surveillance exercise is that it facilitates and revolves around processes of peer and market scrutiny of national policies, based on the discussion and publication of economic data. The reality of this form of three-dimensional governance is that governments are now effectively more responsive to non-citizens for their national macroeconomic policies – international investors, foreign currency traders, and other finance ministries and central banks and international organizations in various multilateral settings, than to their own electorates. This is evident in the daily referendum on national policies in the foreign exchange market and regular multilateral surveillance exercises, while national electorates have had the infrequent opportunity of exercising sanction at the ballot box. One of the major consequences of this is that the demands of societal groupings on exchange rates and to a lesser extent on macroeconomic issues are increasingly ignored. In other words, in the context of diffuse multi-spatial macroeconomic governance, the notion of national accountability is being incontrovertibly diluted and dispersed in two directions simultaneously, while democracy remains constructed almost exclusively around the nation state. The empirical evidence presented in this chapter has pointed towards the ascendancy of the market in the process of three-dimensional governance and in the determination of macroeconomic and exchange rate outcomes, as well as the fortunes of citizens and governments across the globe.[102] The G7 process contributes to this state of affairs by prioritizing technocratic competence ahead of a well-rounded definition of the public good and relying on discourse and declaratory policy to exert influence.

7 The Group of Seven and the global financial architecture

The institutional and ideational foundations of market supremacy

From the outset, the forerunners of the modern-day G7 process were involved in efforts to communicate with and set priorities, agendas and mandates for wider international financial institutions. For example, initial discussions of how to construct a post-Bretton Woods exchange rate regime were held at the meetings of the G4 finance ministers in the library of the White House in 1973, while the subsequent drafting of the Rambouillet declaration in 1976 by the finance ministry deputies made reference to the role of the IMF in monitoring the regime and the responsibilities of national authorities in delivering exchange rate stability.[1] Indeed, Putnam and Bayne's earlier study of summitry contained an entire chapter on relations with wider institutions.[2] However, in more recent times reviewing the activities of wider sets of specialist financial institutions and bodies has become more systematic and has constituted the G7's most significant contribution to global financial governance. Since the mid-1990s this review of wider institutions has been captured by the umbrella term the 'global financial architecture', covering the broad range of institutions, principles, codes and practices that contribute to the governance of the global financial system. For some authors the initiatives on the global financial architecture launched after the Asian financial crisis of 1997–8 were marked by a break with the norm of capital account liberalization, were characterized by growing tensions between the G7 over the normative desirability of open capital accounts, or have presaged a more inclusive and just approach to financial governance.[3] Yet viewed from another perspective, it would be wrong to view the ongoing initiatives relating to the global financial architecture, as some sort of historical punctuation mark in the development of the international financial system, comparable to the radical redesign of Bretton Woods. The current review of the global financial architecture has its roots in G7 reports and proposals that were first presented at the Halifax summit of 1995 as a response to the Mexican peso crisis, at a time when enthusiasm for capital account liberalization was at its high water mark.[4] More recent G7 reports and proposals, and those from related bodies, can be seen as a direct product of these earlier reports, informed by but further elaborating the principles and ideas outlined in the Halifax documentation. Therefore, this chapter identifies the continuity in G7 financial architectural proposals, from Halifax right through to the present day. It argues that the principal characteristic of recent G7 proposals has been 'adaptive incrementalism'. The G7's global financial architectural initiatives have not constituted a qualitative challenge to the norms of free capital mobility and capital account convertibility, but have been informed and driven by the principles outlined at Halifax. Indeed I will argue, as others have, that recent reform efforts effectively promote financial liberalization as the ultimate universal goal of the international financial regime, something all states should be aspiring to and moving towards, by preparing their domestic procedures, institutions and norms for such an eventuality.[5] Furthermore, this global financial architectural exercise has, with one or two notable exceptions, been a remarkably consensual one, enjoying more or less unanimous endorsement from the G7 finance ministries and central banks. In other words, the principal impact of the G7's review of the global financial architecture has been to institutionalize, deepen, extend, but also crucially to refine the prevailing consensual mind-set described in Chapter 4, particularly the normative attachment to a fully liberalized open global financial system and an associated pattern of market supremacy.

Ultimately, global financial governance continues to be driven by financial and monetary imperatives rather than social concerns and is based on a predominantly neo-classical view of financial markets as rational efficiency optimizers. Capital controls, which might allow for the kind of redistributive policies based on seigniorage and a shift in the tax burden towards capital owners that characterized the immediate post-war Keynesian period, have on the whole been rejected both by the G7 countries and emerging markets, as anything other than a short-term temporary measure.[6] Recent developments have on the whole involved an intensification of G7 attempts to persuade countries to accept policies conducive to financial liberalization, while constructing a global institutional apparatus that can cope with the policy challenges produced by financial liberalization. This process of persuasion has been assisted by an accompanying rhetoric that makes reference to social concerns and acknowledges the pitfalls of hasty capital account liberalization. However, simply acknowledging the importance of local conditions and circumstances, as well as the need for financial liberalization to be appropriately sequenced and to be accompanied by political and institutional reform, does not challenge the overall policy goal of financial liberalization. Rather it paves the way for further financial liberalization by promoting the adjustment of domestic arrangements to make them more compatible with a liberalized global market order. Financial liberalization has been promoted as a universal global norm to which domestic peculiarities and differences ultimately have to be subordinated.[7] In short, the G7 finance ministries and central banks have on the whole adopted a strategy of attempting to persuade the world's economies of the value of Anglo-Saxon financial institutions and norms, through a combination of discourse, rhetoric and technical argumentation. This has involved the G7 acting as a transgovernmental coalition in respect of the wider global financial architecture, acting as catalysts and agenda setters for a process of incremental reform of the existing institutions and practices, as the finance ministries and central banks construct an internal consensus before promoting that consensus elsewhere through interactions with wider bodies and states. In this respect, the G7 can be understood as a senior, core transgovernmental coalition in the context of a diffuse global financial architecture.

This chapter goes on to address the kind of authority and power the G7 enjoy in global financial governance, the sources of that power and authority, and how it is exercised. The concern in this chapter is with what was referred to in Chapters 3 and 5 as fourth-dimensional diplomacy, involving the G7 finance ministries and central banks' attempts to communicate with a range of other actors and non-G7 national authorities. Generally, fourth-dimensional diplomacy has been characterized by the G7's efforts to promote institutional arrangements based on and derived from the consensual beliefs referred to in Chapter 4. This involves extending and institutionalizing the pattern of three-dimensional diplomacy, entailing peer and market scrutiny of domestic policies, into other areas of financial governance and into new countries, especially emerging markets under the banner of improved 'transparency'.

Section one of this chapter looks at the G7's Halifax strategy of 1995. It is argued that the G7's approach to the reform of the global institutional architecture was first elaborated through the Halifax reports, which subsequently informed and provided the basis for more detailed proposals in the aftermath of the Asian financial crisis. In particular, one G10 deputies' report on the orderly resolution of sovereign liquidity crises prepared during 1995–6, laid out many of the key features and principles of the current approach. This report provided the platform for all subsequent G7 proposals. However, the implementation record of the Halifax strategy prior to the emergence of problems in Asian financial systems at the end of 1997 was poor. Rather than leading to a substantial revision of the Halifax strategy however, the events in Asia merely led to more detail being built onto the Halifax proposals. It also led to a closer focus on implementation in emerging markets and examination of how information could be better shared and pooled by various agencies and institutions. The next two sections of the chapter both consider the response to the Asian financial crises and develop these arguments, demonstrating how the post-Asian architectural proposals were derived from the broad principles and foundations laid out at the Halifax summit and in various follow-up reports. The second section considers the G7's immediate crisis management of the Asian financial contagion as well as proposals on the broader global institutional architecture that were subsequently developed from early 1998 onwards, while relating these initiatives to the principles outlined at Halifax. A final section considers the most recent initiatives on developing country debt. Recent initiatives on debt relief are suggestive of a qualitative shift in discourse that makes reference to the need to globalize notions of social justice. However, this merely marks the start of a process that will inevitably be a long and arduous one that faces many political obstacles if the initiative is not to be still-born.

Elaborating a common approach: G7 beliefs and the Halifax strategy of 1995

During the 1990s, the G7 focused on responding to resistance to economic and financial globalization and facilitating further liberalization. In the words of one former participant in and author on the process of summitry, the G7 assumed 'a modest and austere role as catalysts in promoting change in wider international institutions'.[8] According to former US G7 Deputy, Lawrence Summers, speaking in 1996:

> One of the paradoxes of the present is that whilst we are in a period of almost unprecedented prosperity, the forces of liberalization and integration that have provided so much of that prosperity are also viewed as being responsible for many of the problems plaguing the industrial world. Our challenge, and the challenge for the G-7 is to continue to find ways to maximize the benefits of these changes in the world economy and international financial markets, while continuing to find ways to effectively address the challenges they bring.[9]

G7 motivation was to resist protectionist pressures and any potential movement towards the widespread use of capital controls, maintaining the momentum of financial market liberalization while ensuring that authorities were better equipped to respond collectively to crises. There was both a political motivation and ideational motivation for this, as discussed in Chapter 4.

Incrementalism and the importance of existing institutional and technical legacies

Following the Mexican peso crisis of 1994–5, G7 policy-makers began drafting reports on 'financial architectural issues' for the Halifax summit of 1995. Unlike discussions at Bretton Woods, those in the lead up to Halifax took place in an existing institutional context that set parameters for any recommendations. As one practitioner at the time commented:

> The Bretton Woods pioneers of 50 years ago had the advantage of an open prairie. They could design from afresh the institutional structure and could introduce radical changes quickly. Today the site is cluttered with institutions, each with their own vested interests, so that the approach to reform today will have to be incremental. There can be no repeat of the institutional revolution of fifty years ago.[10]

In a cluttered institutional context, incrementalism has been a repeated feature of the G7's approach to reforming the global institutional architecture. Existing institutions have an institutional legacy and place a constraint on G7 policy-makers. For example, officials repeatedly stress that the IMF is not merely the 'handmaiden' of the G7 and that the G7 cannot impose their wishes on the institution.[11] G7 officials have to engage in continuous networking, pressurizing and persuading where IMF matters are concerned, although of course the provision of financial resources do provide the G7 collectively, as principal paymaster, with a strategic advantage in influencing IMF policies and procedures, and consequently those of authorities in borrowing countries.

However, the reasons why continuity and incrementalism have been defining characteristics of the G7's approach to global financial architectural issues go far beyond existing institutions seeking to maximize their budgets and role in the policy process out of a sense of bureaucratic self-interest. In a recent seminal article, Tony Porter explains how the review of financial architecture that emerged following the Asian financial crisis was a response to the development of the global financial system as an increasingly complex technical system that required technical responses.[12] In this respect, recent global financial architectural initiatives have built upon the experience of technical collaboration that had been developed during the 1970s and 1980s. Powerful states were constrained by a legacy of existing technical knowledge in responding to the financial crises of the 1990s. This legacy and the robustness of the history of technical collaboration made the approach adopted appear a reasonable, viable and acceptable option. In contrast, more ambitious radical proposals did not have the research, institution building and linkages to the technical system of more modest proposals. In other words, issue areas such as the regulation of global finance, which have the character of a technical system as 'a spatially extended and functionally integrated socio technical network' embedded in a material infrastructure, displaying symptoms of path dependence, and in which scientific and technical expertise is a key source of authority, are predisposed towards incremental development trajectories based on a legacy of accumulated technical knowledge, expertise and collaboration.[13] Porter concentrates on the FSF and the G20 in his article, but even G7 reports had the same incremental dynamic. Not only did these reports draw on work from other technical bodies such as the Basle Committee, IOSCO and the IMF's secretariat, but the G7 process itself has a conservative and incremental dynamic, which as revealed in Chapter 5 is a product of the social practices associated with communiqué drafting, often resulting in the replication or further development of previous passages of text and borrowing from and endorsing the work of other bodies.

The need for reform and the constraints on reform

Any complacency that the existing multilateral institutions were fine as they were was shattered by the Mexican peso episode and highlighted that the procedures and resources of the Bretton Woods institutions needed to be adjusted and reformed.[14] Mexico narrowed the focus for officials.[15] The handling and the prevention of sovereign liquidity crises, the financial resources of the multilateral institutions, and cross-border financial regulation and supervision became key issues. In this respect, US Treasury Secretary Robert Rubin surmised that the task was to make the global institutional architecture 'as modern as the markets'. This notion of institutional adjustment to keep up with or respond to developments in sophisticated globally networked financial markets again appears to support Porter's technical systems analysis.

The finance ministry deputies, their deputy-deputies and the national Executive Directors at the IMF and the World Bank in Washington handled the majority of the workload for the Halifax report on architectural issues. The finance ministers and central bank governors discussed their proposals at meetings in Toronto and Washington in February and April of 1995. The actual proposals however, were to be announced by the heads of state and government at the Halifax summit, to give them a higher profile and greater publicity.

The eventual Halifax communiqué identified a number of constraints on the process of adapting institutions. Fiscal constraints in donor countries, stemming from pressures to reduce public spending and balance budgets throughout the industrialized world, meant that identified needs had to be consistent with the magnitude and specific nature of the resources available to address them. Moreover, existing institutions had grown to the point where there was a case for a concerted effort to eliminate unnecessary overlap, so as to get institutions to focus on areas where they had been most effective. The stated aim was to get multilateral institutions to play a role where the private sector could not, or would not, play a role.

Financial stability was the key focus at Halifax. The strategy consisted of three identifiable components: crisis prevention, the creation of procedures to deal with accidents, and the creation of a system sufficiently robust to absorb shocks.

Crisis prevention

The first priority identified by the G7 finance ministries and central banks in their Halifax report was the need to put in place measures that would enable authorities to spot potential problems early, thus reducing the likelihood of crises. This was known as crisis prevention. Prevention essentially revolved around proposals for an early warning system consisting of a system of intensified multilateral surveillance and new standards on timely data release. Surveillance and data release were intended to improve the quality of information made available by public authorities on the state of their economies, which in turn would enhance the quality, rationality and efficiency of market decision making, thus reducing the likelihood of future crises. These kind of initiatives to improve the information on which market participants made decisions were bracketed under the heading 'transparency'. As discussed in Chapter 4, according to neo-classical theory, information shortages are the principal cause of market failure and improving information flows is therefore the only possible remedy to market failure because markets are always efficient and rational when they have adequate information. This position simultaneously implies that it is always authorities in affected countries that are to blame for financial crises for withholding information, and never market participants. 'Transparency', or improving the collection and publication of economic data and information, has therefore, as Mark Blyth has argued, provided an ideational shield for financial interests by immediately placing the onus of responsibility onto authorities in affected countries. The prominence of transparency in G7 proposals would suggest that they were heavily reliant on and even derived from neo-classical premises and understandings and this in itself is an inherently political state of affairs.

Transparency has become an increasingly fashionable term – a byword for good practice in macroeconomic and financial policy. Better information, the G7 have repeatedly argued in their collective statements, will make the flow of capital from investors to savers a more rational process. Larry Summers stated that the aim of Halifax was to seek 'a change in the culture in the IMF, in the markets, and in developing countries, towards an emphasis on transparency ... as the best way of ensuring that the markets can respond to any problem very quickly'.[16] Such views translated into an aim to create a role for the IMF as administrator of a code of economic information, which would determine what data countries should make available. The Fund would then act as an auditor of information, certifying that figures were an accurate reflection of underlying fundamentals, on which it was assumed markets based their investment decisions.

According to the Halifax communiqué, surveillance served three fundamental purposes. First it provided discipline, ensuring that financial developments were systematically reviewed and their implications clearly identified by multilateral institutions. Second, it provided governments with the opportunity to deliver collective advice to one another with respect to economic policy measures. Third, it permitted the private sector to make informed decisions and perform its role more effectively.[17] In other words, surveillance was integral to the kind of three-dimensional diplomacy between multilateral peers, national authorities and increasingly globalized financial markets, identified in earlier chapters. Surveillance relies on multilateral exchanges between national authorities on suitable national policies, subsequently publishes the data on which those exchanges are based with the purpose of improving market decision making and enhancing market participants' capacity to reach judgements on national economies and policies.

Halifax made a number of specific proposals for the IMF. It called for the establishment of benchmarks for the timely publication of key financial and economic data and a procedure for the regular public identification of countries that complied with these benchmarks. There was also a call for full and timely reporting by member countries of standard sets of data. Suggestions included reporting on a central bank balance sheet on a monthly basis, as well as up-to-date monthly information on government receipts and outlays. US Treasury Secretary Robert Rubin speculated that once standards for disclosure of data existed, it would become very difficult for a country not meeting those standards to raise funds in capital markets, because such a failure would create mistrust and market uncertainty.[18] In other words, it was envisaged from the outset that the implementation of data standards would primarily rely upon the implicit threat of market veto or withdrawal, if countries did not comply with multilateral standards. While consensus would be evident in the agreement of data standards therefore, the subsequent implementation of those standards would rely on a degree of coercion and the implicit threat of market withdrawal.

Four ways in which IMF surveillance could be improved were identified in the Halifax reports. First, the IMF was encouraged to devote greater resources and attention to countries of global significance, including both industrial and emerging economies. Second, the Fund was urged to provide clear and direct policy advice to governments, particularly those avoiding necessary policy measures. Third, patterns of capital flows and their maturity in financial and banking sectors were identified as areas in need of increased IMF attention. Moreover, the Fund was asked to attain a greater balance between cross-cutting issues such as common developments in capital markets and country-specific issues. Fourth, the Fund was encouraged to be more open and transparent in its assessments and policy advice.

Halifax therefore established the importance of timely data release and indicated that the international community would not shy away from whistle blowing countries deemed to have followed imprudent policies. However, officials also acknowledged that there were limits to the extent to which they could force this sort of issue. According to one official, it was never the intention of the G7 to turn the IMF into a sort of credit rating agency.[19] The aim was to give investors time to ponder the situation, while pushing the IMF to do more. This was accompanied by awareness that making the IMF view public became unreasonable at some point. What was aspired to was what officials described as a form of 'escalating candour'.[20] In this respect, the IMF had to be careful not to issue warnings about possible future 'crises' because this might only serve to accelerate a crisis or create one that would otherwise not have happened. This reflected the fact that communicating with the markets, or what has been referred to in earlier chapters as third-dimensional diplomacy, is often both 'awkward' and problematic.[21]

Stephen Gill has provided some insights into the social implications of this intensified surveillance from a critical neo-Gramscian perspective. According to Gill it is akin to what Jeremy Bentham and Michael Foucault have described as *panopticism*, involving a system of normalization that serves to enforce and reproduce the disciplines of global markets.[22] Intensified surveillance provides private investors with greater information, forces states to prove their 'credibility' and thereby enhances the structural power of capital and its ability to force changes on national policy-makers.[23] Indeed, the current macroeconomic regime, its domestic institutional features such as central bank independence and fiscal rules and the concept of credibility on which these institutional features are based, rely on and revolve around a politically encouraged and socially constructed interactive relationship between markets and public authorities.[24] These relationships involve markets engaging in a perpetual opinion poll on national policies and national policy-makers providing symbolic pledges and commitments to reassure markets. Moreover, this ongoing form of interaction between markets and public authorities is encouraged by and rationalized in terms of neo-classical theories of markets and constituent concepts such as 'credibility through pre-commitment' and 'transparency', as the dominant form of economic knowledge used and promoted by finance ministries and central banks.[25]

Improving crisis management: dealing with 'accidents'

Even with improved surveillance and good information, the Halifax proposals effectively contained an implicit acceptance that future financial crises would continue to occur, again suggesting that neo-classical theories are not accepted by the G7 finance ministries and central banks without reservation, but are often applied pragmatically and/or for politically convenient reasons (see Chapter 4). In other words, while promoting the view that liberal and open financial markets provide the most efficient means of allocating capital, the G7 also accept that financial markets are occasionally prone to volatility and herd-like behaviour. In particular, there was a heightened awareness of the dangers of 'moral hazard' following the Mexican experience, when the US government provided funds to provide emergency liquidity and avoid large losses for US financial institutions. For some this suggested that authorities stood ready to act as a lender of last resort and effectively discouraged private sector investors from paying sufficient attention to risk.

Officials openly acknowledged in the post-Mexico period that there was a need for an improved financial safety net, as a partial response to the increased size and speed of international capital flows. Such a safety net would be activated when countries had followed disciplined policies and had sound fundamentals, but were temporarily suffering from adverse market sentiment. At the same time however, the approach was predicated on a need to tightly define the circumstances in which such arrangements might be used, through the imposition of strict conditionality. The IMF practice of disbursing funds only after the negotiation of an acceptable economic policy programme with agreed policy commitments and targets was endorsed in the reports drafted for Halifax. Other proposals included a new standing procedure, the 'Emergency Financing Mechanism'. This involved high up-front access and faster procedures to access Fund resources in crisis situations, under an 'exceptional circumstances' clause. To support the new standing procedure, the G7 asked that the G10 and other countries develop financing arrangements with the objective of doubling as soon as possible the amount available under the General Arrangement to Borrow (GAB). At the same time, they urged continued discussions on a new IMF quota review. A new group of countries with the capacity to support the Fund, including Australia, Austria, Korea, Singapore and Spain, were added to the existing G10. Initially, these countries were prevented from being given an enhanced decision-making role in the GAB.[26] Unsurprisingly, rejection of G7 proposals followed. This rejection forced the G7 to create a 'new' arrangement to borrow (NAB), a parallel facility in which the new countries had a decision-making role. Essentially, these proposals were about enhancing existing institutions' fire-fighting capacity and strengthening the resilience of the existing financial system by creating the institutional foundations required to maintain and preserve a liberalized financial order.

System strengthening

A further issue highlighted by Halifax was the importance of financial regulation and supervision. Halifax made a contribution in the sense that leaders and finance ministers acknowledged the importance of the issue of financial regulation and supervision in ways they had not done before.[27] The G10 were encouraged to intensify their review of work in this area. The Basle Committee and the International Organization of Securities Commissions (IOSCO) were encouraged to work closely together to identify problems and areas of shared concern, and to report back. The information these bodies relayed would then enable ministers to reach conclusions on the extent of systemic risk. For countries in the process of liberalizing capital accounts it was recommended that technical assistance be provided and contacts with regulators in industrialized economies be developed. There were also calls for more work on appropriate guidelines for bank capital and supervisory regimes. Regulators and supervisory agencies were urged to deepen their co-operation in an effort to create an integrated approach on a global basis. The emphasis was on developing standards that encouraged transparent information exchange so as to produce a system capable of monitoring risk. At the same time, this was to be accompanied by continued encouragement to countries to remove capital market restrictions, coupled with strengthened policy advice from international financial institutions on the appropriate supervisory structures. According to one G7 deputy at the time, the real challenge lay in making 'standards operational, in training supervisors to implement them, and in adopting complementary changes that have to occur in bankruptcy regimes, accounting systems, and the examination infrastructure'.[28] Such measures were seen as paving the way for further financial liberalization.

What is notable here is that the finance ministries and central banks did not really debate or contest the technical detail of the reports being produced by more specialist bodies. Rather they settled for setting strategic priorities, deadlines and for catalysing increased communications between technocrats engaged in banking and securities regulation. Inevitably, these networks of regulators built upon their previous work and existing technical knowledge, giving proposals a kind of evolutionary technocratic dynamic that Porter's application of the technical system perspective would anticipate. Furthermore, while the upper echelons of the hierarchies of finance ministries and central banks participated in the G7 meetings and preparations (the G7 deputies and deputy-deputies), those at lower ranks tended to get more involved with the specialist detailed work of the Basle Committee or IOSCO, or else independent national regulatory agencies assumed more regulatory responsibilities at the expense of finance ministries and central banks. This reflects the fact that regulatory issues are mirroring developments in financial systems and are becoming more complex, technical and specialized. In contrast, it has been in macroeconomic matters including exchange rates, and the overall design of the international monetary and financial system, where the hierarchies of finance ministries and central banks involved in the G7 process have been most directly active. The involvement of senior officials should alert us to the fact that there were bigger issues at stake in global financial architectural debates than simple technocratic questions. As Armijo has pointed out, the official G7 community made a strategic decision to prioritize transparency over more interventionist options aimed at financial stabilization.[29]

As far as financial regulatory questions were concerned therefore, the G7 process acted as the most senior of a number of overlapping technocratic transgovernmental networks, that were in turn often embedded in their hierarchies of national administrative structures. Many of the more junior officials involved in specialist Basle committee or G10 work were directly answerable to the finance ministry and central bank deputies who prepared G7 agendas. While the deputies rarely involved themselves in the technical specifics of the work of more specialist regulators, they did set strategic priorities and deadlines for lower-level specialists. Moreover, ministers were on the margins of a lot of G7 work and largely restricted themselves to one or two big issues they had a personal interest in (see Chapter 5).[30] The prominence this gave to senior career officials and lower-level technocratic regulatory specialists in determining G7 agendas and defining legitimate knowledge has given the G7 process a sense of continuity and an incremental and inherently conservative dynamic. Unfortunately, whether such incremental adaptation is suited to an area renowned for the speed of innovation and its fast moving nature, is increasingly questionable.

Follow-up and the G10 report

Finance ministry and central bank officials conducted the more detailed post-Halifax work far from public scrutiny in a range of specially convened working groups and task forces. The role of the leader' summits was to provide a deadline for much of this work and to act as a high-profile event at which to announce progress. In this respect, international financial diplomacy proceeds slowly and in an incremental fashion, partly because of its reliance on consensus, partly because of the constraints of the legacies of inherited technical knowledge and partly because of its reliance on set-piece meetings. An example of the slow pace of progress was the issue of data standards. A year after Halifax, only thirty out of the IMF's 183 members had signed up to the standards the G7 had asked the Fund to formulate. The significant number of countries that had not signed up emphasized the protracted task of persuasion faced by the G7. Yet the interconnectedness of financial systems and the increasing dangers of contagious financial crises has made the implementation of measures in emerging markets so as to make imprudent investment in these locations less likely, a crucial priority for the G7.

The work at Halifax was further developed in a detailed G10 deputies' report. At a length of 71 pages, the report was both detailed and technical. It constituted a statement of G7 policy and has informed subsequent G7 policy on sovereign liquidity crises.[31] In particular, the report was intended to influence and affect the behaviour of a range of actors outside of the G7/G10, by communicating G7 intentions in the event of future crises. In other words, the report was a form of fourth-dimensional diplomacy in its own right.[32] Five staff from the IMF, three from the OECD, a European Commission official and four officials from the secretariat of the Bank for International Settlements also contributed to the report.

The principal focus of the report was on sovereign debt to private creditors, such as internationally traded securities, and its principle conclusion was that in the event of a crisis the terms and conditions of all sovereign debt contracts were to be met in full and market discipline was to be maintained, although a temporary suspension of debt payments could be invoked in exceptional circumstances. Moreover, neither debtor countries nor their creditors were to expect to be insulated from adverse financial consequences by large-scale sources of official financing. It was argued that markets should be equipped to assess the risks involved in lending to sovereign borrowers and should set prices accordingly. Public money would therefore not be readily available to guarantee private sector investments. A case-by-case approach to sovereign liquidity crises was advocated as an appropriate starting point for handling work-out procedures. The report also encouraged bargaining and negotiated settlements between creditors and debtors. Most especially, this placed an onus on the debtor government to put the process on a co-operative footing and to show willingness to subject itself to market discipline.

Three main actors in financial crises were identified: the official community, private creditors, and the sovereign debtor. Financial crises were in turn to be resolved through a series of three-way interactions, or a form of three-dimensional diplomacy between these actors. However, the approach advocated placing principal responsibility onto the individual debtor and their creditors. The report advocated basing responses to crises on the implementation of an IMF-supported sustainable adjustment programme and on an ongoing dialogue between the sovereign debtor and creditors. The overall aim of such dialogue was to prevent a small number of dissident creditors from disrupting or delaying arrangements to support a credible adjustment programme that was acceptable to the vast majority of concerned parties. The private sector was therefore encouraged to collaborate so it could develop collective positions in the event of a crisis. This was the forerunner of what later became known as collective action clauses and would allow the renegotiation of the terms and conditions of debt contracts. Sovereign bond contracts were to have procedures for consultation and co-operation between creditors and debtors written in to them in the event of a default, while the private sector was to appoint a creditors' representative to act on behalf of all creditors, so as to ensure a coherent market response.

Economic adjustment programmes implemented domestically would provide the pivot of work-out processes and would typically involve an immediate tightening of monetary policy, a credible fiscal package and possibly some exchange rate action. In this respect, macroeconomic policy remained a key focus, for the time being at least. The report also stressed that when debtor countries reached an agreement with the IMF it was seen to be the beginning of a continuing partnership for the restoration of macroeconomic balance in crisis-affected countries. In this context however, the official community's role was to facilitate a dialogue between interested parties and to assist in data collection. In other words, the G7 and the IMF were expected to catalyse third-dimensional diplomacy with market actors through an extension of their surveillance processes.

Post-Halifax G7 discussions

After Halifax, multilateral surveillance in the G7 process paid more attention to conditions outside the G7, particularly those countries that potentially posed a risk to the international financial and monetary system. In this respect, dimension I G7 discussions were considering fourth-dimensional issues and strategies more explicitly, and this was a direct consequence of the dynamics associated with the context of decentralized globalization described in Chapter 3.

At the Lyon summit, ongoing co-operative work between the Basle Committee, concerned with the supervision of banks, payments and settlement systems, and IOSCO, concerned with the supervision of securities firms and markets, was applauded. These bodies had managed to establish a common reporting framework since the Halifax meeting. The G7 also called for better organization of co-operation between Basle, IOSCO and the Joint Forum of banks, securities and insurance supervisors. Clarification of the responsibilities and roles of the respective forums was called for, together with a more comprehensive network of bilateral arrangements between authorities. Despite its high level of generality, the G7 was effectively attempting to act as an instigator of or a catalyst for an improvement in the pooling of information by other more specialist bodies.[33] This later crystallized in a more tangible institutional form with the establishment of the Financial Stability Forum.

Two major issues began to dominate the G7 agenda during 1997: capital account convertibility and the strengthening of banking systems. Earlier passing mentions of capital account convertibility had appeared in G7 communiqués from 1994 and 1996, but serious work on a concrete proposal did not begin until the IMF interim committee meeting in 1996. The British Treasury first raised the issue of amending IMF articles of agreement in 1994.[34] According to officials, the proposal would constitute more than a cosmetic change. It reflected national G7 philosophies and one of the fundamental premises of the shared belief system regarding the merits of greater capital mobility. The proposed amendment was intended to provide a constitutional basis for the further removal of restrictions to capital mobility.[35] It was intended to give the IMF a formal mandate for pushing progressive capital account liberalization. Most significantly, it was also intended to prevent backsliding. The IMF could formally discourage countries experiencing sovereign liquidity crises from resorting to the re-imposition of capital controls.[36] In other words, the amendment was intended to enhance the G7's capacity to engage in fourth-dimensional diplomacy with non-G7 states and bodies and promote further capital account liberalization.

By April 1997, the IMF's executive board reached broad agreement on four main principles. Capital account convertibility should be the mandate of the Fund, its articles of agreement should reflect this, countries should be allowed flexibility when moving towards convertibility, and countries should be allowed to impose temporary restrictions on capital inflows and outflows with IMF approval.[37] G7 officials expressed surprise at the ease with which developing countries were willing to accept these principles.[38] Reservations remained about the idea of putting the issue into a big bureaucratic process to be run by the Fund. In this respect, many Federal Reserve officials' grounding in financial regulation and issues relating to the banking system gave them a more cautious, albeit still generally favourable perspective where financial liberalization was concerned.[39] Ultimately, the Asian financial crisis and fears concerning hasty capital account liberalization under conditions of imprudent banking regulation, eventually stalled formal ratification of the amendment. However, this was not based on rejection of capital account liberalization as a principle, but a recognition that liberalization needed to be carefully sequenced and accompanied by adequate regulatory provision. Moreover, such provisions would need to be written into any formal capital account amendment. The failure to approve the amendment was in part recognition of the sensitivities resulting from the Asian financial crisis, particularly the argument that capital account liberalization was itself a cause of the crisis. A formal mandate for the IMF also ran the risk that financial liberalization might be rushed, running the risk of further serious disruption at some point in the future. In other words, the decision to stall formal ratification was effectively born out of a desire to protect the integrity of the principle of capital account liberalization, rather than outright rejection of the principle and a political recognition of a need to proceed more cautiously.

At the Denver summit of 1997, a report from the working group on supervision in emerging markets, including officials from Poland, Hong Kong, Indonesia, Korea and Thailand, was published. It established core principles for banking supervision. This was an illustration of the ad hoc attempts to periodically broaden the G7/G10 nexus to include some authorities in emerging markets. Such attempts have repeatedly characterized the second half of the 1990s and have been an effort to intensify the process of fourth-dimensional diplomacy. The rationale behind these efforts has been to extend G7-approved forms of regulation into these countries and increase the influence of networks of regulators such as the Basle Committee and IOSCO. These exercises in consultation were also the forerunner of more formal efforts to include emerging markets in decision making, such as the G20. Both Basle and IOSCO were also urged by the G7 to develop their work on derivatives disclosure practices. Formal information sharing among different regulatory agencies was also encouraged, as was IOSCO's initiative to identify large firm exposures that would have an effect on the market if the firm defaulted.

The fundamental pillars of the strategy developed at Halifax were therefore taken forward in a whole host of settings, albeit in a fairly protracted fashion. The G7 acted as a catalyst, pushing the process forward by setting objectives, priorities and targets that accorded with the principles of prevention, crisis management and system strengthening. The extension of market discipline, the enhancement of channels of communication between financial markets, authorities in emerging markets and the array of G7-dominated international and transnational bodies were the consistent themes of G7 proposals. In other words, there were clear efforts to deepen the three-way interactions between multilateral surveillance and standards, domestic policy-making and market actors, as a form of three-dimensional governance and to extend this process, while placing it on a firmer institutional footing in emerging markets.

The contribution of Halifax in perspective: elaborating and establishing a common approach

The contribution and impact of Halifax has to be understood in a wider societal context, including the key question of who participated in the Halifax exercise. Finance ministry and central bank officials almost exclusively conducted preparatory groundwork for the Halifax exercise. Wider societal input into the Halifax exercise was almost non-existent. The process of formulating proposals was taken forward mainly in the deputies and deputy-deputies' networks and then channelled into the summit's sherpa networks primarily through financial *sous* sherpas (often deputy's deputies), out of the sight and beyond the reach of electorates and wider social movements. Political scrutiny was conspicuous by its absence, while little publicity surrounded the process until the proposals were formally announced at Halifax. Work by groups such as the Canadian-based Halifax Initiative coalition, comprising a range of church, charitable, social and environmental groupings, was largely ignored, at least by the finance ministries and central banks, despite the production of an extensive report on institutional reform and the record of Halifax. This confirms the point made in Chapter 2 that the process of agenda setting prior to G7 meetings is circumscribed. Agendas generally reflect a narrow set of financial interests and criteria. Moreover, this is part of a wider pattern of underdeveloped dialogues with civil society that characterizes international financial diplomacy and the operations of multilateral institutions such as the IMF.[40] Although the IMF has made moves to improve its consultation process with civil society groupings, this is happening predominantly on an informal basis and there is little evidence to suggest that such consultations are having a major impact on either G7 or IMF policy prescriptions.[41]

Throughout the 1990s, the G7/G8 annual summits were shadowed by a series of events involving various global social movements and NGOs, referred to as the other economic summit or the People's Seven (P7). The main protestation was the absence of a third-world voice at the G7. However, finance ministry and central bank officials have consistently paid little attention to the views of these groupings, at least as far as architectural issues have been concerned.[42] Amongst NGOs, the popular view was that a sweeping review of capital flows and even a possible currency transaction (Tobin) tax was required to protect local currencies and help developing nations. Such ideas are the complete antithesis of the G7 mind-set and have not been seriously entertained by the G7 finance ministry and central banking community, not least because they threaten the strategic interests of the United States and the United Kingdom, primarily their ability to finance persistent long-term current account deficits.

Similarly, in the second-dimensional domestic setting, interactions prior to G7 meetings have been restricted. The input of foreign ministries into the Halifax exercise varied from country to country and depended on the degree of co-ordination between individual national agencies. Leaders were consulted through occasional briefings, but their role was largely restricted to questions of emphasis and to a large extent they merely reiterated the proposals drawn up by finance ministry and central bank officials. Together with more regular meetings, frequent contacts with the staff of the multilateral institutions and greater technical expertise, finance ministries in conjunction with central banks have been able to dominate the process of G7 policy formation on international financial questions. It is in this context that financial and monetary imperatives, rather than a broader set of socially orientated objectives, have driven the G7 policy agenda. In short, G7 finance ministries and central banks have acted as a transgovernmental coalition, closing ranks so as to control or channel debates and agendas in global financial governance on the grounds of their superior technical expertise and authority.

The clearly identifiable rationale of Halifax was to strengthen, reinforce and extend the liberal financial order that had been created in the 1970s and 1980s. It attempted to do so in an incremental, piecemeal and conservative fashion. The Halifax reports were a high-level statement of intent on the future of the global system, which acted as a starting point for a process of adjusting international institutions, so as to make them more compatible and better equipped to deal with a liberalized financial order. During this protracted process the G7 acted as a mechanism for setting agendas and priorities for more detailed work conducted in more specialized and lower-level forums. The official G7 financial community's main fear was that countries affected by financial crises would reintroduce capital controls, shutting off their capital markets to foreign investors, whilst pursuing go-for-growth macroeconomic strategies. There was therefore a strong strategic desire to retain access to markets for financial constituents based in the geographical financial centres located in G7 territories. Moreover, countries such as the US and the UK remained dependent on inflows of foreign capital to finance growing levels of indebtedness. Despite these political motivations, all of the G7's proposals evident in the Halifax exercise were heavily premised on the existing G7 consensus or mind-set, as discussed in Chapter 4.

The rest of this chapter illustrates an essential continuity in the process of global institutional reform in the 1990s. The three fundamental pillars of the Halifax strategy identified here, crisis prevention, procedures to deal with accidents, and a more robust and coherent system, have remained fundamentally unchanged, providing the cornerstone for the G7 approach to the issue of the global institutional architecture throughout the decade. Subsequent developments have progressively built more detail on to these three fundamental pillars, and on the ideas relating to negotiated settlements between private creditors and sovereign debtors outlined in the G10 report of 1996, but the basic approach has remained unaltered. Rather than producing a major rethink, officials have used financial crises in Russia, Latin America and Asia to further deepen and extend the basic constituent beliefs of their approach. In the minds of officials, the Asian crisis revealed that the problem with the Halifax strategy was the process of implementation, rather than the fundamental approach itself.[43] In other words, the record of the 1990s has suggested that fourth-dimensional diplomacy, or persuading multilateral institutions and emerging market authorities to behave in certain ways, has proved to be the most difficult challenge of all for the G7. The poor implementation record of Halifax ultimately reflected the relatively narrow social basis of the G7 process and the limited societal input into the Halifax exercise. In this respect, Halifax was not particularly successful in deepening or extending the G7 mind-set. However, it did provide a starting point for that protracted process by further elaborating and refining the beliefs on which it was based and therefore informing responses to further financial crises throughout the rest of the decade.

The G7 response to the Asian financial crisis

The devaluation of the Thai baht in the summer of 1997 sparked a series of currency crises and problems in equity markets in a host of East Asian economies during 1997–8. These events shook the foundations of global capitalism. However, Asian financial crises had a number of features that distinguished them from earlier debt and currency crises.[44] Most of the countries affected were either at or close to fiscal balance, the stock of government debt was not excessive and monetary policy appeared sensible. Moreover, with the exception of Thailand, current account deficits were not particularly large, while virtually all the economies in the region had well-developed export sectors. More complex causes centred on the financial system have been identified.[45] The 'developmental state' model, consisting of long-term co-operative reciprocal relations between firms, banks and governments, was characteristic of many South East Asian countries. Often there was little government control on domestic companies and no effective banking supervision. Moreover, high domestic savings (often as high as a third of GDP) and high corporate debt equity ratios, combined to allow firms to borrow multiples of their equity.[46] This yielded enormous technological and economic progress for East Asian economies in a relatively short space of time. Financial deregulation together with China's devaluation in 1994 enabled corporations to borrow more cheaply abroad than at home. When the dollar rose from 1995 and exports slowed, East Asian companies engaged in short-term borrowing to cover shortfalls in revenue. Excessive and risky lending resulted. When asset market bubbles in Thailand and Indonesia burst, and when an investment boom in South Korea proved unsustainable, foreign investors, domestic banks, firms and citizens scrambled for dollars to meet their obligations. It was this surge of investor panic that caused pegged exchange rates to collapse. 'Massive increases in debt and the rush of foreign investors to call in these loans – many of which were short term – led to the crisis'.[47]

In short, the Asian crisis was unlike other financial crises. It was not about balance of payments discrepancies, or a need to restructure foreign debt. Financial regulation, corporate governance and 'transparency' were key issues. It is in this context that the response of the G7 to the Asian crisis has to be understood. Essentially, this has involved a concerted attempt to challenge the high debt model of Asian development, or the developmental state model.[48] Something akin to an 'ideas battle' resulted.[49] The G7 process has been at the core of this 'ideas battle' as participants in the process have used the crisis to extend their own beliefs and norms through fourth-dimensional diplomacy.

When the crisis first broke the G7 had two priorities. The first was to stem and manage the initial crisis. The second was to revisit the architectural issues elaborated in the Halifax documentation, to build more detail upon these proposals and look at how implementation of architectural proposals could be improved. The principal focus in this chapter is on the second of these activities, because of their significance for the longer-term design of the global financial system and its relationship to social and economic development options. However, the initial handling of the crisis provided the political context for these architectural discussions, so a brief word is first required on the immediate G7 response to the crisis.

The G7 as crisis manager

As the Asian financial crisis proceeded, G7 relations were characterized by a combination of consensus and conflict. At times conflict and tension in response to the problems in Asia threatened to overwhelm the consensual traditions of the G7 finance ministries and central banks, particularly between Japan and the United States and Europe, but recognition of a mutual interest in successfully resolving the crisis ensured that a collective response was put together and areas of conflict and tension were successfully negotiated.

The G7 were involved in resolving the crisis in three ways. The first way was the provision of emergency financing to stem the crisis, although collective G7 mobilization came somewhat belatedly and only after contagion had spread throughout the region.[50] The lateness of the US and European response was a source of tension because Japan had been contributing finance since the summer of 1997.[51] A $35 billion package of G7 support was agreed in December 1997. On Christmas Eve 1997, the G7 released a statement announcing the intention to accelerate IMF disbursements and the disbursement of one third ($8 billion) of a supplemental financial commitment made by the G10, by early January.[52] In October 1998, the G7 finance ministries provided 90 per cent of a $41 billion package to ease liquidity difficulties in Latin America, as the New Arrangement to Borrow (NAB) funds were utilized for the first time ever, following telephone conference calls amongst G7 finance ministers. Therefore, after initially ignoring the Asian crisis and viewing it primarily as a regional problem, much to the chagrin of Japan, the G7 acknowledged their mistake by providing increasing amounts of official financing in recognition of the global threat posed by the series of financial crises of 1997–8. Collective discussions facilitated the construction of these financial packages and paved the way for a series of reassuring statements that indicated that the G7 governments were prepared to act to minimize the crisis by providing temporary liquidity. Collectively they enjoyed some degree of success in this regard.

Second, the G7 engaged in some limited efforts to catalyse private bail ins, in accordance with the principles of private sector collective responsibility outlined in the G10 report on the orderly resolution of sovereign liquidity crises. The G7 deputies acted as a catalyst for a package that rolled over bank loans on the basis of telephone calls, which in normal markets would have been renewed.[53] Lloyds Bank in the UK were the first to take action, tentatively agreeing to roll over a $US5 million loan to Chung Ho Bank in South Korea, which had been scheduled to mature. Housing and Commercial Bank also reached an agreement with Japan's Bank of Tokyo-Mitsubishi to roll over a ¥1 billion one month loan. However, there was less of a willingness to extend new lines of credit. In return for such agreements, governments in South East Asia had to agree not to protect local financial institutions and to prioritize the repayment of foreign creditors. Somewhat inevitably this caused resentment in South East Asia because international lenders appeared to be bailed out, in return for the minor concession of rolling over some loans.[54]

Third, in accordance with IMF lending procedures, the financing provided by the G7 was accompanied by strict conditionality that was built into IMF support programmes. While IMF loan programmes were discussed collectively by the G7 and approved by the Group as whole, the conditionality associated with them undoubtedly reflected a US bias and this proved to be a source of some tension within the G7. The extent of US dominance of an institution like the IMF is a contentious matter. What is clear is that the conditionality imposed by the IMF in the Asian financial crisis clearly reflected US preferences. Obviously the US was the largest shareholder in the Fund, but there were cultural and social reasons for this US bias, including the location of the Fund's headquarters in Washington, which increased its susceptibility to US influence, and the fact that the majority of Fund economists were sympathetic to neo-classical perspectives and/or were trained by the largest and best US graduate schools.

The conditions in the IMF programmes largely fell into two categories. First, there were reforms targeted at stemming the financial crisis and restoring financial confidence. These included measures to restructure the regulation of the banking and financial sectors, interest rate rises to protect currencies, fiscal retrenchment, which was sometimes seen as excessive, and institutional reforms such as the creation of independent central banks. In other words, most of these measures fitted with and were derived from shared G7 beliefs, and although there was a dispute over details and the extent of some of the reforms, most of these kinds of reforms were not contested too vigorously in principle by the G7. The second set of reforms were however more controversial and included the elimination on limits of foreign holdings of bonds and equities, abolition of restrictions on foreign ownership of land, acceleration of capital account liberalization and a reduction on the restrictions on corporate borrowing. These measures were clearly unrelated to the immediate task of managing and abating the crisis. They were designed to challenge the very nature of Asian capitalism and open the financial sector to increased international competition. International banks made major inroads into the region's banking sectors. In the first four months of 1998 there were mergers and acquisitions in Asian markets to the tune of US$35 billion, with many US and to a lesser extent European banks benefiting. Throughout Asia, most especially in affected South East Asian countries but also in Japan, there was a perception that the United States had aggressively used the IMF and the Asian crisis to leverage open Asian financial markets and seize control of Asian assets at the expense of local businesses and investors. Critics have also maintained that the Asian crisis has not resulted in wealth losses being allocated fairly. Workers and local entrepreneurs have borne a larger brunt of the crisis than foreign investors have. This was compounded by the fact that the IMF packages did not result in capital flows returning to previous levels, while violent movements of capital continued well into the second half of 1998.[55] As Higgott and others have pointed out, the perception that the IMF was an instrument of US power intensified throughout Asia.[56] The IMF's handling of the Asian crisis subsequently became an increasing cause of resentment and tension, not only for emerging markets in South East Asia, but between two key members of the G7 club, the US and Japan. While the US continued to assert throughout the first half of 1998 that the real cause of the Asian financial crisis was crony capitalism of a particular Asian variety, Japanese officials began to point to hasty capital account liberalization and the weaknesses of the global financial system. At the beginning of 1998, there was the potential for the development of considerable rifts and differences between the G7 countries, but the collegiate nature of the deputies' network and their discussions were crucial in ensuring that political differences were minimized and that the eventual response was consensual and even technocratic rather than being politicized, preserving the uneasy and increasingly fragile consensus amongst the G7 finance ministries and central banks on financial and monetary matters.

Architectural discussions and the AMF proposal

It was in the political context of increased tension described above that debates on the longer-term global financial architecture commenced. As in the case of the Halifax exercise, discussions focused on to how create an institutional framework that made crises less likely, while improving the capacity of the official community to manage future crises. From the outset the discussions assumed a technical character, but strategic questions of geopolitics and influence were never far away. The G7 process was the principle setting for taking these debates forward, yet the simmering tension between the club's two leading members, the US and Japan, which the Asian crisis had ignited, was soon brought into the open by a Japanese proposal to create an Asian Monetary Fund with capital resources of $100 billion and no seat at the table for the United States. The Japanese aim was to create a countervailing force to perceived western supremacy and to avoid situations where the IMF and western officials told Asian governments what to do, despite having little acquaintance with the region.[57] The US remained concerned that an Asian Monetary Fund would diminish its capacity to impose conditionality on national authorities in Asia.[58] For these reasons, the US sought to protect the IMF's central role in handling the crisis. Initially the US did not express any opposition to the AMF proposal when it was first discussed at an OECD meeting in Paris in early September, assuming that it too would be a member of the new AMF.[59] Lawrence Summers later learned that the US was to be excluded from the proposed AMF and telephoned his fellow G7 deputy Eisuke Sakakibara to express strong objections. The Japanese press even reported that Summers personalized the issue by referring to their friendship.[60] In other words, Summers worked through the deputies' network and used its collegiality as a means of expressing and highlighting the extent of US opposition to the proposal. The US had no formal way of vetoing the AMF proposal and had to rely on persuasion.

It is not clear why the Japanese eventually dropped the AMF proposal, given that it did not depend on US financing. One interpretation is that MOF officials valued the collegiality and the consensual nature of the relations they enjoyed with their colleagues at the US Treasury and feared that this might be damaged by pressing ahead with the AMF. Certainly, Japanese officials were reluctant to push ahead with the AMF initiative without US blessing, and ultimately it appears that respect for the consensual-based norms of G7 financial diplomacy were placed above the extension of geo-strategic influence. However, domestic financial concerns and opposition from the Chinese also contributed to the Japanese decision to drop the AMF proposal.[61]

In the period after the crisis a putative form of Asian monetary regionalism began to emerge. In place of an AMF, the so-called Manila Framework was agreed amongst the ASEAN countries in December 1997. This provided for IMF-style multilateral surveillance of Asian economies, albeit in a specific regional setting. In other words, the eventual outcome of the AMF proposal was an initiative that was entirely consistent with the kind of initiatives proposed in the Halifax reports, given their emphasis on enhanced surveillance. The Manila Framework was accompanied by the Miyazawa Plan, which made $30 billion available to countries in Asia, and an enhanced swap network among central banks in the region was implemented that was designed to enable Asian countries to address crises themselves without resort to the IMF.[62] This more modest initiative did not encounter US opposition, indicating that American endorsement and consensus remains important for the MOF and the BOJ.[63]

US endorsement is important precisely because a breakdown in the consensual collegiality that characterizes the G7 deputies' network will minimize Japanese influence in global monetary and financial affairs. G7 finance ministry and central bank interaction based on persuasion and argumentation so as to arrive at consensus, provides Japanese officials with a very real way of making their views heard, influencing important global financial debates and making the United States Treasury and Federal Reserve listen to a Japanese perspective. Any Japanese action that wilfully angered the US and damaged that consensual mode of operation would make it more difficult for the Japanese to make their voice heard in monetary and financial affairs. These were the kind of calculations influencing Japanese responses to the Asian financial crisis. In time, a role as a regional leader of an incipient form of Asian monetary regionalism may provide Japan with more leverage with the United States, making it just as important for American officials to have the ear of Japanese officials as it currently is for the Japanese to have the ear of their American counterparts. For the time being, however, despite G7 financial diplomacy being based on persuasion and consensus, some notable asymmetries based on structural power resources such as levels of liquidity, the importance of the dollar, the intellectual position and location of the leading multilateral lending agencies, continue to underpin G7 otherwise collegiate discussions, and make it more important for the Japanese to have good relations with the US than the other way round.

The durability of the consensus on capital controls

In the context of the US and IMF handling of the crisis and the rise of Asian monetary regionalism, US–Japanese relations were characterized by increasing tension during 1997 and 1998. For some authors, there was a breakdown of the G7 consensus on the use of capital controls and questions of monetary order more generally. Robert Wade predicted a coming fight between the US and Europe over the use of capital controls that never quite materialized.[64] John Kirton has argued that following Canadian promptings there was diminished enthusiasm for the principle of capital account liberalization amongst the G7.[65] Paul Martin's proposal for an emergency standstill mechanism clause on short-term capital inflows provides some evidence of this. However, a consensus on the selective use of Chilean-style controls on short-term inflows into banking systems had existed since Lawrence Summers made reference to their usefulness in 1996 and this was consolidated in the period after the Asian financial crisis.[66] The issue for debate and discussion was not the desirability of capital account liberalization as such, or the need to overturn this as the principal norm in the international financial order, but the circumstances in which short-term controls on capital inflows and standstill mechanisms should be activated. Certainly, Canada was a more enthusiastic supporter of the use of such methods than the United States, but differences on detail did not mean that the broad G7 consensus was crumbling. On the contrary, a consensus that financial liberalization was a desirable goal to be worked towards continued to set the parameters for G7 discussions on the global financial architecture.

As evidence of a growing Asian–US rift, Jonathon Kirshner has highlighted how US officials including Summers and Alan Greenspan heaped scathing criticism on the Malaysian government for implementing more comprehensive style controls, while Japan fully supported the measure.[67] It was certainly the case that Malaysia was the first country to receive assistance under the new Miyazawa initiative, but there was never any official endorsement of Malaysian style controls, even if the condemnation that came from the United States was not repeated by the Japanese. Japan was anxious to avoid antagonizing Asian neighbours, given their desire to act as leaders of Asian monetary regionalism. Pragmatic strategic considerations were more significant reasons for the Japanese silence on Malaysian capital controls than any ideational disagreement with the United States. Moreover, prominent individuals from the Japanese financial sector and academia reported that Japanese officials were bewildered by the Malaysian controls.[68] Ultimately, there is little evidence to suggest that the Japanese, or any other G7 country, supported more stringent controls either in principle or in practice. There was never any formal on-the-record promotion of Malaysian style capital controls in the official documentation of any of the G7 finance ministries and central banks. Indeed, a closer look at the architectural proposals that followed would seem to suggest these proposals were informed by the objective of institutionalizing a liberal financial order and securing further capital account liberalization.

Japan's vice minister for international affairs (MOF), Dr Eisuke Sakakibara, was even prepared to explicitly reject the notion of a rift between the US and Japan on the issue of capital controls and pointed to the durability of the evolving G7 consensus by referring to the report on the global financial architecture issues at the Cologne summit:

> It has sometimes been suggested by the press and others that Japan is advocating more controls on capital flows while other G7 countries are arguing for free capital movements. This is simply not true. If one reads the Miyazawa speech of last December carefully, it is clear that Japan's position from the

> outset was that maintaining market friendly controls that would prevent turbulent capital inflows should be justified when a country wants to keep capital inflows at a manageable level according to the stage of development of its financial sector, and there might be some cases that would justify the re-introduction of controls on capital outflows as an exception, for example in order to avoid bail out by IMF loans. As the report shows this stance is shared by all G7 countries.[69]

This message of support for some limited market-friendly controls on capital inflows from across the G7 corresponds with the analysis forwarded in Chapter 4. Japan's greater willingness to endorse controls on capital outflows in exceptional circumstances was a slight departure, but exceptional circumstances was something emphasized throughout in official Japanese policy documentation and the Japanese were happy for the IMF to conduct research and reach judgements on what constituted appropriate exceptional circumstances.[70]

There was certainly some evolution of the G7 consensus on capital account liberalization post-Asia, and Japan was at the forefront of promoting refinements to this consensus, but the Japanese remained unequivocal in their overall support for capital account liberalization and these incremental refinements to existing beliefs were not representative of a broader paradigm shift. Japan repeatedly acknowledged that active cross-border capital flows realized a more efficient allocation of world resources and helped to increase the productivity and economic development of emerging markets and other capital receiving countries, while providing high returns for investors.[71] The general approach to capital account liberalization derived from such views was that while excessive capital inflows had contributed to the Asian crisis, there was no merit in ruining the whole of the net advantages of capital account liberalization by correcting a small fault.[72] Japan consequently began to promote an approach designed to harness the benefits of capital account on the basis of assessments conducted on a country-by-country basis, so as to ascertain the specific circumstances faced by each country, rather than the blanket approach that was implicit in the proposal to amend the articles of the IMF to promote capital account liberalization in the mid-1990s.[73] Consequently, the G7 consensus evolved from promoting the liberalization of capital transactions as broadly and as speedily as possible, to a situation where it is now acknowledged that capital liberalization has to be properly sequenced and should be proceeded by certain pre-conditions, including a well-established market economy; trade liberalization; a strong financial sector supported by an efficient supervisory system that was capable of monitoring the risks involved in exposure to foreign currency denominated loans; and a macroeconomic framework consistent with a liberalized financial system. Japanese views were instrumental in producing this refined G7 consensus, which remained supportive of capital liberalization and even saw it as a priority that first required reform to existing domestic institutional arrangements.

The continuous and circumspect approach, and in most cases opposition, of the G7 to the use of capital controls was also accompanied by widespread hesitation and rejection of capital controls in emerging markets. The reasons for this rejection are not hard to find. Ultimately, the responsibility for operating such controls would fall on finance ministries and central banks. Elites in these agencies have tended to be sympathetic and orientated towards a range of constituents who have benefited from financial liberalization, such as big tradable goods producers, banks and other financial services and large private asset holders. These interests have gained improved access to loanable funds and lower borrowing costs, while being able to engage in portfolio diversification and more profitable investments. Such benefits would be lost if capital controls were re-imposed. The precise nature of these state–society coalitions vary from state to state, but in almost every case important domestic commercial interests have had good links with finance ministries and central banks, who themselves enjoyed considerable autonomy in relation to other government agencies. In Mexico for example, Sylvia Maxwell has identified a 'bankers alliance', while in the case of South Korea and Taiwan large-scale manufacturers engaged in capital-intensive activities have been key in bringing pressure to bear, so as to preserve access to competitive sources of international financing.[74] In this respect, Benjamin Cohen's analysis as to why states hesitated in implementing capital controls is compelling. He argues that 'a coalition of political opposition from within emerging markets, a comparably influential bank–industry–wealth holder complex interacted in a mutually reinforcing fashion with the Wall Street–Treasury complex as a powerful de facto transnational coalition to bar any retreat from the Washington consensus'.[75]

The comparative political economy literature on financial liberalization in emerging markets has therefore repeatedly identified influential state–society coalitions that support financial liberalization and resist efforts to restrain it. In a similar fashion we can identify a similar state–society coalition in the industrialized world in all G7 countries. This state–society coalition extends beyond the Anglo-Saxon world to include the German finance ministry, the Bundesbank and internationally active concerns such as Volkswagen, Daimler-Benz, BMW and Deutsche bank, who all had growing concerns in a range of Latin American and Asian markets and therefore had an interest in ensuring that capital accounts remained open. Likewise in Japan with Nomura International, Toyota and Tokyo-Mitsubishi Bank, there were a similar range of interests whose views were well represented by the Ministry of Finance and the Bank of Japan. This is not to say there were no voices in each of the G7 countries that were more sympathetic to the use of capital controls. Even in the United States, which has traditionally been strongest in its opposition to the use of capital controls, sympathetic voices for the use of a range of capital controls do exist.[76]

Unfortunately those voices advocating financial stabilization have not been as well connected to the finance ministry–central banking policy community, which has largely dominated and controlled the debate on the global financial architecture as the coalition that supports financial openness.[77] This is something that Wade, Kirton and others often overlook and consequently they tend to overestimate the extent of Japanese, Canadian and European opposition to financial openness.

Ultimately, the predominantly technocratic finance ministry and central banking community has almost exclusively controlled architectural debates. They have been the principal authors of official proposals. Indeed, this is the principal reason why these proposals have been so modest, technical and incremental. Wider distributive political projects that could be aided by the use of capital controls are unlikely to receive due consideration in debates on the global financial architecture until the coalition of social forces sympathetic to such controls are more actively involved in these debates. In particular, control of architectural debates need to be wrestled from elite networks of finance ministry and central bank officials, regardless of whether these networks are restricted solely to the G7 or include selected groups of emerging markets such as the recent G22 and G20 initiatives. While finance ministries, central banks and regulators have supposedly increased their outreach activities on architectural issues,[78] the kind of discussions that have resulted have been muted, have had limited influence on official documentation and have more often than not taken the form of a 'dialogue of the deaf'. Any mutual learning processes are undoubtedly proceeding at a slow place. Until a broader range of interests are included in key decision-making networks, debates on the governance of global finance will remain predominantly technical, with scant concern paid to social and political considerations, other than expressions of the normative case for capital liberalization and its institutional pre-requisites. For the time being, the limited use of capital controls is explained by the fact that finance ministries and central banks, who are most sympathetic to internationally active commercial concerns, control debates on the use of these controls and have constructed a technical consensus that practically ignores the interests of a wider range of social groupings, but is by its very nature an inherently political and partisan consensus. Within these processes of consensus formation the G7 finance ministries and central banks have acted as a core transgovernmental coalition, overseeing and setting agendas and priorities for a range of other institutions and networks of regulators.

Further areas of contention

There were three further areas of contention amongst the G7 as debates on the global financial architecture proceeded. The first of these was the role of the IMF. The Japanese had implicitly challenged the role of the IMF with its proposal for the establishment of the AMF, but they later relented and accepted that the IMF had a central role to play in global financial governance.[79] Several elements became part of a new G7 consensus such as focusing IMF surveillance more explicitly on large-scale cross-border capital flows, restricting the IMF's involvement in structural policies to matters directly relating to financial crises and to improve the transparency of IMF decision making. Some Japanese proposals on this last point eventually contributed to the consensus, such as the publication of more IMF staff papers and the establishment of an evaluation unit reporting direct to the global financial and monetary committee, formerly the interim committee. However, there were also more contentious proposals such as inviting representatives of programme countries to participate in Board discussions on programmes and calls for the Fund to avoid fiscal and monetary policies that prioritized financial stability at the expense of an excessive contraction of the economy. This last proposal made little headway as conditionality has been retained in Fund programmes and the macroeconomic elements of this conditionality has been focused on the prioritization of price stability, evident in the conditionality accompanying financial assistance for Turkey and Argentina. Both the US and the German Bundesbank argued the importance of retaining the principle of macroeconomic conditionality attached to IMF loans.[80] Japan also called for a redistribution of the IMF quota system. Given that such a move would also lead to a reconfiguration of IMF decision making, this proposal was perhaps unsurprisingly opposed by the United States. Japan's response to the issue of the IMF was clearly informed by the perception that the Fund had imposed unsuitable policies in Asia following the financial crisis, had engaged in little consultation with Asians and had essentially promoted the interests of western creditors in its dealings with the region. The Japanese position was clearly motivated by a desire to avoid a repeat performance and in this respect Japan was successful in achieving some of its priorities in relation to the Fund even if macroeconomic conditionality has continued. However, there is little sign that the asymmetrical system of decision making that characterizes the Fund will be addressed in the near future, even if the US has realized the need to respond to concerns about the US-centred nature of decision making in global financial governance. The G7 provided the principal vehicle for the Japanese to promote their interests and its collegiality and consensual mode of operation gave Japan, Canada and the UK opportunities to display intellectual leadership and influence the debate on the global financial architecture.

The second contentious area was the issue of standstill. This was an area where the Bank of Canada and the Bank of England displayed intellectual leadership as they engaged in joint work that established a framework for resolving financial crises that consisted of three elements.[81] The first element was that the limits of available official financing in the event of crises should be known well in advance, creating 'presumptive limits' for any public financial rescue. The second element consisted of exceptional official financing if a crisis threatened global financial stability, to be based on explicit criteria and procedures. The final element allowed for a temporary suspension of debt service repayments under certain conditions. The principle of orderly standstill of debt repayments is designed to give distressed debtors some time to take steps, including debt rescheduling, to address their problems. US opposition to the standstill principle resulted in its dilution, although the experience of Argentina in 2002 served to convince the United States that there was a need to increase the predictability and reduce the uncertainty of official G7 policy actions in relation to emerging markets. As a consequence the G7 adopted an action plan in April 2002 based on the work of the Bank of Canada and the Bank of England. The plan recognized the need for clear limits to official financing and made the minimal concession of promoting rules in loan contracts to allow a cooling off, in the form of 'collective action clauses', which would prevent small groups of rogue creditors from blocking a reasonable offer by authorities in emerging markets for a debt-restructuring deal. This action plan and its recognition of collective action causes was a concession, albeit a minor one, from the G7 towards emerging markets and placed rather more responsibility on private investors to participate in the resolution of financial crises than had hitherto been the case. Collective action clauses were a recognition that more had to be done to modify and manage some of the more extreme consequences of market volatility and irresponsibility even if they placed only minor constraints on private actors. While we must be careful not to overstate the extent of the change in G7 attitude, or its significance, the acceptance of collective action clauses by the G7 went some of the way towards redressing the imbalances of a crisis-prone globalized financial system that had repeatedly placed obligations on emerging markets while seemingly bailing out private financial concerns. In this respect, the Action Plan constituted an important symbolic acknowledgement that the global financial system was prone to crisis, excess and speculative activities, the extremes of which needed to be curbed. It was in effect another example of the G7's pragmatic departure from neo-classical theory.

The third issue of contention that has resulted in an uneasy G7 consensus was the issue of hedge funds. The Japanese position was particularly pronounced. They leaned towards the view that hedge funds influenced other market participants so greatly that when large-scale hedge funds take a position in a market, it practically determines the direction of market movements, distorting the working of the markets and leading to herd-like behaviour.[82] Consequently, the official Japanese position at the end of 1998 was that there was a case for appropriate prudential rules and reporting requirements for financial institutions investing in or lending to hedge funds, especially those operating in offshore financial centres.[83] By April 2000, the Japanese position had softened and they were accepting the consensus reached by the Financial Stability Forum (FSF), which merely called for enhanced disclosure by all market participants, while direct regulation initially favoured by the Japanese and Germany but opposed by the Americans, was rejected.[84] The FSF findings, for all their technical character, were clearly the product of political compromise because while US opposition to the regulation of hedge funds was represented in the report, this was accompanied by the proviso that if the report's recommendations did not address concerns about hedge fund instability and herd behaviour, direct regulation would be reconsidered. This appeared to appease Japanese and German concerns and maintained an uneasy G7 consensus. It also kept open the possibility that hedge funds would be directly regulated at some point in the future, which directly contradicted the US position that it was not possible to regulate hedge funds.

These episodes demonstrate several things about global financial governance. First, while global financial governance is certainly not characterized by an equality of capability among the major powers, it is overstating the case to claim that the outcomes of global financial diplomacy amongst the G7 perfectly mirror US preferences. The US has had to modify its position on several matters and has often been persuaded to do so by other G7 finance ministries and central banks. Therefore, while the US remains ascendant in global financial governance, ascendancy is not the same thing as outright domination. Despite this, the US usually does get its way on key issues and this was evident in the shelving of the Sovereign Debt Restructuring Mechanism. Second, the pace of change in global financial governance is slow, incremental and builds upon existing technical knowledge and reports, which tend to be refined and adjusted rather than overturned on a wholesale basis. Those predicting rapid change or paradigm shifts misunderstand the nature of global financial governance and the preference for consensual relations amongst the world's leading finance ministries and central banks, which in turn creates a dynamic of adjustment and refinement in reform discussions, due to the inherent conservatism of these institutions and their relatively narrow technical outlook. Third, contrary to some claims, the Japanese and the Canadians did not sit outside the broader G7 consensus on the issue of capital controls and capital liberalization, but contributed to the refinement and adjustment of that consensus through participation in G7 discussions, even if they did so on predominantly US terms. Ultimately, however they continue to have a belief in liberal financial order and a faith in capital liberalization as a goal to be worked towards. As we shall see, other architectural proposals were largely informed by this objective and the Japanese participated fully in these debates and have more or less been content with consensual outcomes and moderate adjustments that have resulted.[85]

Continuity from Halifax: Halifax II

By February 1998, an inquest into the longer-term implications of the Asian crisis was under way. The G7 process systematically revisited the issue of the global institutional architecture. Officials sought to identify long-term lessons from the crisis and then adjust institutional arrangements accordingly. A review of the global financial institutional architecture similar to that initiated at Halifax was undertaken.

The first and most important lesson drawn from the Asian crisis was that the work done after Halifax was fundamentally sound.[86] Halifax was viewed by officials as having moved the system along, ensuring that they were 'one or two steps behind instead of three or four'.[87] The whole issue was viewed as being 'less one of approach and more a question of implementation – of persuading countries to actually do certain things'.[88] For this reason, US officials were quite openly referring to the process of scrutinizing the global institutional architecture post-Asia as Halifax II, indicating that they saw the latest discussions as being a continuation and a direct successor of the earlier discussions held at Halifax.[89] Bretton Woods II was also considered as a title for these discussions, but this was rejected for having the wrong connotations.[90]

The climate of financial crisis provided the opportunity to place many of the principles elaborated at Halifax on a firmer institutional footing, as well as institutionalizing the processes of market scrutiny and consultation with authorities in less-developed countries. Exploring how to enhance implementation of G7 initiatives in emerging markets was therefore one of the overriding concerns informing G7 discussions on the global financial architecture. More active consultation with authorities in these emerging markets was already underway, albeit on a rather ad hoc basis, and were seen as an obvious route to enhancing implementation in emerging markets, particularly if the kind of collegiate, consensual, technocratic discussions that characterized the G7 deputies' network could be extended to a similar professional network with a broader membership that also included representatives from emerging markets.

In the eyes of G7 officials, the Asian crisis revealed that Thai, Indonesian and Malaysian authorities had been less than open in the release of data. Therefore surveillance highlighted at Halifax had not worked as well as it might because of the requirement for countries to voluntarily engage in data release. There was consequently a need for the G7 to investigate ways of putting surveillance on a firmer institutional footing. This focus on transparency fitted with a broad American position that the root cause of the crisis was crony capitalism consisting of inadequate domestic institutions, poorly capitalized banks with huge portfolios of questionable loans to politically well-connected businesses and opaque financial reporting of total foreign national liabilities. However, the focus on transparency was also compatible with a Japanese position that reform of the global financial system was required to lessen the risk of future financial crises. Ultimately, attempts to create international standards to improve transparency, together with a more qualified and cautious approach to financial liberalization and efforts to improve the lending procedures of multilateral institutions, provided the major thrust of reform proposals. A consensus formed around this approach that was compatible with the seemingly diametrically opposed positions of the US in relation to crony capitalism and the Japanese on flaws in the global financial system. Both countries softened their initial positions and accepted a compromise that involved both international and domestic change and produced initiatives that entailed reform to multilateral institutions and the formulation of new global codes and standards that also required emerging markets to reform their own existing financial governance practices and procedures.

During the process of formulating architectural proposals, officials remained upbeat about what Halifax had actually achieved. Their initial verdict on the crisis was that Thailand and Indonesia's problem were picked up relatively quickly and that the new 'Emergency Financing Mechanism' worked relatively well.[91] At the same time however, the reckless private sector investment that the G10 report of 1996 had attempted to discourage, was acknowledged as a contributory factor in the Asian situation. In other words, the G7 had not been particularly successful in its efforts to persuade markets actors, multilateral institutions, or authorities in emerging markets, to behave in particular ways. Therefore, the G7 needed to look at ways of improving their capacity to engage in what was referred to in Chapter 3 as third and fourth dimensional diplomacy, or communicating with states outside of the G7, with international institutions and with market actors. In retrospect, officials acknowledged that the 'transparency' issue had not been pushed hard enough and the message should have been made more loudly and consistently.[92] Essentially, the Halifax II exercise was an investigation of ways of doing this, but the continuity with the earlier Halifax exercise was clear from the sort of proposals that came forward.[93]

Transparency and codes of practice: institutionalizing, deepening and extending three-dimensional diplomacy

The crucial focus of Halifax II was to build a broader constituency for 'transparency' as a basis for more informed and more responsible market activities, while investigating precisely how increased 'transparency' could be put into practice in institutional terms.[94] With this objective in mind, the US Treasury convened a Group of Twenty-two countries at the start of 1998 to consider some of these issues. The G22 included numerous emerging market economies and was part of an effort to expand input into the process of reviewing the global financial architecture. However, officials considered the G7 to be the pre-eminent forum for doing business, or 'first among equals'.[95] Once a G7 consensus was obtained, the objective was to promote this consensus in wider settings and to give a larger group of countries a sense of ownership of that consensus. It was in this sense that the Group of Seven acted as a core transgovernmental coalition in the review of the global financial architecture. The rationale behind the G22 was that by enlarging the number of participants contributing to the review of architectural proposals, the prospects for implementation of those proposals would in turn be improved, while the proposals themselves would enjoy wider legitimacy. Lawrence Summers, US G7 deputy at the time, alluded to this when he stated that the crucial task remained one of 'building an institutional architecture that links the industrialized and developing world and unites them in the way the industrialized world is already united'.[96] In effect, the aim was to create the basis for agreement on the desirability of sound money policies and open capital markets, whilst broadening the constituency for transparency. The G22 was in essence therefore an example of a group of powerful states creating a body in an effort to obtain the voluntary compliance of weaker states through an active process of consultation and discussion.[97] In part, the lesson of the relatively narrow series of contributions to the Halifax exercise had been learnt as participation in key global financial governance debates was broadened, albeit on an ad hoc and arbitrary basis. Criticisms of the G22 followed however, and the Managing Director of the IMF, Michael Camdessus, argued that it was unrepresentative of his organization's 183 members. The problem for the G22 was that they were seen as selected friends of the US because there were representatives from Latin America and Asia but none from Africa.

The broad process of reviewing the international financial architecture – post-Asia – was a diffuse one taken forward in a number of settings including the G7, G22, ASEAN, the so-called 'Manila Group' and more specialist bodies like Basle and IOSOCO. During 1998, three G22 working parties prepared reports on transparency, strengthening financial systems and involving the private sector in crisis resolution. The fact that the G7 finance ministries and central banks were communicating with sympathetic elites from finance ministries and central banks elsewhere, ensured that the debate retained more of a technocratic character than a political one and enabled finance ministries and central banks to dominate and control the debate.

The G7 finance ministries and central banks shared the view that one of the principal causes of the Asian financial crisis was the disclosure of previously withheld data in affected countries. This is not to say there were no differences on the issue of the causation of the Asian financial crises amongst the G7 countries. As we have already seen, the US diagnosis focused more heavily on the internal workings and failings of the Asian developmental model and the Japanese attributed a greater role to the workings of the global financial system, but the gap between the two positions was not as great as is often asserted and it was not so large that it could not be bridged. Most notably, there was agreement within the G7 deputies' network that there was a need for greater transparency in the global financial system. For example, the South Korean central bank was criticized by the G7 for not disclosing the extent of short-term borrowing by private sector Korean banks until December 1997.

Behind the subsequent promotion of transparency was the belief that authorities in emerging markets had to establish lasting relationships with private sector investors and achieve 'an honest and open dialogue in which hard questions could be asked and bad news was difficult to conceal'.[98] In other words, the G7 were investigating ways of deepening what was referred to in Chapter 3 as third-dimensional diplomacy between national authorities and markets.

A number of codes of practice emerged from the G22 working groups' dialogue with the G7. These included codes of practice on monetary and fiscal policy, which the British Treasury had been pushing strongly. Areas that were identified as being particularly important for incorporation under the new codes of practice were forward transactions in foreign exchange transactions, foreign currency liabilities of foreign banks, and indicators of the health of the financial sector. A code of practice for corporate governance was to involve principles for auditing, accounting and disclosure in the private sector. These codes of practice were the centrepiece of G7 proposals. The proposals eventually translated into twelve key standards for sound financial systems, which were recognized and promoted by the Financial Stability Forum (created by the G7 as one of their post-Asian initiatives) as the basis for good financial practice. The twelve codes included monetary and financial transparency, fiscal transparency, special data dissemination standard/general data dissemination system, all presided over by the IMF; principles of corporate governance monitored and evaluated by the OECD; international accounting standards reported on by the International Accounting Standards Board (IASB); international standards on auditing monitored by the International Federation of Accountants (IFAC); core principles for systemically important payments systems and recommendations for securities settlement systems overseen by IOSCO; core principles for effective banking supervision evaluated by the Basle Committee; objectives and principles of securities regulations monitored by IOSCO; and insurance core principles evaluated by the International Association of Insurance Supervisors (IAIS). The governance implications of these various codes of practice remains to be deciphered and evaluated. The Group of Seven have however promoted these standards and on request receive reports on their progress from specialist bodies such as the Basle Committee's report on the progress of International Accounting Standards for Banks in April 2000.[99]

However, the collection of codes catalysed and stimulated by the G7's promotion of transparency have no formal enforcement mechanism. Rather they operate through the threat of investor withdrawal if countries failed to comply with the data standards and core principles spelt out in the codes of practice. In this respect, markets look to public authorities for guidance on standards. The G7 are of course one step removed from the dissemination and evaluation of the codes, but it is their promptings and the strategic decision to prioritize transparency that has led to an approach to global financial governance which currently relies heavily on this array of codes. Crucially, codes not only provide guidance for emerging markets on what they need to do to avoid financial disruption, they also give markets a clearly stated standard by which to judge countries' macroeconomic policies and financial sectors. In this respect, the codes and standards provide, facilitate and encourage the process of continuous market scrutiny, providing a loose institutional foundation for the process of three-dimensional diplomacy.

The IMF's role in relation to the codes is to publicize concerns about gaps in information disclosure where the public sector and macroeconomic data are concerned.[100] The G7 also publicly argued in favour of making compliance with codes and standards a condition for countries needing to borrow from the Fund, but there has been no formal inclusion of the standards and codes in IMF Article IV surveillance or the formulation of conditionality.[101] The Basle Committee was to perform a similar role to that of the IMF in the case of the publication of banking sector standards and IOSCO similarly for securities markets. Since 1999, the IMF has been publishing Country Reports on the Observance of Standards and Codes (ROSCs), while joint IMF–World Bank teams have been preparing Financial Sector Assessment Programmes (FSAPs), which are expected to lead to the voluntary publication of Financial System Stability Assessment Reports (FSSAs). All of these developments have had the effect of placing the processes of peer and market review of national macroeconomic and financial sector policies on a firmer institutional footing.

However, the standards and codes do remain voluntary and it remains unclear how successfully they have been implemented. There has been resistance to them. The G24 group of developing nations have complained about their lack of representation in the setting of standards in communiqués to the IMF. They have also complained about the cost of implementing the standards, suggested that they are not appropriate for all national contexts and retained a right to prevent the publication of ROSCs and FSAPs.[102] Moreover, the Fund has provided flexible assessments based on national specifics, rather than simple numerical pass or fail scorecards that the markets would prefer. Market discipline has been similarly problematic and the extent to which markets have made use of the standards and codes is unclear. At best they appear to have treated the standards and codes as simply another source of information.[103] On the other hand, Fitch ratings reported a significant relationship between publication of ROSCs and changes in sovereign ratings between 1999 and 2002, suggesting that compliance with standards and codes have a positive impact on perceptions of creditworthiness. Even if codes do not have the disciplinary impact the G7 was perhaps envisaging, there are clear incentives for countries to comply with the standards and codes and by the end of 2002 close to half of the IMF's 184 members had completed at least one ROSC module.[104] As Thirkell-White has argued, the codes claim to provide authoritative statements of best practice which means they are an exercise in persuasion as much as power.[105] By choosing to go down the route of transparency and codes which rely on a combination of market incentives and threats, the G7 have sought to create an institutional foundation and basis for the process of market scrutiny, or third-dimensional diplomacy, but simultaneously this enhances the market's capacity to reach judgements and define national best practice in accordance with its own preferences. Whether the combination of G7 and market persuasion will be sufficient to deliver a successful record of implementation in relation to the codes remains to be seen, but the recent record of G7 finance ministry–central banks' response to architectural questions and financial crises, suggests that if setbacks are encountered, the G7 are unlikely to drop their technocratic focus and their efforts to keep politics at arms length from financial governance debates. If anything we can probably expect them to intensify their efforts at persuasion, their consultations with technocrats from systemically significant emerging markets and their investigations of how to implement policies oriented towards financial stability. Over the last decade they have demonstrated a persistent and determined incremental approach to institutionalizing a liberal financial order, progressively intensifying their efforts to create the institutional foundations for a liberal financial order by focusing on the definition and subsequent implementation of market-friendly policies. In this respect, the overwhelming rationale behind the G7 finance ministries and central banks' activities has been 'to assist emerging markets in their preparations for the process of liberalization'.[106] Technocratic use of codes and standards and the provision of technical assistance by multilateral institutions and industrialized countries has undoubtedly provided a cloak for some quite intrusive interventions into domestic policy-making and political arrangements in emerging markets.

Therefore, the long-term G7 response to the Asian crisis has involved the initiation of a series of international institutional mechanisms and processes that enhanced market discipline and the pattern of three-dimensional diplomacy. A series of technical standards, practices and principles have been spawned. The net impact of this has been to extend the influence and oversight capacity of the technocratic specialists with connections to the broad G7 finance ministry–central bank policy community and the power of transnational market players to scrutinize national policy structures and economic performance. In other words, the initiation of the codes of practice are an attempt to create only one possible future development trajectory for countries across the world, involving prudent independent supervision of financial actors according to internationally market-defined standards, capital account liberalization and the prioritization of sound money and price stability in macroeconomic policy. As Jacqueline Best has argued, codes of practice represent an attempt to universalize western or Anglo-Saxon norms on a global basis.[107]

The Financial Stability Forum, the G20 and complex stratified transgovernmentalism

Apart from President Clinton's announcement and endorsement of contingent IMF funds designed to get ahead of contagion, rather than react to it, by creating a line of credit that countries could call upon as they needed to, there were two other major thrusts to the G7's post-Halifax proposals. The first of these was to improve communications between various regulatory bodies and between these bodies and the macroeconomic policy-making community, because many financial firms were now operating as financial supermarkets, eroding the distinction between previously discrete sectors, impinging upon financial stability and the macroeconomic outlook more generally. The second element involved recognition of the need to regularize communications between the G7 and significant emerging markets, creating a channel for permanent dialogue between these two groups of countries. The Financial Stability Forum (FSF) was created in response to the first consideration and the G20 in response to the second.[108]

Neither of these two institutional innovations constituted fundamental reform. Rather they have been incremental and piecemeal adaptations designed to further institutionalize a system based on sound money policies, liberalized capital markets, a floating exchange rate regime and market disciplinary forms of regulation.

The first institutional innovation – the Financial Stability Forum – resulted from a proposal from a working group chaired by Hans Tietmeyer, President of the Bundesbank. It was aimed at bringing the IMF and World Bank together with bank, insurance and securities market supervisors, thus enhancing exchanges of information between macroeconomic and financial regulatory communities. Each G7 country was to be allowed three representatives on the forum, one each from the finance ministry, central bank and senior supervisory authority. The IMF, World Bank, the Basle Committee and IOSCO were to have two members each. The BIS, OECD, Committee on Payment and Settlement Systems and the Committee on the Global Financial System (under the auspices of the BIS) were to have one member each.

The Financial Stability Forum meets twice a year. Since its inception the Netherlands, Australia, Hong Kong and Singapore have been given one representative each. Despite this, the Financial Stability Forum remains G7-centric in terms of membership and is using its technical specialist knowledge to inform debates on global financial governance. This was evident in one of its first published reports on hedge funds and highly leveraged institutions. More importantly, Hong Kong and Singapore's inclusion in the new forum can be considered a function of the fact that they are countries of systemic significance in financial terms and remain favourably predisposed to the principle of capital account liberalization and open market access. Their inclusion in the FSF can been seen as a step towards extending G7 regulatory standards and practices into Asia by involving them in the formulation of the G7-dominated Financial Stability Forum's proposals.

The overall aim of the forum, according to the G7 communiqué issued after the Bonn meeting, was to ensure that national authorities, multilateral institutions, relevant international supervisory bodies and expert groupings can more effectively foster and co-ordinate their respective responsibilities.[109] Tietmeyer maintained that the forum was intended to improve the pooling of information and help develop early warning indicators of crises. Tietmeyer also highlighted additional reporting and disclosure of hedge funds and other highly leveraged institutions as a priority. In effect, the Financial Stability Forum was the culmination of efforts to improve communication between national authorities, overlapping multilateral bodies and private investors.

The first major contribution from the FSF was on the issue of hedge funds, which as we have seen essentially endorsed the US position that for the time being there was no need to directly regulate hedge funds.[110] While in theory the debate remains open, it appears that continental Europe has neither the energy nor the enthusiasm to push the Americans much further on the issue, although this may reflect the fact that policy recommendations have been entrusted to officials and technocrats in the FSF rather than to politicians.

It is notable that where financial regulatory questions are concerned the G7 process has acted as the most senior of a number of overlapping technocratic networks that in turn have conducted more detailed work. Basle Committee and specialist G10 and FSF committee work has usually been conducted by middle-ranking officials who are usually directly answerable in national administrative terms to the finance ministry and central bank deputies who prepare for G7 meetings. What has resulted from the review of the global financial architecture carried out by the G7 and initiatives such as the FSF, is an increasingly stratified form of complex transgovernmental governance, involving a complex division of labour and functional specialisms. Within this context we can see how the G7 itself has assumed the role of a senior core co-ordinating transgovernmental coalition as described in Chapter 5, exercising a loose oversight function in the field of global financial governance, offering strategic direction to a series of more specialist and partially autonomous junior transgovernmental networks that engage in technical problem solving, setting agendas, priorities and deadlines for the technical work of these networks.

Recent G7 initiatives in spawning new technical standards and bodies have increased technocrats' grip and monopoly on global financial governance and ring-fenced debates as technical rather than political matters. It has had the effect of institutionalizing the narrow participation that characterizes global financial governance and has made it more difficult for a wider range of social groupings to participate in debates and contest the complex, technical findings of the technocrats in their reports, despite the fact that these findings often have significant political implications. The G7 finance ministries and central banks have consequently kept the key debates on global financial governance within their own purview and have restricted access to them, making it difficult for outsiders to penetrate or influence global financial governance, by operationalizing a series of junior technical transgovernmental networks which they periodically direct and set priorities for.

The second institutional innovation is the creation of a Group of Twenty, which is essentially a permanent version of the earlier G22. The G7 had periodically consulted with emerging markets by convening various working groups following the Halifax reports and the Asian financial crisis. The creation of the G20 was seen as a means of permanently institutionalizing these consultations. The forum was similar to the G7 in that it was primarily intended to act as a deliberative forum that would facilitate consensus. Finance ministers from Australia, Brazil, China, India, Indonesia, Mexico, Russia, Saudi Arabia, South Africa, South Korea and Turkey, together with the G7 and senior representatives from the IMF, World Bank and the EU, comprise the G20. The aim of the G20 is to provide a forum in which authorities from non-G7 countries, particularly emerging markets, can engage with their G7 counterparts on crucial global financial issues, so as to provide extra legitimacy for many of the proposals being forwarded on architectural issues and to improve the prospects for implementation of those proposals. However, as with the IMF, the G7 are not in a position to command the G20 to do certain things, but have to engage in a continuous process of persuasion. The G20 has consequently become a principal site for fourth-dimensional diplomacy.

Notably, the G7 have not only created the G20, but have also vetted membership, vetoing those states with a marked hostility to the principle of capital account liberalization, such as Malaysia. In other words, members of the G20 have had to be deemed to be sympathetic to the broad principles and parameters of the G7 beliefs. Certainly, there is little evidence based on current debates to suggest that the formation of the G20 is leading to a qualitative shift in the normative and causal beliefs that inform global financial governance. Therefore, the creation of a new grouping of states to increase the inclusive nature of deliberations on global financial issues does not necessarily imply a shift in the prevailing mode of governance, but simply reflects changing patterns of systemic significance. In this respect, the G20 can be seen to represent the institutionalization of a long-standing form of G7 diplomacy, namely efforts to persuade emerging markets to accept certain G7 initiatives.

An alternative interpretation of the G20 is that it breaks new ground in allowing for the more prominent participation of emerging markets in global financial governance and might therefore give rise to a more inclusive and democratic form of governance.[111] Unfortunately, the G20's one or two yearly meetings set against the G7's three or four meetings, suggest that the G7 will continue to act as the caucus group, because the G20 does not have the same momentum or regularity as the G7 process. Furthermore, existing historical and technical legacies, together with well-established procedures and routines, mean that the G20 tend to look to the G7 for leadership, rather than the other way round, although this may change over time. It is also interesting to note that the G7 chose only to consult with finance ministries from emerging markets, rather than a wider range of state agencies and this was a deliberate attempt to replicate the kind of informal collegial deliberations that the G7 finance ministries and central banks are themselves involved in. As we have already noted, the literature on financial liberalization in emerging markets has identified key state–society coalitions that have connected elites in finance ministries and central banks to key internationally active commercial concerns that in turn have benefited from capital account liberalization.[112] In other words, the G7 finance ministries and central banks have natural allies in central banks and finance ministries in emerging markets who are generally supportive of a liberalized financial order. Consequently, the G7 finance ministries and central banks have chosen to engage in a dialogue with sympathetic technocratic elites from finance ministries and central banks. Notably, these carefully selected elites invariably have a formal neo-classical economics training. In short, the G20 has constituted a deliberate attempt to expand the logic of G7 transgovernmentalism.[113] It is therefore difficult to believe that this modest institutional development will make global financial governance substantially more inclusive in terms of the range of social and political voices represented in key debates, but it does offer some prospect of authorities in emerging markets having some sense of ownership of global norms and standards, thereby enhancing the implementation record of G7-generated initiatives.[114] Moreover, prevailing beliefs amongst the finance ministries that advocate the statutory independence of central banks and regulatory agencies, make it difficult to see how the G20 will lead to more inclusion and greater democratic scrutiny in global financial governance. If anything, the pattern of three-dimensional diplomacy which characterizes global financial governance and which the G20 appears to be contributing to through the endorsement of G7 proposals, suggests that governments are becoming more accountable to multilateral peers, standards and codes and to global investors, than to their own citizens.[115]

Debt and development

No discussion of the G7's contribution to the functioning and design of the contemporary global financial system would be complete without considering one of the most pressing issues in the modern world – the issue of developing country debt and how it has impeded development and contributed to extreme poverty and deprivation. The G7's contribution on debt issues has taken two principal forms. First, there has been the consideration of procedures for dealing with sovereign debt defaults in relation to debts owed to private creditors. Second, there has been the provision of debt relief on official obligations to other governments and multilateral institutions.

The defeat of the SDRM proposal

Following the Argentinean default on sovereign bond repayments to private creditors in 2001, the G7 began encouraging the IMF to report on possible approaches to dealing with sovereign debt default. What emerged from the Fund was a proposal for a sovereign debt restructuring mechanism (SDRM) forwarded by Deputy Managing Director Anne Krueger. The mechanism entailed a new international legal framework, the equivalent of a corporate bankruptcy court, that would overrule the laws of all nations and supersede the contracts of all existing debt, reminiscent of Chapter 11 of US bankruptcy law. Under the IMF plan, a country in financial crisis would be able to suspend payments on its debt and seek protection from litigation by its creditors in return for entering a judicial arbitration process. The motivation behind the proposal was the recognition that orderly work out processes needed to be placed on a firmer institutional footing, not least because IMF bail outs of debtor defaults were expensive and damaging, while rogue creditors could hold restructuring efforts hostage. Simultaneously, pressure was coming from campaign groups such as Jubilee 2000 for a fair and independent arbitration process, which would determine which debts should be repaid.[116] A clearly delineated, more orderly work out process was required. Under the SDRM proposal the IMF would not only determine which countries were deserving of entering the SDRM process, they would then protect countries from litigation and adjudicate in the renegotiation process with private sector creditors. In short, the SDRM proposal envisaged a considerably enlarged role for the IMF in debt work outs as an independent adjudicator based on prior conditions and clearly laid out procedures.

However, such a proposal required an amendment to IMF articles of agreement and a vote amongst member countries, which put finance ministries and central banks from the G7 countries in a powerful position to determine the future of the proposal. The SDRM proposal eventually ran into opposition from a number of quarters. Understandably, there was suspicion about the nature of the role the IMF envisaged for itself from developing countries and debt campaign groups, concerned about the wider conditionality that might be attached to participation in the mechanism. Finance ministries and central banks in emerging markets were particularly concerned that the very existence of the mechanism would make investors more reluctant to lend to them. The fiercest opposition however came from the private sector and financial interests who were opposed to the idea that the IMF would dictate to them the terms and conditions on which they could access their money.

At the time of the G7's publication of their sovereign debt action plan for emerging markets in April 2002, the G7 finance ministries and central banks' attitude towards the plan could be described as ambiguous agnosticism, as they seemed to favour a position of keeping their options open. Within the G7, support for the SDRM was warm from Canada and the UK, with the Bank of England and the Bank of Canada, as principal drafters of the action plan, being supported by finance ministers Gordon Brown and Paul Martin. The departure of Paul O'Neill as Treasury Secretary in the United States and his replacement by John Snow, saw a much cooler attitude from the United States, reflecting the position of G7 deputy John Taylor who was in favour of a more market-oriented approach. The wording of the action plan left considerable room for doubt that the SDRM would ever get off the ground as it called for a market-oriented approach, consisting of contingency clauses in debt contracts, describing as precisely as possible what would happen in the event of a debt restructuring. Clauses were to include super-majority decision making so as to prevent a 'tyranny of the minority' (rogue creditors) blocking the swift settlement of claims, a description of the restructuring process, including a cooling-off or standstill process, and a description of how creditors should engage with borrowers. Despite this, the position of the SDRM in the action plan was decidedly non-committal as the G7 pledged to 'support further work by the IMF on proposed approaches to sovereign debt restructuring that may require new international treaties, changes in national legislation, or amendments of the Articles of Agreement of the IMF'.[117] This was a clear reference to the SDRM proposal, which was described as 'complementary' to the market-oriented approach and reflected the fact that further work on the SDRM was being conducted in response to criticisms from the private sector and developing countries.

In the final eventuality, it was a further twelve months before the G7 explicitly killed off the SDRM proposal, but what had happened in the intervening period to move the G7 from lukewarm and tacit support to categorical and unanimous opposition? The worry amongst the private sector was that the SDRM might encourage strategic defaults, a distortion of the market value of debt instruments and a general weakening of the role creditors enjoy under domestic bankruptcy laws. Aggressive political mobilization duly followed with the American financial sector writing to Paul O'Neill and advocating collective action causes and criticizing the SDRM for detracting from such an approach. A writing campaign was similarly directed at Gordon Brown as chairman of the IMF's International Monetary and Financial Committee.[118] But this process of political mobilization was not restricted solely to the Anglo-Saxon countries. A similar process of lobbying took place across the industrialized world. Pressure from ABN and ING Barings brought a sudden and abrupt shift in the position of the Dutch finance ministry from one of support to implacable opposition to the SDRM and Deutsche Bank was exerting similar pressure in Germany.[119] While opposition to the SDRM was strongest in the United States, G7 finance ministries and central banks eventually came to share this position collectively, as they responded to pressure from financial interests with whom they have traditionally shared the closest relationship and on whose behalf they have often operated.

The G7 statement that effectively killed the SDRM proposal came on 12 April 2003, ahead of an IMF ministerial meeting. First, the statement outlined a commitment to collective action clauses (CACs), similar to those discussed in the 2002 action plan. Second, in the first explicit reference to the SDRM in a G7 statement, a brief section on the Sovereign Debt Restructuring Mechanism argued that after experience with implementing CACs it was recognized that it was now not feasible to implement the SDRM proposal.[120] However, work has continued on some of the issues raised by the SDRM discussions and the most recent proposal involves aggregating and valuing debt in terms of growth indexed bonds.

The significance of the decision to strategically choose CACs over the SDRM is that creditors remain in control of their loans to debtors at times of crisis and effectively will in theory leave jurisdiction to courts in the country where a bond was initially issued, placing London and New York in a powerful position. The G7 have strategically chosen an approach to sovereign debt restructuring that resolves problems informally through creditor–debtor negotiations, in which the market will have the upper hand.[121] In short, the SDRM episode has provided another example of the G7 acting as a transgovernmental coalition. In this instance, the G7 acted collectively to veto an alternative non-market-based solution, which would have in part subordinated market actors to legislative oversight. Ultimately, the G7 finance ministries and central banks bowed under the weight of concerted pressure from private financial interests within their own territories, demonstrating that while they are on the whole insulated from wider societal interests, they continue to be most susceptible to influence by globally active financial interests. Moreover, they form an effective state–society coalition with these interests and control global financial governance, by acting as collective gatekeepers determining which financial governance strategies can be pursued, producing a narrow pattern of transgovernmental politics. Quite simply, proposals such as the one proposed by the IMF are reliant on majority support from IMF shareholders. Alternatives to the *de facto* institutionalization of market supremacy cannot proceed without the consent of the G7 finance ministries and central banks. Changing this situation not only requires changes to IMF voting procedures, but a broadening of the decision-making structures of global financial governance, to include a wider range of state agencies who are not as closely aligned with a speculative financial sector to quite the same extent as the finance ministries and central banks.

Official debt relief

It should come as no surprise that the area in which the Group of Seven's ideas have been most progressive is official debt relief. This has been the area in which the finance ministries and central banks have had most meaningful dialogue with church and charitable groups and campaigning organizations such as Jubilee 2000. It is also an area in which the finance ministries have had most scope to take action independently of other actors. Most significantly, the G7 are able to write off or reduce the amounts of money they are owed without directly impacting or relying upon private sector actors, to whom they have appeared in awe of and beholden to in other areas of financial governance. Private financial interests, it could even be reasoned, might be expected to approve of efforts to reduce the amount of money owed to public authorities, based on the calculation that it will improve the prospects for timely regular repayment of amounts owing to them. With debt relief and the problem of developing country debt becoming increasingly high-profile issues due to celebrity campaigns pioneered by Bono and Bob Geldof, and with initiatives to reduce debt increasingly supported by western publics, there is no notable constituency of opposition to the provision of debt relief, other than the finance ministries themselves for fiscal reasons, and other government agencies fearful of how debt relief might impact on their own budgets.

On the whole, individuals directly involved in G7 meetings have been one step removed from the provision of debt relief, restricting themselves to setting targets and priorities. Lower-ranking officials have handled most of the technical details of debt relief negotiations in the context of the Paris Club. The Baker plan and the Brady plan were the first attempts to secure a restructuring and rescheduling of official obligations, with the emergence of Brady bonds marketizing much of this debt. That there has been a continuous need to revisit and renegotiate debt obligations is sufficient evidence to suggest that successive rounds of debt relief have not necessarily generated the anticipated gains in terms of prosperity, growth and the reduction of poverty anticipated by western creditor nations. In 1995 at Halifax, the G7 launched the Heavily Indebted Poor Countries Initiative (HPIC), which consisted of co-ordinated efforts by governments and multilateral institutions to reduce to 'sustainable levels' the external debt burden of the most heavily indebted poor countries. At the Cologne summit in 1999, the finance ministers announced an 'Enhanced Debt Initiative' to build upon HPIC. The G7 proposed that those countries demonstrating a commitment to 'good governance' and the targeting of poverty alleviation would be given faster, broader and deeper debt relief. Debt relief was in effect being used as an incentive to persuade countries to reform governance structures in a direction desired by the G7. This was no mere act of altruistic generosity. The new enhanced initiative was to double the amount of debt relief to over $27 billion, increase the number of eligible countries from twenty-nine to thirty-six and promised up to 90 per cent and more in bilateral debt forgiveness for the poorest eligible countries. Eligible countries had to be an International Development Association (IDA) country, meet debt sustainability criteria and be engaged in an IDA or Enhanced Structural Adjustment Facility reform programme.[122]

HPIC has not been an unreserved success and further debt and development initiatives have continued to be pursued. Notably, the G8 published an African Action Plan implementation report based on the New Partnership for Africa's Development (NPEAD). Assistance under this programme depended on a peer-review process relating to entirely subjective judgements on good governance, the rule of law, investing in people, and policies that spur growth and alleviate poverty.[123] Debt-relief programmes that reward countries for pushing reform programmes endorsed by the G7 are still suggestive that the G7 have been using debt relief as means of advancing strategic interests, rather than being entirely motivated by humanitarian concerns. Moreover, a reading of G7 documentation on debt reveals a self-congratulatory tone, providing lists of various generous instances of financial assistance, without discussing the roots of the problems developing countries continue to face, or the developed world's ethical obligations and responsibilities to assist. The tone of G7 statements on debt relief is suggestive of the industrialized nations as benevolent knights coming to the rescue of hapless developing country governments and citizens, who are incapable of managing their own affairs. It is understandable that such a conceited and self-congratulatory discourse would alienate the populations and elites of developing countries.

In its approach to debt, the Bush administration has pursued an increasingly bilateral track and in the process has taken conditionality to a new level, thus increasing its own leverage over key features of the domestic political economies of developing countries. This has been evident in the formation of a Millennium Challenge Account (MCA) by President Bush in 2002 in recognition of the fact that 3 billion people continued to live in poverty. While the MCA allows developing countries to construct their own plans based on how they will achieve development priorities and tackle constraints to growth and productivity, this is accompanied by strict conditionality involving judgements on governing justly, investing in people and encouraging economic freedom.[124] The Bush administration has chosen six indicators relating to governing justly, four in relation to investing in people, and six encouraging economic freedom, including indicators of the length of time it takes to start a business, a reduction in which is just as likely to benefit American investors as indigenous populations. The MCA increases the capacity of the US to choose who gets debt aid in a fairly arbitrary way, based on those countries following US-friendly policies. While Bush's laudable stance of supporting more grants rather than loans is certainly being welcomed in developing countries,[125] this is being accompanied by concerted efforts to promote and spread American values through a very specifically American form of conditionality.

Nevertheless, an account of the G7 and US approaches to debt and development issues, such as the one presented above, would be churlish and one-sided if it failed to acknowledge that the G7 and the United States have been increasingly generous in their provision of debt relief. Unfortunately, they have also been slow to recognize the scale of the problem, while their responses have been protracted and incremental. Rather like the G7 approach to the global financial architecture, periodic reviews and a monitoring of progress have revealed that previous initiatives, while sound in principle, have not achieved quite as much as initially hoped for and have therefore had to be revisited, modified and adjusted. In short, the very conservative and incremental nature of the G7 process, due to its reliance on the reports of technocrats who build on existing bodies of technical knowledge, results in a conservative and incremental approach to debt relief, which has made that process a great deal more drawn out and protracted than it has needed to be, with devastating and catastrophic consequences for the populations of developing countries.

At the start of 2005 however, there were indications that a much-needed shift in G7 discourse might be on the horizon. British Chancellor Gordon Brown has pledged to make debt relief the centrepiece of the UK's chairing of the G8 in 2005 and will work through the G7 process to build a coalition of support amongst his finance ministry colleagues for new debt relief initiatives that he has termed a Marshall plan for the developing world in the twenty-first century.[126] Brown's plans have three components. First, full debt relief for developing countries, going beyond the mere writing off of bilateral debt owed to industrialized governments, but also including multilateral debt relief on money owed to the IMF and the World Bank, with the G7 countries establishing and contributing to a World Bank trust fund, and a revaluation and/or an off-market sale of further IMF gold to fund the IMF share of debt relief. However, this proposal faces opposition from Japan and Germany, not least because the Germans have large reserves of gold, and budget deficit reduction efforts in Germany will depend on the price of gold on world markets as Germany pursues a policy of gold sales to increase public revenues. Second, a trade round targeted at the needs of the developing world. Third, the establishment of a new International Financial Facility (IFF) providing long-term aid for developing countries, funded by commitments from individual governments and leveraging in additional funds from international capital markets, doubling aid with the aim of halving poverty. However this proposal has received a decidedly lukewarm reaction in Washington from the US Treasury. In other words, Brown and the British Treasury face a protracted task of persuasion in obtaining the support of other G7 finance ministries and progress is likely to be slow.

Periodically, finance ministers have emerged with radical multilateral ideas but they have usually floundered on the basis of consensual opposition from other finance ministries and the dynamic of adaptive incrementalism and the inherent conservatism of the G7 process. Usually, finance ministries pursuing radical or innovative proposals either lose credibility with their peers or become socialized into a more modest and conservative way of thinking. What is different about Brown is that he is not new in post, but is well respected amongst his peers as a long-standing member of the finance ministry community, who is well acquainted with G7 norms. In this respect, while Brown faces a protracted and arduous process of persuasion, which will in all likelihood lead to the adjustment and dilution of his proposals, those proposals have marked a significant shift in tone. Brown has made references to a shared moral universe, the developing world's duty to others and the need to see strangers as neighbours. What is morally wrong, Brown has argued, cannot be economically right and tackling world poverty is the most important challenge for the current generation.[127] This is the language of globalizing social justice.[128] For the first time it makes moral obligation rather than economic rationality as the starting point for future G7 action on debt and for this reason it should be viewed as a significant shift and a promising development. It is however merely the starting point for a longer process of humanizing global financial governance and placing social justice rather than technocratic concerns at the centre of debate. Unfortunately, the transgovernmental nature of the G7 process is not conducive to the emergence of debates that prioritize social justice over technocratic concerns and if this promising development is not to be suffocated by the inherent conservatism of the G7, it may be necessary to broaden participation in key decision making and debating arenas in the field of global financial governance, to include a broader range of state agencies than just finance ministries and central banks for the reasons discussed throughout this chapter.

Conclusions

Three separate but related substantive points or arguments have been made in this chapter. First, a combination of elite interviews and an extensive reading of official G7 documentation on the global financial architecture, reveal that officials do believe they are engaged in a predominantly technocratic exercise. The patterns described by Tony Porter in his work on global finance as a technical system, certainly seem to be supported by the evidence. Officials respond to developments in a highly technical global financial system embedded in and partly determined by advances in information technology and electronic computer networks. Previous specialist technical reports have informed and provided the basis for new initiatives on the global financial architecture, with officials viewing their principal role as building more detail on to existing reports, investigating ways of improving implementation and engaging in a protracted task of persuasion to convince actors to behave in certain ways and to publish and share information more freely. At no time have the fundamental premises on which this approach has been based, been openly challenged, discussed or questioned in a serious or fundamental fashion. As a consequence, the G7 process has assumed an inherently conservative dynamic and its approach to the global financial architecture has been one of adaptive incrementalism. The current approach has been heavily derived from neo-classical ideas and has involved a heavy focus on transparency or the release of more information for the benefit of market actors. Such an approach is supposed to encourage an open ongoing dialogue between creditors and debtors, and governments and markets, but as Chapter 4 argued, transparency provides a *de facto* ideational shield for financial interests. It is based on the notion that market participants behave rationally and will only make inefficient decisions if inadequate information is available. From the outset therefore, an approach based on transparency creates a fundamental asymmetry in the power relations of financial diplomacy by implicating public authorities and regulators in crisis-affected countries and absolving foreign investors of responsibility. Despite claims to the contrary therefore, G7 proposals on the global financial architecture are not simply technocratic, but are inherently political, based on market-friendly solutions and ideas, which facilitate a fundamental asymmetry in financial diplomacy involving market supremacy and the need for public authorities to reassure market sentiment. Beneath the mask of their gradual, technocratic, reform trajectory, the finance ministries and central banks have therefore displayed a continuous ideational bias towards the interests of large-scale international financial investors.

Second, because of an approach to the global financial architecture that has primarily been based on transparency, the G7 have laid the institutional and ideational foundations for a global financial system characterized by market supremacy, in which market actors are able to engage in asymmetrical negotiations with debtors and demand reassurance in the form of institutional arrangements and policies and have the final say in the determination of repayment schedules. Complete financial and capital account liberalization is being promoted as a universal norm that all states should be working towards and the recently introduced twelve codes and standards that have resulted from the G7's review of global financial architecture are designed to produce the kind of domestic institutional practices and norms that will facilitate such an eventuality. The codes and standards are designed to enhance processes of market scrutiny and discipline, although the success they are enjoying in this regard will need to be the subject of further research, because currently the evidence is mixed. By vetoing the SDRM proposal, the G7 also acted as a formidable transgovernmental gatekeeper, preventing the emergence of a proposal that would have challenged market supremacy and taken sovereign debt work out processes out of the hands of market actors and placed them into a supranational judicial process. In short, the G7's capacity to oppose and reject such proposals and favour more market-friendly solutions, in this case CACs, has enabled the G7 to operate as a filtering device, vetting architectural reform proposals and effectively reinforcing and maintaining the current status quo of market supremacy.

Third, relations between the G7 finance ministries and central banks have been remarkably consensual and collegiate due to shared beliefs, understandings and social practices. On several occasions, the UK, Japan and Canada have all exercised leadership on architectural debates, and have modified or restrained US positions through a process of technical argumentation and deliberation. At the same time however, the US has enjoyed a power of veto not really enjoyed to the same extent by any other G7 state, and anything the United States has been strongly opposed to has been defeated. Ultimately, despite the fact that G7 meetings continue to display some intergovernmental characteristics as well as occasional tensions and differences of emphasis between the G7 finance ministries and central banks, the G7 is best characterized as a transgovernmental coalition in respect of the global financial architecture. They have constructed a consensus revolving around transparency and the universal norm of capital account liberalization and promoted it in relation to other bodies, actors and groupings. Differences between the G7 finance ministries and central banks on architectural questions have certainly existed and have been discussed in this chapter, but they have often been overstated and they have frequently been resolved by dialogue, deliberation and compromise. Finance ministries and central banks remain close, politically, ideationally and socially, to internationally active financial sectors and the ideas and institutional innovations they have promoted have reflected this. In short, the finance ministries and central banks have largely monopolized debates on global financial governance and conducted these debates on narrow consensual technocratic terms, which has given global financial governance an overwhelmingly technocratic and transgovernmental character. Recent institutional initiatives, the G20 and FSF, have been designed to preserve this technocratic transgovernmental character. The G7 have decided to consult with predominantly sympathetic like-minded agencies in emerging markets in a *de facto* extension of G7 transgovernmentalism characterized by consensual technocratic deliberation. The G20 is about intensifying and institutionalizing efforts, channels of communication and persuasion with emerging markets, so as to improve the implementation record where G7 standards and codes are concerned. What has resulted from these recent institutional initiatives is a more complex stratified form of transgovernmentalism consisting of various networks of regulators and technical specialists who report to the finance ministry and central banking community and retain a certain degree of autonomy based on their technical expertise. Nevertheless the G7 finance ministries and central banks retain a co-ordinating role, orchestrating, catalysing and setting agendas and priorities for these networks of regulators and officials. The net result of this has been to institutionalize the technocratic character of global financial governance, ring-fencing debates and excluding outsiders by basing future governance on technocratic reports and findings that are difficult to contest. Recent G7 initiatives have been a conscious effort to place an avowedly political issue, which determines the fortunes and life chances of a range of citizens around the world, outside of the formal political process and beyond political contestation. Until the institutional foundations of the complex stratified transgovernmental approach to global financial governance can be challenged and a broader range of interests can be brought to the decision-making table, social justice is always likely to be a secondary consideration rather than at the centre of the debate.

8 Conclusions

Global financial governance and the Group of Seven as a senior transgovernmental coalition

In this concluding chapter the three empirical research agendas highlighted in the introduction are revisited. In the first section, there is a discussion of the factors influencing G7 interaction and behaviour. In the second section, the implications of G7 interactions and outcomes for US power in global financial governance are examined. The third section assesses the overall contribution of the G7 finance ministries and central banks to global financial governance, examines the collective authority they enjoy, how that authority is exercised and the implications of this for how we think about the contemporary financial order. A final section discusses normative criticisms of the G7 and of global financial governance more generally and looks at what kind of reforms will be required to produce a more just and inclusive form of governance.

The form and determinants of G7 interaction and co-operation

Many of the main approaches to IR and IPE have become embroiled in theoretical controversies concerning the causal status of different variables in international politics, such as societal preferences in key states, the structure of the international system and the norms and ideas that characterize particular issue areas. While such parsimonious controversies and debates might lead to academic and theoretical clarity, they are not necessarily the most reliable route to accurate representations of reality. This study of finance ministries and central banks' contribution to global financial governance has sought to avoid the pitfalls of theoretical parsimony and has adopted an approach derived from theoretical complexity, which accepts the proposition that two or more independent variables can operate in explanations of international governance. Drawing on John Hobson's neo-integrationist insight concerning the need to give 'equal ontological status to international and global social, normative, economic and political structures on the one hand, but also the state and state–society relations on the other',[1] the multi-spatial analysis conducted in this book has sought to examine the interactions of a number of variables across a range of spatial dimensions, which have influenced the collective decisions and behaviour of the G7 finance ministries and central banks. In this regard, the first empirical research agenda in this book has sought to examine which factors explain and determine the form that G7 interaction and co-operation takes.

One of the principal arguments made throughout this book is that the G7 finance ministries and central banks have developed a loose consensus based on a belief in the value of, and a normative preference for, the basic principles of sound money and open markets. In its current form this consensus involves a faith in independent central banks that target low inflation; a general scepticism of the benefits of pegged exchange rates; a belief in long-term fiscal consolidation; a view that capital account liberalization is beneficial but needs to be accompanied by appropriate sequencing and adequate regulatory provision; recognition of the need for financial crisis prevention mechanisms such as multilateral surveillance and data transparency that facilitate a more rational financial order and ultimately pave the way for further liberalization; a growing commitment to private sector involvement in the international community's responses to financial crises; and a basic approach to financial crises that involves debtors taking steps to put the right measures in place, including keeping financial markets open, macroeconomic policies designed to support national currencies and the initiation of negotiations with creditors. These basic shared beliefs act as a frame of reference for the G7 finance ministries and central banks' interactions, set the parameters for their collaboration on financial and monetary issues and provide the common ground for them to operate as a collective transgovernmental coalition.

What the operation of the G7 process over the last decade has brought into sharp focus is that ideas, interests and institutions have effectively dovetailed in a mutually reinforcing fashion in global financial governance and none of these factors can be attributed single causal status. A *de facto* transnational coalition between financial interests and finance ministries and central banks, with a shared mutual interest in promoting sound money and open capital markets, what is sometimes referred to as the US Treasury, Wall Street, UK Treasury, Bank of England, City of London axis, but which also exists to varying extents in other G7 states, has supported and advocated a predominantly neo-classical reading of financial markets. As the financial sectors of G7 states have expanded, so those states have developed a greater stake in the continuation and extension of the current financial system. States with large financial interests can attract more resources from a larger available pool of capital, avoiding domestic trade-offs by rent seeking from the rest of the world and deflecting risks and adjustments costs on to other states.[2] In short, the development of a country's financial sector determines a state's interest in the current financial regime. Clearly, this interest is strongest in the US and the UK. However, creeping financialization in states such as Japan and Germany (which in part is being cultivated by finance ministries and central banks) helps to explain these states' continuing commitment to the current regime and to the G7 consensus (described above and in more detail in Chapter 4), even though they continue to run current account surpluses and are not financially dependent on capital account liberalization in quite the way deficit states such as the US and the UK are.[3]

The G7 finance ministries and central banks have attempted to rationalize and justify the current global financial system by invoking a predominantly neo-classical reading of financial markets as rational decision-making entities that produce efficient outcomes. This basic, albeit questionable, intellectual assumption has provided the basis for a common approach to global financial governance based on transparency, which assumes that financial markets will only be subject to disruption when inadequate information is available on the state of an economy. Automatically this places responsibility for resolving a financial crisis on to authorities in crisis-affected countries and provides an effective ideational shield for financial interests that may have been the cause of the disruption in the first place.[4] In this sense there is no neat division between ideas and interests in the operation of contemporary financial governance and we might be reasonably reminded of Robert Cox's famous observation that 'theory is always for someone and some purpose'.[5]

However, a simple interest-based explanation of finance ministries and central banks' neo-classical bias is insufficient. Finance ministries and central banks also tend to employ large numbers of economists who often have formal neo-classical training, which in turn informs their specialist reports and briefings. Officials in these institutions have a technocratic bent rooted in their training and their sense of professional identity. Furthermore, these neo-classical positions are further strengthened by socialization processes within their own institutions, through international networks such as the G7 and a series of traditionally close relationships and contacts with financial interests and economists who share their perspective. Finally, neo-classical prescriptions in relation to the most reliable institutional routes to low inflation also invariably advocate greater powers for finance ministries and central banks, which further strengthens the commitment of officials working in these institutions to neo-classical theory. Technical, professional, institutional and social explanations of finance ministries and central banks' commitment to neo-classical ideas therefore need to accompany interest-based explanations, if we are to understand the source of the ascendancy of the current financial orthodoxy and how that ascendancy is sustained.

Despite evidence that questions many of the assumptions inherent in the G7 consensus and the repeated occurrence of financial crises over the last decade, it is notable how durable and resilient the current consensus has proved to be. One of the reasons for this durability is that the finance ministries and central banks have always had a rather more pragmatic, qualified and nuanced, but also more intellectually inconsistent approach to financial governance than that of extreme free market fundamentalism. This has allowed room for refinements and qualifications to G7 beliefs, as the current consensus has been continuously adjusted in an incremental fashion. Furthermore, talk of consensus should not be mistaken for convergence. As the discussion in Chapters 4 to 7 established, there are key differences between the political economies of G7 countries, even if there are signs that Japan and Germany are becoming more like the US and the UK. The current consensus is sufficiently broad to allow for discussion and deliberation over detail and questions of emphasis, over which there are frequent differences (see Chapters 6 and 7). Nevertheless, the consensus is sufficiently well established and accepted by the finance ministries and central banks to define what is to be negotiated over or debated in the current world financial order.

While intergovernmental negotiation and bargaining, where states attempt to realize a specific national self-interest, clearly continues to take place at G7 meetings, transgovernmentalism, which involves bureaucratic agencies identifying shared objectives and constructing a consensus on the basis of this, is becoming a far more significant form of activity. One of the principal arguments made in this book is that the finance ministries and central banks share sufficient ground in terms of their institutional position, the responsibilities and tasks with which they are charged and their basic normative and causal beliefs, to encourage them to reach common positions on a range of financial and monetary issues. Once they have arrived at a consensual position, the finance ministries and central banks attempt to communicate that position to a wider audience, in an effort to steer decision making, expectations and agendas in their own domestic settings (as envisaged by the original transgovernmental concept), a range of specialist multilateral bodies, emerging markets and private sector market actors. In short, it is the structural context, described by Germain as decentralized globalization[6] (see Chapter 2), in which there is simultaneously a diffusion of responsibility and mutual vulnerability stemming from systemic interconnectedness between different markets and different territorial locations, that has provided multiple incentives for the finance ministries and central banks to collaborate and arrive at collective positions. In this respect, I have argued that the multiple communications the G7 finance ministries and central banks are involved in, can be conceived of as a form of four-dimensional diplomacy, including interactions with one another, with domestic actors, with trans-border financial markets and a broader range of institutions, bodies, committees and states outside of the G7.

Crucially, in this context of decentralized financial globalization where no single financial centre is able to control the dynamics of the system as a whole, consensus is essential because of the need for a variety of states and bodies to implement shared initiatives if the omnipresent threat of systemic contagion and financial crisis is to be minimized. This was evident after the Asian financial crisis when the G7 revisited their Halifax strategy, but increased their consultations with sympathetic finance ministries and central banks in emerging markets and intensified their efforts to persuade them to implement G7 initiatives. However, the G7's preference for operating through consensus also reflects the specialist nature of global finance as an emerging technical system, characterized by a reliance on technology and technical authority.[7] Finance ministry and central bank officials engage in processes of technical deliberation at their meetings, using argument, reason and evidence as guiding precepts for debate.[8] There is a shared recognition that decisions should be reached on the basis of the technical merits of a particular case and consequently officials attempt to rationalize their preferences in technical (mainly neo-classical) terms, rather than simply on the basis of political motivation. In this respect, the authority of individual G7 deputies amongst their peers is a product of technical expertise and a demonstrable track record in forwarding convincing and accurate technical analyses and arguments over time. The deputies' regularity of contact engenders familiarity and a sense of collegiality or *esprit de corps*, revolving around shared professional respect, shared understandings and social practices, enhancing their capacity to arrive at consensus, while reducing mistrust, tension and conflict.[9] This collegiality and the shared understandings and social practices that constitute a very distinct deputies' working method, have had an impact on G7 interactions and outcomes in four principal ways.

First, there is a clear understanding that the finance ministries and central banks do not make precise demands of one another's macroeconomic policies. They can express broad opinions on the general direction in which policy should proceed, based on evidence and analysis, but to make more precise demands of another country's macroeconomic policy would constitute a breach of appropriate G7 practice. There is a clear recognition that macroeconomic decisions are made nationally. Macroeconomic fine-tuning, or package deals based on a clear bargain or agreement to generate a co-ordinated global macroeconomic stimulus, or to manage exchange rates, such as the Bonn or Plaza agreements, are not seriously contemplated. As Bergsten and Henning have noted, fiscal rules and independent central banks with domestic price stability mandates have effectively immobilized macroeconomic policy.[10] More precisely, concerns over the credibility of central bank independence and a recognition that central bank governors cannot give commitments on the future course of monetary policy, mean that no bargaining over interest rate decisions takes place at G7 meetings. Behaviour that contravenes this unwritten rule is viewed as inappropriate conduct. In other words, domestic institutional arrangements create a sense of appropriate G7 social practice, and while this is not the principal reason for the demise of co-ordination (prevailing shared beliefs and associated national institutional arrangements are), current appropriate G7 social practice does act as an additional barrier to macroeconomic policy co-ordination.

Second, the collegiality, familiarity and personal friendships that the deputies' network fosters allow the network to act as a mechanism for managing and minimizing tensions and conflicts that arise from opposing national positions. In other words, the personal relationships that the G7 process fosters are an important aspect of contemporary monetary and financial diplomacy and help to facilitate a consensual mode of operation. For example, as we saw in Chapter 7, tensions between the US and Japan, brought about by the AMF proposal, different diagnoses of the cause of the Asian financial crisis and the initial US handling of the crisis through the IMF, were diffused through debates conducted by the G7 deputies' network on the global financial architecture. Ultimately these debates proved to be a remarkably consensual exercise as the Japanese and the US contributed fully to the exercise and expressed satisfaction with greater transparency, support for the use of controls on capital inflows and a more cautious approach to capital account liberalization based on a greater number of pre-conditions. Initial acrimony and tensions following the Asian financial crisis were managed and minimized through the collegiate nature and professional norms of the deputies' network, which allowed all G7 states to contribute to the debate and facilitated Japanese, British and Canadian intellectual leadership at key stages.

Third, the Group of Seven's consensual mode of operation, together with its informality, have produced a form of co-operation based on strategic signalling to other actors in an effort to convey the G7 consensus. This strategic signalling has taken three principal forms. In relation to macroeconomic policy, the finance ministries and central banks use their meetings to highlight future priorities and challenges, often with the aim of reinforcing positions they are intent on pursuing. They also use statements on macroeconomic policy to influence the expectations of domestic and market actors, to occasionally catalyse broader domestic policy debates and more generally to circumscribe what can be thought and done in macroeconomic policy. The most specific example of this kind of strategic macroeconomic signalling involved efforts to influence domestic monetary policy in the direction of concerted interest rate easing in 1998 and 2001, following the exogenous shocks of the Asian financial crisis and 9/11. On those occasions the G7 sought to collectively influence the domestic debates that would determine future interest rate decisions, but they did not engage in interest rate co-ordination as such. The second form of strategic signalling has involved the periodic release of collective statements on exchange rates, in an effort to minimize excessive volatility and avoid long-term currency misalignments. This has involved the formulation of joint positions on prevailing market conditions based on an analysis of underlying fundamentals, followed by an effort to present this analysis to the market in a form of persuasion that I have referred to as declaratory policy. The current reliance on declaratory policy is based on domestic institutional arrangements and existing normative and causal beliefs, but it is also compatible with and derived from the technical argumentation that is the predominant mode of interaction between the G7 finance ministries and central banks. The G7 have consequently managed to strategically steer exchange rates on several occasions over the last decade, even if their record has been decidedly mixed in this regard. Finally, the G7 formulated joint proposals on the global financial architecture. They created new bodies, catalysed new channels of communication between existing bodies and authorities, and generally settled for setting strategic priorities, agendas and deadlines for the work of more specialist committees. This is without doubt an important directional role, because if senior personnel from the G7 finance ministries and central banks reach a collective view on a matter, it carries weight, simply because they provide many of the resources, personnel and expertise that enable wider more specialist organizations to operate, but again this directional role is dependent on G7 capacity to arrive at consensual collective positions.

Fourth, the G7 deputies have continuously displayed a professional respect for technical expertise. This has been evident in their communications with one another on exchange rates, on macroeconomic policy and on the wider global financial architecture, which on the whole have been fairly narrow technical debates. More especially, it has also been evident in their reaction to the reports of more specialist committees and bodies. With one or two notable exceptions, such as their reaction to the IMF's SDRM proposal (see Chapter 7), the G7 have not really disputed or contested the detail and content of technical reports produced by more specialist bodies and committees. As we saw in Chapter 7, a wider technocratic machinery, or a complex stratified transgovernmental system of governance, has come to characterize international financial governance. An array of technocrats predominates and the specialist reports they produce invariably build upon previous reports and accumulated technical knowledge. Consequently, global financial governance is characterized by conservative, evolutionary incremental adaptations, rather than sudden, rapid changes. The G7 finance ministries and central banks provide the crucial political support for this technocratic approach, through their efforts to privilege technical expertise over political concerns. This has enabled a neo-classical reading of markets and monetary and financial affairs to predominate in global financial governance, in turn producing institutional gains for finance ministries and central banks, and benefits for the financial interests to which they are closest.

In short, despite claims to the contrary, interests are never far away where financial governance is concerned. Reigning causal and normative beliefs set the parameters for G7 interactions, but those causal and normative beliefs also favour financial interests and translate into specific forms of institutional and social practice, which further determine and circumscribe governance agendas and the range of possible outcomes in monetary and financial affairs. Ideas, institutions, interests and elite social practices have dovetailed in financial governance, circumscribing agendas and making it difficult for wider social groupings and interests to penetrate and influence this issue area. Ultimately, shared normative and causal beliefs have been the most significant factors influencing G7 co-operation and interaction, but it is difficult to separate these beliefs from interests, developments in financial markets (financial globalization) and institutional factors. What we have seen in this study is how beliefs have combined with institutional changes, elite social practices and discourses and changed material circumstances (capital market integration based on large-scale private international capital flows through extensive electronic computer networks) in a mutually reinforcing fashion to produce a self-fulfilling and socially constructed single structural dynamic of market supremacy that is often referred to as financial globalization.[11]

Authority and power within the Group of Seven: is the G7 a US-dominated coalition or a concert of modern international powers?

Scholarly debates on the extent to which the United States dominates the Group of Seven and exercises hegemony in global financial affairs have been polarized between a position that views the G7 as an irrelevance, other than as a further expression of US dominance, and a position which views the G7 as a modern concert of equal powers exercising effective collective management of the global financial system. In this book, I have argued that both positions are extreme and misrepresent the realties of G7 diplomacy and its various subtleties. The evidence presented in this study has supported a middle course between these two extreme positions.

'Decentralized globalization', involving the existence of large liquid credit markets in Europe, Asia and Latin America as well as North America, means that no single financial centre is able to provide guidance and direction to the entire global financial system.[12] Despite this, the United States continues to enjoy an unprecedented capacity to delay macroeconomic adjustment and finance budget and trade deficits by attracting finance from abroad.[13] Likewise movements in the dollar and in US interest rates continue to have a disproportionate impact on economic activity in other states. Moreover, no initiative in global finance has much chance of success without the consent and participation of the state that is home to and regulator of the world's leading financial institutions and most liquid financial markets. This translates into an effective power of veto for the United States in global financial governance debates. When these capacities are added to the US's voting share in the IMF and the fact that the US hosts and chairs a disproportionate share of G7 meetings (somewhere between half and two-thirds), and consequently drafts more G7 statements than any other country, exerting the biggest impact on G7 consensus and discourse, we can see that international monetary and financial affairs are characterized by some quite fundamental asymmetries. There is little evidence to suggest that G7 powers enjoy an equality of capability in international monetary affairs and plenty of evidence to support the view that the United States remains an exceptional power.

Yet despite these asymmetries, deliberations at the meetings of G7 finance ministries and central banks take place on a relatively equal footing. Debates between the G7 finance ministries and central banks have an appearance of equality based on a mutual appreciation and recognition of professional expertise and competence, and the resulting preference for collegiality and decisions based on consensus, even if the broad parameters of these debates are defined by the United States. Within these parameters there is a good deal of significant detail to be debated and argued over, meaning that, as John Kirton has noted, lesser G7 powers such as Canada and the UK do have the capacity to critically influence G7 debates and exercise intellectual leadership. However, acknowledging the opportunities that arise from a collegiate and technical mode of operation is not the same thing as saying that the G7 represents a modern international concert of powers with each member enjoying an effective equality of capability.[14] The collegiate and technical nature of interactions between the finance ministries and central banks, together with the mutual vulnerability of 'decentralized globalization', means that the United States finds it increasingly difficult to act alone in international financial affairs. The United States has to listen to other G7 states, and does listen to other states, which provides opportunities for these other G7 states to critically influence debates on financial and monetary governance through their finance ministries and central banks.

In Chapter 6, we saw how the US is constrained in relation to dollar exchange rate policy. The evidence of G7 co-operation on exchange rates in the 1990s suggested that Peter Gowan's claims that the US Treasury secretary can talk the value of the dollar up or down simply by opening his or her mouth, and therefore arbitrarily influence economic conditions throughout the world by using exchange rate policy to engage in politically advantageous aggressive economic statecraft, are exaggerated.[15] Indeed, it is a great deal more difficult for US policy-makers to move the dollar exchange rate than is frequently assumed. Exchange rate movements do not simply occur because the US Treasury wants them to and the Treasury cannot simply wish exchange rate movements into existence, but has to present a convincing technical case that persuades officials at other G7 finance ministries and central banks and more crucially convinces market analysts and sentiment more generally that there are grounds for a currency movement. This is a real constraint on the United States and means that exchange rate policy cannot simply be formulated on the basis of US political preferences or strategic objectives. Of course, the United States can continue to exploit currency movements and fluctuations for political and economic gain, but as we saw in Chapter 6 there is a finite potential for politically expedient strategies if some degree of technical credibility is to be retained. Furthermore, movements in the value of the dollar also proved to be a source of a frustration for the Treasury when markets did not respond to the views forwarded by officials. Both the Europeans and the Japanese have catalysed collective G7 exchange rate action in the last decade, but this is a much less common occurrence than the US doing likewise and ultimately the concert equality model is a hugely overstated expression of the fact that Japan and Europe can influence G7 exchange rate policy and that a certain exchange rate policy is much more likely to succeed if it is collectively backed by the G7 as a group.

Exchange rate policy is in fact a complex area, characterized by a multi-spatial (three-dimensional) governance process that no one single actor is able to control. A complex combination of factors is required to move an exchange rate in a particular direction. The G7 have been most successful in influencing exchange rates when three conditions have been in place: a strong technical argument for an exchange rate movement has existed; there has been strong domestic support for such a movement, most especially in the United States, so as to avoid the risk of market confusion brought about conflicting domestic signals; and finally a successful exchange rate outcome has been most likely when a broad consensus has existed among G7 authorities. The need to build up a track record of technical competence and cultivate technical authority where exchange rate matters are concerned, places a very real constraint on the United States and limits the possibilities of the US arbitrarily influencing exchange rates. Moreover, it creates incentives for the US to conform with the accepted social practices of finance ministries and central banks and engage in technically grounded multilateralism. The capacity of US monetary authorities to engineer monetary and economic outcomes through the act of currency manipulation should therefore not be overestimated, while the willingness of the finance ministries and central banks to respond to societal demands on exchange rates appears to have diminished. The discussion in Chapter 6 revealed that the record of an administration with a sound economic record that paid close attention to macroeconomic credibility and on the whole respected technical authority, was decidedly mixed in terms of its ability to achieve desired exchange rate outcomes through a combination of interventions and declaratory policy (the Clinton administration). An administration that has displayed little interest in economic policy beyond populist tax cuts (the Bush administration) could be about to suffer the consequences of its earlier disinterest and find painful macroeconomic adjustment unavoidable. In the event of such a scenario, US monetary exceptionalism will have been significantly eroded.

Further examples of multilateral constraints on the United States were evident in G7 debates on the global financial architecture. The United States did not have things entirely their own way in the debates that followed the Asian financial crisis. For example, the G7 consensus evolved from promoting the liberalization of capital transactions as broadly and as speedily as possible, to a situation where it is now acknowledged that capital liberalization has to be properly sequenced and should be proceeded by certain pre-conditions, including a well-established market economy, trade liberalization, a strong financial sector supported by an efficient supervisory system that was capable of monitoring the risks involved in exposure to foreign currency denominated loans, as well as a macroeconomic framework consistent with a liberalized financial system. Japanese views were instrumental in producing this refined G7 consensus. Moreover, on the basis of a Japanese proposal, the US also agreed that the IMF's involvement in structural policies should be restricted to matters directly relating to financial crises. This was a direct recognition of the sensitivities arising from the IMF's handling of the Asian financial crisis. In other words, US positions on several key issues softened as a consequence of G7 discussion. However, it is also worth noting that the US achieved several victories on key issues, notably on retaining IMF conditionality and in the rejection of the SDRM proposal, although in the case of the latter, even though opposition was strongest in the US, financial interests from across the industrialized world mobilized against the proposal and the eventual decision was the result of experiences with CACs based on work conducted by the Bank of England and the Bank of Canada.

Ultimately, on those issues on which the United States successfully achieved their objectives, they did so not by acting in a unilateral manner, but usually on the basis of varying degrees of support from other G7 finance ministries and central banks. For example, opposition to Japan's doomed AMF proposal came not only from the US, although opposition was undoubtedly strongest in Washington, but also from European states. In short, while the US remains the most important power in the G7, for reasons already discussed, it has on occasion had to modify and temper its position, while in the areas in which it has enjoyed success it has usually enjoyed varying degrees of support from other G7 states.

While it is clearly an exaggeration to claim that the G7 represents a concert of equal powers, the G7's reliance on a mode of operation that involves exercising influence through persuasion and argumentation, based on the presentation of evidence, means that it is not simply a state's political interests that determine G7 outcomes, but the strength of a given argument. All G7 states have some capacity to influence debates and outcomes depending on the expertise, competence and reputation of key personnel at any given time. Consequently, G7 positions are not determined by US preferences, while US preferences and positions in the field of global financial governance are not fixed, but are sometimes modified as a consequence of interactions and discussions with G7 finance ministry and central bank counterparts. In this regard, while the US retains its pre-eminent position in the G7 and in some respects has even enhanced its capability to achieve its objectives under financial globalization,[16] in other respects it has found itself constrained by growing market authority and shared multilateral norms, including the preference for governance by multilateral consensus in the field of money and finance. A crucial implication of this is that studying the exercise of power and authority in global financial governance requires a sensitivity to the particular multilateral setting under consideration and the norms and social practices of the elites that operate in these settings. Until now, consideration and analysis of these kind of factors has barely figured in debates on US power in international monetary affairs. This has not only impeded our understanding of the true extent of US power, it has also restricted our understanding of the nature of global financial governance and the contribution of particular multilateral processes.

How important is the G7 process? The wider collective authority of the G7 in an era of decentralized globalization

The third principal research question pursued in the book asked what contribution the G7 makes to global financial governance, how much authority the G7 has and how that authority is exercised. As we have seen, the principal rationale for the G7 process is that it creates opportunities for finance ministries and central banks to arrive at consensual positions on a range of monetary and financial issues. They are then able to promote that consensus collectively, thus enhancing their capacity to influence decisions reached elsewhere in the global political economy through a form of strategic signalling. The logic behind this mode of operation is simple. If the world's leading finance ministries and central banks, as repositories of considerable wisdom on monetary and financial affairs, arrive at a collective position and come to a shared conclusion on a particular issue, other actors will take this view more seriously than if it was held by one or two finance ministries and central banks. In this way the G7 can set agendas and priorities in relation to the diverse decision-making processes and complex range of actors that comprise global financial governance.

Yet it is precisely the G7's supposed strength that is also its crucial weakness. Limited participation in terms of both individual representatives and country membership, results in relatively small numbers attending G7 meetings. Small numbers have the advantage of facilitating a genuine exchange of views, a process of arguing back and forth and an enhanced potential for constructing consensus. But limited participation and restricted membership also means that the G7 struggle to arrive at binding decisions, precisely because much decision making in the global financial system is dependent on actors who do not attend G7 meetings. It is for this reason that the G7 rely on strategic signalling to exert influence and this in turn means that the G7 will exert most influence and have most authority if they are able to develop convincing arguments based on persuasive analysis. For example, while the G7 cannot reach decisions on national macroeconomic policies, arriving at a common view on the overall orientation of macroeconomic policy in a particular state will clearly inform the terms on which national policy debates subsequently take place, especially when the advocates of a shared G7 view are also key figures in national policy-making. In this respect, G7 finance ministers and central bank governors can use the G7 as a resource to provide backing from their G7 colleagues for a position they intend to pursue nationally.

Strategic signalling of this sort might appear a relatively benign form of influence and authority, but it has a very distinct social and political purpose. Strategic signalling by the G7 has facilitated and institutionalized the supremacy of the market actors in financial governance in two principal ways. First, through their choice of declaratory policy as the principal means of influencing exchange rates, the G7 have facilitated a situation whereby market actors have become authorities in their own right and are increasingly able to determine macroeconomic priorities. Market operators are often swept along by the exuberance of the market. Declaratory policy relies on some degree of self-awareness amongst market actors to acknowledge and correct excessive movements. Yet the experience of the last decade, involving repeated large gyrations between the major currencies, suggests that faith in the foreign exchange market's capacity to behave reasonably may be unwarranted. Market actors can simply reject policy-makers' analyses or arguments on the grounds that prevailing market thinking is superior to that of public officials. Declaratory policy leaves policy-makers with no real response in such circumstances. When the market refuses to respond to policy-makers' statements, the impotency of declaratory policy becomes all too apparent, and the belief that financial markets are all-powerful is further consolidated and augmented. In the absence of any feasible public sanction, market operators can offer alternative views to those of G7 policy-makers, while claiming they have a better feel for market dynamics. A growing reliance on declaratory policy has cast the market as judge and jury in the determination of exchange rates and macroeconomic priorities, effectively inviting the market to engage in an ongoing referendum or opinion poll on national macroeconomic policies. Consequently, current G7 beliefs and social practices have encouraged and facilitated a continuous form of communicative diplomacy and signalling between private markets and public authorities, which is a key defining feature of the contemporary international monetary order – what I have referred to as a form of third-dimensional diplomacy. The empirical evidence presented in Chapter 6 points towards the ascendancy of the market in the resulting form of three-dimensional governance, based on market and peer scrutiny of national macroeconomic policies, and in the determination of macroeconomic and exchange rate outcomes, as well as the fortunes of citizens and governments across the globe. In summary, the G7 process contributes to this state of affairs by viewing markets as rational, efficient entities, by prioritizing technocratic competence ahead of a well-rounded definition of the public good and by relying on declaratory policy to exert influence in financial markets.

Second, the finance ministries and central banks have also facilitated market supremacy in their work on the global financial architecture. Their heavy focus on transparency has been designed to encourage an open ongoing dialogue between creditors and debtors, but places an onus on national authorities and governments to prove their market-friendly credentials. From the outset, an approach based on transparency creates a fundamental asymmetry in the power relations of financial diplomacy by implicating public authorities and regulators in crisis-affected countries and largely absolving foreign investors of responsibility. Despite claims to the contrary therefore, G7 proposals on the global financial architecture are not simply technocratic but are inherently political. Beneath the mask of their gradual, technocratic, reform trajectory, the finance ministries and central banks have displayed a continuous ideational bias towards the interests of large-scale international financial investors. They have laid the institutional and ideational foundations for a global financial system characterized by market supremacy, in which market actors are able to engage in asymmetrical negotiations with debtors and demand reassurance in the form of institutional arrangements and policies that are market friendly, while having the final say in the determination of debt repayment schedules. This contrasts starkly with a progressively generous approach to debt relief on sums of public money owed by developing countries to G7 governments, illustrating the degree of apprehension with which the G7 approach matters relating to private financial interests. Furthermore, the recent architectural proposals treat complete financial and capital account liberalization as a universal norm that all states should be working towards and the recently introduced twelve codes and standards have been designed to create a procedural and institutional basis for further orderly liberalization processes.

However, the key element of G7 power in global financial governance is not related to the extent to which they can influence others through collective statements–strategic signalling, but through their capacity to prevent certain things from happening. Withdrawal of support is a crucial strategy the G7 can employ to prevent governance initiatives they oppose coming to fruition. This power of veto has been most evident in the case of the SDRM proposal. A G7 argument that the proposal was unworkable and incompatible with CACs, not only damaged the credibility of the proposal but also removed the political will and consent for the IMF to press ahead. Quite simply, any initiative in global financial governance is doomed to fail without the backing and support of the major finance ministries and central banks. In this respect, the G7 are able to collectively define the limits of the possible in the public sphere of global financial governance. The G7's capacity to oppose and reject such proposals and favour more market friendly solutions, have enabled the finance ministries and central banks to operate as a collective filtering device, vetting architectural reform proposals and effectively reinforcing and maintaining the current status quo of market supremacy. The G7 consequently operate as a transgovernmental gatekeeper, defining the terms on which global financial governance is conducted.

Recent institutional initiatives proposed by the G7 under the auspices of the architecture debate, have also had the effect of defining the terms on which global financial governance is conducted, the language used and most crucially who has a legitimate right to participate in key debates. The biggest impact of recent G7 architectural proposals, I have argued, has been to institutionalize the predominantly technocratic and transgovernmental nature of global financial governance. In the case of the G20, the G7 now consult with predominantly sympathetic like-minded agencies in emerging markets in a *de facto* extension of G7 transgovernmentalism. The G20 is about intensifying and institutionalizing channels of communication and persuasion with finance ministries and central banks in emerging markets, who are on the whole sympathetic to neo-classical premises. The principal motivation behind this appears to have been to improve the implementation record of G7 standards and codes. In the case of the FSF, a number of specialist regulators and bodies have been brought together under one roof and have been asked to provide technical reports to the G7 on a number of matters. Crucially however, the FSF also represents an attempt to control debates on issues such as hedge funds and offshore financial centres by monopolizing technical expertise and in this context, the findings of technical FSF reports become difficult to contest. A more complex stratified form of transgovernmentalism, consisting of various networks of regulators and technical specialists who report to the G7 finance ministries and central banks but retain a certain degree of autonomy based on their technical expertise, is the net result of these proposals. In this context, the G7 finance ministries and central banks retain a co-ordinating role, orchestrating, catalysing and setting agendas and priorities for these networks of regulators and officials. Meanwhile, debates are effectively ring-fenced and outsiders excluded as governance depends on highly technical reports and findings that pay scant attention to wider social and political considerations.

In short, the G7 process is as much about catalysing developments elsewhere, and formulating and endorsing approaches and ideas, as it is about reaching decisions in its own right. In this respect, the Group of Seven itself does not represent a form of governance in its own right, but plays a particular niche role in a broader diffuse process of global financial governance. The G7 have initiated a wider machinery of global financial governance – a series of mechanisms, forums, codes, practices, principles and norms that are monitored and implemented by specialist technocrats and officials, some of whom are directly answerable to the G7 deputies, in national administrative terms. Most of the consensual norms, ideas, approaches and principles that inform contemporary global financial governance, are either authored or approved by the G7, and G7 approval is crucial if these practices are to enjoy authority, simply because the rest of the world look to the G7 for leadership on these issues. Many voices may not like G7 leadership and may be critical of it, but a sufficient number of actors, including markets, the financial press, emerging markets, the staff of various multilateral institutions and bodies, continue to expect the G7 to develop ideas, approaches, priorities, strategies and to catalyse action in response to financial governance challenges, to keep the G7 in a leadership role. It is these expectations that partly confer authority on the G7 in this field, even if questions concerning the sustainability of the G7 in its current form are beginning to gain momentum.

Strategic meetings of senior figures from finance ministries and central banks enable them to catalyse their bureaucratic and technical capability, urging their bureaucracies to work together and share findings, experiences and information. This is made easier by a legacy of dialogue and collaboration stretching over thirty years. Since the breakdown of Bretton Woods, the finance ministries and central banks have established a rhythm of meetings and consultations which gives a momentum and sense of routine to their ongoing activities, and in turn contributes to the climate of expectation amongst outsiders. For all that we can criticize the G7 for its exclusive qualities and the lack of legitimacy arising from this, in the absence of the G7 a similar sort of process would in all likelihood have to be established. The advantage of the G7 process is that it has well-established procedures for consultation, dialogue and collaboration amongst the most senior officials and politicians with direct responsibility for monetary and financial governance.

Even if relatively little beyond the definition and endorsement of broad approaches is achieved at G7 meetings, the G7 does sit at the apex of the diverse specialist committees and networks that populate the domain of global financial governance. Ultimately, the day-to-day detailed work that informs the governance of global finance is conducted and formulated elsewhere. The Group of Seven remains reliant on this more detailed work and can offer direction to the bodies producing this work, but cannot dictate to them for fear of undermining their technical credibility, which the G7 may need to draw upon at a later date. The G7 can of course prioritize and selectively promote the lessons and findings of these committees and bodies, but the relationship is best characterized as one of mutual dependence. For example, the technocrats owe their existence to senior figures involved in the G7, but at the same time the G7 are dependent on the information, analysis and recommendations provided by the technocrats. The G7 do set deadlines, priorities and agendas for this broad array of technocrats and therefore define the parameters of their debates, but within these parameters the technocrats have considerable discretion. In this regard, the G7 can be characterized as a senior co-ordinating transgovernmental coalition providing strategic direction for, but not controlling, an increasingly complex and stratified transgovernmental system of financial governance.

One of the consequences of understanding the G7's role in this way is that it brings into focus the problems associated with examining the G7 finance ministries and central banks' record in terms of compliance, which is the favoured approach of the Toronto school of thought pioneered by John Kirton. G7 meetings rarely attempt to reach specific agreements that require 'compliance'. Communiqués are often written in code and are frequently vague and ambiguous, making it difficult to assess the extent to which countries comply with them. Moreover, when G7 policy-makers express a collective view it can have a protracted and delayed impact, influencing national agendas, market behaviour, or the agendas of international bodies, in ways that are not easily measurable. For example, the collective expression of a G7 view may trigger a debate in a legislature or put something on the agenda of an international body, but the proposal might take time to come to fruition.

However, ultimately, there is no secretariat at G7 meetings and the process has no legal basis, meaning that binding agreements are rare. The lack of legal powers and the lack of binding agreements should not be mistaken for a lack of influence or an absence of authority. The G7 finance ministries and central banks continue to strive to reach consensus and then promote that consensus in technical and increasingly in normative terms.[17] Mutual endorsement and reinforcement of shared G7 ideas and approaches, or continuous normative persuasion, is a necessity precisely because the insulation of finance ministries and central banks from political pressures has created increasing legitimacy problems and a growing number of critics opposed to neo-liberal globalization. Finance ministries and central banks have responded to resistance by using the G7 process as a platform for intensifying the promotion of further capital liberalization and macroeconomic austerity and instigating procedures and mechanisms designed to sustain a liberalized financial order, while simultaneously ring-fencing global financial governance as a technocratic issue rather than an inherently political one.

Overall therefore, the Group of Seven are a transgovernmental coalition. Elsewhere I have suggested that this transgovernmental coalition have acted as a global 'ginger group'.[18] The ginger group in the nineteenth-century British Liberal Party operated as an influential caucus group that worked through the party machinery to ensure that party policy remained intellectually and ideologically coherent and consistent with the core principles of political liberalism. In the 1990s, G7 finance ministries and central banks have used the G7 process to similar effect. They have promoted their own beliefs or consensus in an effort to ensure that policy-making in a variety of settings throughout the global political economy is consistent with the fundamental premises of that consensus in the area of macroeconomic policy and financial governance. The framework of four-dimensional diplomacy has illustrated how the G7 performs this function in the context of domestic opposition and resistance, unstable and uncooperative markets, resistance from authorities in emerging market authorities, and multilateral institutions and transnational policy communities that have their own agendas and turf to protect. Crucially however, one vital issue remains unresolved and has continuously been overlooked by the G7. It is that too many important voices remain excluded from global financial governance, which as a consequence has too narrow and technocratic a basis for it too enjoy legitimacy with the wider public.

Prospects for a more inclusive and socially just form of global financial governance

This last point raises the issue of what needs to be done. The most commonly articulated criticism of global financial governance relates to a so-called democratic deficit or a lack of inclusion.[19] This lack of democracy is a result of global finance being presented as something that involves highly complex private transactions, best handled by technical experts operating free from political interference. Consequently, there are concerns that recent adjustments to global financial governance have been predominantly technical in nature (even if they can be potentially intrusive where domestic governance structures are concerned), broadly market-based and have institutionalized a neo-liberal agenda.[20] Certainly the new financial architecture agenda has been limited in extent and intent, while reform debates have been couched in apolitical terms that serve to obfuscate the political dynamics underpinning global financial governance.[21] Moreover, there are concerns that recent initiatives do not leave sufficient room for local practices and traditions, but impose a set of western 'universal' financial norms.[22] We have seen in the discussion in this book how private financial market interests dominate the formulation of economic policies and how the G7 finance ministries and central banks have facilitated market ascendancy in determining economic outcomes. These are not new observations. In a seminal article ten years ago, Geoffrey Underhill pointed out that crucial decisions about the structure of global financial markets have often been made in transnational policy communities, dominated by private interests, while broader segments of society are excluded.[23] Little has changed in the intervening time.

The problem with all of this is that global finance is unavoidably political. As the Asian financial crisis starkly demonstrated, global finance and its governance affects the lives and livelihoods of millions throughout the developing world.[24] Yet participation in key debates has been restricted and reform proposals have favoured interests in leading financial centres and their preferences for further liberalization based on initiatives to enhance transparency, derived from neo-classical theory. If concerns of equality, social justice, employment and poverty reduction are to become genuine concerns in global financial governance and feature alongside more technocratic concerns, current institutional arrangements for governing global finance will need to be reformed in a way that challenges the status quo in quite fundamental ways.

One argument that is gathering steam is that the G7 is a dated grouping, reflecting the conditions of a previous era and as its proportion of the global economy and population diminishes it is no longer possible to indefinitely exclude such a large proportion of the world's population (the developing world and emerging markets) from such a key forum. One proposal has been to extend the current G20 so that it operates at the leaders' level, as well as acting as a mechanism for finance ministry–central bank communications.[25] This is certainly a proposal that might broaden the dialogue between the global North and South, and potentially move us beyond the G20's current technocratic focus. Another proposal backed by a recent G7 deputy is to reconfigure the G7 as the principal mechanism for facilitating exchange rate co-operation in relation to the world's major currencies, so that the composition of representatives more accurately reflects the significance of certain currencies. Under this proposal the G7 would be replaced by a G4, in which European states would be represented by a Eurozone delegation, which would continue to meet with the US and Japan, with China being added as a fourth leading monetary power.[26] Given that future Chinese policies may determine the fate of the dollar, there is an obvious rationale for such a move.

However, if global financial governance is really to be made more progressive and inclusive, it is its overwhelmingly transgovernmental character that needs to be addressed. Some see the G20 as a promising development because it increases the participation of emerging markets in a key decision-making forum.[27] I would suggest that we should not hold out too many hopes for the G20 in its current institutional format. The restriction of the G20 to finance ministries and central banks is unlikely to deliver a more progressive debate, or produce a significant shift away from the current technocratic focus of global financial governance. Many officials in finance ministries and central banks in emerging markets remain sympathetic to neo-classical positions and premises and are regarded by their G7 counterparts as reliable and competent individuals possessing technical expertise for precisely this reason. Moreover, these agencies have been instrumental in forming a key state–society with financial and commercial interests, which in turn advocates financial liberalization and opposes the use of capital controls.[28] As Benjamin Cohen has argued, to reinstate capital controls as a legitimate tool of economic management, and by association to tackle the supremacy of unstable private financial markets, it will be necessary to build a more effective transnational coalition of proponents.[29] Furthermore, any such transnational coalition will need to be given access to key deliberative processes such as the G7 and G20 that effectively define the parameters of global financial governance debates. It will not be sufficient to restrict these key deliberative forums to finance ministries and central banks because this will only perpetuate the ascendancy of key financial interests and of a technocratic approach to global financial governance derived from neo-classical premises.

Crucially, as market supremacy was about to be partially reined in through the SDRM proposal, the finance ministries and central banks showed themselves susceptible to pressure from financial interests and changed their position to one of opposition. The episode brought into stark focus the simple truth that the finance ministries and central banks remain far too closely aligned with key private financial interests. Consequently, a wider range of government agencies representing a wider range of key societal interests need to be included in global financial governance debates, and possibly even NGO and civic associations (if state centrism is to be overcome).[30] I would hold out most hope for a mixture of government agencies from the developed and developing world being represented in a broad agenda-setting process, similar to the current G7, so as to break up the current finance ministry–central bank monopoly of debate. Ultimately, reconfiguring global financial governance will require broadening the national delegations that participate in the IMF, the FSF and other key decision-making processes as well as the G7. As Richard Higgott has pointed out, we need new discursive spaces where the policies and actions of global financial institutions can be discussed in a more open manner.[31] Crucially however, the range of voices represented in these key discursive spaces need to be extended beyond finance ministries and central banks and the financial interests they tend to represent. Without this global financial governance is unlikely to become substantially more inclusive or reflect concerns with social justice. Nor, given the current dominance of the finance ministries and central banks and their general neo-classical bias, is global financial governance likely to avoid financial crises that are often rooted in the very nature of the financial markets whose behaviour is determined by market trends as much as by underlying fundamentals. For the G7, the very real danger is that continued financial volatility may ultimately produce a dramatic backlash from the excluded and the dispossessed, imposing the highest costs on those who benefit most from the current system. A pressing question over the next decade is whether the G7 will be sufficiently enlightened to curtail the finance ministries and central banks current control of global financial governance and extend participation in key debates and dialogues to a wider range of government agencies and societal interests.

Notes

1 Introduction

1 Bank for International Settlements, 2001.
2 On the unique geography of financial markets see Cohen's distinction between spaces of place and spaces of flows; Cohen, 1998. For historically informed accounts of financial globalization see Eichengreen, 1996; Strange, 1998; McKenzie and Lee, 1991; Helleiner, 1994. Note that reference to financial globalization was also frequently made in the speeches of officials and politicians. A more sceptical position is evident in Hirst and Thompson, 1996.
3 For historical accounts of the evolution of the G7 see Putnam and Bayne, 1987; Pauly, 1997; James, 1996.
4 Porter and Wood, 2002, p. 243.
5 Bergsten and Henning, 1996.
6 For examples of the much-needed work in the Toronto G8 governance series on the G7 and global financial governance see Fratianni, Savona and Kirton, 2002; Kirton and von Furstenberg, 2001; Kaiser, Kirton and Daniels, 2000; Kirton, Daniels and Freytag, 1999. For further analysis of global financial architectural issues see Noble and Ravenhill, 2000; Armijo, 2002; Special Issue of *Global Governance* (7) 2001; Underhill and Zhang, 2003b; Soederberg, 2004a.
7 The absence of a detailed monograph on the G7 process is further surprising because one of the major works in the field of IPE in the 1980s looked in detail at the dynamics of the G7 summit and tracked its record in the first decade of its existence; Putnam and Bayne, 1987. Funabashi, a Japanese journalist, wrote a comprehensive account of the Plaza agreement and Louvre accord reached between finance ministries and central banks in the 1980s; Funabashi, 1989. While histories of the international system and international monetary co-operation have touched on the work of the G7, none has provided a comprehensive account of the politics and norms of the G7 process; Pauly, 1997; James, 1996; Webb, 1995.
8 Multilateralism refers to the conduct of relations between three or more states in accordance with certain principles. In contrast to macro-regionalism this would involve the states coming from more than one trading bloc, see Ruggie, 1992. Transnational refers to non-state actors that operate across borders. This should not be confused with transgovernmental which refers to governmental sub-units or bureaucracies from more than one country that come together to pursue and promote shared interests in relation to other parts of the state apparatus, or international organizations. For example see Keohane and Nye, 1974, pp. 39–62. Supranational refers to multi-national bureaucracies that perform a governance function in a particular international policy area. In relation to the issue of the relationship between what is referred to as 'financial globalization' and the state the literature is considerable. For good examples of the argument that globalization has and is eroding state capacities see Strange, 1996,

1998; Cerny, 1990; Cerny, 1995, pp. 595–625; Frieden, 1991, pp. 427–33; Moses, 1994, pp. 125–48. For the opposite view see Weiss, 1998; Hirst and Thompson, 1996; Garrett, 1998.

9 On the subject of legitimacy and inclusion in global financial governance see Germain, 2001, pp. 411–26; Porter, 2001, pp. 427–39.
10 Cooper, 1968. Also see Putnam and Bayne, 1987.
11 For an account of how this applied to the G10 in the 1960s see Russell, 1973, pp. 431–64.
12 Putnam and Bayne 1987. Pauly, 1997; James, 1996.
13 On the Bonn Summit see Putnam and Henning, 1989, pp. 12–140. On the Plaza and Louvre agreements see Funabashi, 1989; Henning and Destler, 1988, pp. 317–33.
14 Putnam and Henning, 1989; Cooper, 1985; Bryant, 1980.
15 Putnam and Henning list other forms of co-ordination such as unilateral adjustment, consultation and reinforcement, but note that these might be better described as co-operation. This is the approach adopted here because policy-makers tend to associate policy co-ordination with what Putnam and Henning refer to as package deals, while calling other types co-operation. Putnam and Henning, 1989, pp. 14–16. Point gleaned from confidential interviews with officials.
16 For a discussion see Webb, 1991, pp. 309–42.
17 For a full discussion see Putnam and Henning, 1989, pp. 14–16.
18 Webb, 1991.
19 Bergsten and Henning, 1996.
20 Henning, 1994.
21 Dore, 2000.
22 Henning and Destler, 1988. For a similar argument see Frieden, 1994, pp. 81–103.
23 Cox, 1992a, pp. 161–80. This approach also draws on Hobson, 2000.
24 A point made repeatedly to me in confidential interviews with officials between 1997 and 2000.
25 Strange, 1986; Cohen, 1998; Seabrooke, 2001; Walter, 1993; Gowan, 1999; Gill, 2003.
26 Germain, 2004.
27 Kirton first made the argument in 1989; Kirton, 1989. For a more recent application of this argument see Kirton, 2002.
28 Putnam and Bayne, 1987; Webb, 1995; Henning and Destler, 1988.
29 Kirton, 1989, 2000.
30 Kirton, 2000.
31 A common expression of this are references to a Treasury–Wall Street axis or Dollar–Wall Street regime, see Gowan, 1999. Also see Wade, 1999.
32 Gowan, 2001, pp. 359–74.
33 For an argument that the G20 does constitute an important step forward in relation to inclusion in global financial governance see Germain, 2001.
34 Kirton and Kokotsis, 1997–8, pp. 38–56.
35 Keohane and Nye, 1974.
36 Cerny, 2002.
37 Partial autonomy is probably a better description of this relationship.
38 Rosenau 1995, p.16.
39 Kirton and Kokotsis, 1997–8; Chayes and Chayes, 1993, pp. 175–205.
40 Again see Cox's notion of the internationalization of the state and the neo-Gramscian approach more generally; Cox, 1987, also Gill, 1993a.
41 On the G7 and debt see Bayne, 2000 and Wood, 2000.
42 Mundell, 1960, 1963, pp. 475–85; Flemming, 1962.
43 Underhill, 1997a, pp. 10–11.
44 See Underhill, 1997b, pp. 313–18.
45 Underhill, 1997c, pp. 17–50.

46 Cerny, 1994b.
47 Bank for International Settlements, 1996.
48 Point made in confidential interview with official, January 1999.
49 The multi-dimensional approach also has a role to play here. Examinations of the national institutional factors affecting G7 interactions makes it possible to identify the limits of the possible at G7 meetings and this assists in the task of spotting distorted press commentary.
50 Lowenthal, 1972.

2 The evolution of the Group of Seven

1 Henning and Destler, 1988, pp. 317–33; Webb, 1995.
2 For a commentary on how the liberal financial order of the 1920–1930s was discredited and used by Keynes as a justification for the construction of a more restrictive financial order after WWII see Helleiner, 1994.
3 Keynes, 1930.
4 Gardener, 1981.
5 This problem was first identified by Triffin, 1961.
6 De Ceco, 1986, pp. 381–99.
7 Webb, 1995.
8 Webb refers to symptom management policies as direct efforts to reduce exchange rate and payments imbalances through the use of public money, i.e. a focus on addressing the symptoms rather than the cause of any imbalances.
9 Webb, 1995.
10 Webb, 1991.
11 Michaely found that fiscal policy was not responsive to balance of payments data in any of the G7 countries, whilst monetary policy was only consistently responsive in Japan and Britain; Michaely, 1973.
12 Strange, 1986.
13 Helleiner, 1994.
14 Mundell, 1960; Flemming, 1962.
15 Odell, 1979, pp. 57–81.
16 Strange, 1986.
17 Helleiner, 1994. This was less evident in the field of macroeconomic policy, although the Federal Reserve was experimenting with forms of monetary control as early as 1971. The broad outlook was oriented towards growth and macroeconomic expansion as evidenced in the Bonn locomotive strategy of 1978, which represented a form of international Keynesianism in which the US was instrumental.
18 Such views are represented in Machlup, 1968.
19 This was evident in the case of the European countries in the context of the EMU process. See McNamara, 1998.
20 Calleo, 1982.
21 Hall, 1989.
22 Webb, 1995. Webb cites the cases of the Bonn locomotive strategy and the Plaza and Louvre agreements to support this argument. These instances of policy co-ordination are briefly covered elsewhere in this chapter.
23 Tsoukalis, 1997.
24 Helleiner, 1994.
25 Cerny, 1990.
26 Several volumes could be devoted to debating the extent to which rising international capital mobility has genuinely restricted the macroeconomic policy autonomy of states. This is certainly disputed in the literature. For dissenting voices which argue that governments retain more macroeconomic discretion than is commonly assumed see

Hirst and Thompson, 1996; Garrett, 1998; Hay, 2000, pp. 138–52; Notermans, 1994, pp. 133–67. I do not wish to enter into the terms of the long and complicated debate on what is possible in macroeconomic policy other than to note the rise of a discourse and rhetoric among policy-makers during the 1980s and 1990s that emphasized that there was no alternative to macroeconomic discipline. I also wish to highlight the institutional shift towards macroeconomic discipline in the 1990s evident in a rise in central bank independence and fiscal rules in advanced capitalist states.

27 Bank for International Settlements, 1996.

28 Confidential interview with official February 1998.

29 Russell, 1973, pp. 431–64.

30 There were actually eleven members of the G10, the current G7 together with Belgium, Netherlands, Sweden and Switzerland.

31 WP-3, 1966, p. 8.

32 Cooper, 1968.

33 Russell, 1973.

34 James, 1996, p. 183.

35 Effectively these individuals were the first deputies that were to become so influential as a consequence of their regular behind the scenes negotiations and interactions; James, 1996, pp. 266–7.

36 This account of the origins of the Library Group is taken from Volcker and Gyohten, 1992, p.126.

37 The growth in the G7 apparatus began at the Ottawa summit when the heads of state and government asked trade ministers to start meeting regularly ahead of GATT negotiations. This group became known as the Quadrilateral due to a membership of four. The European countries were represented by a single representative from the European Commission, because of the EC's concern to develop the single market and represent the Community as a single trading bloc.

38 This was partly because the leaders themselves had begun to disengage from the discussion of macroeconomic issues.

39 A three- or four-line statement was released in January 1985, but the association with the Plaza agreement has meant that G5 meetings began to attract considerable media attention from this point on.

40 For accounts of this see Putnam and Bayne, 1987 and Lawson, 1992.

41 Point made repeatedly in confidential interviews with officials between 1997 and 1998.

42 Putnam and Bayne, 1987. Such an argument reflects the liberal or neo-liberal institutionalist position in international relations. See Keohane, 1984.

43 The fact that Putnam and Bayne's extensive research on the G7 summits from 1975 to 1986 supports such a conclusion, makes it all the more curious why they place so much emphasis on interdependence and trilateralism as explanations for the emergence of the G7. Certainly these factors played a role in the establishment of the G7 process, but they should not obscure the fact that the G7 was primarily US inspired, motivated by a belief that the G7 would better enable the US to pursue its objectives than the existing G10.

44 Putnam and Bayne, 1987.

45 Putnam and Bayne, 1987, p. 29; Lawson, 1992, pp. 546–56.

46 Putnam and Bayne, 1987, p. 39; James, 1996.

47 In this respect the US Treasury had to submit an annual report to Congress on the behaviour of foreign governments in exchange rate matters.

48 In a sense this was a forerunner of the more developed form of three-dimensional diplomacy evident in the operation of the G7 process today. See Chapter 5.

49 Firm preceded the word surveillance in the actual text on French insistence.

50 Pauly, 1997.

51 See Communiqué released by the leaders of the G6 at the Rambouillet Summit, 15–17 November 1975. The full text of the agreement is available at http://www.library.utoronto.ca/g7/summit/index.htm.
52 It also provided endorsement for certain regional exchange rate regimes such as the European monetary snake. The successor of the snake, the EMS, has been orientated towards price stability because of the Deutschmark's anchor status within the system largely because of the Bundesbank's impeccable anti- inflationary record.
53 More detailed accounts of this and the operation of multilateral surveillance in the 1970s are to be found; James, 1996, pp. 265–337; Putnam and Bayne, 1987, pp. 25–48; Pauly, 1992, pp. 293–327. The new mandate of the Fund contained some ambiguities and there was some degree of division amongst the G7 powers as to how to interpret it. France and Germany called for the Fund to promote broad policy objectives by taking a view on the correctness of particular exchange rates. On the other hand, the US, Canada and the UK favoured an approach that would defer to market forces with a narrow definition of market disorder. They also favoured focusing the Fund's mandate on avoiding exchange rate manipulation by governments. On this basis, it was agreed that a 'guidelines' approach might allow specific principles to evolve out of practice. This ambiguity placed a special emphasis on the process of G7 consensus formation.
54 Baker, 1999, pp. 79–100.
55 Bryant and Hodgkinson, 1989. For a case study of this paradigmatic case of co-ordination which led to the development of the idea of two level games see Putnam and Henning, 1989.
56 Putnam and Bayne, 1987.
57 Nolke, 2004.
58 Putnam and Henning, 1989.
59 See Holtham, 1989.
60 Communiqué of G7 leaders, Bonn summit 1978.
61 Japan and the US have at various times continued to pursue Keynesian-style policies.
62 Point made by former official in a confidential interview, January 1998.
63 In sterilized intervention official purchases or sales of foreign currency are offset by domestic transactions so as to leave the monetary liabilities of both home and foreign monetary authorities unchanged. This works by changing the denomination of bonds held by the public. Such a purchase would reduce private sector holdings of foreign assets and increase private sector holdings of the home currency. This increase has the effect of expanding the monetary base unless the central bank removes an equivalent amount from the market by, for example, selling an equivalent amount of own-currency denominated bonds to the public. The benefit of sterilized intervention therefore is that it does not conflict with other policy objectives, although it can affect the stock of foreign exchange reserves. Its principal advantage is that it conveys signals about future policy intentions to financial markets.
64 Unsterilized intervention occurs more than signalling because it affects the size of the money supply; this implies that unsterilized intervention is more likely to conflict with other policy objectives, particularly that of controlling inflation.
65 Point made in confidential interview with official, January 1998.
66 Confidential interview with British official, January 1998; Henning and Destler, 1988.
67 Points made by former British official in an interview with the author, January 1998.
68 Funabashi, 1989.
69 Feldstein, 1994.
70 Mussa, 1994.
71 Confidential interview former British official, January 1998.
72 Artis and Ostry, 1983.
73 Mulford, 1998, p. 12.
74 Henning and Destler, 1988, p. 330.

75 Funabashi, 1989, p. 241.
76 Lawson, 1992, p. 554. Louvre was actually agreed by the G6 because the Italians had walked out of the meeting in protest at the fact that the G5 were continuing to meet ahead of G7 meetings.
77 Statement issued by G6 finance ministers, Louvre, 22 February 1987.
78 Dobson, 1991, p. 69. Often this was because participants could not agree on a suitable level by any other means.
79 Funabashi, 1989, p. 2.
80 Dobson, 1991, p. 67.
81 Dobson, 1991, p. 119; also see Lawson, 1992.
82 Bergsten and Henning, 1996; Bergsten, 1996; Merlini, 1994, pp. 5–26; Gill, 1993b; Ikenberry, 1993, pp. 132–9; Smyser, 1993; Dornbusch, 1996, pp. 41–2.
83 US contributions alone were inadequate, while Japan and Germany as losers in WWII were excluded from western security institutions.
84 Generally, debt relief has not been characterized by the same degree of consensus or shared belief system amongst the G7 that has been evident in macroeconomic, exchange rate and financial issues. At the Cologne summit in 1999 a new debt relief initiative was announced.
85 Webb, 1995. One could even advance the argument that ultimately international capital mobility reaches the point where it gives rise to a series of ideas and institutional arrangements that actually make policy co-ordination more difficult.
86 Cerny, 1995, pp. 595–625.
87 Bergsten and Henning, 1996.
88 The traditional leitmotiv of economic policy in the G7 countries have differed substantially and these has been a further source of inaction and occasional conflict.
89 For arguments and evidence relating to the effectiveness of foreign exchange market intervention see Dominguez and Frankel, 1993.
90 Gill, 1993b, p. 104.
91 Pauly, 1997.
92 Balance of payment imbalances between the US and Germany fell in the early 1990s, due to the effects of German unification. Towards the end of the 1990s they began to increase again as the US trade deficit reached record levels. Low consumer demand in Japan and cheap exports stemming from the Asian crisis have been contributory factors here. Ultimately this reflects the reality that G7 officials have become less concerned with current account imbalances in an era of international capital mobility and more concerned with capital account developments and the balance of saving and investments.
93 Bergsten and Henning, 1996.
94 The definitive statement of this position is Strange, 1996.

3 Situating the Group of Seven in a context

1 Cox, 1992a, p. 161.
2 A similar point about the pitfalls of considering a global level of analysis as exogenous has recently been made by Cerny, 2001b, pp. 397–410.
3 Multilateralism is used here as a general term to refer to processes based on relations and interaction between three or more states. See Ruggie, 1992.
4 Wendt, 1987, pp. 335–370; Hollis and Smith, 1991, pp. 393–410.
5 Ruggie, 1992, p. 568.
6 Strange, 1994.
7 Langley, 2005, pp. 85–101.
8 Germain, 1997.
9 On disintermediation see Langley, 2005. Also see Chapter 5.
10 Langley, 2002.

11 Randall Germain takes this one step further and argues that the very act of creating credit is reliant on symbolism and voluntary exchanges, including future promises to pay. If they are not to be compromised, these exchanges and the operation of the financial system as a whole, have to be underpinned by some form of consensual decision making; Germain, 2004.
12 Porter, 2003, pp. 520–51.
13 Strange, 1994.
14 On the contemporary politics of the IMF, particularly the institution's role in the Asian Financial crisis see White, 2005a. Also see Pauly, 1993.
15 On IOSCO see Underhill, 1995, pp. 251–78.
16 On the BCBS see Kapstein, 1994; Wood, 2000.
17 On the G30 see Tsinigou, E 'Transnational policy communities and financial governance: the role of private actors in derivatives regulation', *Centre for the Study of Globalisation and Regionalisation Working Paper,* No.111/03. Available online at http://www.warwick.ac.uk/fac/soc/CSGR/abwp11103.html (9 April 2004).
18 Sinclair, 2005.
19 On the G20 see Germain, 2001, pp. 411–26; Baker, 2000, pp. 165–89.
20 For the classic statements of realist, neo-realist and modified neo-realist positions see Morgenthau, 1948; Waltz, 1979; Gilpin,1981.
21 Keohane and Nye, 1974.
22 Keohane and Nye, 1974.
23 For such an argument see Baker, 2000.
24 For a discussion of the way finance ministries and central banks dominate other state agencies see a discussion of what Robert Cox calls the internationalization of the state; Cox, 1994, pp. 45–59; Panitch, 1996, pp. 83–116.
25 Scholte, 1997.
26 Wicks, 1994a.
27 See Keohane and Nye, 1974, pp. 39–62.
28 Russell, 1973, pp. 431–64.
29 For a recent systematic attempt to apply transgovernmentalism see Nolke, 2004.
30 Slaughter, 2004; Nolke, 2004.
31 For an account of this see Strange, 1994.
32 Soros, 1987.
33 Kirshner, 1995.
34 Funabashi, 1988; Destler and Henning, 1989.
35 Gowan, 1999.
36 Cohen, 2004.
37 Gowan, 2001, pp. 359–74.
38 Cohen, 2004.
39 Aykens, 2002, pp. 359–80.
40 Arendt, 1958.
41 Arendt, 1958; Risse, 2000, p. 1.
42 The emergence of the euro may challenge this supremacy eventually. Throughout the 1990s well over 60 per cent of world currency transactions involved the dollar.
43 Point made repeatedly in interviews with finance ministry and central bank officials involved in G7 preparations throughout 1997 and 1998.
44 Cohen, 2003.
45 Aykens, 2002, pp. 64–5.
46 On the rise of polycentic governance see Scholte, 2004.
47 Hobson, 2000.
48 A possible notable exception is the neo-Gramscian tradition inspired by the work of Robert Cox. Cox sought further understanding of the role of the state in the structuration of the global economic order. Patterns of global order were seen by Cox as being directly related to the balance of social forces across the system,

particularly those within dominant states. Cox attempted to overcome reductionism by emphasizing the power of ideas and urged researchers to investigate the relationships between material capabilities, ideas and institutions and between states, social forces and world orders in an open-ended fashion with no assumption of one-way determinism; Cox, 1987.

49 See Hobson, 2000. For similar approaches see Mann's notion of four power sources – ideological, economic, military and political; Mann, 1993. Also see Susan Strange's idea that financial, production, security and knowledge structures hold one another in place; Strange, 1994.

50 Hobson, 2000, p.204.

51 Underhill, 2000, pp. 805–24.

52 Cerny, 2000a, pp. 453–63.

53 Cerny, 2000a, p. 436; Giddens, 1984.

54 Hobson, 1997; Gamble, 1988.

55 Hobson, 2000.

56 Hobson, 2000, p. 230. For the classic outside-in statement see Waltz, 1979. Also see Gourevitch, 1978, pp. 281–313. For a classic inside-out statement see Bull, 1977.

57 Hobson, 2000, p. 234.

58 Moravcsik, 1997, pp. 513–53.

59 Putnam and Henning, 1989, pp. 12–140.

60 Dyson, 1994; Putnam and Henning, 1989.

61 Putnam, 1998, pp. 429–60. It is important to discuss the notion of the two-level game because it has become something of a metaphor for G7 co-operation, and because the idea emerged out of Putnam's research on the G7 summits; Putnam and Bayne, 1987.

62 Throughout the course of the rest of this study this proposition is questioned. For an expression of the argument that independent central banks increase the potential for international monetary co-operation see Artis and Ostry, 1983.

63 Correspondence from and discussions with Robert Putnam. A 'win-set' is the range of conditions that win, or make an international agreement possible. One such proposition arrived at through a case study of the Bonn Summit of 1978 as discussed in the previous chapter, is that division between domestic political forces increases the likelihood of reaching an international agreement, because negotiators favouring an agreement can exploit these divisions and promote their own favoured course of action.

64 Keohane, 1984; Wallich, 1984, pp. 85–99.

65 More advanced and sophisticated discussions of two-level games have attempted to consider what would happen if level I negotiators developed independent preferences, or if a state was represented by more than one negotiator. See Evans *et al.*, 1993. However, the assumption that the principal form of multilateral interaction is 'hard bargaining' remained unchallenged, whilst the definition of what constituted a level remained narrow and restrictive, preventing multilateral processes from being located in a wider world context.

66 Cox, 1987; Cox, 1983, pp. 162–75. Others have built upon the work of Cox and have developed the notion of the growing authority of actors in private financial markets; Sinclair, 1994, pp. 133–59; Harmes, 1998, pp. 92–121.

67 Cox, 1999; O' Brien *et al.* 2000.

68 Giddens, 1982, p. 32.

69 Amin and Palan, 2001, p. 567.

70 Amin, 2001.

71 Cohen, 1998; Woodward, 2005, pp. 49–61.

72 There are a range of constructivist perspectives. Space prevents a detailed treatment here. For sense of some of the variation see Christiansen, Jorgensen and Wiener, 2001. For some of the main constructivist statements see Wendt, 1999; Ruggie, 1998.

73 Risse, 2000, p. 1.
74 McNamara, 1998.
75 March and Olsen, 1998, pp. 943–69.
76 This is one of the basic conclusions of Putnam and Bayne's study of summitry; Putnam and Bayne, 1987.
77 March and Olsen, 1988.
78 McNamara, 1998.
79 Henning, 1994.
80 Significantly, it is not possible to have a chapter on each national finance ministry and central bank, but there will be a general discussion of these issues in Chapter 5.
81 Agnew, 1994, pp. 53–80.
82 Cohen, 1998.
83 Taylor, 1996, pp. 917–28.
84 Castells, 1996; Cohen, 1998.
85 There is a need for more research into the influence of various policy-makers and market analysts over a long period of time, focusing on the cult of personality and reputation.
86 Soros, 1987; Thrift and Leyshon, 1994, pp. 299–327.
87 Wriston, 1998.
88 Cohen, 2004.
89 Sinclair, 2005.
90 See for example Webb, 1991; Cerny, 1994b; Moses, 1995, pp. 407–26. Of course, an alternative body of literature suggests otherwise see Hirst and Thompson, 1996; Garrett, 1998. While it may be true that states retain greater autonomy in macroeconomic policy than is frequently assumed, the discourse of policy-makers during the 1990s, together with the movement towards independent central banks and fiscal rules, suggest policy-makers have been unconvinced by such arguments. In this respect the impact of ideational factors in driving and sustaining international capital mobility and macroeconomic discipline should not be under-estimated. Moreover, the real rapid increase in international capital mobility came after 1989, which means that the data used by Garret from the 1980s to demonstrate that states have continued to follow fiscal activism might be dated and inappropriate for assessing the true impact of international capital mobility.
91 Cerny, 1994b; McNamara, 1998.
92 Andrews, 1994.
93 See Porter, 2003. His definition is partly derived from Mayntz and Hughes, 1988.
94 Porter, 2003, p. 526.
95 Porter, 2003, p. 526.
96 Crockett, 1988, p. 22.
97 Point made repeatedly in confidential interviews with officials in 1997–8.

4 The Group of Seven and the politics of financial ideas

1 There is a considerable tradition of highlighting the importance of the ideas policy-makers hold as a determining influence on monetary and financial policy. For some examples see Odell, 1982; McNamara, 1998; Verdun, 2000.
2 Watson, 2002b, pp. 183–96; Blyth, 2003, pp. 239–59; Kirshner, 2003b.
3 Underhill and Zhang, 2003a, p. 382.
4 Note that two hundred years of industrial and post-industrial economic development had served to make the application of the principles of sound money and open markets tolerable for advanced capitalist societies. Often, developing countries were urged to

adopt policies informed by these principles without the preparation of industrialized societies; Underhill and Zhang, 2003a.

5 Helleiner, 1994.
6 Williamson, 1994; Krugman, 1995.
7 Krugman, 1995.
8 Wicks, 1994b.
9 Summers, 1999, pp. 3–18.
10 The empirical evidence in studies by economists is mixed. Indeed, there is a strong case to make against free capital mobility. For a review see Felix, 2002. Also see Stiglitz, 2002; Bhagwati, 1998, pp. 7–12; Sachs and Wing Thye Woo, 2000.
11 Bleaney, 1985.
12 Fama, 1970, pp. 383–417.
13 Blyth, 2003.
14 Blyth, 2003; Kirshner, 1999, pp. 313–37; Keynes, 1936.
15 Strauss-Kahn, 1998.
16 For further evidence of this see Verdun's study of European finance ministries and central banks perceptions of EMU. Capital market integration and liberalization and the institutionalization of sound money (to varying degrees) were identified as two particular benefits by French, German and Italian officials; Verdun, 2000.
17 For a more far-reaching discussion of the Japanese position see Chapter 7. Japanese positions on capital account liberalization are outlined in Haymani, 2000; Vice Minister's speech on 'The Future International Financial Architecture and Regional Capital Market Development,' at the Round Table on Capital Market Reform in Asia, Tokyo, 11 April 2000; Nakao, 1999; speech by Dr Eisuke Sakakibara, 1999.
18 Halifax Communiqué G7 Summit 1995, Background Document: Institutions, Section 5: 'Promoting Financial Stability in a Globalized Economy'. Written by the Finance Ministers and Central Bank Governors.
19 Halifax Communiqué G7 Summit 1995, Background Document.
20 Halifax Communiqué G7 Summit 1995, Background Document.
21 Halifax Communiqué G7 Summit 1995, Background Document.
22 All of these points are contained in the Finance Ministers' Report to the Heads of State and Government at the Halifax Summit, 1995.
23 See the Finance Ministers' Report to the Heads of State and Government at the Halifax Summit of 1995.
24 Group of Ten, 1996.
25 'Clinton's intellectual power broker,' *The International Economy*, March/April 1999, p. 9.
26 'Clinton's intellectual power broker,' *The International Economy*, March/April 1999, p. 9.
27 Stiglitz, 2002. Stiglitz has argued that this is in fact based on an intellectually incoherent economic agenda and is a political agenda designed to protect foreign creditors enhancing the possibilities of repayment, while minimizing their losses. The effects of such policies on employment prospects in the countries concerned are often disastrous, while social programmes are often the first to be targeted and cut, resulting in considerable economic and social distress and turmoil for lower income groups. Chapter 8 – The IMF's Other Agenda.
28 Summers, 1996a.
29 Private sector involvement was first highlighted in Group of Ten, 1996.
30 Group of Ten, 1996.
31 Group of Ten, 1996.
32 See Cohen, 2003.
33 Summers, 1996a.
34 Summers, 1996a.
35 Points made by US Treasury official in confidential interview, January 1998. Also see Fischer, 1997.

36 Doubts on the wisdom of putting capital account liberalization as s standard fit policy into a large bureaucratic process run by the Fund were being expressed as early as Spring 1998, even by US officials. This was the beginning of the later more public acknowledgement that capital account liberalization needed to proceed at different paces in different places and be accompanied by adequate sequencing and regulatory reform. Confidential interviews at the US Treasury and Federal Reserve, February, March and April 1998.
37 Balls, 1998, pp. 113–32.
38 Hall, 1989; Baker, 1999, pp. 79–100.
39 Friedman, 1968.
40 Blanchard and Summers, 1990.
41 Romer, 1986.
42 Stiglitz, 2002, p. 27.
43 International Monetary Fund, 1994.
44 Pauly, 1997.
45 Tobin, 2003.
46 Stiglitz, 2002.
47 Summers, 1996a.
48 Larry Summers quoted in Delamaide, 1993, p. 71.
49 Stark, 1995, pp. 53–4.
50 Summers, 1996a.
51 Confidential interview with senior US Treasury official, Feburary 1998.
52 Bergsten and Henning, 1996.
53 Summers, 1996a.
54 Summers, 1996b.
55 Confidential interview with senior US official, February 1998.
56 Balls, 1998.
57 The Bank of Canada, the European Central Bank and the Bank of England all have inflation targets. The Bank of Japan and the Federal Reserve have more discretion. The Bank of Japan's mandate is defined merely as price stability, while the Fed is supposed to take growth and employment into consideration as well, although debates about the introduction of an inflation target have taken place in both countries.
58 Watson, 2002b.
59 Watson, 2002b.
60 Gill, 1997.
61 Gill and Law, 1989, pp. 475–500.
62 Sassen, 2002.
63 There is no clearer expression of this than in the arguments of Ed Ball, the architect of the UK macroeconomic framework after 1997, concerning the importance of credibility for macroeconomic policy. Balls, 1998.
64 Balls, 1998, p. 122.
65 Stiglitz, 2002; Bhagwati, 1998; Eichengreen, 1999; Krugman, 1995.
66 Kirshner, 2003b; Cohen, 2003; Blyth, 2003; McNamara, 1998.
67 Blyth, 2003.
68 Grabel, 2003.
69 This was particularly evident in Alan Greenspan and Lawrence Summers' analyses and explanations of the Asian financial crisis.
70 Grabel, 2003; Kirshner, 2003b; Blyth, 2003.
71 Blyth, 2003.
72 Stiglitz, 2002, p. 27.
73 Kirshner, 2003b.
74 Kirshner, 2003b.
75 Maxfield, 1997.
76 Watson, 2002b.

77 Bhagwati, 1998.
78 Gowan, 2001, pp. 359–74; Wade and Veneroso, 1998; Baker, 1999, pp. 79–100.
79 Dore, 2002, pp. 116–17.
80 On the British case see Baker, 2005b.
81 Henning, 1994.
82 This argument is also developed by Watson, 2002a.
83 Cohen, 2004.
84 Blyth, 2003.
85 Holtham, 1989, pp. 141–77.
86 Willamson and Miller, 1987.
87 In the 1980s, while the new right rhetoric of the Reagan administration made reference to less state and more market, the US's international economic policy still placed an emphasis on growth, particularly after 1985 when the US became involved in proactive attempts to manage the dollar through the Plaza agreement and the Louvre accord. Periodically this involved attempts to pressurize Japan and Germany to stimulate their economies in order to reduce the US current account deficit. In reality the current account deficit had more to do with the high dollar, which was a function of domestic policy, particularly high short-term interest rates required to offset the budget deficit run up by Reagan's tax-cutting policies. Rather than address its domestic policy the US chose to attempt to manage the dollar and pressurize foreign partners to go for growth. In the 1990s, the US Clinton administration in contrast adopted an international financial policy based on domestic economic fundamentals, involving a sustained effort to reduce the budget deficit.
88 Bergsten and Henning, 1996, p. 57.
89 The growing support for and conversion to the principle of sound money in the 1990s was also evident in discussions in Congress about the introduction of a balanced budget resolution and a reform to the Humphrey Hawkins act to give the Federal Reserve an inflation target.
90 Langley, 1997.
91 Dore, 2000.
92 Henning, 1994.
93 Zysman, 1983; Story and Walter, 1998; Langley, 2002.
94 Henning, 1994.
95 Bergsten and Henning, 1996.
96 These domestic institutional arrangements were in part a product of a shared international consensus on the desirability of central bank independence, which was in turn a response to perceptions of rising international capital mobility and capital market integration. This domestic institutional response to material and ideational shifts – central bank independence, restricts the range of alternatives open to participants at G7 meetings to those of the prescriptions of sound money open market consensus, described earlier in this chapter, that above all else values low national inflation and capital market integration, thus reinforcing and subordinating other policy objectives to the imperatives of open global financial markets. Thus we can appreciate that the relationship between the first three dimensions referred to in the previous chapter are at the same time mutually reinforcing and interactive.
97 Flemming, 1962.
98 Point made repeatedly in interviews with officials. Also see Dyson, 1994; Bergsten and Henning, 1996; Stark, 1995, pp. 53–4; Strauss-Kahn, 1998.
99 *Financial Times*, 30 October 1998. Klaus Gretschmann, acting as the Chancellor's economic adviser and 'sherpa' for Germany's summit preparations for the Cologne event of 1998, refused to circulate a policy paper prepared by Lafontaine's deputy Flassbeck to the other summit sherpas, for fear it might cause Germany embarrassment on the international stage.
100 Schroder, 1997, pp. 6–10.
101 Cerny, 2000b; Lütz, 2000.

102 Point made repeatedly in interviews with finance ministry and central bank officials.
103 Albert, 1991.
104 For a more thorough exploration of these arguments see Engelen, 1998, pp. 42–5.
105 Engelen, 1998.
106 Most powerfully by former World Bank Chief Economist Stiglitz, 2002. But the list of critics of the IMF in particular was long and varied.
107 Most notably this line of argument has been applied to the G7 by John Kirton. Kirton, 2000, pp. 65–94.
108 Kirton, 2000, p. 87.
109 Stiglitz, 2002, p. 213.
110 Kirton, 2000, p. 77.
111 In accordance with G7 behavioural norms, the US have avoided making precise demands of European macroeconomic policies and they have not bargained over monetary or fiscal policy, but they have expressed the view that a looser macroeconomic stance could help growth prospects in Europe.
112 Watson, 2002b.
113 The United States can lead but it cannot create G7 consensus alone. The implications of this observation for the concert equality model of G7 consensus formation will be discussed further in Chapter 5. The US has also been supported in questioning macroeconomic austerity by Canada, as Kirton points out. However, in the case of Canada this has had more to do with a softer stance on IMF programmes. Canadian macroeconomic institutional frameworks show a greater commitment to the principle of sound money than US ones, evident in repeated budget surpluses and an inflation target for the Bank of Canada.
114 Wade, 1998–9, pp. 41–53.
115 Kirton, 2000.
116 Some countries did use Chilean-style controls. Cohen, 1993, pp. 60–76. Soederberg reports that fourteen emerging markets experimented with Chilean style controls. Soederberg, S., 2002, pp. 490–512.
117 Summers, 1996a.
118 Cerny, 2001a; Lütz, 2000.
119 Kirton, 2000, p. 79.
120 The most recent G7 statements may not openly laud capital account liberalization as they did in the mid-1990s, but proposals on crisis prevention, transparency and surveillance are all designed to make capital account liberalization work better and involve an implicit acceptance that capital account liberalization is beneficial and is something to be either protected, reinforced, or aspired to. Statement of G7 Finance Ministers and Central Bank Governors 22 February 2003, Paris. Statement of G7 Finance Ministers and Central Bank Governors, 12 April 2003, Washington, DC.
121 Interview with Federal Reserve official, January 1998.
122 Note that various codes and standards introduced in response to the Asian financial crisis have been designed to improve the G7 and IMF's capacity to manage a liberalized global financial system, to better enable the IMF to judge the appropriate time for emerging markets to liberalize and have been part of a process ensuring that countries have met the standards required for a liberalized financial order.
123 Stiglitz, 2002, p. 225.
124 Stiglitz, 2002, p. 234.
125 Kohler, 2003.
126 Rogoff, 2003.
127 Underhill and Zhang, 2003a.
128 Kirton, 2002, pp. 45–74.
129 On the Wall Street–Treasury axis see Gowan, 1999.
130 Scholte, 1997; White, 2005b, pp. 147–70.
131 Interview with Canadian finance minister Paul Martin, conducted by Candida Tamar Paltiel, University of Toronto G8 Research Group, 18 November 2001, Ottawa. On

University of Toronto's G8 website at http://www.g7.utoronto.ca/oralhistory/.
132 Higgott and Phillips, 2000, pp. 359–81.
133 Interview with David Dodge, Governor of the Bank of Canada, conducted by Candia Tamar Paltiel, G8 Research Group, 18 November 2001, Ottawa. On University of Toronto's G8 website at http://www.g7.utoronto.ca/oralhistory/.
134 Stiglitz, 2002, p. 222.

5 The Group of Seven as a multi-spatial transgovernmental actor

1 Snidal, 1985, pp. 579–614.
2 Kirton and Kokotsis, 1997–8, pp. 38–56.
3 Kirton, 1998.
4 Gill, 1994a, pp. 169–99; Gill, 1994b.
5 Cox, 1992b.
6 Germain, 2004.
7 Kirton, 1989. For a more recent application of this argument see Kirton, 2002, pp. 45–74.
8 On international concerts see Elrod, 1976, pp. 159–74.
9 Kirton, 1989.
10 While we might focus on the issue of measurement, all the criteria can be questioned for various reasons.
11 Kirton, 1989.
12 Kirton, 2000, p. 68.
13 Kirton, 1989, 2000.
14 As alluded to in the introduction to this book, interpreting G7 statements is one of the principal methodological difficulties in studying the G7 because these statements are ambiguous, are difficult to take at face value and often represent a form of code. When individual state's detailed understanding of the nuances of G7 statements differ, it is not surprising to see this pattern repeated in the academic world. It is this that makes the G7 such an interesting area of study, because it acts as a laboratory for testing some of the differing interpretations of the international system and of state behaviour that characterize IR and IPE.
15 Risse, 2000.
16 Bhagwati, 1998, pp. 7–13; Gowan, 1999; Wade and Veneroso, 1998.
17 Japanese and European banks have often been bigger, more significant international players than US commercial banks, but money markets outside of London and New York have been much smaller and American investment banks have played the dominant role in providing clients with access to these funds.
18 Kirton, 2000.
19 The position adopted here is therefore an attempt to find a middle ground between notions of the G7 as a modern concert of powers and as merely a demonstration and instrument of US power. For the latter perspective see Gowan, 1999, p. 32.
20 Wicks, 2003, pp. 261–74.
21 Kirton, 2000.
22 Risse, 2000, p. 11.
23 Interview with Paul Martin, Canada's Minister of Finance and chair of the G20, Conducted by Candida Tamar Paltiel, University of Toronto G8 Research Group, 18 November 2001, Ottawa. On University of Toronto's G8 website at http://www.g7.utoronto.ca/oralhistory/.
24 Interview with David Dodge, Governor of the Bank of Canada, Conducted by Candia Tamar Paltiel, G8 Research Group, 18 November 2001, Ottawa. On University of Toronto's G8 website at http://www.g7.utoronto.ca/oralhistory/.

25 Interview with Paul Martin, Canada's Minister of Finance and chair of the G20, Conducted by Candida Tamar Paltiel, University of Toronto G8 Research Group.
26 Delamaide, 1993.
27 Confidential interview with officials, July 1998.
28 For a brief discussion of this in the case of Paul Martin the incoming Treasury Secretary under the Bush administration see Kirton, 2002, pp. 45–74.
29 Wicks, 1994a.
30 Pauly, 1997.
31 Confidential interview, July 1997.
32 At the G7's instigation, the IMF is also becoming concerned with information on private sector balance sheets, accounting standards and how supervisory and regulatory structures feed into the macroeconomic picture.
33 Confidential interview with officials, January 1998.
34 Confidential interview with officials, January 1998. Recently, since the establishment of the central bank deputies' group, the central bank deputies have become more involved in the surveillance exercise. The thinking behind this is that it will enable the G7 to identify problems in the world economy at an earlier stage.
35 Confidential interviews with officials, May 1997.
36 Pauly, 1997.
37 Some authors might consider that logics of arguing and appropriateness are incompatible and either one or the other represents some sort of theoretical panacea or end game. However, we should at least allow for the possibility that something resembling these two logics can co-exist and overlap in practice in various specific multilateral settings. Therefore in the case of the G7 process we can point to a situation whereby a process of arguing and deliberation is accompanied by a shared sense of appropriateness concerning the limits of that process. This sense of appropriateness might be the product of shared beliefs, a common mind-set or discourse and is probably the product of earlier instances of arguing, but which also simultaneously facilitates an ongoing process of arguing and deliberation within commonly understood parameters.
38 For the first, second and third order distinctions see Chapter 3. Also see Hall, 1993, pp. 275–96.
39 Japan was the exception that proved the rule, but this was due to the unique and desperate circumstances of the Japanese economy.
40 Lawson, 1992.
41 Mosely, 1997.
42 Watson, 2002b, pp. 183–96.
43 McNamara, 1998; Dyson, 1994.
44 Confidential interview with UK Treasury officials, February 1997.
45 Central bank deputies have only been meeting since 1994. Finance ministry and central bank deputies meet together but also separately.
46 Yergin and Stanislaw, 1998.
47 Pauly, 1997 provides the outstanding statement of problems of legitimacy in the international monetary system. On regulatory capture in the financial sector see Underhill, 1997c, pp. 17–49; Coleman, 1990, pp. 91–117; Moran, 1991; Oatley and Nabors, 1998, pp. 35–54.
48 Point made repeatedly in confidential interviews with officials.
49 Confidential interview with official, February 1997.
50 It is rarer for central bank officials to meet at deputy-deputy level, although this is becoming more common.
51 Point made repeatedly in interviews 1997–9. The deputies do de-brief colleagues but minutes are not formally recorded and transcripts of discussions are not taken. Since 1994, the deputies have been assisted in their preparatory work by deputy-deputies, usually the second most senior international financial official in finance ministries, so

as to increase the speed of consensus formation and build up a greater momentum of co-operative relations between G7 finance ministries.

52 Confidential interview with official, July 1997.
53 Confidential interview with official, July 1997.
54 Confidential interviews with officials, February, July 1997 and March 1998.
55 Confidential interview with officials, January 1998.
56 Every third year the IMF holds its annual autumn meeting in a non-US city.
57 Kirton, 1989, 2000.
58 Confidential interview with official, February 1997.
59 Confidential interview with official, July 1997.
60 Confidential interview with official, July 1997.
61 Confidential interview with official, July 1997.
62 It is worth noting that in his study that refuted the analytical use of the concept of transgovernmentalism in the study of international monetary affairs, Robert Russell only considered domestic politics, but in an era of decentralized globalization and a diffuse decision-making complex characterizing global financial governance, finance ministries and central banks face multiple incentives to engage in transgovernmental coalition building; Russell, 1973.
63 Confidential interviews with officials, July 1997.
64 This has been synonomous with the work of the G8/G7 Research Centre at the University of Toronto. Kokotsis, 1995, pp. 117–33; Daniels, 1993.
65 Hodges, 1998.
66 Kirton, 2002.
67 Only in Canada does the Finance Minister retain the right to have a decisive say in monetary policy.
68 It is worth noting that national central bank governors from Eurozone countries have now stopped attending G7 meetings and are represented by the Managing Director of the ECB, although national finance ministry representatives continue to participate in the process. In central bank terms the Group of Seven is now a Group of Five.
69 For example the Bank of Canada's mandate is to keep inflation at a 2 per cent target, the midpoint of a 1 to 3 per cent inflation control target range. The Bank of England has to keep inflation in a range between 1.5 and 2.5 per cent. The ECB's mandate is to deliver inflation below 2 per cent.
70 Dobson, 1991.
71 On regulatory issues in the US see Cerny, 1994a, pp. 425–38; Garten, 1997, pp. 294–312.
72 Mulford, 1998, pp. 10–13; Smyser, Bergsten and Henning, 1996.
73 See the collection of articles in the special issue of Legalization and World Politics, *International Organization*, 54(3), summer 2000; Chayes and Chayes, 1993, pp. 175–205. Kirton's perspective which sees the G7 as an effective governance institution is also partly derived from the liberal institutionalist perspective and he has attempted to calculate and measure actual instances of compliance with G8 summit communiqués. See summit record cards at http://www.g7.utoronto.ca/.
74 Cox, 1992b.
75 Gowan, 1999; Bhagwati, 1998; Wade and Veneroso, 1998.
76 See Gowan, 1999.
77 This argument is developed by Peter Gowan. See Gowan, 1999.
78 Phillips, 1997.
79 Gowan, 1999, p. 124.
80 Confidential interview, February 1997.
81 Dore, 2000; Story and Walter, 1998.
82 It should be noted that the process of reforming labour markets is path dependent. The institutional legacies of powerful trade unions and the legal frameworks that govern in labour markets in a heavily regulated country such as Germany has meant

the process of German labour market reform is a protracted one based on negotiation between social partners. This has not prevented repeated debate on the subject of reform of labour markets, with the finance ministry and the Bundesbank at the forefront of those arguing for more flexible labour markets, particularly those officials working on the international side.

83 Teague, 1999, pp. 33–62.
84 Grossman, 2005, pp. 130–46.
85 Gowan, 1999, p. 131.
86 Frieden, 1994, pp. 81–103.
87 McNamara, 1999.
88 Jackson, 2002.
89 For evidence and further discussion of reformist forces and agendas see Dore, 2000; Kosai, 2002, p. 124–5. Interview with Gerhard Schroder, 1997, pp. 6–7.
90 The different intellectual assumptions and educational backgrounds of different finance ministry and central bank officials, the struggles and contests between them is an under researched aspect of contemporary political economy. Unfortunately, this book is unable to do little more than scratch the surface in this regard.
91 This is Ronald Dore's definition of financialization, see Dore, 2002, pp. 116–17.
92 Thain, 1984, pp. 581–95; Hall, 1989.
93 Hall, 1992, pp. 90–113.
94 Keegan and Pennant Rae, 1979; Brittan, 1967; Baker, 1999.
95 For discussion of this see Scholte, 1997; White, 2005b; Cohen, 2003; Stiglitz, 2002.
96 Confidential interviews conducted by the author in Washington, DC and London in 1997–8.
97 Confidential interviews with officials, London and Washington, DC, 1997 and 1998.
98 One example was Oskar Lafontaine of Germany and his proposal for a system of target zones for the G3 currencies, which was rejected by the G7. Paul Martin's proposal for a standstill mechanism prompted much debate, but all that has resulted is the relatively modest initiative of collective action clauses.
99 Moses, 1997, pp. 382–415.
100 This development mirrors domestic developments as central banks are given increasing capacity to determine domestic monetary policy independently of government, whilst finance ministries' capacity to police domestic public expenditure processes are enhanced by the establishment of fiscal rules.
101 This will be demonstrated in more detail in the next section.
102 Bank for International Settlements, 1997.
103 See Leyshon and Thrift, 1997.
104 Germain, 1997.
105 Porter, 2003, pp. 520–51.
106 Vrolijk, 1997.
107 Martin, 1994, p. 270.
108 Martin, 1999, p. 11.
109 Budd, 1999, p. 116.
110 Kurtzman, 1993, p. 47.
111 Warf, 1999.
112 Soros, 1987.
113 Thrift and Leyshon, 1994, pp. 299–327.
114 Heath, 1993.
115 Cohen, 2004.
116 Blinder, 1999.
117 Watson, 2002b.
118 Balls, 1998.
119 More generally in macroeconomic policy the idea of credibility through pre-commitment involves third-dimensional diplomacy as the act of creating central banks

with price stability mandates and fiscal rules is an implicit attempt to symbolically communicate with international investors and reassure them of policy-makers' good intentions; Baker, 2005a.

120 Wicks, 1994b. Similar point made in confidential interview with US official, March 1998.
121 Confidential interview with UK official, February 1997.
122 Mosely, 1997.
123 Confidential interview with official, February 1997.
124 Confidential interview with official, March 1998.
125 Confidential interview with official, March 1998.
126 Confidential interview with official, February 1998.
127 Stiglitz, 2002.
128 A point made repeatedly in confidential interviews for this study.
129 Woods, 2000.
130 Stiglitz, 2002, p. 41.
131 Underhill, 1997c, pp. 17–49.
132 Porter, 1999.
133 Germain, 2000.
134 Underhill, 1995, pp. 251–78.
135 Porter, 1999.
136 On the relationship between IOSCO and governments see Underhill, 1995, pp. 251–78.
137 Slaughter, 2004. For a critique of earlier work see Woodward, 2001.
138 Porter, 2003.

6 The Group of Seven and macroeconomic governance

1 Dobson, 1991.
2 Balls, 1998, pp. 113–32.
3 Mosely, 1997.
4 The notable exception was the Japanese case where stagnation meant interest rate easing and periodic fiscal expansion became the norm throughout the 1990s in response to exceptionally slack consumer demand and low growth.
5 That is not to say that data and evidence will not reflect societal and political bias inherent in the norms of a particular technical profession. Theory, as Robert Cox remarked, is always for someone and for some purpose.
6 See Cox's notions of *nébuleuse* and the 'internationalization of the state', involving a process of consensus formation among states and various international agencies; Cox, 1987.
7 G7 Finance Ministers and Central Bank Governors' statements 7 April 1990, Paris and 6 May 1990, Washington, DC.
8 Statement of G7 Finance Ministers and Central Bank Governors, Washington, DC, 22 September 1990.
9 Statement of G7 Finance Ministers and Central Bank Governors, Washington, DC, 28 April 1991.
10 The notable exception was Japan where it was noted that inflation was under control and that there was a need to increase domestic demand such as to reduce the Japanese trade surplus. See Statement of G7 Finance Ministers and Central Bank Governors, 29 April 1993.
11 G7 Finance Ministers and Central Bank Governors' Statement, 3–4 February 1995.
12 G7 Finance Ministers and Central Bank Governors' Statement, Berlin, February 1997. G7 Finance Ministers and Central Bank Governors' Statement, 27 April 1997.
13 Statement of G7 Finance Ministries and Central Banks, London, 21 February 1998.

14 Indeed, one of the principal features in European industrial relations in the 1990s was the rise of credibility wage bargaining, designed to deliver wage restraint as one of the components of the drive towards low inflation; Teague, 1998.
15 As Chapter 4 noted, while there has been a basic sound money open markets consensus since the early 1980s, that consensus has not been static, but has been progressively refined, adjusted and ultimately institutionalized in domestic policy-making arrangements.
16 Kirton, 2000, p. 45–74.
17 Kirton, 1999.
18 Statement of G7 Finance Ministers and Central Bank Governors, 14 September 1998.
19 Statement of G7 Finance Ministers and Central Bank Governors, October 1998.
20 Hall, 1993, pp. 275–96.
21 Statement of G7 Finance Ministers and Central Bank Governors, Washington, DC, 26 April 1999.
22 Statement of G7 Finance Ministers and Central Bank Governors, Washington, DC, 26 April 1999.
23 Stiglitz, 2002.
24 Statement of G7 Finance Ministers and Central Bank Governors, 25 September 1999, Washington, DC.
25 Statement of G7 Finance Ministers and Central Bank Governors, Tokyo, 22 January 2000.
26 Statement of G7 Finance Ministers and Central Bank Governors, 16 April 2000, Washington, DC.
27 Statement of G7 Finance Ministers and Central Bank Governors, 12 September 2001.
28 Statements of G7 Finance Ministers and Central Bank Governors, 6 October 2001, Ottawa; 9 February 2002, Paris; 15 June 2002, Halifax, Nova Scotia; 27 September 2002, Washington, DC.
29 Statements of G7 Finance Ministers and Central Bank Governors, 9 February 2002, Paris; 12 April 2003, Washington, DC.
30 Statement of G7 Finance Ministers and Central Bank Governors, Dubai, 20 September 2003.
31 Statement of G7 Finance Ministers and Central Bank Governors, Dubai, 20 September 2003.
32 Although they had both done so in accordance with special political approval.
33 Informal discussions with finance ministry officials. I'm also grateful for informal discussions on these kind of issues with Uwe Putter, a former PhD student at the Institute of European Studies, Queen's University of Belfast, who was involved in the preparations for Euro Group meetings as part of the field work for his thesis, and with Professor Kenneth Dyson.
34 One of the major conclusions of Bergsten and Henning's short study of the G7 in the mid-1990s was that a new non-aggression pact in which states avoided being critical of one another's policies, had come to characterize macroeconomic diplomacy, while the G7 consensus more generally gravitated towards the traditional German position which emphasized the control of inflation and fiscal discipline. See Bergsten and Henning, 1996.
35 Kirton, 2002, pp. 45–74.
36 Higgott, 2003.
37 Cohen, 2004.
38 Harvey, 2003.
39 'US Tax Cut Plan Attacked at G7 talks', *Financial Times*, 24 Feburary 2003. 'Rift Between EU and US over Falling Dollar', *Financial Times*, 14 January 2004.
40 Bergsten and Henning, 1996.

41 Nolke, 2004. Transnational Politics Section, Panel on the 'Transnationalization of the State'.
42 For a similar type of argument see Tony Porter's recent work on technical systems; Porter, 2003, pp. 520–51.
43 Generally, finance ministries and central banks do not require the consent of political actors or legislatures to authorize exchange market interventions, although they may have to account for their actions at a later date. Following the bail out of the Mexican peso in 1995, Congress froze the US Treasury's exchange stabilization fund. See Table 5.3 for more details.
44 Finance Ministers' Report on International Monetary Stability, to the Heads of State and Government, at the Lyon summit, 28 June 1996.
45 The only challenge to the G7 belief system came with proposals for a system of target zones from German Finance Minister Oskar Lafontaine in 1998. However, the rest of the G7 were unanimous in their condemnation of Lafontaine's proposals. Other senior members of the G7 rejected Lafontaine's target zone proposals. Federal Reserve chairman Alan Greenspan, Robert Rubin and Wim Duisenberg all publicly dismissed calls for managed exchange rates as unworkable. French presidential aides were also concerned that such proposals would alienate the US and damage the existing G7 consensus on exchange rate policy.
46 Rubin and Weisburg, 2003, p. 183.
47 Bergsten and Henning, 1996.
48 *Financial Times*, 27 February 1993.
49 *Financial Times*, 7 April 1993.
50 Rubin and Weisberg, 2003, p. 182.
51 Federal Reserve Board of Governors, 1994.
52 *Financial Times*, 4 May 1999.
53 Gowan, 1999.
54 Federal Reserve Board of Governors, 1994. See also Bergsten and Henning, 1996, p. 33.
55 Scholte, 2000. See the essays in Baker *et al.*, 2005.
56 Bergsten and Henning, 1996.
57 Bergsten and Henning, 1996.
58 G7 Finance Ministers and Central Bank Governors' Statement, Washington, DC, 25 April 1995.
59 Bergsten and Henning, 1996.
60 Summers, 1996a.
61 Gowan, 2001, pp. 359–74. Gowan offers one of the few coherent recent discussion of US power in the area of dollar policy.
62 Barone, 1998, pp. 46–50.
63 Statement of G7 Finance Ministers and Central Bank Governors, Berlin, 8 February 1995.
64 The US Treasury's exchange stabilization fund for exchange market interventions had been frozen by a Republican Congress following the Mexican bail out of 1995.
65 View of economic consultancy forecast, *Financial Times*, 15 April 1995.
66 Stephen Roach, chief economist for Morgan Stanley Dean Witter quoted in *Financial Times*, 20 April 1998.
67 Peter Chambers, managing director, investment strategy at HSBC Securities quoted in *Financial Times*, 17 April 1998.
68 Comments of Nick Parsons of Paribus Capital Markets, *Financial Times*, 8 June 1998.
69 Comments of Robin Marshall of Chase Morgan, *Financial Times*, 8 June 1998. In part, this monetary expansion reflected traditional Japanese institutional difficulties where macroeconomic policy is concerned. The MOF's refusal to engage in fiscal expansion meant that when a macroeconomic expansion was required it usually had

to come through monetary policy and the subordinate Bank of Japan. Indeed this was the root cause of the so-called bubble economy.

70 *Financial Times*, 8 June 1998, 9 June 1998.
71 Rubin and Weisburg, 2003, p. 186.
72 Rubin and Weisburg, 2003, p. 186.
73 Statement of G7 Finance Ministers and Central Bank Governors, Prague, Czech Republic, 23 September 2000.
74 Statement of G7 Finance Ministers and Central Bank Governors, Dubai, 20 September 2003.
75 See for example articles in *Financial Times*, 3 October 2003.
76 *Financial Times*, 13 January 2004.
77 Statement of G7 Finance Ministers and Central Bank Governors, Boca Raton, 8 February 2004. See also *Financial Times*, 9 February 2004.
78 The dollar did eventually start to strengthen in early March, primarily against the yen although this appeared to be on the basis of data suggesting a recovery in the US labour market together with interventions by the Bank of Japan, rather than as a belated response to G7 statements; *Financial Times*, 3 March 2004.
79 For the classic exposition of the former position see Keohane, 1984. For the latter position see Strange, 1986.
80 Kirton, 2000, 2002; Gowan, 1999, 2001.
81 Kirton, 2000.
82 Gowan, 1999.
83 Underhill, 2001.
84 *Guardian*, 15 September 1998.
85 *Financial Times*, 17 September 1998.
86 Statement of G7 Finance Ministers and Central Bank Governors and Statement of G7 Leaders on the World Economy, issued 30 October 1998.
87 Comments of Hans Teitmeyer and Eddie George reported in *Financial Times*, 5 October 1998.
88 Baker and Barber, 2001
89 Baker and Barber, 2001.
90 Bergsten and Henning, 1996.
91 Confidential interview with official, April 1998.
92 Dyson, 1994.
93 Bergsten and Henning, 1996.
94 One European G7 Deputy expressed a preference for the informality of the G7, viewing it as a welcome antidote to the proceduralism and formality of EU meetings; confidential interview, February 1997.
95 Confidential interviews, 1997–8.
96 Summers, 1997. Confidential interview with official, April 1998.
97 Confidential interview with the author, Washington, DC, April 1998.
98 Summers, 1997.
99 Bergsten and Henning, 1996.
100 Alan Greenspan, a long-standing Republican, has been an altogether more enthusiastic advocate of Bush's tax cuts.
101 Baker, 2005a.
102 Story, 2003, pp. 21–40.

7 The Group of Seven and the global financial architecture

1 Putnam and Bayne, 1987; Pauly, 1997; James, 1996.
2 Putnam and Bayne, 1987.

3 Kirton, 2002, pp. 45–74; Kirton, 2000, p. 45–74; Wade, 1998–9, pp. 41–53.
4 Cohen, 2003, pp. 60–76.
5 For similar arguments see Best, 2003, pp. 363–84.
6 Cohen, 2003; Schulze, 2000.
7 Best, 2003.
8 Bayne, 1995, pp. 492–509.
9 Summers, 1996a, p. 9.
10 Wicks, 1994b, p. 3.
11 Confidential interview with official, February 1998.
12 Porter, 2003, pp. 520–51.
13 Porter, 2003.
14 Confidential interview with official, July 1997.
15 Confidential interview with official, March 1998.
16 *Financial Times*, 19 June 1995.
17 Halifax Communiqué G7 Summit 1995, Background Document: Institutions, Section 5: 'Promoting Financial Stability in a Globalized Economy'.
18 *Financial Times*, 19 June 1995.
19 Confidential interview with officials, February 1998.
20 Confidential interviews with officials, February 1998.
21 Interview with Stanley Fischer, 1998, pp. 6–9, 59. For examples of the difficulties encountered by the G7 in the case of exchange rate policy see the previous chapter.
22 Gill, 1997.
23 Gill and Law, 1989, pp. 475–99.
24 See Baker, 2005a, pp. 102–29.
25 Balls, 1998, pp. 113–32.
26 The GAB originated in 1962. Essentially it has been a mechanism for the G10 to lend additional resources to the IMF. Each G10 member undertook to lend to the Fund, beyond its own quota, specified amounts of its own currency. Generally, when a country wants to draw on the GAB it consults the Managing Director of the IMF. The Managing Director, after consultation with the Executive Board and GAB members, can propose activation. The proposal becomes effective once the GAB participants and the Executive Board accept the proposal. Once funds are transferred to the IMF they are re-lent to a borrowing country under an IMF programme. The IMF therefore serves as intermediary between lender and borrower and as GAB administrator imposes conditionality on the borrowing country. This conditionality is at the core of contemporary fourth-dimensional diplomacy.
27 Confidential interview with official, March 1998.
28 Summers, 1996a.
29 Armijo, 2001, pp. 379–96.
30 Point made repeatedly in interviews with officials.
31 Group of Ten, 1996.
32 Officials directly involved conceded that many of the report's targets failed to pay much attention to the content of the report; confidential interviews with the author, 1998.
33 It was clear from the tone of statements that issues of financial regulation and the precise jurisdiction remained unclear to finance ministries involved in the G7 process.
34 Confidential interview with official, July 1997. Fund officials had favoured this for some time but needed the issue to be promoted by the G7. The issue was initially aired by a British Treasury official acting as deputy-deputy following a spell as UK IMF executive director in Washington.
35 Point made repeatedly in confidential interviews with officials in 1997–8. OECD codes had performed a similar role in the 1980s.
36 Confidential interview with official, February 1998; Fischer, 1997.
37 *Financial Times*, 28 April 1997.

38 Confidential interview with official, July 1997.
39 Confidential interview, April 1998.
40 Scholte, 1997.
41 Thirkell-White, 2005a.
42 A dialogue of sorts has been opened up on the issue of developing country debt.
43 Confidential interview with US official, February 1998.
44 Haggard and MacIntyre, 1998, pp. 381–92. Also see Goldstein, 1998.
45 Krugman, 'What happened to Asia?' at http://web.mit.edu/krugman/www.
46 Wade and Veneroso, 1998.
47 Higgott, 1998, p. 337.
48 Wade and Veneroso, 1998.
49 Higgott, 1998.
50 Two informative accounts of the short-term handling of the Asian financial crisis are Kirton, 1999 and Higgott, 1998.
51 Japan contributed $4 billion, Korea and Taiwan provided $2 billion each and further $1 billion came from Australia in a package to help the Thai baht.
52 The provision of financing was also evident in another form. Prior to the G7 finance ministers and central bankers' meeting in London in February 1998, G7 export credit agencies met to discuss a common response to the Asian situation. An agreement was reached to continue providing and even extend short-term insurance to creditworthy buyers in the region. Short-term credits of this nature were vital if countries affected by the crisis were to continue trading. Businesses had been unable to attract letters of credit from banks in the affected countries. Without such letters of credit producers were unable to import raw material or get working capital to finance exports. The agencies vowed to continue to co-operate sharing information on market developments and progress on reform measures agreed with the IMF.
53 *Financial Times*, 27 December 1997.
54 Higgott, 1998.
55 Higgott, 1998.
56 Higgott, 1998; Bowles, 2002, pp. 244–70; Gowan, 1999; Tadokoro, 2003; Katada, 2001; Hughes, 2000, pp. 241–58.
57 Confidential interview with official, February 1998.
58 For a more thorough treatment of this see Higgott, 1998. On the Treasury–Wall Street complex see Bhagwati, 1998.
59 Tadokoro, 2003, p. 225.
60 *Sakakibara*, Yomiuri Shimbun, 26 November 1999.
61 Katada, 2001, p.169; Tadokoro, 2003; Katada, 2002.
62 Bowles, 2002, p. 253
63 Tadokoro, 2003.
64 Wade, 1998–9. See also Chapter 4 for a discussion.
65 Kirton, 2000.
66 Summers, 1996a.
67 Kirshner, 2004.
68 Kiuchi, 2002.
69 Speech by Dr Eisuke Sakakibara, 1999.
70 Nakao, 1999.
71 Haymani, 2000; Vice Minister's speech on 'The Future International Financial Architecture and Regional Capital Market Development,' at the Round Table on Capital Market Reform in Asia, Tokyo, 11 April 2000; Nakao, 1999; speech by Dr Eisuke Sakakibara, 1999.
72 Vice Minister's speech on 'The Future International Financial Architecture and Regional Capital Market Development'.
73 Nakao, 1999.
74 Maxfield, 1991, pp. 419–58; Woo-Cummings, 1997, Ch. 3.

75 Cohen, 2003, p. 72.
76 Council on Foreign Relations, 1999.
77 Armijo, 2001.
78 Germain, 2004.
79 Speech by Dr Eisuke Sakakibara, 1999.
80 Deutsche Bundesbank, 2000.
81 Remarks by David Dodge, 2002.
82 Speech by Dr Eisuke Sakakibara, 1999; Nakao, 1999.
83 Miyazawa, 1998.
84 Vice Minister's speech on 'The Future International Financial Architecture and Regional Capital Market Development'.
85 Kiuchi, 2002.
86 Point made repeatedly in interviews with officials throughout 1997 and 1998.
87 Confidential interview with official, February 1998.
88 Confidential interview with official, April 1998.
89 Point made repeatedly in confidential interviews with officials in 1998.
90 Confidential interview with officials, February and March 1998.
91 Confidential interviews with officials, March and April 1998.
92 Confidential interview with official, January 1998.
93 G7 discussions on the issue of the global institutional architecture in 1998 took place against the uncomfortable backdrop of US domestic institutional gridlock. Congressional opposition to the extra funding agreed for the IMF at a meeting in Hong Kong in September 1997, in the form of the new GAB and the US's quota increase, was a cause of great anxiety for both US Treasury department and IMF officials. The US was being asked to contribute a total of $17.5 billion in the form of a quota increase and a new emergency fund. Following squeezes on public expenditures in a Congressional election year, few in Congress were willing to be seen to be openly supporting IMF funding for fear of an electoral backlash from important constituents. Involvement with Congress doubled for staff in the Treasury's IMF office, from 25 per cent of their time to 50 per cent of their time dealing with Congressional matters in the first half of 1998; confidential interview with official, February 1998.
94 Point made repeatedly in confidential interviews, 1997 and 1998.
95 Confidential interview with official, February 1998.
96 Summers, 1996a.
97 For an application of this argument to the FSF and the G20 see Porter, 2000.
98 Brown, 1998.
99 Basle Committee on Banking Supervision, 2000.
100 Note that these proposals were not just supported by Anglo-Saxon countries but the G7 as a whole. Dominique Strauss-Khan for example was advocating two particular improvements in data release – the external liabilities of the private sector and the off balance sheet commitments of central banks. He also favoured making a country's ability to borrow from financial markets dependent on the ability to fulfil international data dissemination standards monitored by the IMF.
101 Thirkell-White, 2004.
102 Mohammed, 2003.
103 Thirkell-White, 2004.
104 Bretton Woods and Related Agreements Act, Report 2002, Canadian Ministry of Finance.
105 Thirkell-White, 2004.
106 Central Bank Official, *Financial Times*, 31 October 1998.
107 Best, 2003.
108 The G7 were also forging contacts with the International Accounting Standards Board (IASC), urging the board to finalize proposals for a full range of international accounting standards, which in turn would be presented to IOSCO for endorsement.

However, opposition from the Securities Exchange Commission in the US and the US financial Accounting Standards Board to the application of such standards on the New York stock market stalled such attempts.

109 Communiqué of G7 Finance Ministers and Central Bank Governors, 20 February 1999.

110 Working Group on Highly Leveraged Institutions, 2000. Also see Working Group on Highly Leveraged Institutions, 2001; Group of Seven Finance Ministers and Central Bank Governors, 2000, 2001.

111 Germain, 2001, pp. 411–26.

112 Maxfield, 1991; Woo-Cummings, 1997.

113 Porter, 2003.

114 For a more optimistic assessment see Germain, 2001.

115 The most recent G7 initiative is a financial action plan announced in April 2002. This emphasizes the extent to which national governments are becoming accountable to global investors and revisits the principle of private sector burden sharing first outlined in the G10 report of 1996. The plan proposes that all governments in emerging markets add a special clause to their bonds, which will specify what will happen in the event of a need for sovereign debt restructuring, including descriptions of how creditors will engage with borrowers. Mexico, a G20 member, expressed opposition to the proposal on the grounds that it will in all likelihood increase the cost of government borrowing in emerging markets, and other developing countries followed suit.

116 Ambrose, 2003.

117 Action Plan in Statement of G7 Finance Ministries and Central Bank Governors, 20 April 2002.

118 Soederberg, 2004b.

119 Confidential conversations with colleagues and officials, September and October 2004.

120 Statement of G7 Finance Ministers and Central Bank Governors, 12 April 2003.

121 Soederberg, 2004b.

122 Department of Finance, Canada, 1999.

123 Implementation Report by African Personal Representatives, 2003.

124 Taylor, 2004b.

125 Taylor, 2004a.

126 Speech by Rt. Hon Gordon Brown, Chancellor of the Exchequer, 2005.

127 Brown, 2005.

128 On the theoretical and normative case for globalizing social justice see Caney, 2005.

8 Conclusions

1 Hobson, 2000, p. 234.

2 Blyth, 2003, pp. 239–59.

3 On creeping financialization see Dore, 2002, pp. 116–17.

4 Blyth, 2003; Grabel, 2003.

5 Cox, 1996.

6 Germain, 1997.

7 Porter, 2003, pp. 520–51.

8 Porter, 2003; Germain, 2004.

9 Confidential interview with official, February 1997.

10 Bergsten and Henning, 1996.

11 The standard but most sophisticated account of globalization as a political, cultural and economic phenomenon identifies a similar structural dynamic brought about by the interaction of a range of factors as driving and causing globalization; Scholte, 2000.

12 Germain, 2004.
13 Cohen, 2004.
14 Kirton, 2000, p. 45–74.
15 Gowan, 1999.
16 Gowan, pp. 359–374.
17 On the rise of normative discourse in global financial governance see Best, 2003, pp. 363–83.
18 Baker, 2000, pp. 165–89.
19 Porter, 2001, pp. 427–39; Wood, 2000; Germain, 2001, pp. 411–26.
20 Soederberg, 2004a; Best, 2003.
21 Underhill and Zhang, 2003a, pp. 360–83.
22 Underhill and Zhang, 2003a; Best, 2003.
23 Underhill, 1995, pp. 251–78.
24 Wade and Veneroso, 1998; Higgott, 1998, p. 337.
25 Bradford and Linn, 2004.
26 Kenen, 2004.
27 Germain, 2001.
28 Maxfield, 1991, pp. 419–58; Woo-Cummings, 1997, Ch. 3.
29 Cohen, 2003.
30 I'm a little sceptical of the benefits and possibilities of including civil society groupings in global financial governance as a means to resolving issues of representation and legitimacy, although any debate that offers the potential of widening participation in global financial governance is to be broadly welcomed. For a more optimistic assessment of the potential for civil society participation see Germain, 2004.
31 Higgott, 2004.

Bibliography

African Personal Representatives to Leaders (2003) Implementation Report by on the G8 Africa Action Plan, Evian, 1 June.

Agnew, J. (1994) 'The territorial trap: the geographical assumptions of international relations theory', *Review of International Political Economy*, 1(1): 53–80.

Albert, M. (1991) *Capitalism against Capitalism*, Paris: Seuil.

Ambrose, S. (2003) 'The IMF's latest ruse: sovereign debt restructuring mechanism', *50 Years is Enough – Economic News Justice Online*, 6(1), April.

Amin, A. (2001) 'Spatialities of globalisation', *Environment and Planning*, 33.

Amin, A. and Palan, R. (2001) 'Towards a non-rationalist international political economy', *Review of International Political Economy*, 8(4): 567.

Andrews, D. (1994) 'Capital mobility and state autonomy: towards a structural theory of international monetary relations', *International Studies Quarterly*, 38(2): 193–218.

Arendt, H. (1958) 'What was authority?', in Fredreich, C. (ed.) *Authority*, Cambridge, MA: Harvard University Press.

Armijo, L. (2001) 'The political geography of world financial reform', *Global Governance*, 7: 379–96.

Armijo, L. (ed.) (2002) *Debating the Global Financial Architecture*, Albany, NY: SUNY Press.

Artis, M. and Ostry, S. (1983) *International Economic Policy Co-ordination*, London: Routledge and Kegan Paul.

Aykens, P. (2002) 'Conflicting authorities: states, currency markets and the ERM crisis of 1992–93', *Review of International Studies*, 28: 359–80.

Baker, A. (1999) 'Nébuleuse and the "internationalization of the state" in the UK: the case of HM Treasury and the Bank of England', *Review of International Political Economy*, 6(1): 79–100.

Baker, A. (2000) 'The G7 as a global ginger group: plurilateralism and four-dimensional diplomacy', *Global Governance*, 6(2): 165–89.

Baker, A. (2005a) 'The three-dimensional governance of macroeconomic policy in the advanced capitalist world', in Baker, A., Hudson, D. and Woodward, R. (eds) *Governing Financial Globalization: International Political Economy and Multi-level Governance*, London: Routledge, pp. 102–29.

Baker, A. (2005b) 'The political economy of the UK competition state: committed globalism, selected Europeanism', in Stubbs, R. and Underhill, G. (eds) *Political Economy and the Changing Global Order*, Oxford: Oxford University Press.

Baker, G. and Barber, T. (2001) 'Central banks did not co-ordinate rate cuts', *Financial Times*, 19 September.

Baker, A., Hudson, D. and Woodward, R. (eds) (2005) *Governing Financial Globalization: International Political Economy and Multi-Level Governance*, London: Routledge.

Balls, E. (1998) 'Open macroeconomics in an open economy', *Scottish Journal of Political Economy*, 45(2): 113–32.

Bank for International Settlements (1996) *Central Bank Survey of Foreign Exchange and Derivatives Markets Activity 1995*, Basle.

Bank for International Settlements (1997) *Central Bank Survey of Foreign Exchange and Derivatives Market Activity 1996*, Basle.

Bank for International Settlements (2001) 'Central Bank survey of foreign exchange and derivatives market activity in April 2001: preliminary global data', 20 December.

Barone, M. (1998) 'Wealth accumulation and American politics: how stock ownership is changing the political game', *The International Economy*, September/October: 46–50.

Basle Committee on Banking Supervision (2000) *Report to G7 Finance Ministers and Central Bank Governors on International Accounting Standards*, Basle, April.

Bayne, N. (1995) 'The G7 Summit and the reform of global institutions', *Government and Opposition*, 30: 492–509.

Bayne, N. (2000) 'The G7 summit's contribution: past, present and prospective', in Kaiser, K., Kirton, J. and Daniels, J. (eds) *Shaping a New International Financial System*, Aldershot: Ashgate.

Bergsten, F. (1996) 'Grade F for the G7', *International Economy*, November/December: 19.

Bergsten, F. and Henning, R. (1996) *Global Economic Leadership and the Group of Seven*, Washington, DC: Institute of International Economics.

Best, J. (2003) 'From the top down: the new financial architecture and the re-embedding of global finance', *New Political Economy*, 8(3): 363–84.

Bhagwati, J. (1998) 'The capital myth: the difference between trade in widgets and trade in dollars', *Foreign Affairs*, 77(3): 7–12.

Blanchard, O. and Summers, L. (1990) 'Hysteresis and the European unemployment problem', in Summers, L. (ed.) *Understanding Unemployment*, Cambridge, MA: MIT Press.

Bleaney, M. (1985) *The Rise and Fall of Keynesian Macroeconomics*, London: Macmillan.

Blinder, A. (1999) *Central banking in theory and practice*, Cambridge, MA: MIT Press.

Blyth, M. (2003) 'The political power of financial ideas: transparency, risk and distribution in global finance', in Kirshner, J. (ed.) *Monetary Orders: Ambiguous Economics, Ubiquitous Politics*, Ithaca, NY: Cornell University Press, pp. 239–59.

Bowles, P. (2002) 'Asia's post crisis regionalism: bring the state back in, keeping the United States out', *Review of International Political Economy*, pp. 244–270.

Bradford, C. and Linn, J. (2004) 'Global economic governance at the cross roads: replacing the G7 with the G20', *Policy Briefing 131*, Washington, DC: Brookings Institution.

Brittan, S. (1967) *Steering the Economy: The Role of the Treasury*, London: Secker & Warburg.

Brown, G. (1998) Speech to the Kennedy School of Government, Harvard University, December.

Brown, G. (2005) British Chancellor of the Exchequer at the National Gallery Scotland, 'International Development in 2005: the Challenge and the Opportunity', 6 January.

Bryant, R. (1980) *Money and Monetary Policy in Interdependent Nations*, Washington, DC: Brookings Institution.

Bryant, R. and Hodgkinson, E. (1989) 'Problems of International Co-operation', in Cooper, R., Eichengreen, B., Holtham, G. and Putnam, R. (eds) *Can Nations Agree? Issues in International Economic Co-operation*, Washington, DC: Brookings Institution.

Budd, L. (1999) 'Globalisation and the crisis of territorial embeddedness of international financial markets', in Martin, R. (ed.) *Money and the Space Economy*, Chichester: Wiley.

Bull, H. (1977) *The Anarchical Society*, London: Macmillan.

Calleo, D. (1982) *The Imperious Economy*, Cambridge, MA: Harvard University Press.

Caney, S. (2005) *Justice Beyond Borders: A Global Political Theory*, Oxford: Oxford University Press.

Castells, M. (1996) *The Information Age: Economy, Society and Culture, Vol. 1 – The Rise of the Network Society*, Oxford: Blackwell.

Cerny, P. (1990) *The Changing Architecture of Politics: Structure, Agency and the Future of the State*, London: Sage.

Cerny, P. (1994a) 'Gridlock and decline: financial internationalisation, banking politics and the American political process', in Stubbs, R. and Underhill, G. (eds) *Political Economy and the Changing Global Order*, London: Macmillan, pp. 425–38.

Cerny, P. (1994b) 'The infrastructure of the infrastructure? Towards "embedded financial orthodoxy" in the international political economy', in Palan, R. and Gills, B. (eds) *Transcending the State-Global Divide: A Neostructuralist Agenda in International Relations*, Boulder, CO: Lynne Reinner, pp. 223–49.

Cerny, P. (1995) 'Globalization and the changing logic of collective action', *International Organization*, 49(4): 595–625.

Cerny, P. (2000a) 'Political agency in a globalising world: towards a structurational approach', *European Journal of International Relations*, 6(4): 453–63.

Cerny, P. (2000b) 'The Big Bang in Tokyo, financial globalization and the unravelling of the Japanese model', in Harukiyo, H. and Hook, G. (eds) *The Political Economy of Japanese Globalization*, London: Routledge.

Cerny, P. (2001a) 'Financial globalization and internalising neo-liberalism in Japan: a new Meiji revolution?' Paper presented at the Annual Meeting of the American Political Science Association, San Francisco, 30 August – 2 September.

Cerny, P. (2001b) 'From "iron triangles" to "golden pentangles"? Globalizing the policy process', *Global Governance*, 7: 397–410.

Cerny, P. (2002) 'Webs of governance: National authorities and transnational markets', in Andrews, D., Henning, R. and Pauly, L. (eds) *Organizing the World's Money: Essays in Honour of Benjamin Cohen*, Ithaca, NY: Cornell University Press.

Chayes, A. and Chayes, A. (1993) 'On compliance', *International Organization*, 47(2): 175–205.

Christiansen, T., Jorgensen, K. and Wiener, A. (eds) (2001) *The Social Construction of Europe*, London: Sage.

Cohen, B. (1998) *The Geography of Money*, Ithaca, NY: Cornell University Press.

Cohen, B. (2003) 'Capital controls: the neglected option', in Underhill, G. and Zhang, X. (eds) *International Financial Governance under Stress: Global Structures versus National Imperatives*, Cambridge: Cambridge University Press, pp. 60–76.

Cohen, B. (2004) 'The meaning of monetary power', Paper presented at the annual meeting of the International Studies Association, Montreal Canada, March.

Coleman, W. (1990) 'The banking policy community and financial change', in Skaogstad, G. and Coleman, W. (eds) *Policy Communities and Public Policy in Canada*, Toronto: Clark Pittman, pp. 91–117.

Cooper, R. (1968) *The Economics of Interdependence: Economic Policy in the Atlantic Community*, New York: McGraw-Hill.

Cooper, R. (1985) 'Economic interdependence and co-ordination of economic policies', in Jones, R. and Kenen, P. (eds) *Handbook of International Economics*, Vol. 2, Amsterdam: North Holland.

Cooper, R., Eichengreen, B., Holtham, G., Putnam, R. and Henning R. (eds) (1989) *Can Nations Agree? Issues in International Economic Co-operation*, Washington, DC: Brookings Institution.

Council on Foreign Relations (1999) *Safeguarding Prosperity in a Global Financial System: The Future International Financial Architecture*, Report of an Independent Task Force, New York Council on Foreign Relations.

Cox, R. (1983) 'Gramsci, hegemony and international relations: an essay in method', *Millennium: Journal of International Studies*, 12(2): 162–75.

Cox, R. (1987) *Production, Power and World Order: Social Forces in the Making of History*, New York: Columbia University Press.

Cox, R. (1992a) 'Multilateralism and World Order', *Review of International Studies*, 18: 161–80.

Cox, R. (1992b) 'Global Peristroika', in Miliband, R. and Panitch, L. (eds) *The Socialist Register 1992*, London: Merlin Press.

Cox, R. (1994) 'Global restructuring: making sense of the changing international political economy', in Stubbs, R. and Underhill, G. (eds) *Political Economy and the Changing Global Order*, London: Macmillan, pp. 45–59.

Cox, R. (1996) 'Social forces, states and world orders: beyond international relations theory', in Cox, R. with Sinclair, T. (eds) *Approaches to World Order*, Cambridge: Cambridge University Press.

Cox, R. (1999) 'Civil society at the turn of the millennium: prospects for an alternative world order', *Review of International Studies*, 25(1): 3–28.

Crockett, A. (1988) 'Indicators and international economic cooperation', *Finance and Development*, 25(3): 22.

Daniels, J. (1993) *The Meaning and Reliability of Economic Summit Undertakings, 1975–1989*, London: Garland.

De Ceco, M. (1986) 'International financial markets and US domestic policy since 1945', *International Affairs*, 52(3): 381–99.

Delamaide, D. (1993) 'The coming of age of G7', *Euromoney*, September, p. 71.

Department of Finance, Canada (1999) 'G7 Enhanced Debt Initiative', Press Backgrounder Cologne, 18–22 June.

Destler, I. and Henning, R. (1989) *Dollar Politics: Exchange Rate Policy Making in the United States*, Washington, DC: Institute for International Economics.

Deutsche Bundesbank (2000) *Annual Report.*

Dobson, W (1991) *Economic Policy Co-ordination: Requiem or Prologue*, Washington, DC: Institute for International Economics.

Dodge, D. (2002) Governor of the Bank of Canada, Remarks to the Canadian Club of Ottawa and the Canadian Institute of International Affairs, Ottawa, Ontario, 14 May.

Dominguez, K. and Frankel, J. (1993) *Does Foreign Exchange Market Intervention Work?* Washington, DC: Institute for International Economics.

Dore, R. (2000) *Stock Market Capitalism: Japan and Germany versus the Anglo-Saxons*, Oxford: Oxford University Press.

Dore, R. (2002) 'Stock market capitalism and its diffusion', *New Political Economy*, 7(1): 116–17.

Dornbusch, R. (1996) 'The ridiculous G7', *International Economy*, September/October: 41–2.

Dyson, K. (1994) *Elusive Union: The Process of Economic and Monetary Union in Europe*, London: Longman.

Eichengreen, B. (1996) *Globalizing Capital: A History of the International Monetary System*, Princeton, NJ: Princeton University Press.

Eichengreen, B. (1999) *Toward a New International Financial Architecture: A Practical Post-Asian Agenda*, Washington, DC: Institute for International Economics.

Elrod, R. (1976) 'The concert of Europe: a fresh look at an international system', *World Politics*, 28: 159–74.

Engelen, K. (1998) 'Why Germans still hate the IMF', *The International Economy*, September/October: 42–5.

Evans, P., Jacobsen, H. and Putnam, R. (eds) (1993) *Double Edged Diplomacy: Domestic Politics and International Bargaining*, Berkeley, CA: University of California Press.

Fama, E. (1970) 'Efficient capital markets: a review of theory and empirical work', *Journal of Finance*, 25(2): 383–417.

Federal Reserve Board of Governors (1994) *Record of Policy Actions of the Federal Open Market Committee*, Washington, DC.

Feldstein, M. (1994) 'American economic policy in the 1980s: a personal view', in Feldstein, M. (ed.) *American Economic Policy in the 1980s*, Chicago, IL: Chicago University Press.

Felix, D. (2002) 'The economic case against free capital mobility', in Armijo, L. (ed.) *Debating the Global Financial Architecture*, New York: SUNY Press.

Fischer, S. (1997) 'Capital account liberalization and the role of the IMF', IMF Working Paper.

Fischer, S. (1998) Interview with Stanley Fischer, 'The IMF fights back', *The International Economy*, January/February: 6–9, 59.

Flemming, J. (1962) 'Domestic financial policies under fixed and floating exchange rates', *IMF Staff Papers*, 9, March.

Fratianni, M., Savona, P. and Kirton, J. (eds) (2002) *Governing Global Finance: G7 and IMF Contributions*, Aldershot: Ashgate.

Frieden, J. (1991) 'Invested interests: the politics of national economic policies: in a world of global finance', *International Organization*, 45(4): 427–33.

Frieden, J. (1994) 'Exchange rate policies: contemporary lessons from American history', *Review of International Political Economy*, 1(1): 81–103.

Friedman, M. (1968) American Economics Association, Presidential Address.

Funabashi, Y. (1988) *From the Plaza to the Louvre*, Washington, DC: Institute for International Economics.

Funabashi, Y. (1989) *Managing the Dollar: From the Plaza to the Louvre*, Washington, DC: Institute for International Economics.

Gamble, A. (1988) *The Free Economy and the Strong State*, Macmillan: London.

Gardener, R. (1981) *Sterling-Dollar Diplomacy in Current Perspective*, New York: Columbia University Press.

Garrett, G. (1998) *Partisan Politics in a Global Economy*, Cambridge: Cambridge University Press.

Garten, H. (1997) 'The United States, financial reform and the new world order in international finance', in Underhill, G. (ed.) *The New World Order in International Finance*, London: Macmillan, pp. 294–312.

Germain, R. (1997) *The International Organization of Credit*, Cambridge: Cambridge University Press.

Germain, R. (2000) 'The long road to reform: current political obstacle's to reforming the international financial architecture', Paper on the website of the G8 Research Centre, University of Toronto.

Germain, R. (2001) 'Global financial governance and the problem of inclusion', *Global Governance*, 7: 411–26.

Germain, R. (2004) 'Financial governance and the public sphere: recent developments', Paper delivered to the annual conference of the International Studies Association, Montreal, Canada, 17–20 March.

Giddens, A. (1982) *Profiles and Critiques in Social Theory*, London: Macmillan, p. 32.

Giddens, A. (1984) *The Constitution of Society: An Outline of the Theory of Structuration*, Cambridge: Polity Press.

Gill, S. (ed.) (1993a) *Gramsci, Historical Materialism and International Relations*, Cambridge: Cambridge University Press.

Gill, S. (1993b) 'Global finance, monetary policy and co-operation among the Group of Seven, 1944–92', in Cerny, P. (ed.) *Finance and World Politics: Markets, States and Regimes in the Post-Hegemonic Era*, Aldershot: Edward Elgar.

Gill, S. (1994a) 'Political economy and structural change: globalizing elites in the emerging world order', in Sakamoto, Y. (ed.) *Global Transformations*, New York: United Nations University Press, pp. 169–99.

Gill, S. (1994b) 'Structural changes in multilateralism: the G7 nexus and the global crisis', in Schechter, M. (ed.) *Innovation in Multilateralism*, New York: Macmillan for United Nations University Press, pp. 113–65.

Gill, S. (1997) 'Analysing new forms of authority: New constitutionalism, panopticism and market civilization', paper presented at Non State Actors and Authority in the Global System Conference, University of Warwick, 31 October–1 November.

Gill, S. (2003) *Power and Resistance in the New World Order*, London: Palgrave.

Gill, S. and Law, D. (1989) 'Global hegemony and the structural power of capital', *International Studies Quarterly*, 36: 475–99.

Gilpin, R. (1981) *War and Change in World Politics*, New York: Cambridge University Press.

Goldstein, M. (1998) *The Asian Financial Crisis: Causes, Cures and Systemic Implications*, Washington, DC: Institute for International Economics.

Gourevitch, P. (1978) 'The second image reversed: the international sources of domestic politics', *International Organization*, 32(4): 281–313.

Gowan, P. (1999) *The Global Gamble: Washington's Faustian Bid for Global Dominance*, London: Verso.

Gowan, P. (2001) 'Explaining the American boom: the roles of "globalization" and United States global power', *New Political Economy*, 6(3): 359–74.

Grabel, I. (2003) 'Ideology, power and the rise of independent monetary institutions in emerging markets', in Kirshner, J. (ed.) *Monetary Order*, Ithaca, NY: Cornell University Press, pp. 25–54.

Grossman, E. (2005) 'European banking policy: between multi-level governance and Europeanization', in Baker, A., Hudson, D. and Woodward, R. (eds) *Governing Financial Globalization*, pp. 130–46.

Group of Seven Finance Ministers (1995a) Halifax Communiqué Background Document: Institutions, Section 5: 'Promoting financial stability in a globalized economy'.

Group of Seven Finance Ministers (1995b) Report to the Heads of State and Government at the Halifax Summit of 1995.

Group of Seven Finance Ministers (1996) Report on International Monetary Stability, to the Heads of State and Government, at the Lyon Summit, 28 June.

Group of Seven Finance Ministers (2002) Statement, 15 June, Halifax, Nova Scotia.

Group of Seven Finance Ministers and Central Bank Governors (2000) 'Strengthening the international financial architecture', report to the Heads of State and Government, Fukuoka, 8 July.

Group of Seven Finance Ministers and Central Bank Governors (2001) 'Strengthening the international financial system and multilateral development banks', Rome, 7 July.

Group of Seven Finance Ministers and Central Bank Governors' Statement, 7 April 1990, Paris.

Group of Seven Finance Ministers and Central Bank Governors' Statement, 6 May 1990, Washington, DC.

Group of Seven Finance Ministers and Central Bank Governors' Statement, 22 September 1990, Washington, DC.

Group of Seven Finance Ministers and Central Bank Governors' Statement, 28 April 1991, Washington, DC.

Group of Seven Finance Ministers and Central Bank Governors' Statement, 29 April 1993, Washington, DC.

Group of Seven Finance Ministers and Central Bank Governors' Statement, 3–4 February 1995, Ottawa.

Group of Seven Finance Ministers and Central Bank Governors' Statement, 8 February 1995, Berlin.

Group of Seven Finance Ministers and Central Bank Governors' Statement, 25 April 1995, Washington, DC.

Group of Seven Finance Ministers and Central Bank Governors' Statement, February 1997, Berlin.

Group of Seven Finance Ministers and Central Bank Governors' Statement, 27 April 1997, Washington, DC.

Group of Seven Finance Ministers and Central Bank Governors' Statement, 21 February 1998, London.

Group of Seven Finance Ministers and Central Bank Governors' Statement, 14 September 1998, Washington, DC.

Group of Seven Finance Ministers and Central Bank Governors' Statement, October 1998.

Group of Seven Finance Ministers and Central Bank Governors' Statement, 20 February 1999.

Group of Seven Finance Ministers and Central Bank Governors' Statement, 26 April 1999, Washington, DC.

Group of Seven Finance Ministers and Central Bank Governors' Statement, 25 September 1999, Washington, DC.

Group of Seven Finance Ministers and Central Bank Governors' Statement, 22 January 2000, Tokyo.

Group of Seven Finance Ministers and Central Bank Governors' Statement, 16 April 2000, Washington, DC.

Group of Seven Finance Ministers and Central Bank Governors' Statement, 23 September 2000, Prague, Czech Republic.

Group of Seven Finance Ministers and Central Bank Governors' Statement, 12 September 2001.

Group of Seven Finance Ministers and Central Bank Governors' Statement, 6 October 2001, Ottawa.

Group of Seven Finance Ministers and Central Bank Governors' Statement, 9 February 2002, Paris.

Group of Seven Finance Ministers and Central Bank Governors' Action Plan on Sovereign Debt, 20 April 2002, Washington, DC.

Group of Seven Finance Ministers and Central Bank Governors' Statement, 27 September 2002, Washington, DC.

Group of Seven Finance Ministers and Central Bank Governors' Statement, 22 February 2003, Paris, France.

Group of Seven Finance Ministers and Central Bank Governors' Statement, 12 April 2003, Washington, DC.

Group of Seven Finance Ministers and Central Bank Governors' Statement, 20 September 2003, Dubai.

Group of Seven Finance Ministers and Central Bank Governors' Statement, 8 February 2004, Boca Raton, Florida.

Group of Ten (1996) 'The resolution of sovereign liquidity crises: A report to the ministers and governors under the auspices of the deputies', May.

Haggard, S. and MacIntyre, S. (1998) 'The political economy of the Asian economic crisis', *Review of International Political Economy*, 5(3): 381–392.

Hall, P. (1989) *Governing the Economy: The Politics of State Intervention in Britain and France*, Oxford: Oxford University Press.

Hall, P. (1992) 'The movement from Keynesianism to monetarism: institutional analysis and British economic policy in the 1970s', in Steinmo, S., Thelen, K. and Longstreth, F. (eds) *Structuring Politics: Historical Institutionalism in Comparative Perspective*, Cambridge: Cambridge University Press, pp. 90–113.

Hall, P. (1993) 'Policy paradigms, social learning and the state: the case of economic policy making in Britain', *Comparative Politics*, April: 275–96.

Harmes, A. (1998) 'Institutional investors and the reproduction of neoliberalism', *Review of International Political Economy* 5(1): 92–121.

Harvey, D. (2003) *The New Imperialism*, Oxford: Oxford University Press.

Hay, C. (2000) 'Globalization, social democracy and the persistence politics: a commentary on Garrett', *Review of International Political Economy*, 7(1): 138–52.

Haymani, M. (2000) 'Globalization and regional co-operation in Asia', Speech given by the Governor of the Bank of Japan, at Asian Pacific Bankers Club, 17 March.

Heath, C., Jirotka, M., Luff, P. and Hindmarsh, J. (1993) 'Unpacking collaboration: the international organisation of trading in a city dealing room', *Proceedings of the European Conference on Computer Supported Co-operative work* (CSCW), Milan.

Helleiner E. (1994) *States and the Re-emergence of Global Finance: From Bretton Woods to the 1990s*, Ithaca, NY: Cornell University Press.

Henning, R. (1994) *Currencies and Politics in the US, Japan and Germany*, Washington, DC: Institute for International Economics.

Henning, R. and Destler, I. (1988) 'From neglect to activism: American politics and the 1985 Plaza Accord', *Journal of Public Policy*, 8(3/4): 317–33.

Higgott, R. (1998) 'The Asian economic crisis: a study in the politics of resentment', *New Political Economy*, 3(3): 337.

Higgott, R. (2003) 'American unilateralism, foreign economic policy and the "securitization" of globalisation', Centre for the Study of Globalisation and Regionalisation, Working Paper No.124/03, University of Warwick, September.

Higgott, R. (2004) 'Multilateralism and the limits of global governance', CSGR Working Paper, University of Warwick, May.

Higgott, R. and Phillips, N. (2000) 'Challenging triumphalism and convergence: the limits of global liberalisation in Asia and Latin America', *Review of International Studies*, 26(3): 359–81.

Hirst, P. and Thompson, G. (1996) *Globalization in Question: The International Economy and the Possibilities of Governance*, Cambridge: Polity Press.

Hobson, J. (1997) *The Wealth of States: A Comparative Sociology of International Economic and Political Change*, Cambridge: Cambridge University Press.

Hobson, J. (2000) *The State and International Relations*, Cambridge: Cambridge University Press.

Hodges, M. (1998) 'What future for the summits?' Concluding remarks at Conference on Jobs, Money and Crime: Challenges for the G8 in 1998, Plaisterers' Hall, London, organised by LSE, University of Toronto G8 Research Group and Clifford Chance, 13 May.

Hollis, M. and Smith, S. (1991) 'Beware of gurus: structure and action in international relations', *Review of International Studies*, 17(4): 393–410.

Holtham, G. (1989) 'German macroeconomic policy and the 1978 Bonn Summit', in Cooper, R *et al.* (eds) *Can Nations Agree?* Washington, DC: Brookings Institution.

Hughes, C. (2000) 'Japanese policy and the East Asian crisis: abject defeat or quiet victory?' *Review of International Political Economy*, 7(2): 241–58.

Ikenberry, J. (1993) 'Salvaging the G-7', *Foreign Affairs*, 72(4): 132–9.

International Monetary Fund (1994) *International Capital Markets: Developments and Prospects*, Washington, DC: IMF, September.

Jackson, G. (2002) 'Corporate governance in Germany and Japan: liberalisation pressures and responses', in Streek, W. and Yamamura, K. (eds) *Germany and Japan: The Future of Nationally Embedded Capitalisms*, Ithaca, NY: Cornell University Press.

James, H. (1996) *International Monetary Co-operation Since Bretton Woods*, Washington, DC: International Monetary Fund; New York: Oxford University Press.

Kaiser, K., Kirton, J. and Daniels, J. (eds) (2000) *Shaping a New International Financial System: Challenges of Governance in a Globalizing World*, Aldershot: Ashgate.

Kapstein, E. (1994) *Governing the Global Economy*, Cambridge, MA: Harvard University Press.

Katada, S. (2001) 'Determining factors in Japan's co-operation and non co-operation with the United States', in Miyashita, A. and Sato, Y. (eds) *Japanese Foreign Policy in Asia and the Pacific: Domestic Interests, American Pressure and Regional Integration*, Palgrave: New York.

Katada, S. (2002) 'Japan and Asian monetary regionalism: cultivating a new regional leadership role after the Asian financial crisis', *Geopolitics*, 7:1.

Keegan, W. and Pennant Rae, R. (1979) *Who Runs the Economy? Control and Influence in British Economic Policy*, London: Maurice Temple Smith.

Kenen, P., Shafer, J., Wicks, N. and Wyplosz, C. (2004) *International Economic and Financial Co-operation: New Issues, New Actors, New Responses*, London: Centre for Economic Policy Research.

Keohane, R. (1984) *After Hegemony: Co-operation and Discord in the World Economy*, Princeton, NJ: Princeton University Press.

Keohane, R. and Nye, J. (1974) 'Transgovernmental relations and international organizations', *World Politics*, 27(1): 39–62.

Keynes, J. (1930) *A Treatise on Money*, London: Macmillan.

Keynes, J. (1936) *The General Theory, Employment, Interest and Money*, New York: Harcourt, Brace and World.

Kirshner, J. (1995) *Currency and Coercion: The Political Economy of International Monetary Power*, Princeton, NJ: Princeton University Press.

Kirshner, J. (1999) 'Keynes, capital mobility and the crisis of embedded liberalism', *Review of International Political Economy*, 6(3): 313–37.

Kirshner, J. (ed.) (2003a) *Monetary Orders: Ambiguous Economics, Ubiquitous Politics*, Ithaca, NY: Cornell University Press, pp. 239–59.

Kirshner, J. (2003b) 'Explaining choices about money: disentangling power, ideas and conflict', in Kirshner, J. (ed.) *Monetary Orders*, Ithaca, NY: Cornell University Press, pp. 260–80.

Kirshner, J. (2004) 'Currency and coercion in the twenty-first century', Paper presented at the International Studies Association Annual Conference, Montreal, 17–20 March.

Kirton, J. (1989) 'Contemporary concert diplomacy: the seven power summit and the management of the international order', Paper presented at the International Studies Association Annual Meeting, London, 29 March–1 April.

Kirton, J. (1998) 'What future for the summits?' Concluding comments made at 'Jobs, Crime and Money: Challenges for the G8 Summit in 1998', Conference at the Plaisterers' Hall, London, organized by LSE, University of Toronto, G8 Research Group and Clifford Chance, 13 May.

Kirton, J. (1999) 'Canada and the global financial crisis of 1997–98: G7 and APEC diplomacy', Paper presented at National Chengchi University, Taipei, Taiwan, 18 December, Version: 5 January.

Kirton, J. (2000) 'The dynamics of G7 leadership in crisis response and system reconstruction', in Kaiser, K., Kirton, J. and Daniels, J. (eds) *Shaping a New International Financial System*, Aldershot: Ashgate.

Kirton, J. (2002) 'Consensus and coherence in G7 financial governance', in Fratianni, M., Savona, P. and Kirton, J. (eds) *Governing Global Finance*, Aldershot: Ashgate.

Kirton, J. and Kokotsis, E. (1997–98) 'Revitalising the G7: prospects for the Birmingham Summit', *International Journal*, Winter: 38–56.

Kirton, J. and von Furstenberg, G. (eds) (2001) *New Directions in Global Economic Governance: Managing Globalisation in the Twenty-First Century*, Aldershot: Ashgate.

Kirton, J., Daniels, J. and Freytag, A. (eds) (1999) *Guiding Global Order: G8 Governance in the Twenty-First Century*, Aldershot: Ashgate.

Kiuchi, T. (2002) 'Japan, Asia and the rebuilding of the financial sector', in Fratianni, M., Savona, P. and Kirton, J. (eds) *Governing Global Finance: New Challenges, G7 and IMF Contributions*, Aldershot: Ashgate.

Kohler, H. (2003) 'The challenges of globalisation and the role of the IMF', Speech at the Annual Meeting of the Society of Economics and Management, Humboldt University, Berlin, 15 May.

Kokotsis, E. (1995) 'Keeping sustainable developments: the recent G7 record', in Kirton, J. and Richardson, S. (eds) *The Halifax Summit: Sustainable Development and International Institutional Reform*, Ottawa: National Round Table on the Environment and the Economy, pp. 117–133.

Kosai, Y. (2002) 'A reformist's view of Japanese reform', *New Political Economy*, 7(1): 124–5.

Krugman, P. (1995) 'Dutch tulips and emerging markets', *Foreign Affairs*, July/August: 28–44.

Krugman, P. (1998) 'What happened to Asia?', at http://web.mit.edu/krugman/www.

Kurtzman, J. (1993) *The Death of Money*, Boston, MA: Little Brown, p. 47.

Langley, P. (1997) 'Globalisation, regionalisation and the world financial order: London, Frankfurt and the European financial area', Paper presented at 'Globalisation versus Regionalisation: New Trends in World Politics', Centre for the Study of Globalisation and Regionalisation, University of Warwick, 10–11 December.

Langley, P. (2002) *World Financial Orders: An Historical International Political Economy*, London: Routledge.

Langley, P. (2005) 'The everyday life of global finance: a neglected level of governance', in Baker, A., Hudson, D. and Woodward, R. (eds) *Governing Financial Globalization*, London: Routledge, pp. 85–101.

Lawson, N. (1992) *The View From No. 11: The Memoirs of a Tory Radical*, London: Bantam Press.

Leyshon, A. and Thrift, N. (1997) *Money Space: Geographies of Monetary Transformation*, London: Routledge.

Lowenthal, A. (1972) *The Dominican Intervention*, Cambridge, MA: Harvard University Press.

Lütz, S. (2000) 'From managed to market capitalism? German finance in transition', Max Plank Institut für Gesellschaftsforschung Discussion Paper, 00/2.

Machlup, F. (1968) *Remaking the International Monetary System: The Rio Agreement and Beyond*, Baltimore, MD: Johns Hopkins University Press.

Mann, M. (1993) *The Sources of Social Power, Vol. II*, Cambridge: Cambridge University Press.

March, J. and Olsen, J. (1988) *Rediscovering Institutions: The Organisational Basis of Politics*, London: Macmillan.

March, J. and Olsen, J. (1998) 'The institutional dynamics of international political orders', *International Organization*, 52(4): 943–69.

Martin, R. (1994) 'Stateless monies, global financial integration and national economic autonomy: the end of geography', in Corbridge, S., Martin, R. and Thrift, N. (eds) *Money, Power and Space*, Cambridge: Basil Blackwell, p. 270.

Martin, R. (1999) 'The new economic geography', in Martin, R. (ed.) *Money and the Space Economy*, Chichester: Wiley, p. 11.

Maxfield, S. (1991) 'Bankers alliances and economic policy patterns: evidence from Mexico and Brazil', *Comparative Political Studies*, 23(4): 419–58.

Maxfield, S. (1997) *Gatekeepers of Growth: The International Political Economy of Central Banking in Developing Countries*, Princeton, NJ: Princeton University Press.

Mayntz, R. and Hughes, T. (eds) (1988) *The Development of Large Technical Systems*, Boulder, CO: Westview.

McKenzie, R. and Lee, D. (1991) *Quicksilver Capital: How the Rapid Movement of Wealth Has Changed the World*, New York: Free Press.

McNamara, K. (1998) *The Currency of Ideas: Monetary Politics in the European Union*, Ithaca, NY: Cornell University Press.

McNamara, K. (1999) 'Consensus and constraint: ideas and capital mobility in European integration', *Journal of Common Market Studies*, 37(3): 462.

Merlini, C. (1994) 'The G7 and the need for reform', *International Spectator*, Special Issue 'The Future of G7 Summits', April–June, xxix(2): 5–26.

Michaely, M. (1973) *The Responsiveness of Demand Policies to Balance of Payments: Post War Patterns*, New York: National Bureau of Economic Research.

Miyazawa, K. (1998) 'Towards a new international financial architecture', Speech by the Minister of Finance, at the Foreign Correspondents Club of Japan, 15 December.

Mohammed, A. (2003) 'Implementing codes and standards through the Bretton Woods institutions: an overview of the developing country perspective', in Schneider, B. (ed.) *The Road to International Financial Stability: Are Key Financial Standards the Answer?* Basingstoke: Palgrave.

Moran, M. (1991) *The Politics of the Financial Services Revolution*, London: Macmillan.

Moravcsik, A. (1997) 'Taking preferences seriously: a liberal theory of international politics', *International Organization*, 51(4): 513–53.

Morgenthau, H. (1948) *Politics Among Nations*, New York: Alfred Knopf.

Mosely, L. (1997) 'International financial markets and government economic policy: the importance of financial market operations', Paper presented at the Annual meeting of the American Political Science Association, Duke University.

Moses, J. (1994) 'Abdication from national policy autonomy: what's left to leave', *Politics and Society*, 22(2): 125–48.

Moses, J. (1995) 'The social democratic predicament in the emerging European Union: a capital dilemma', *Journal of European Public Policy*, 2(3): 407–26.

Moses, J. (1997) 'Trojan horses: Putnam, ECU linkage and the EU ambitions of Nordic elites', *Review of International Political Economy*, 4(2): 382–415.

Mulford, D. (1998) 'Mulford memorandum: America has blown it with the G7', *The International Economy*, January/February: 12.

Mundell, R. (1960) 'The monetary dynamics of international adjustment under fixed and floating exchange rates', *Quarterly Journal of International Economics*, 74.

Mundell, R. (1963) 'Capital mobility and stabilisation policy under fixed and flexible exchange rates', *Canadian Journal of Economics and Political Science*, 30: 475–85.

Mussa, M. (1994) 'Exchange rate policy', in Feldstein, M. (ed.) *American Economic Policy in the 1980s*, Chicago, IL: Chicago University Press.

Nakao, T. (1999) 'Hedge funds and international financial markets', Paper prepared by the Direction of the International Organization Division, International Finance Bureau, Ministry of Finance, July.

Noble, G. and Ravenhill, J. (eds) (2000) *The Asian Financial Crisis and the Architecture of Global Finance*, New York: Cambridge University Press.

Nolke, A. (2004) 'Bringing transgovernmental relations back in', Paper presented at ECPR Pan European International Relations Conference, Den Haag, 9–11 September.

Notermans, T. (1994) 'The abdication of national policy autonomy: why the macroeconomic policy regime has become so unfavourable to labour', *Politics and Society*, 21(2): 133–67.

Oatley, T. and Nabors, R. (1998) 'Redistributive co-operation: market failure, wealth transfers and the Basle accord', *International Organization*, 52(1): 35–54.

O'Brien, R., Goetz, A.M., Scholte, J.A. and Williams, M. (2000) *Contesting Global Governance: Multilateral Economic Institutions and Global Social Movements*, Cambridge: Cambridge University Press.

Odell, J. (1979) 'The US and the emergence of flexible exchange rates: an analysis of foreign policy change', *International Organization*, 33(1): 57–81.

Odell, J. (1982) *US International Monetary Policy*, Princeton, NJ: Princeton University Press.

Panitch, L. (1996) 'Rethinking the role of the state', in Mittleman, J. (ed.) *Globalization: Critical Reflections*, Boulder, CO: Lynne Rienner, pp. 83–116.

Pauly, L. (1992) 'The political foundations of multilateral economic surveillance', *International Journal*, 48(2): 293–327.

Pauly, L. (1993) 'From monetary manager to crisis manager: systemic change and the International Monetary Fund', in Morgan, R. *et al.* (eds) *New Diplomacy in the Post-Cold War World: Essays for Susan Strange*, London: Macmillan.

Pauly, L. (1997) *Who Elected the Bankers: Surveillance and Control in the World Economy*, Ithaca, NY: Cornell University Press.

Phillips, K. (1997) *Arrogant Capital: Washington, Wall Street and the Frustration of American Politics*, New York: Little Brown.

Porter, T. (1999) 'Representation, legitimacy and the changing regime for global financial regulation', Paper presented at the 1999 Annual Meeting of the American Political Science Association, Atlanta Hilton, 2–5 September.

Porter, T. (2000) 'The G-7, the financial stability forum and the politics of international financial regulation', Paper Presented at the International Studies Association Annual Meeting, Los Angeles, March.

Porter, T. (2001) 'The Democratic deficit in the institutional arrangements for regulating global finance', *Global Governance* 7(4): 427–39.

Porter, T. (2003) 'Technical collaboration and political conflict in the emerging regime for international financial regulation', *Review of International Political Economy*, 10(3): 520–51.

Porter, T. and Wood, D. (2002) 'Reform without representation: the transnational and international dialogue on the global financial architecture', in Armijo, L. (ed.) *Debating the Global Financial Architecture*, New York: SUNY Press.

Putnam, R. (1998) 'Diplomacy and domestic politics: the logic of two-level games', *International Organization*, 42(3): 429–60.

Putnam, R. and Bayne, N. (1987) *Hanging Together: Co-operation and Conflict in the Seven Power Summits*, London: Sage.

Putnam, R. and Henning, R. (1989) 'The Bonn Summit of 1978: a case study in co-ordination', in Cooper, R. *et al.* (eds) *Can Nations Agree? Issues in International Economic Co-operation*, Washington, DC: Brookings Institution, pp. 12–140.

Risse, T. (2000) 'Let's argue!: communicative action in world politics', *International Organization*, 54, 1.

Rogoff, K. (2003) 'The IMF strikes back', Carnegie Endowment for International Peace, February.

Romer, P. (1986) 'Increasing returns and long run growth', *Journal of Political Economy*, 94(5): 1002–36.

Rosenau, J. (1995) 'Governance in the twenty-first century', *Global Governance*, 1: 1–28.

Rubin, R. and Weisburg, J. (2003) *In an Uncertain World: Tough Choice from Wall Street to Washington*, New York: Thompson Texere.

Ruggie, J. (1992) 'Multilateralism: the anatomy of an institution', *International Organization*, 46(3): 568–80.

Ruggie, J. (1998) 'What makes the world hang together? Neo-utilitarianism and the social constructivist challenge', *International Organization*, 52(4): 855–85.

Russell, R. (1973) 'Transgovernmental interaction in the international monetary system 1960–1972', *International Organization*, 27(3): 431–64.

Sachs, J. and Wing Thye Woo (2000) 'Understanding the Asian financial crisis', in Wing Thye Woo, Sachs, J. and Schwab, K. (eds) *Understanding the Asian Financial Crisis: Lessons for a Resilient Asia*, Cambridge, MA: MIT Press.

Sakakibara, E. (1999) 'Reform of the international financial architecture: main elements of the G-7 report on the architecture', Vice Minister for International Affairs, Ministry of Finance, at the Symposium on Building the Financial System of the 21st Century, Kyoto Japan, 25 June.

Sassen, S. (2002) 'Globalization and the state', in Hall, R. and Biersteker, T. (eds) *The Emergence of Private Authority in Global Governance*, Cambridge: Cambridge University Press.

Scholte, J. (1997) 'The IMF and civil society: an underdeveloped dialogue', Paper presented at ESRC Centre for the Study of Globalisation and Regionalisation, 'Non State Actors and Authority in the Global System', University of Warwick, 31 October–1 November.

Scholte, J. (2000) *Globalization: A Critical Introduction*, London: Macmillan.

Scholte, J. (2004) 'Globalization and governance: from statism to polycentrism', Centre for the Study of Globalisation and Regionalisation (CSGR) Working Paper no.103/04.

Schroder, G. (1997) 'The dark side of EMU', *The International Economy*, November/December: 6–10.

Schulze, G. (2000) *The Political Economy of Capital Controls*, New York: Cambridge University Press.

Seabrooke, L. (2001) *US Power in International Finance: The Victory of Dividends*, London: Palgrave.

Sinclair, T. (1994) 'Passing judgement: credit rating processes as regulatory mechanisms of governance in the emerging world order', *Review of International Political Economy*, 1(1): 133–59.

Sinclair, T. (2005) *The New Masters of Capital: American Bond Rating Agencies and the Global Economy*, Ithaca, NY: Cornell University Press.

Slaughter, A.M. (2004) *A New World Order*, Princeton, NJ: Princeton University Press.

Smyser, W. (1993) 'Goodbye G-7', *Washington Quarterly*, 16(1): 15–28.

Smyser, W., Bergsten, F. and Henning, R. (1996) *Global Economic Leadership and the Group of Seven*, Washington, DC: Institute for International Economics.

Snidal, D. (1985) 'The limits of hegemonic stability theory', *International Organization*, 39: 579–614.

Soederberg, S. (2002) 'A historical materialist account of the Chilean capital control: prototype policy for whom?' *Review of International Political Economy*, 9(3): 490–512.

Soederberg, S. (2004a) *The Politics of the New International Financial Architecture: Reimposing Neoliberal Domination in the Global South*, London and New York: Zed Books.

Soederberg, S. (2004b) 'The transnational debt architecture and emerging markets: the politics of discipline and punish', Paper presented at ISA Annual Conference, Montreal, March.

Soros, G. (1987) *The Alchemy of Finance*, New York: Wiley.

Stark, J. (1995) 'The G7 at work', *The International Economy*, September/October: 53–4.

Stiglitz, J. (2002) *Globalization and Its Discontents,* London: Penguin.

Story, J. (2003) 'Reform of the international financial architecture: what has been written?' in Underhill, G and Zhang, X (eds) *International Financial Governance Under Stress: Global Structures versus National Imperatives*, Cambridge: Cambridge University Press, pp. 21–40.

Story, J. and Walter, I. (1998) *The Political Economy of Financial Integration in Europe: The Battle of the Systems*, Manchester: Manchester University Press.

Strange, S. (1986) *Casino Capitalism*, Oxford: Blackwell.

Strange, S. (1994) *States and Markets*, London: Pinter.

Strange, S. (1996) *The Retreat of the State: The Diffusion of Power in the World Economy*, Cambridge: Cambridge University Press.

Strange, S. (1998) *Mad Money*, Manchester: Manchester University Press.

Strauss-Kahn, D. (1998) 'Personal view', *Financial Times*, 16 April.

Summers, L. (1996a) 'US policy toward the international monetary system on the eve of the Lyon summit', Remarks to Emerging Markets Traders Association, 24 June, p. 9.

Summers, L. (1996b) 'In Defense of the G7', *The International Economy*, July/August.

Summers, L (1997) 'The Euro will be good for the US if it helps strengthen and modernise Europe's economy', comment and analysis, *Financial Times*, 22 October.

Summers, L. (1999) 'Reflections on managing global integration', distinguished lecture on economics in government, *Journal of Economic Perspectives*, 13(12): 3–18.

Tadokoro, M. (2003) 'The Asian financial crisis and Japanese policy reactions', in Underhill, G. and Zhang, X. (eds) *International Financial Governance Under Stress: Global Structures versus National Imperatives*, Cambridge: Cambridge University Press.

Taylor, J. (2004a) 'Implementing reforms that drop the debt of the heavily indebted poor countries', Under Secretary of Treasury for International Affairs, Remarks at the Poverty and Debt Relief Photo Exhibit, United States Senate, 14 October.

Taylor, J. (2004b) Under Secretary for International Affairs Remarks at the Cleveland Council on World Affairs, Case Western Reserve University, Cleveland OH, 'Getting international economic development right: is effective foreign assistance possible?' 26 October.

Taylor, P. (1996) 'Embedded statism and the social sciences: opening up to new spaces', *Environment and Planning*, 28(11): 917–28.

Teague, P. (1998) *Economic Citizenship in Europe*, London: Routledge.

Teague, P. (1999) 'Reshaping employment regimes in Europe: policy shifts alongside boundary change', *Journal of Public Policy*, 19(1): 33–62.

Thain, C. (1984) 'The Treasury and Britain's decline', *Political Studies*, XXXII: 581–95.

Thirkell-White, B. (2004) 'The international financial architecture: soft law, power and legitimacy', IPEG Papers in Global Political Economy, 13 June.

Thirkell-White, B. (2005a) 'The IMF, middle income countries and the Asian financial crisis: multi-level governance as adaptation', in Baker, A., Hudson, D. and Woodward, R. (eds) *Governing Financial Globalization*, pp. 147–70.

Thirkell-White, B. (2005b) *The IMF and the Politics of Globalisation: From the Asian Financial Crisis to a New Financial Architecture*, Basingstoke: Palgrave.

Thrift, N. and Leyshon, A. (1994) 'The phantom state? The de-traditionalisation of money, the international financial system and international financial centres', *Political Geography*, 13: 299–327.

Tobin, J. (2003) *World Finance and Economic Stability: Selected Essays of James Tobin*, Cheltenham: Edward Elgar.

Triffin, R. (1961) *Gold and the Dollar Crisis: The Future of Convertibility*, New Haven, CT: Yale University Press.

Tsingou, E. (2003) 'Transnational policy communities and financial governance: the role of private actors in derivatives regulation', *Centre for the Study of Globalisation and Regionalisation Working Paper*, No. 111/03. Available online at http://www.warwick.ac.uk/fac/soc/CSGR/abwp11103.html.

Tsoukalis, L. (1997) *The New European Economy Revisited*, Oxford: Oxford University Press.

Underhill, G. (1995) 'Keeping government out of politics: transnational securities markets, regulatory co-operation and political legitimacy', *Review of International Studies*, 21(3): 251–78.

Underhill, G. (1997a) *The New World Order in International Finance*, London: Macmillan.

Underhill, G. (1997b) 'Conclusion: global markets, macroeconomic instability and exchange rate crises: the political economy of the new world order in international finance', in Underhill, G. (ed.) *The New World Order in International Finance*, London: Macmillan, pp. 313–18.

Underhill, G. (1997c) 'Private markets and public responsibility in a global system: conflict and co-operation in a transnational banking and securities regulation', in Underhill, G. (ed.) *The New World Order in International Finance*, London: Macmillan, pp. 17–50.

Underhill, G. (2000) 'State, market and global political economy: geneaology of an (inter?) discipline', *International Affairs*, 76(4): 805–24.

Underhill, G. (2001) 'States, markets and governance: public interests, the public good and the democratic process', inaugural lecture, University of Amsterdam, 21 September.

Underhill, G. and Zhang, X. (2003a) 'Conclusion: towards the good governance of the international financial system', in Underhill, G. and Zhang, X. (eds) *International Financial Governance Under Stress*, Cambridge: Cambridge University Press, pp. 360–83.
Underhill, G. and Zhang, X. (eds) (2003b) *International Financial Governance Under Stress: Global Structures versus National Imperatives*, Cambridge: Cambridge University Press.
Verdun, A. (2000) *European Responses to Globalization and Financial Market Integration: Perceptions of Economic and Monetary Union in Britain, France and Germany*, London: Macmillan.
Volcker, P. and Gyohten, T. (1992) *Changing Fortunes: The World's Money and the Threat to American Leadership*, New York: Times Books, p. 126.
Vrolijk, C. (1997) 'Derivative affects on currency transmission', Working Paper of the International Monetary Fund, WP/97/121.
Wade, R. (1998/9) 'The coming fight over capital controls', *Foreign Policy*, 113: 41–53.
Wade, R. (1999) 'National power, coercive liberalism and global finance', in Art, R. and Jervis, R. (eds) *International Politics: Enduring Concepts and Contemporary Issues*, Ithaca, NY: Cornell University Press.
Wade, R. and Veneroso, F. (1998) 'The Asian crisis: the high debt model versus the Wall Street–Treasury–IMF complex', *New Left Review*, 228, March/April: 3–23.
Wallich, H. (1984) 'Institutional co-operation in the world economy', in Frankel, J. *et al.* (eds) *The World Economic System: Performance and Prospects*, Dover, MA: Auburn House, pp. 85–99.
Walter, A. (1993) *World Power and World Money* Brighton: Harvester Wheatsheaf.
Waltz, K. (1979) *Theory of International Politics*, New York: McGraw-Hill.
Warf, B. (1999) 'The hypermobility of capital and the collapse of the Keynesian state', in Martin, R. (ed.) *Money and the Space Economy*, Chichester: Wiley, p. 230.
Watson, M (2002a) 'Sand in the wheels, or oiling the wheels of international finance? New Labour's appeal to a new Bretton Woods', *British Journal of Politics and International Relations*, 4(2): 193–221.
Watson, M. (2002b) 'The institutional paradoxes of monetary orthodoxy: reflections on the political economy of central bank independence', *Review of International Political Economy*, 9:1.
Webb, M. (1991) 'International economic structures, government interests and international co-ordination of macroeconomic adjustment policies', *International Organization*, 45(3): 309–42.
Webb, M. (1995) *The Political Economy of Policy Co-ordination*, Ithaca, NY: Cornell University Press.
Weiss, L. (1998) *The Myth of the Powerless State*, Ithaca, NY: Cornell University Press.
Wendt, A. (1987) 'The agent-structure problem in international relations theory', *International Organization*, 41: 335–70.
Wendt, A. (1999) *Social Theory of International Politics*, Cambridge: Cambridge University Press.
White, B. (2005a) *The IMF and the Politics of Globalisation: From the Asian Financial Crisis to a New Financial Architecture*, Basingstoke: Palgrave.
White, B. (2005b) 'The IMF, middle income countries and the Asian financial crisis: multi-level governance as adaptation', in Baker, A., Hudson, D. and Woodward, R. (eds) *Governing Financial Globalization: International Political Economy and Multi-level Governance*, London: Routledge, pp. 147–70.
Wicks, N. (1994a) 'G7 co-ordination: an empty box?' Speech to the Bank of England's Advanced Development Course, 1 September.

Wicks, N. (1994b) 'The development of international financial institutions and the G7 co-ordination process', Speech at the Groucho Club London, December.

Wicks, N. (2003) 'Governments, the international financial institutions and international co-operation', in Bayne, N. and Woolcock, S. (eds) *The New Economic Diplomacy: Decision Making and Negotiations in International Economic Relations*, Aldershot: Ashgate, pp. 261–74.

Williamson, J. (ed.) (1994) *The Political Economy of Policy Reform*, Washington, DC: Institute for International Economics.

Willamson, J. and Miller, M. (1987) *Targets and Indicators: Blueprints for International Economic Policy Co-ordination*, Washington, DC: Institute for International Economic Policy.

Woo-Cummings, M. (1997) 'Slouching towards the market: the politics of liberalization in South Korea', in Loireaux, M. *et al.* (eds) *Capital Ungoverned: Liberalising Finance in Interventionist States*, Ithaca, NY: Cornell University Press.

Wood, D. (2000) 'The G7, international finance and developing countries', in Kaiser, K., Kirton, J. and Daniels, J. (eds) *Shaping a New International Financial System*, Aldershot: Ashgate.

Wood, D. (2005) *Governing Global Banking: The Basel Committee and the Politics of Financial Globalisation*, Aldershot: Ashgate.

Woods, N. (2000) 'Making the IMF and the World Bank more accountable', *International Affairs*, 77(1): 83–100.

Woodward, R (2001) 'Slaughtering the British state? Transgovernmental networks and the governance of financial markets in the City of London', Global Studies Association Conference, Manchester Metropolitan University, July.

Woodward, R. (2005) 'Money and the spatial challenge: multi-level governance and the territorial trap', in Baker, A., Hudson, D. and Woodward, R. (eds) *Governing Financial Globalization: International Political Economy and Multi-Level Governance*, London: Routledge, pp. 49–61.

Working Group on Highly Leveraged Institutions (2000) Report to the Financial Stability Forum, March.

Working Group on Highly Leveraged Institutions (2001) 'Progress on implementing the recommendations of the Working Group on Highly Leveraged Institutions', March.

WP-3 (1966) *The Balance of Payments Adjustment Process*, A Report by the Working Party No.3 of the Economic Policy Committee of the Organization for Economic Co-operation and Development, Paris OECD, August, p.8.

Wriston, W. (1998) 'Dumb networks and smart capital', *Cato Journal*, 17(3): 333–44.

Yergin, D. and Stanislaw, J. (1998) *The Commanding Heights: The Battle Between Government and Marketplace that is Remaking the Modern World*, New York: Simon Schuster.

Zysman, J. (1983) *Governments, Markets and Growth: Financial Systems and the Politics of Industrial Change*, Ithaca, NY: Cornell University Press.

Index

ABN, 221
Aichi, Kiichi, 24
Al-Qaeda, 150
Andrews, David, 61
Anglo-Saxon financial practices, 85
Arendt, Hannah, 48
Argentina, 208; debt default, 218
Armijo, Leslie, 192
ASEAN, 203, 212
Asian financial crisis, 2, 71–2, 109, 131, 195, 201, 232
Asian Monetary Fund, 202, 207, 232
Australia, 191, 218
Austria, 191

Bahrain, 132
Baker, James, 26, 32
Baker plan, 222
Balanced Budget Act (US), 119
Bank of Canada, 84, 89, 118, 208, 237
Bank of England, 81, 89, 123, 149, 208, 229, 237; Monetary Policy Committee, 118, 175–6
Bank for International Settlements (Basle), 23, 111, 132, 193, 216
Bank of Japan, 85, 123, 203, 206; Policy Board, 118
Bank of Tokyo, 133, 200, 206
Barber, Anthony, 24
Barclays, 133
Barings, 1
Basle II negotiations, 86, 97
Basle Committee on Banking Supervision, 63, 86, 136, 138–9, 140, 187, 191, 216; core principles for effective banking supervision, 139; International Accounting Standards for Banks, 214
balance of payments surpluses, 82
Bennett, Ian, 113
Bentham, Jeremy,
Bentsen, Lloyd, 156–7
Bergsten, Fred, 5, 34, 153, 232
Best, Jacqueline, 215
Blyth, Mark, 68, 78, 188
BMW, 206
Boca Raton, 167
Bonn locomotive strategy, 3, 29–30, 82, 232
Bonn summit, 109
Bono, 222
Brazil, 218
Bretton Woods, 19, 21–2, 84, 242
Brady bonds, 222
Brady plan, 34, 222
Brossolette, Claude Pierre, 24
Brown, Gordon, 220–1, 224–5
bubble economy (Japan), 34
Bundesbank, 206, 208, 215; Board of, 175
Burns, Arthur, 24
Bush administration, 88, 167, 223, 237; tax cuts, 173

Camdessus, Michel, 212
Canadian Congress, 121
capital account liberalization, 68,77–8, 93, 205, 229; universal norm, 227
capital controls, 71, 72, 92, 205
Carter administration, 36
central bank independence, 76, 78, 97, 110
Cerny, Philip, 60
Chase Manhattan, 133
Chatham House rules, 16,
China, 165–6, 218
Christmas Eve package 1997, 200
Chung Ho Bank, 200
Citicorp, 133
City of London, 1, 20, 22, 40, 81, 129–30, 229

civil society, 64, 130, 197
Clinton administration, 13, 144, 237; fiscal consolidation strategy, 88
Clintonomics, 73, 83
Cohen, Benjamin, 48, 60, 134, 151, 206
collective action clauses, 208, 221, 226, 237, 240
Cologne consensus, 95
Cologne Summit, 140
Commerce Department (US), 158
Committee on the Global Financial System, 216
Committee on Payment and Settlement Systems, 216
communiqués, 116, 242
compliance, 117, 242
concert of powers thesis/ concert equality model, 6, 7, 49, 102–5, 137, 141–2, 181, 235
Conservative party (UK), 22
control total, 119
COREPER, 178
corporate scandals, 1
Cox, Robert, 52–3, 56, 64, 100, 124, 229
credibility, 76, 135, 144, 190
Crockett, Andrew, 63,
crony capitalism, 211
current account deficits, 79

Daimler-Benz, 206
Darman, Richard, 32
de Larosiere, Jacques, 28
decentralized globalization, 7, 38–41, 50, 133, 194, 231, 235, 238
declaratory policy, 162, 169–70, 172, 180, 233
deputies, 112, 115, 197; G5/G7, 28, 45, 111–16, 192, 197, 202, 231–3, 244
Destler, Ian, 32
Deutsche Bank, 206, 221
deutschmark, 32, 159
disintermediated financial markets, 40
Dodge, David, 106
dollar, 32; appreciation 157–62; rout, 173; stabilization of, 33; Wall Street Regime, 165, 169
Dubai, 150, 165–6

ECOFIN, 110–11, 123, 178
Economic Fiscal Plans (Italy), 121
embedded financial sectors of Japan and continental Europe, 5
Emergency Financing Mechanism, 191, 211
Enron, 1
environmental lobbyists, 91
Euro 12 Group, 177–8
Eurocentrism, 25
Eurodollar markets, 20
European Central Bank, 84, 89–90, 123, 152, 176, 178; Governing Council, 118
European Commission, 193
European Monetary System, 12, 22–3, 33, 85; ERM crisis, 123, 144
European Monetary Union, 85, 110, 144, 177–8, 182
European Union, 218; Economic and Financial Committee, 115
exchange market intervention, 32, 122; sterilized and unsterilized, 31
exchange rate stability, 28
Exchange Stabilization Fund (US), 122
exogenous shocks, 173
Expenditure Management System, 121

Federal Reserve, 19, 48, 82, 89, 116, 161, 195; Bank of New York, 123; Federal Open Market Committee, 118, 175–6
Financial Action Task Force, 94
financial crises, 23
financial globalization, 37, 234; decentralized, 38–41, 45
financial liberalization, 12
Financial Sector Assessment Programmes (FSAPs), 214
Financial Services Authority (UK), 124
Financial Stability Forum, 63, 86, 187, 209, 216–17, 241, 244
Financial System Stability Assessment Report (FSSAs), 214
Financial Times, The, 61
financialization, 80, 129
fiscal consolidation, 97
fiscal policy, 44
fiscal rules, 110
fiscal structural reform act (Japan), 119
Foucault, Michel, 190
four-dimensional framework, 54–65; four spatial dimensions, 55–6, 64
Frankfurt, 40, 132
French socialists (1983), 21
Friedman, Milton, 21, 73

G5, 1, 24
G7: Action Plan, 209, 221; approval, 241; ideas/beliefs/belief system 15, 87, 94, 118, 180, 189, 230, 243; conflict,

82–7; consensus, 67, 77–8, 87–8, 92–3, 98, 205, 209, 229–30, 233, 237; co-operation, 18, 33, 39, 234–5; debates/deliberations/discussions/interactions, 45–6, 49, 58, 64, 67, 96, 101–18, 180–1; leadership, 241; meetings, 46, 64, 78, 94, 101, 104, 106–8, 111, 117–18, 130, 136, 143, 181, 231–2, 238; mind-set, 98–9, 118, 130; nexus, 100; proposals, 66; social practices, 102, 107–11, 189, 232; statements, 102, 116–18, 143, 235
G8 summits, 45, 112, 131
G10, 1, 23–4, 140, 191; deputies' report, 185
G20, 9, 41, 187, 207, 217–19, 244
G22, 207, 212, 217
G24, 214
Geldof, Bob, 222
General Arrangement to Borrow (GAB), 23, 191
Germain, Randall, 7, 38, 133, 231
German Ministry of Finance, 206
Gill, Stephen, 76, 100, 190
ginger group, 243
Giscard d'Estaing, Valéry, 24–5
global financial architecture, 14
Globex, 133
Goldman Sachs, 155, 161
Gowan, Peter, 47, 158, 160, 168–9, 235
Gramm–Rudmann–Hollings Act, 119
Greenspan, Alan, 49, 89, 167, 174, 204
Gulf war (first), 34, 145

Halifax II, 210–12
Halifax Initiative Coalition, 197
Halifax summit, 140, 188, 196; report on architectural issues, 187–93, 196–8; strategy, 231
Hall, Peter, 88, 148
Hannoun, Hervé, 113
Hayek, Friedrich von, 21
Heavily Indebted Poor Countries Initiative (HPIC), 223
hedge funds, 126, 209
Henning, Randall, 4, 5, 32, 34, 84, 153, 232
Higgott, Richard, 96, 201, 244
Hobson, John, 51–2, 228
Hong Kong, 40, 196, 216
Housing and Commercial Bank, 200
Humphrey Hawkins Act of 1978, 82

ideas battle, 199
ideology, 77
India, 218
Indonesia, 196, 199, 211, 218
ING Barings, 221
Instinet, 133
International Accounting Standards Board, 41, 213
International Association of Insurance Supervisors (IAIS), 41
International Development Association (IDA), 223
International Federation of Accountants (IFAC), 213
International Financial Facility (IFF), 224
International Monetary Fund, 19, 23, 36, 41, 63, 111, 136–8, 140, 190, 194, 201, 205, 207, 216, 245; article IV, 28, 214; conditionality, 50; director of research, 94; Enhanced Structural Adjustment Facility, 149, 223; executive board 195; executive directors, 111–12, 187; International Monetary and Financial Committee, 221; lending policies, 58; Managing Director, 25, 94, 134, 212; point iv article I, 94; Poverty Reduction and Growth Facility, 149
International Organization of Securities Commissions (IOSCO), 41, 63, 136, 139, 187, 191–2, 196, 213, 216
International Securities Market Association, 41
Iranian revolution, 28

Japanese Ministry of Finance, 69, 123, 206
Jenkins, Paul, 113
Joint Forum, 139, 195
Jubilee 2000, 222
Jurgensen Report, 31,

K-group, 100
Kato, Koichi, 147
Kato, Takatoshi, 114
Kelley, Edward, 114
Keohane, Robert, 10, 38, 42, 52, 53, 56, 64, 117, 130, 140, 168
Keynes, John Maynard, 19
Keynesian, 20, 29, 34, 79, 129, 184
King, Mervyn, 116,
Kirshner, Jonathon, 47, 204
Kirton, John, 7, 49, 58, 87–9, 92, 100, 102, 116, 168, 181, 203, 206, 235, 242
Kohl, Helmut, 30

Kohler, Horst, 87
Krueger, Anne, 219

Labour government (UK), 21
Lafontaine, Oskar, 85, 181
LDP (Liberal Democratic Party of Japan), 147
Lemierre, Jean, 113
Liberal Party (UK), 243
Library Group, 25–8
Lloyds Bank, 200
logic of appropriateness, 57
logic of arguing, 57, 105
London, 132
Louvre accord, 3, 33, 36, 144
low inflation, 78
Lyon summit, 155

Maastricht convergence criteria, 177
macroeconomic austerity, 12; discipline 15
Malaysia, 92, 211, 218
Manila Framework, 203
March, James 57
market authority, 50
Martin, Paul, 106–7, 111, 204, 220
Maxwell, Sylvia, 206
Medium-term Fiscal Plan (Germany), 119
Mer, Francis, 166
Merrill Lynch, 133
Mexico, 218; peso crisis, 128, 160, 183
Millennium Challenge Account (MCA), 223–4
Mitchell, Derek, 24
Miyazawa Plan, 203; speech, 204
modern theory of markets, 68
monetary orthodoxy, 78
Montreal consensus, 95–6
moral hazard, 71
multilateralism, 6, 39; multilateral consensus formation, 117, 238
multi-dimensional diplomacy, 6, 50, 55
multi-level governance, 55
Mundell-Flemming dilemma, 11, 20, 85

Nagashima, Aikra, 114
Nakasone, Yasuhiro, 30
Naples terms of debt relief, 34
National Economic Council, 161
National Westminster, 133
nébuleuse, 56, 101
neo-classical economic ideas/ theory, 44, 71, 75, 112, 230
neo-conservatives, 152
neo-functionalist, 64
neo-Gramscian, 190
neo-integrationist, 39, 52, 228
neo-realists, 46
New Arrangement to Borrow, 191, 200
new constitutionalism, 76,
New Partnership for Africa's Development (NPEAD), 223
New York, 22, 40
Nomura International, 206
non-governmental organizations (NGOs), 197, 245
Nye, Joseph, 10, 38, 42, 52, 56, 64, 117, 130, 140

O'Neill, Paul, 151–2, 220–1
OECD, 20, 23, 193, 202, 216
Olsen, Johan, 57
open markets, 72

panopticism, 190
Paris Club, 140, 222
People's Seven (P7), 197
Phillips, Nicola, 96
Plaza agreement, 3, 5, 32–3, 36, 232
plurilateral, 60
Pohl, Karl Otto, 24
Poland, 196
Porter, Tony, 52, 64, 133, 187, 192, 225
power to delay, 134
Prague, 165
pre-commitment, 75
prisoner's dilemma, 117
private sector burden sharing, 71
public authority, 50
Putnam, Robert, 4, 53

Rambouillet summit, 1975, 28, 154, 183
Reagan, Ronald, 30; administration, 32–3; tax cuts, 31
Regan, Donald, 31–2
rentier activity, 132
Reports on Observance of Standards and Codes (ROSCs), 214–15
Reuters, 133
Risse, Thomas, 57, 105–6
Rubin, Robert, 152, 155–7, 161, 164, 187, 189
Russell, Robert, 46,
Russia, 218

Sakakibara, Eisuke, 202, 204
Saudi Arabia, 218
Schieber, Helmut, 113,
Schioppa, Padoa, 114

Schmidt, Helmut, 24–5
Schroeder, Gerhard, 166
Schultz, George, 24
second wave Weberian historical sociology, 51, 64
securitization agenda of Bush administration, 151–2
September 11, 94, 174, 233
shareholder value, 59
sherpas, 112
Singapore, 132, 191, 216
Slaughter, Anne-Marie, 140
Snow, John, 89
social justice, 185, 225, 227
Soros, George, 47
sound money, 72
South Africa, 218
South Korea, 191, 196, 199, 206, 218; central bank, 213
Sovereign Debt Restructuring Mechanism, 92, 210, 219–22, 226, 234, 237, 240, 244
spaces of flows, 60
Spain, 191
Special Drawing Rights (SDR), 23
Sprinkel, Beryl, 31–2
stability programme (France), 120
standstill mechanism, 92, 208
Stark, Jürgen, 74, 113
state-market condominium, 51
Stiglitz, Joseph, 93, 98, 149
Strange, Susan, 41
strategic signalling, 238
Strauss-Khan, Dominique, 68
strong dollar policy, 161
Summers, Lawrence, 74, 107, 114, 152, 160, 186, 189, 202, 204, 212
surveillance, 28, 36, 75, 97, 107–12, 134, 188–90, 194, 207
symptom management policies, 22

Taiwan, 166, 206
Taylor, John, 220
technical argument, 170
technical authority, 49–50, 172
technical systems, 52
technocratic discourse, 91
Thailand, 196, 199, 211
Thatcher, Margaret, 30
theoretical complexity, 39, 51
third-dimensional diplomacy,134–5
Thirkell-White, Ben, 215
three-dimensional governance, 236, 239
Tietmeyer, Hans, 174, 216–17
Tokyo, 40, 132
Toronto, 132
Toyota, 206
trade unionists, 91
transgovernmentalism, 42–6, 52, 130, 140–1, 219, 227; gatekeeper, 240; policy co-ordination, 43; senior or master transgovernmental coalition, 140–1, 184; transgovernmental coalition, 10, 43–6, 56, 117, 131
transnational coalition, 229, 245
transparency, 68–9, 97, 135, 188, 190, 207
Treasury–Wall Street–IMF axis/ complex, 95, 125, 206
Trichet, Jean-Claude, 166
Tripartite Group, 139
Turkey, 208, 218
two-level games, 39, 50, 52–4

UBS, 133
UK Treasury, 72, 81, 90, 107, 116, 123, 126, 129, 195, 213, 225, 229
Underhill Geoffrey, 51, 244
unholy trinity, 11
University of Toronto G8 Research Centre, 2, 107,
US Congress, 28, 31
US Trade Representative (USTR), 158
US Treasury, 19, 72, 81, 157, 161, 169, 229, 235 secretary, 24, 104
USA: ascendancy, 209; hegemony, 7–8, 27, 104, 234; monetary exceptionalism, 173; power, 2; structural power, 41, 49

Vanhala, Matti, 176
verbal signalling, 157
Versailles summit 1982, 25
Volcker, Paul, 24, 31
Volkswagen, 206

Wade, Robert, 203, 206
Wallich, Henry, 53
Wall Street, 81, 105, 126, 130, 229
Warburg, 133
Washington consensus, 67, 71, 87, 97, 98, 116, 206
Watson, Matthew, 90
Webb, Michael, 5, 24, 34
Weimar Germany, 82
Whitehall, 129
Wicks, Nigel, 107, 114
win-sets 53; analysis, 59

Woods, Ngaire, 138
World Bank, 34, 63, 112; Development Committee, 111
working group on supervision in emerging markets 1997, 196
WP-3, 23, 115
Wriston, Walter, 61

yen, 159; appreciation, 162–4
Yeo, Edwin, 28

Zodda, Augusto, 114